WILLIAM HENRY HUNT
(1790-1864)

WILLIAM HENRY HUNT

(1790-1864)

Life and Work

with a Catalogue

John Witt

BARRIE & JENKINS
London Melbourne Sydney Auckland Johannesburg

Barrie & Jenkins Ltd

An imprint of the Hutchinson Publishing Group

17–21 Conway Street, London W1P 6JD

Hutchinson Group (Australia) Pty Ltd
30–32 Cremorne Street, Richmond South, Victoria 3121
PO Box 151, Broadway, New South Wales 2007

Hutchinson Group (NZ) Ltd
32–34 View Road, PO Box 40-086, Glenfield, Auckland 10

Hutchinson Group (SA) (Pty) Ltd
PO Box 337, Bergvlei 2012, South Africa

Distributed in the United States of America by Abner Schram, 36 Park St, Montclair, N.J., 07042

First published 1982

Filmset in Monophoto Bembo
and printed in Great Britain by
BAS Printers Limited
Over Wallop, Hampshire

British Library Cataloguing in Publication Data

Witt, John
William Henry Hunt.
1. Hunt, William Henry 2. Water-colourists-
England – Biography
I. Title
759.2 ND1931.H/

ISBN 0 09 146690 3

Abner Schram ISBN 0 8390-0290-4

Contents

Appendixes

Illustrations

Works are undated except where dates are given.
In size, height precedes width, inches precede millimetres. Bracketed numbers refer to the Catalogue.

Where locations of works illustrated are not evident from the names of the owners as listed below, see Catalogue entries or captions to the Plates beginning on page 79.

Abbreviations:

Fry Collection *Mr and Mrs Cyril Fry Collection, London*

Huntington Library, San Marino *Henry E. Huntington Library and Art Gallery, San Marino, California*

Witt Collection *Sir John and Lady Witt Collection, London*

Yale Center for British Art *Yale Center for British Art, Paul Mellon Collection, New Haven, Connecticut*

Plates in Colour

Between pages 40 *and* 41

Plates in Monochrome

2 (158) Twickenham
Oil on millboard, $12\frac{3}{4} \times 6\frac{1}{2}$ (329×168)
Tate Gallery, London

3 (109) Windsor Castle
Oil on canvas, 20×26 (508×660)
The National Trust—Anglesey Abbey, Cambridgeshire, Fairhaven Collection

4 (134) A Scene in Venice – Crowds Watching the Comedy Players
Reed pen, brown ink and grey wash, $8\frac{1}{8} \times 12\frac{1}{2}$ (206×319)
Ashmolean Museum, Oxford

5 (179) Saltwood Castle, Kent
Pencil and watercolour, $5\frac{7}{8} \times 8$ (148×206)
Witt Collection

6 (137) View of Hastings
Pencil and watercolour, $11\frac{1}{2} \times 15\frac{1}{4}$ (291×393)
Ashmolean Museum, Oxford

7 (250) The Flagstaff, Margate
Pencil and watercolour, $7\frac{15}{16} \times 11\frac{5}{8}$ (201×295)
Yale Center for British Art

8 (239) Building Waterloo Bridge
Reed pen and brown ink with brown and grey wash, $9\frac{7}{16} \times 15\frac{5}{8}$ (252×396)
Yale Center for British Art

9 (58) Rebuilding London Bridge
Watercolour, $6\frac{3}{4} \times 9\frac{1}{8}$ (160×233)
Courtesy of the Provost and Fellows of Eton College, Windsor

10 (244) St Paul's Cathedral and Blackfriars Bridge
Reed pen, brown ink and watercolour, $9 \times 13\frac{3}{8}$ (228×340)
Yale Center for British Art

11 (31) London Bridge with Pool of London Beyond
Reed pen, brown ink and watercolour, $13\frac{3}{8} \times 21\frac{3}{8}$ (342×544); dated 1825
British Museum, London

12 (23) Dr Monro Inspecting his Burnt-out Stables at Bushey
Reed pen, brown ink and watercolour, $13\frac{7}{8} \times 10\frac{1}{4}$ (354×262)
British Museum, London

13 (246) The Lecture House, Watford
Watercolour, $12\frac{7}{8} \times 16\frac{13}{16}$ (327×427)
Yale Center for British Art

14 (243) A Farm House
Pencil and watercolour, $11\frac{13}{16} \times 15\frac{3}{4}$ (300 × 400)
Yale Center for British Art

15 (240) Bushey Church from the South-West
Pencil and watercolour, $7\frac{1}{4} \times 10\frac{1}{8}$ (183 × 251)
Yale Center for British Art

16 (47) Houses at Watford
Watercolour, $10\frac{1}{2} \times 14\frac{13}{16}$ (267 × 376)
Courtauld Institute of Art, London

17 (8) The Water Mill, Bushey
Reed pen, ink and watercolour, $13\frac{1}{4} \times 16\frac{7}{8}$ (335 × 427)
The Trustees, Cecil Higgins Art Gallery, Bedford

18 (247) Village Street in St Albans
Pencil and watercolour, $9\frac{3}{8} \times 11\frac{3}{4}$ (237 × 297)
Yale Center for British Art

19 (245) A Lodge at Cassiobury
Reed pen, ink and watercolour, $10\frac{5}{8} \times 15$ (271 × 381)
Yale Center for British Art

20 (26) The Village in the Valley
Watercolour, $10\frac{1}{2} \times 14\frac{3}{4}$ (267 × 375)
British Museum, London

21 (210) Snow Scene
Watercolour, $4 \times 6\frac{1}{2}$ (102 × 166)
Witt Collection

22 (375) The Dining Room at Cassiobury Park
Watercolour, $9\frac{5}{8} \times 13\frac{1}{4}$ (245 × 336); dated 1821
Fry Collection

23 (376) The Drawing Room at Cassiobury Park
Watercolour, $8\frac{3}{8} \times 10\frac{3}{4}$ (211 × 270); dated 1823
Fry Collection

24 (141) The Portico of St Martin-in-the-Fields
Reed pen, brown ink and sepia wash, $19\frac{1}{2} \times 13\frac{7}{8}$ (494 × 353); dated 1822
Ashmolean Museum, Oxford

25 (252) Bushey Churchyard
Reed pen, brown ink and watercolour, $12\frac{1}{4} \times 16\frac{1}{4}$ (312 × 413)
Yale Center for British Art

26 (17) The Nave, Bushey Church
Reed pen, ink and watercolour, $16\frac{5}{8} \times 12\frac{1}{2}$ (423 × 317)
Art Galleries and Museums, Bradford

27 (24) Bushey Church, South Side
Reed pen, ink and watercolour, $12\frac{5}{8} \times 16\frac{1}{2}$ (322×420)
British Museum, London

28 (197) Interior of the Belfry, Bushey Church
Reed pen and brown ink, $10\frac{7}{8} \times 8$ (277×203)
Witt Collection

29 (251) Interior of the Belfry, Bushey Church
Pencil, reed pen, brown ink and watercolour, $14\frac{7}{16} \times 10\frac{5}{16}$ (366×266)
Yale Center for British Art

30 (362) Self Portrait Aged 25 Years
Pencil and watercolour, $3\frac{3}{4} \times 3\frac{1}{8}$ (95×80)
Fry Collection

31 (540) Stable Boy
Watercolour, $10\frac{7}{8} \times 7\frac{1}{4}$ (276×184); dated 1815
Witt Collection

32 (271) Farmer in a Barn
Watercolour heightened with white, $10\frac{3}{4} \times 7\frac{1}{8}$ (274×182)
Birmingham Museums and Art Gallery

33 (544) Young Girl Standing Barefoot
Reed pen, ink and watercolour, $7\frac{1}{2} \times 3\frac{7}{8}$ (190×97)
Witt Collection

34 (258) Old Man Fishing by a Lock Gate
Reed pen, brown ink and watercolour, 11×15 (280×382); dated 1822
Mrs B. Asprey, London

35 (324) The Vegetable Seller
Reed pen, ink and watercolour, $15 \times 10\frac{3}{8}$ (381×264)
Courtauld Institute of Art, London

36 (272) A Miller in his Mill
Reed pen, ink and watercolour, $15\frac{1}{4} \times 11\frac{7}{8}$ (387×303)
Birmingham Museums and Art Gallery

37 (473) Portrait of a Man
Pencil, reed pen, brown ink and watercolour, $15\frac{1}{2} \times 11\frac{1}{2}$ (394×293)
Lady Lever Art Gallery, Port Sunlight

38 (470) Young Woman Standing
Watercolour, $10\frac{7}{8} \times 7\frac{1}{8}$ (276×180)
Ashmolean Museum, Oxford

39 (293) Group of Three Women
Pencil and watercolour, $7\frac{1}{8} \times 5\frac{5}{8}$ (180×142)
British Museum, London

40 (391) Portrait of a Girl
Watercolour, 7×4 (177×100)

Bankfield Museum, Halifax

41 (266) Young Girl Reclining on a Couch
Watercolour, $14 \times 10\frac{1}{4}$ (354×260)
The Trustees, Cecil Higgins Art Gallery, Bedford

42 (430) A Radish Stall
Watercolour heightened with white, $8\frac{3}{4} \times 10\frac{7}{8}$ (223×277); dated 1829
City of Manchester Art Galleries

43 (379) Girl Reading by Lamplight
Watercolour, $12\frac{1}{4} \times 8\frac{1}{2}$ (312×220)
Fry Collection

44 (429) Boy Blowing a Horn
Watercolour, $14 \times 10\frac{1}{4}$ (356×262); dated 1829
City of Manchester Art Galleries

45 (334) The Gallery, Chiswick House
Watercolour, $12\frac{3}{4} \times 10$ (325×255);
Devonshire Collection Chatsworth. This and Plates 46 and 47 reproduced by permission of the Trustees of the Chatsworth Settlement

46 (351) The Long Gallery, Hardwick
Watercolour, $11\frac{1}{4} \times 16\frac{3}{4}$ (286×427); dated 1828
Devonshire Collection Chatsworth

47 (332) The Saloon, Devonshire House
Watercolour, $10\frac{3}{8} \times 12\frac{1}{4}$ (265×310); dated 1822
Devonshire Collection Chatsworth

48 (748) Cock and Hens in a Barn
Watercolour heightened with white, $12\frac{1}{8} \times 16$ (307×408)
Mr C. W. Witt, Bucks

49 (642) Dog Studies
Pencil and brown wash, $10\frac{3}{4} \times 7\frac{1}{4}$ (274×184)
Huntington Library, San Marino

50 (736) Studies of a Dog
Pencil and watercolour, $5\frac{7}{8} \times 8\frac{1}{4}$ (148×210)
Mrs G. M. Tuff, London

51 (773) Still Life: Copper Jug, Blue Vase, Blue and White Ginger Jar, Pepper Pot and Basket
Pencil and watercolour, $7\frac{1}{2} \times 10$ (190×255)
Yale Center for British Art

52 (685) Study of Copper Pot and Horn Mug
Watercolour heightened with white, $4\frac{1}{2} \times 5\frac{1}{4}$ (116×133); dated 1825
Ashmolean Museum, Oxford

53 (686) Study of a Woodcock

Watercolour, brown and yellow, heightened with white, $5\frac{1}{8} \times 8\frac{5}{8}$ (129 × 220); dated 1825
Ashmolean Museum, Oxford

54 (759) White Grapes in a Basket
Watercolour heightened with white, $7\frac{7}{8} \times 11\frac{1}{4}$ (198 × 287); dated 1827
Witt Collection

55 (774) A Dead Hare and a Cooked Lobster on a Bench
Pencil, reed pen, brown ink and watercolour, $4\frac{1}{4} \times 8\frac{15}{16}$ (108 × 227)
Yale Center for British Art

56 (665) Still Life: Turtle, Crab and Fish
Reed pen, brown ink and watercolour, $7 \times 13\frac{3}{4}$ (177 × 348)
Whitworth Art Gallery, University of Manchester

57 (437) A Shrimper
Watercolour, $15\frac{1}{8} \times 12\frac{1}{8}$ (384 × 307); dated 1835
Whitworth Art Gallery, University of Manchester

58 (419) The Turnip Lantern
Watercolour heightened with white, $13\frac{1}{8} \times 8\frac{7}{8}$ (336 × 225); dated 1838
Leicestershire Museums and Art Galleries

59 (530) Boy and Goat
Watercolour heightened with white and surface scratching, $12\frac{1}{4} \times 16$ (312 × 407); dated 1836
Victoria and Albert Museum, Crown Copyright

60 (420) Puzzled
Pencil and watercolour slightly heightened with white, $13\frac{1}{8} \times 8\frac{3}{4}$ (333 × 223); dated 1839
Leicestershire Museums and Art Galleries

61 (410) The Young Artist
Watercolour heightened with white, $17\frac{7}{8} \times 12\frac{3}{4}$ (456 × 324)
Huntington Library, San Marino

62 (323) A Young Cricketer
Watercolour, $18\frac{1}{8} \times 14\frac{1}{8}$ (462 × 360)
From the collection of the late Sir Jeremiah Colman, Bt

63 (510) The Artist's Wife
Pencil, $3\frac{7}{8} \times 3\frac{1}{2}$ (98 × 90)
Sheffield City Art Galleries

64 (514) An Old Man's Head
Watercolour, $9\frac{1}{4} \times 8$ (235 × 203)
Tate Gallery, London

65 (387) Musical Party with Three Young Girls Dancing
Pen, $5\frac{1}{8} \times 7\frac{1}{4}$ (130 × 184)
Fry Collection

66 (539) An Interesting Letter
Watercolour, $13\frac{1}{4} \times 9\frac{3}{4}$ (337 × 246)
Mr C. W. Witt, Bucks

67 (408) At the Cottage Door
Watercolour, $12\frac{1}{2} \times 7\frac{1}{4}$ (324 × 184); dated 1835
Huntington Library, San Marino

68 (490) Woman Reading by Candlelight
Pencil and watercolour, $13\frac{3}{8} \times 9\frac{1}{2}$ (340 × 242)
Mrs A. Reed, London

69 (388) The Orphan
Watercolour heightened with white, $11\frac{1}{2} \times 13\frac{1}{4}$ (297 × 355)
Fry Collection

70 (400) Portrait of a Young Lady
Watercolour, $10\frac{3}{8} \times 5$ (263 × 127)
Huntington Library, San Marino

71 (571) Girl with a Black Dress
Watercolour, $7\frac{11}{16} \times 3\frac{7}{8}$ (195 × 98)
Yale Center for British Art

72 (411) The Sisters
Watercolour, $12\frac{1}{8} \times 9\frac{1}{4}$ (308 × 235)
Huntington Library, San Marino

73 (328) The Young Apple Seller
Watercolour, $13\frac{5}{8} \times 9\frac{1}{2}$ (346 × 242)
Mr A. Cuthbertson, London

74 (407) Sunday Morning
Watercolour, $15\frac{3}{8} \times 21\frac{7}{8}$ (391 × 556); dated 1833
Huntington Library, San Marino

75 (267) The Maid and the Magpie
Watercolour slightly heightened with white, $17\frac{3}{8} \times 22\frac{3}{8}$ (441 × 569)
Courtesy of the Trustees, Cecil Higgins Art Gallery, Bedford

76 (472) In Val Crucis Abbey: The Interior used as a Barn
Pencil and watercolour heightened with white with surface scratching, $23\frac{3}{8} \times 15\frac{3}{4}$ (593 × 402); dated 1836
Ashmolean Museum, Oxford

77 (274) Slumber
Watercolour, $13\frac{5}{8} \times 16\frac{7}{8}$ (342 × 428)
Birmingham Museums and Art Gallery

78 (458) Girl Reading at a Window
Watercolour, $8 \times 10\frac{1}{2}$ (203 × 267); dated 1832
Courtesy of His Grace The Duke of Norfolk, Arundel Castle, Sussex

79 (439) A Bedchamber

Watercolour, $11\frac{3}{8} \times 17\frac{3}{8}$ (288 × 443); dated 1839
Whitworth Art Gallery, University of Manchester

80 (451) Self Portrait
Watercolour, $14\frac{3}{4} \times 11$ (374 × 279)
National Portrait Gallery, London

81 (593) Still Life of Slaughtered Goose and Basket
Watercolour heightened with white, $10\frac{1}{4} \times 10\frac{1}{4}$ (261 × 261)
Bolton Museum and Art Gallery

82 (763) Carrots, Celery, Mushrooms, Cheese and a Jug
Watercolour slightly heightened with white, $6\frac{3}{4} \times 12\frac{1}{2}$ (173 × 318)
Witt Collection

83 (675) Bird's Nest with Blossom
Watercolour heightened with white, $7\frac{1}{2} \times 12$ (191 × 305); dated 1831
Laing Art Gallery, Newcastle-upon-Tyne, Tyne and Wear County Council Museums

84 (614) Study of a Rose
Watercolour heightened with white, $5\frac{3}{8} \times 9\frac{1}{4}$ (138 × 235); dated 1835
Fitzwilliam Museum, Cambridge

85 (586) Black Grapes and Pear
Watercolour on prepared ground, $7\frac{3}{4} \times 11$ (197 × 280)
Birmingham Museums and Art Gallery

86 (145) Rock on the Downs near Hastings
Watercolour, $24\frac{1}{2} \times 20$ (622 × 508)
Harris Museum and Art Gallery, Preston

87 (219) Fishing Boats on the Beach at Hastings
Pencil, $8\frac{1}{8} \times 10$ (206 × 254)
Witt Collection

88 (215) Sunset off Hastings Beach
Watercolour, $4\frac{3}{4} \times 6\frac{5}{8}$ (121 × 167)
Witt Collection

89 (105) Fishing Smack
Pencil, pen, ink and watercolour, $14\frac{5}{8} \times 10\frac{1}{4}$ (377 × 261)
Leeds City Art Gallery

90 (99) Hastings Beach
Watercolour, $9\frac{1}{4} \times 12\frac{3}{4}$ (235 × 323)
Huntington Library, San Marino

91 (399) Light and Shade
Watercolour heightened with white, $13 \times 9\frac{1}{2}$ (330 × 242)
Huddersfield Libraries and Museum

92 (390) Interior
Watercolour heightened with white, $17\frac{1}{8} \times 12\frac{3}{4}$ (434 × 323)

Glasgow Art Gallery and Museum

93 (452) Self Portrait
Oil on paper stuck on card, $5\frac{1}{4} \times 4\frac{1}{4}$ (135 × 110)
National Portrait Gallery, London

94 (557) Portrait of his Daughter
Watercolour heightened with white, $5\frac{1}{8} \times 3\frac{3}{8}$ (130 × 86)
Witt Collection

95 (518) The Artist's Daughter Holding a Jug
Watercolour, $10\frac{1}{2} \times 7\frac{1}{8}$ (267 × 182)
Mrs G. M. Tuff, London

96 (535) Portrait of the Artist, his Daughter and Niece
Pen, ink and watercolour, $4 \times 5\frac{5}{8}$ (102 × 143)
Victoria and Albert Museum, Crown Copyright

97 (633) Flowers in a Pewter Mug
Watercolour heightened with white, $10\frac{5}{8} \times 6\frac{7}{8}$ (270 × 175)
Fry Collection

98 (728) Blossom
Watercolour heightened with white, $7\frac{3}{4} \times 5\frac{1}{2}$ (197 × 140); dated 1860
Sheffield City Art Galleries

99 (626) Fruit
Watercolour on prepared ground, $9\frac{1}{2} \times 13$ (242 × 330); unfinished
Dudley Museum and Art Gallery: Dudley Metropolitan Borough

100 (616) Study of Fruit
Watercolour on prepared ground, $8 \times 11\frac{1}{2}$ (203 × 292)
Fitzwilliam Museum, Cambridge

101 (668) Fruit and Tankard
Watercolour on prepared ground, $14\frac{3}{8} \times 12$ (366 × 306)
Whitworth Art Gallery, University of Manchester

102 (726) Still Life: Grapes and Pineapple
Watercolour on prepared ground heightened with white,
$8\frac{1}{8} \times 11$ (205 × 280)
Sheffield City Art Galleries

103 (637) Fruit Piece
Watercolour heightened with white, $8\frac{1}{4} \times 15\frac{1}{2}$ (209 × 395)
Shipley Art Gallery, Gateshead

104 (599) Peach and Grapes
Watercolour on prepared ground, $8 \times 10\frac{3}{4}$ (203 × 273) oval
The Brantwood Trust, Brantwood, Coniston, Cumbria

105 Ruskin's Bedroom at Brantwood – Engraving, April 1900 from a drawing by Arthur Severn

106 (673) Fruit Piece

Watercolour on prepared ground, $5\frac{1}{4} \times 7\frac{3}{4}$ (133 × 197)
National Museum of Wales

107 An Apple by William Hough, $4\frac{5}{8} \times 5\frac{1}{2}$ (117 × 140)
Witt Collection

108 (658) Spring Flowers and Birds' Nests
Watercolour, $8\frac{1}{2} \times 13\frac{1}{2}$ (216 × 343)
City of Manchester Art Galleries

109 (676) Bird's Nest
Watercolour heightened with white, $6 \times 8\frac{3}{4}$ (152 × 223)
Laing Art Gallery, Newcastle-upon-Tyne, Tyne and Wear County Council Museums

110 (659) Bird's Nest and Blossom
Watercolour heightened with white, $11\frac{1}{2} \times 13$ (293 × 330) oval
City of Manchester Art Galleries

111 (653) John Ruskin's Dead Chick
Watercolour heightened with white, $4\frac{1}{4} \times 6\frac{1}{8}$ (108 × 154)
Walker Art Gallery, Liverpool

112 (630) Study of Two Onions
Watercolour, $5\frac{1}{2} \times 8\frac{1}{4}$ (145 × 220)
Fry Collection

113 (620) Shells
Watercolour heightened with white, $4\frac{1}{2} \times 6\frac{1}{2}$ (114 × 165)
Fogg Art Museum, Harvard University: Bequest – Grenville L. Winthrop, Cambridge, Mass.

Foreword and Acknowledgements

I have been interested in the work of William Henry Hunt for many years. Indeed I acquired, as a schoolboy in the 1920s, my first examples of his work, six small pencil sketches for 1*s.* each, from that kind and friendly dealer, now long since departed, F. R. Meatyard.

Hunt was, throughout his long life, an immensely prolific artist. During his almost forty years of membership of the Old Water-Colour Society he exhibited there just under 800 finished works. But he also produced numerous unexhibited works which he sold direct to his various patrons. He also made, from time to time, several copies of many of his more successful drawings, as well as producing countless small pencil and watercolour sketches of his beloved Hastings where he would spend so many winters. In short, his pencil, pen and brush were seldom idle during the fifty-eight years of his working life, from the time he joined John Varley's studio as a pupil in 1806 to his death in 1864.

I wish at the outset to emphasise most strongly that the Catalogue which forms Part II of this work in no way claims to be complete. A large number of works remain untraced, many of which are likely to come to light in the future. I have included in the Catalogue only works where their present ownership in a national, public or private collection is known to me. Inevitably this has involved the omission of many works whose titles are known but whose present ownership is not. I would ask the indulgence of owners of such works for their omission, coupled with a request to provide relevant details for inclusion in any future supplement.

I am greatly indebted to numerous museums and galleries and their trustees, corporate bodies, and staff, and to private owners for help and advice, and for a generous response to my requests for information.

I wish to record my thanks where reproduction rights have been granted and particularly when granted on a free or modest basis and I hope that the acknowledgements in the list of illustrations will be accepted as an expression of my gratitude.

Many people have made important contributions in one way or another to this book and while it must seem invidious to refer only to some, I wish to convey my special thanks to the following: Mr Kenneth Garlick, Mr Gerald Taylor and Mr David Brown of the Ashmolean Museum, Oxford; Mr John Baskett; Miss Lindsay

Stainton and Mr Paul Goldman of the Department of Prints and Drawings, British Museum; Mrs Joan Linnell Burton; Mr Peter Day and Mr Michael Pearman of the Devonshire Collection Chatsworth; Mr John Sunderland, Mrs Priscilla Latham and Miss Elizabeth Hasloch of the Courtauld Institute of Art; Mr Noel Annesley and Mr Francis Russell of Christie, Manson and Woods Ltd; Dr Robert Wark of the Henry E. Huntington Library and Art Gallery, San Marino, California; Dr F. J. G. Jefferiss; Mr Tom Jones; Mr E. Grant Longman; Mr Jeremy Maas; Mr D. L. T. Oppé; Mr Malcolm Fry of The Royal Society of Painters in Water-Colours; Mr Dudley Snelgrove; Mr James Miller and Mr Henry Wemyss of Sotheby Parke Bernet & Co; Mr John Murdoch and Mr Lionel Lambourne of the Victoria and Albert Museum; Miss Mary Bennett of the Walker Art Gallery, Liverpool and The Lady Lever Art Gallery, Port Sunlight; Miss Jane Farington of the City Art Gallery, Manchester; Mr Francis Hawcroft of the Whitworth Art Gallery, University of Manchester; Mr Patrick Noon of the Yale Center for British Art (Paul Mellon Collection), New Haven, Connecticut; and Mr Antony Wood of Barrie and Jenkins Ltd.

I would like to express my special thanks to my friend Mr Cyril Fry who has over the years formed an outstanding private collection of Hunt's works and who, I have reason to suspect, would have embarked in the fullness of time on a similar study of Hunt. He has been unstinting in placing at my disposal his knowledge and material connected with Hunt, and I am deeply grateful to him.

Finally, I would like to thank my daughter-in-law, Elizabeth Witt, my grand-daughter, Frances Witt, and my friend Mrs Sarah Cater for sharing the arduous task of typing this work, and for their skill and patience in creating relative order from often disordered material. But most of all, I owe a deep debt of gratitude to my wife who has not only made a number of valuable suggestions and improvements, but has amiably tolerated over a considerable period my absorption in this undertaking.

Introduction

William Henry Hunt, contrary to his generally accepted reputation as an artist specialising mainly in the subject of birds' nests (hence his nickname 'Bird's Nest Hunt'), was in fact an artist of considerable versatility both of style and subject-matter. For nearly forty years, from the date of his election as a member of the Old Water-Colour Society in 1825, when he ceased to paint in oils, until his death in 1864, Hunt was an artist of the highest technical virtuosity and a respected, influential and financially successful practitioner of the art of watercolour. He was also the inventor of a new process in the use of body-colour or Chinese white which proved of great value to later artists.

In many respects Hunt can be regarded as a bridge between the school of English watercolour artists of the second half of the eighteenth century and the Victorian school of the middle and latter half of the nineteenth, such as John Frederick Lewis, Myles Birket Foster and the Pre-Raphaelites.

Watercolour painting in England can be said broadly speaking to date from the second half of the eighteenth century. Earlier artists had used that medium on occasions, but no definite school of watercolour painters existed before that period. The leading members of this school were the brothers Thomas and Paul Sandby, Alexander Cozens and his son John Robert Cozens, Francis Towne, Thomas Hearne and Edward Dayes (to whom Girtin was apprenticed). Most of these artists were essentially topographers and produced what were often described as stained drawings by means of drawing the outlines in indian ink which were then coloured with flat washes of pure watercolour. These washes produced a clear and transparent effect suitable for the purpose for which watercolours were chiefly used at that time, namely the production of drawings from which copper-plate engravings and aquatints were made.

The purpose of these engravings and aquatints was to meet a need among country gentlemen for views of their houses, school or university, or of buildings of special architectural interest in their county, perhaps for distribution among family or friends or used as illustrations in what would now be called 'coffee-table' books. Such works were easier to acquire and far less costly in money and time than portraits of themselves or of members of their family or even of their horses or dogs which would normally have been done in oil.

Gradually a demand developed for the original drawings or watercolours (for the two terms were synonymous) from which the engravings were made, and by a natural development of this, for drawings which had no relation whatsoever to engravings. During the last quarter of the century the collecting of drawings or watercolours in their own right assumed considerable proportions. It was one aspect of the increase of interest in landscape art in all its forms that occurred in this period.

The next generation of artists were to benefit greatly from this new trend and were well qualified to do so. Hunt was one of them, and the fifteen years preceding his birth in 1790 produced a galaxy of talent in a group of artists many of whom became the outstanding watercolourists of the first half of the nineteenth century. Among this group were (in order of date of birth), Girtin, Turner, Constable, John Varley (to whom Hunt was apprenticed), Cotman, Prout, Cox, de Wint and Copley Fielding.

Hunt, as mentioned earlier, may be considered an important link between the watercolourists of the second half of the eighteenth century and those of the subsequent century. For this he possessed particular qualifications. First, he had the advantage of being a pupil of John Varley. Varley was spiritually and technically a product of the eighteenth century. His work was marked by careful draughtsmanship and subdued colouring reminiscent in many respects of the eighteenth-century topographers. Varley's instruction to his pupils was based on these characteristics which are clearly reflected in Hunt's early work.

Secondly, Hunt was a member of the Monro Academy, of which Girtin, Turner and Varley himself were early members. It is hard to overestimate the enormous importance that Dr Thomas Monro and his 'Academy' possessed for so many artists who were starting their careers in the last ten years of the eighteenth century and the first quarter of the nineteenth. Monro, himself an amateur landscape artist, was an essentially eighteenth-century father figure to the young watercolour artists who formed his Academy. He possessed a fine collection of drawings by Old Masters and also artists nearer his own time, including Canaletto, Gainsborough, and John Robert Cozens. It was particularly works by these three artists that Dr Monro would set the young artists of his Academy to copy. From Canaletto, for example, Hunt derived his lively reed pen, ink and wash technique which he was to use so effectively in many of his early drawings.

Hunt, therefore, in his early impressionable days was steeped in the spirit of the eighteenth century, and in his early landscapes and views of churches, many done with reed pen and watercolour, and others in pure watercolour, his best qualities as an artist can be seen. He possessed an innate and unobtrusive sense of composition which never deserted him. There is a liveliness and spontaneity in these early landscapes and in his seascapes and shore scenes around Hastings which he gradually lost as he came in his later years, and for good financial reasons, to concentrate on plums and grapes and birds' nests. These early works which have only recently begun to become widely known and appreciated should rank far higher in the hierarchy of nineteenth-century watercolours.

Gradually, however, Hunt changed both his technique and his subject-matter. His reed pen and pure watercolour landscapes virtually ceased and were replaced first by his often elaborate figure works inspired by his boy models from Hastings who sat for him throughout the 1830s, and then by his grapes, plums and birds' nests which were to feature so largely and to prove so financially successful in his later years.

For his figure subjects he developed a special technique of breaking up his washes into detached and separately defined touches and patches which could be described as a kind of stippling or even as a forerunner of the Pointillism of Seurat, Signac and Pissarro. He also developed, as did Turner, the use of the knife in scratching out points and lines to provide highlights from the paper which he would either leave untouched or modify by dotting with watercolour. Indeed, as will be discussed later, there are strong grounds for asserting that Hunt's stippling technique had a strong and direct influence on these three leaders of the Neo-Impressionist school.

For his fruit pieces and birds' nests which became so greatly esteemed by collectors and particularly by business men of the latter half of the nineteenth century, such as the rich cotton merchants of Lancashire and the wool merchants of Yorkshire, a special new technique was essential. By this time Hunt had become an artist of outstanding technical skill, but he needed something new, especially for his fruit pieces, by which it would be possible both to work in the greatest detail and also to obtain the highest degree of finish. Necessity would seem to have become the mother of invention, and he devised a new process in the use of body-colour or Chinese white which enabled him to achieve the effects he desired and needed. It was by this new process, described in detail in Part I, Chapter 4, 'Technique', involving mixing gum with Chinese white and laying this admixture as a hard priming on which he would then paint or stipple in pure watercolour, that Hunt was able to obtain his amazing bloom on a peach, plum or grape.

This technical invention confirms how close a link came to be forged between Hunt and later Victorian artists such as J. F. Lewis, Birket Foster and the Pre-Raphaelites with their insistence on detail and almost obsessive determination to obtain a high degree of finish. Without it they would have been hard put to realise their objectives, for by no other method could Lewis have painted the eye of a camel, Birket Foster one of his meticulous cottage scenes, or Millais a blade of grass.

In short, Hunt began his artistic career in 1806 with the background and with a technique shaped by the eighteenth century, and as the years went by he changed both his technique and his subject-matter as mentioned above until at his death in 1864 he had become in all basic respects a typical Victorian artist, and a figure whose technical impact on a number of his fellow artists was significant.

Nevertheless Hunt must be one of the most neglected and underdocumented watercolourists of the nineteenth century. Indeed, apart from the long article on Hunt by the Pre-Raphaelite critic F. G. Stephens published in *Fraser's Magazine* in 1865 a year after Hunt's death; numerous admiring references in Ruskin's works, particularly his Notes to the Loan Exhibition of Prout and Hunt which Ruskin organised in 1879–80 (see Appendix II); valuable biographical sections on Hunt in

J. L. Roget's *History of the Old Water-Colour Society* (1891); William Collingwood's article 'Reminiscences: William Hunt' (1898), and an important account of Hunt in Martin Hardie's great work *Water-colour Painting in England* (1966–68), there is comparatively little published material about him. Certainly no full-length monograph and catalogue solely devoted to his work has been published before now.

In his lifetime Hunt was well regarded by his contemporaries and succeeded in making a comfortable living from his painting so that at his death he left an estate of some £20,000. He regularly exhibited at the Old Water-Colour Society's exhibitions and between 1824, when he became an Associate Member, and his death in 1864 he had exhibited no less than 791 works. Thackeray began his essays on the Old Water-Colour Society's exhibitions in 1839 and referred to Hunt's works in these terms: 'If you want to see *real* nature, now, real expression, real startling home poetry, look at every-one of Hunt's heads. Hogarth never painted anything better than these figures taken singly.'[1] On another occasion Thackeray wrote: 'If I were the Duke of Devonshire, I would have a couple of Hunts in every room in all my houses; if I had the blue devils (and even their Graces are, I suppose, occasionally so troubled) I would but cast my eyes upon these grand, good-humoured pictures and defy care.'[2]

Hunt also exhibited in several other exhibitions of distinction. He had eleven works in the Exposition Universelle at the Paris Salon in 1855 and was awarded a Certificate of Merit. He received a favourable comment by Baudelaire in his review of the Salon. Baudelaire expressed his great pleasure at having seen the works of various British artists including, among others, 'the two Hunts, the one a stubborn realist, and the other the passionate and self-willed creator of Pre-Raphaelitism'.[3] Edmond About, another French art critic, wrote: 'Les petites études de M. Hunt qui frisent de près [run close to] la caricature, se vendent plus cher que les tableaux de M. Ingres et de M. Delacroix.'[4]

The following year Hunt was awarded the honorary title of Member of the Royal Academy of Amsterdam. Then in 1857 he had thirty works in the Exhibition of Art Treasures of the United Kingdom at Manchester. Only Turner and David Roberts had a greater number of works exhibited.

Shortly after Hunt's death in 1864 W. M. Rossetti paid tribute to his work in the Water-Colour Society's Second Winter Exhibition in the *Fine Arts Quarterly Review*:

> The very deplorable loss which English Art has sustained in the death of that sturdy and gentle humourist, poet of literalism and unrivalled prince of still-life painters, Hunt, gives to his contributions, the last which he lived to see upon the walls of any gallery, a sad interest.

James Holland, fellow artist and friend and himself a flower painter in his early days, paid tribute in these words: 'Take it from me there is only one great flower painter in the world and that is old Billy Hunt.'

Similar praise was bestowed by Samuel Palmer who wrote in 1872, eight years after Hunt's death: 'The only quite certain way of making money by watercolours is, I fancy, to do such figures, fruit and flowers as William Hunt did and to do them as well. This again wants a whole life.'[5] Birket Foster also admired Hunt's work[6] and his drawing room at Witley was adorned by eight of Hunt's watercolours.

Ruskin was a great admirer of Hunt and a personal friend, and owned a number of his works. For Ruskin, Hunt was one of the greatest exponents of English Naturalism, possessed of a supreme ability to find beauty and interest 'in . . . things themselves . . . for their own sake.'[7] There are numerous references to Hunt throughout Ruskin's writings. For example, in *Praeterita* he writes that the breakfast room at his house on Denmark Hill 'opening on the lawn and farther hills was extremely pretty when the walls were mostly covered with lakes by Turner and doves by Hunt';[8] while in *The Elements of Drawing* Hunt is pronounced 'The best painter of still life that ever existed'.[9]

Ruskin, in the Preface to his Notes to the Exhibition of Prout and Hunt which he organised at the Fine Art Society in 1879–80 (contained in Appendix II), writes that

> drawings of this simple character were made for these same middle classes, exclusively; and even for the second order of the middle classes, more accurately expressed by the term *bourgeoisie*. The great people always bought Canaletto, not Prout, and Van Huysum, not Hunt. There was indeed no quality in the bright little watercolours which could look other than pert in ghostly corridors, and petty in halls of state; but they gave an unquestionable tone of liberal-mindedness to a suburban villa, and were the cheerfullest possible decorations for a moderate-sized breakfast-parlour opening on a nicely-mown lawn.[10]

There was good reason for Ruskin's admiration of Hunt. Ruskin had a passion for accurate detail, for example in his architectural drawings and in his drawings of birds and minerals, and Hunt was a master of detail. Ruskin also had a profound respect for artists who acquired a technical mastery over their medium: this criterion Hunt again achieved in full measure.

Ruskin was also a great devotee of colour and in this respect too he was a great admirer of Hunt. In his lecture in 1859 on the 'Unity of Art' he discusses the relative merits of the Pre-Raphaelites and Hunt as teachers of colour:

> In the particular gifts of colour there are only one or two of the Pre-Raphaelites and William Hunt of the Old Water-Colour Society who would be safe guides. And as quite a safe guide, there is nobody but William Hunt because the Pre-Raphaelites are all more or less affected by enthusiasm and by various morbid conditions of intellect and temper: but old William Hunt – I am sorry to say 'old', but I say it in a loving way, for every year that has added to his life [Hunt was then 69] has added also to his skill – William Hunt is as right as the Venetians, so far as he goes, and what is more, nearly as inimitable as they.[11]

Ruskin's exaggerated comparison of Hunt with the Venetians should not be allowed to obscure his just perception of Hunt's mastery of colour.

Ruskin also wrote of Hunt: 'simplicity and intensity both of the highest character – simplicity of aim and intensity of power and success are involved in that man's unpretending labour'.[12]

Ruskin, nearly thirty years Hunt's junior in age, took lessons from Hunt first in 1854[13] and then again in 1861 as appears from the Diaries of George Price Boyce, himself an artist as well as a contemporary and close personal friend of Rossetti and his circle. In his diary entry for 4 January 1861, Boyce records that 'Ruskin is now hard at work mastering the manipulations of painting under old Wm. Hunt. He expects to be 8 or 10 years at this: meantime does not mean to write or lecture'.[14]

Another interesting and admiring tribute, which to this writer seems very much to the point, comes from yet another artist, W. R. Sickert. In an article written in 1910, Sickert refers to Hunt and his work in the following terms:

> I was looking at the exquisite examples of [Hunt's] work at Agnew's the other day, and thinking how he had anticipated the Impressionist technique, in his multitude of small touches, building up a sensitive whole. I was thinking of him, and of Pissarro, and of how the extreme division into small touches in each case brought about this desirable result. The more touches, provided they are dictated by sensation and observation, the more frequent is the revision. Hence the juster sum. Both painters mirror the life of their country with intense local and national character and tenderness of general observation. And then I reflected how just a taint of smiling toleration clung, in this country, even to the appreciation of Hunt's work. Due to what? To the patronising tone of the praise of the wealthy wine-merchant's son [John Ruskin] who wielded so able and interesting a pen. But in those days at least, if they patronised, the brutes bought![15]

In the opinion of the present writer it seems reasonable to compare Hunt's still-life work in pure watercolour to that of Chardin in oil. At its best there is the same impeccable sense of composition when nothing looks contrived, however much conscious struggle has been needed to produce such apparently effortless simplicity. The reader is referred to Chardin's 'Still Life with Plums' in oil (Colour Plate 20) and Hunt's 'Study of Copper Pot and Horn Mug' (685, Plate 52) and 'Still Life with Earthenware Pitcher, Coffee Pot and Basket' (684, Colour Plate 21) in watercolour, both the latter being part of the Ruskin Art Collection in the Ashmolean Museum, Oxford, in support of this comparison.

But Hunt was far more than a fine painter of still lifes. Many of his figure studies of women show great tenderness, sensitivity and charm; while his studies of men and boys display an earthiness and vigour which are happily combined with an intimate understanding of the countryside and its often simpler and more modest inhabitants.

Yet for the present writer, Hunt's finest and most memorable works are his early landscapes and farmyard scenes around Bushey and Cassiobury, and the church exteriors and interiors at Bushey and its neighbouring village churches. These by their directness and unerring sense of composition best convey Hunt's passionate love of nature and his skill in portraying it in loving and simple terms. His talents as an all-round watercolourist deserve a far greater and wider recognition than they have hitherto been accorded.

PART I

Life and Work

1

First Period: to 1830

William Henry Hunt, commonly known as William Hunt, was born in London on 28 March 1790 at 8 Old Belton Street, now Endell Street. He was the son of John and Judith Hunt, his father being in a small manufacturing way of business as a tin-plate worker making canisters, tin boxes and such-like goods. He was also a japanner and decorated his goods in the traditional colours of green, black, gold, and red. He was much employed by the numerous theatrical establishments in the neighbourhood.

The house and adjoining workshops were occupied by the Hunt family for many years but have long since been demolished together with other buildings in the same street. At the time of William Hunt's birth the immediate neighbourhood was unattractive: Old Belton Street itself was narrow and the roadway at its northern end was not more than ten feet wide. No doubt its nearness to some of the important London theatres was a compelling reason for the family to remain.

Here William Hunt spent his early childhood. He was a sickly child, his legs being weak and puny and his knees and toes turned in so that he could only walk with difficulty and had to shuffle along.[1] Little is known of his mother Judith Hunt except that she was a kind and domesticated woman who looked after her sickly son with exemplary attention.

William Hunt as a young boy had only limited schooling but spent much of his time drawing and painting at home. As Ruskin wrote later, 'you get your Prout, your Hunt your Turner not indeed any of them well able to spell English.'[2] Probably concern for his health caused his mother to take him to the country to stay with her family who lived in the neighbourhood of Bramley near Basingstoke, Hampshire. He would thus have had the opportunity at an early age of seeing and sketching the open countryside and to have developed that fondness for nature and landscape which never left him.

At the age of sixteen William Hunt persuaded his father to allow him to start a career as an artist. His father must have felt that his son's feeble health would not stand up to the rigours of tin-plate working. Roget records a remark made by William Hunt's uncle, a butcher, some years later, who said that his 'nevvy little Billy Hunt was always a poor cripple, and as he was fit for nothing, they made an artist of him'.[3]

In any event in 1806 his father made the fortunate choice of apprenticing his son to John Varley for a term of seven years. According to Roget again, the seven-year term was chosen because the father did not believe that a knowledge of the arts could be acquired in a shorter period than was normally required to make a proficient tin man.[4] His father paid Varley a premium of £200.[5]

John Varley was in every way an excellent choice. Born in 1778 and thus twelve years older than Hunt, he exercised from a comparatively early age a notable influence on the art world of his day. He possessed to a remarkable degree the art of making friends – among many others he became a close friend of Blake. Varley was a man of unbounded energy and of unselfish generosity, not only financial but also in giving practical help in their work to his brother artists. He was a founder member of the Society of Painters in Water-Colours, commonly known as the Old Water-Colour Society, which was formed in 1805. It is said to have been due to Varley that William Holman Hunt gave up the drudgery of a clerkship for the more congenial life of an artist. Copley Fielding was among those who benefited from his advice without direct pupillage. De Wint had much free help and was probably indebted to Varley for his introduction to Dr Monro's Academy. David Cox began a course of instruction with him at ten shillings an hour, and Varley, having learned after two or three lessons that Cox was not an amateur, insisted on his coming as often as he liked without paying any fee. In short Varley was a central figure in a wide circle of London artists.

When William Hunt joined the studio Varley was living and working at Harris Place, Oxford Street, and subsequently moved to 18 Broad Street, Golden Square. Of Hunt's fellow pupils, the leader was undoubtedly the Irishman William Mulready (born in 1786). He was married to Varley's sister Elizabeth (although the marriage did not last long), and acted as a kind of unofficial instructor to his fellow pupils. Shortly after Hunt's arrival the studio was joined by John Linnell (born in 1792). The following account in John Linnell's unpublished autobiographical notes describes how Linnell met Hunt at the Varleys.

> Here [at John Varley's] I became acquainted with William Hunt who had just been placed under J. Varley – Hunt whose father was a tin man. His shop was in Belton Street, Long Acre, a very low dirty place (now altered). Hunt and I were constant companions in sketching from nature. I looked up to him wondering if I should ever be able to accomplish as much as he had then attained to – he was so far in advance of me in general knowledge of Art.[6]

Both Hunt and Linnell in fact lived for a year in Varley's house at 18 Broad Street and quickly became firm friends, going on numerous sketching expeditions together, as will be more fully described later.

In 1807 Hunt and Linnell were employed by an older artist George Dawe to work upon a large transparency for an illumination to celebrate a victory over the French. In the same year Hunt began to exhibit at the Royal Academy, then situated at Somerset House. He sent in three landscapes of scenes near Hounslow, Reading and

Leatherhead, all in oils. In 1808 both Hunt and Linnell entered the Royal Academy Schools as students.

Undoubtedly the best account of Hunt's early years in Varley's studio and at the Royal Academy Schools is contained in the article on the artist by the Pre-Raphaelite critic F. G. Stephens which was published in *Fraser's Magazine* in November 1865, the year after Hunt's death.[7] The following is an extract.

As I have said, Mulready was the leading spirit at Varley's, he was very intimately connected with the family of his master and concerned in their interests. It was by Mulready's advice that both Hunt and Mr. Linnell entered the Academy in order to study, with greater severity than the loose ways of Varley's house permitted, from the human form, in the antique and the life. Mulready, although the pupil of a landscape painter, and at that time mainly practised in that branch of the art, saw the necessity that anyone who desired to excel should study the figure. We all know how his love of such study made him work all his life as if he were, to use his own words, 'drawing for a medal.' That work was mostly carried on in the Life School of the Royal Academy, where he was not only the best draughtsman, but the most persevering student. It is remarkable that the respective degrees of earnestness with which this notion of the importance of study from the life was carried out by Mulready, Mr. Linnell, and Hunt, are distinctly impressed on their manners of drawing and even of painting, especially in dealing with solid forms. Hunt's pictures, particularly those executed in oil, display his comparative neglect of the precept. Even those in Water-colour, produced when nearly half a century of study had made his hand precise when dealing with a limited range of subjects, confirm the loss. Hunt entered the Academy soon after Haydon arrived there; Wilkie also came within a short time. The school contained many men of note. Hunt, as an old fellow student tells me, drew the 'Gladiators', and his early entrance to the Life School was confidently predicted. It is not certain if Hunt ever drew from the life in the Academy school, and I am disinclined to believe that he could have had at any period of his career much practice from the nude. Excellent as was his drawing of figures in drapery, it is deficient in that precision and firmness of treatment which characterize the accomplished draughtsman from the naked form. This shortcoming shows itself at many points. In this respect I fancy he must have resembled Turner.

Mr. Linnell was Hunt's companion in this part of his life. The pair, as Turner and Girtin had done before them, were accustomed during the summer time to sketch on the banks and in the neighbourhood of the Thames. Teddington, Richmond, Hammersmith (near the mall of which place Turner was then living), Chiswick, Millbank and Lambeth, each in turn offered a school and means of practice. Mr. Linnell possesses a considerable number of studies made by Hunt and himself at this period (1805–9); these are all in oil colours, copies of bits of scenery, hedgerows, banks, little landscapes, comprising trees and cottages; water is frequently introduced.

The study of Twickenham (158, Plate 2) is a good example and an almost identical view by John Linnell is also in the Tate Gallery [T.934].

Hunt's and Linnell's early out-door 'Sketches from Nature' or 'Studies from Nature', as Hunt chose to title them, are of considerable merit and deserve greater recognition than they have hitherto received. They show Hunt's deep affection for and understanding of 'Nature' in landscape painting and reflect the same philosophy of Naturalism as Constable's and Turner's oil sketches of the first two decades of the century. Examples of Hunt's oil paintings of this period are 'Windsor Castle' (109, Plate 3), 'Twickenham' (158, Plate 2), and 'The Reaper' (361, Colour Plate 1).

In 1809 Hunt was sketching with Linnell at Hastings and in the same year was employed with other young artists in the decoration of the interior of Drury Lane Theatre 'where he executed part of the drop scene, which represented "the Temple of Apollo", and did a good deal to the Corinthian columns, tripods, and so forth. His handling is said to have been very effective.'[8]

Meanwhile Hunt continued to exhibit at the Royal Academy. His name appears in the catalogue for 1809 and 1810 when in each year he exhibited a single 'sketch' or 'landscape' in oil. His address, which had previously been included as at Varley's house in Broad Street, is given in 1811 as 8 Old Belton Street, his father's house. It would seem that he served only five years of his seven-year apprenticeship.

There is no doubt that Hunt benefited greatly from his pupillage with John Varley. A good example of his work during his early days with Varley is of Saltwood Castle (179, Plate 5) in pure watercolour. Cornelius Varley, John's brother and three years his junior, made the interesting comment some time later that his brother gained credit because both Hunt and Linnell 'distinguished themselves without showing any likeness to their master.'

In 1814 an important event occurred in Hunt's career. He joined the Society of Painters in Oil and Water-Colours. This was a newly formed society which came into being as a result of a serious dispute which had occurred among the members of the Old Water-Colour Society. Between the date of the foundation of the Old Water-Colour Society in the year 1805 and its temporary demise in 1814, the Society had found it increasingly difficult to pay its way solely by exhibiting watercolours. A number of the members were anxious that oil paintings should be included in the exhibitions and when this step was successfully opposed by the Council of the Society a number of the leading members seceded. These included de Wint, Gilpin, Nash, Reinagle and Pugin. These artists and some others decided to change the name of the Old Water-Colour Society to the Society of Painters in Oil and Water-Colours.

Up to 1814, although Hunt had worked in both oil and watercolour, he had exhibited only in oil at the Royal Academy. It was therefore as a promising young painter in oil that he was invited to contribute works to the exhibitions of the renamed Society. Accordingly, in 1814 he exhibited two works in oils at the Society's premises in Spring Gardens, the above-mentioned view of Windsor Castle (National Trust, 109, Plate 3) and a view of the Bell Tower, Windsor. In 1815 he exhibited six works: two views at Hastings, a view from Richmond Hill, two portraits, and a view of a country house. The present whereabouts of these is unknown but the probability is that some at least were in watercolour.

Between 1815 and 1819 Hunt did not exhibit either at Spring Gardens or at the Royal Academy. During this period he produced several fine views on the Thames. Two examples are of building Waterloo Bridge (239, Plate 8)[9] and of St Paul's

Cathedral and Blackfriars Bridge (244, Plate 10). In 1819 he exhibited at Spring Gardens a sketch from the East Cliff, Hastings. This is the beautiful watercolour 'View of Hastings' (137, Plate 6) in the Ashmolean Museum, Oxford. Another fine work, 'Hastings from White Rock' done at the same time (July 1818), is in the Museum and Art Gallery, Hastings (84).

By his mid-teens Hunt, like so many other contemporary artists, had found a generous patron in Dr Thomas Monro. Dr Monro (born in 1759) was a man of standing and culture who succeeded his father as principal physician to Bethlem Hospital and attended professionally for insanity such diverse patients as George III and John Robert Cozens.

Dr Monro had formed, around 1794, what became known as the 'Monro Academy' consisting of a number of young artists, mainly watercolourists of promise. Among their number over the years were found Turner, Girtin, Hearne, Edridge, John and Cornelius Varley, Cotman, de Wint, Linnell and Hunt. Dr Monro's motives for starting and continuing his Academy over many years were probably mixed. Perhaps his wish to help young and struggling artists of promise was predominant. They could study and copy works from his large and varied collection of drawings, which included a number, as already mentioned, by Canaletto and Gainsborough. As an amateur landscape artist himself – of respectable though derivative qualities, in the manner of Gainsborough – he could guide their brush or pencil with practical advice. But he could also derive material benefit in retaining the copies they made of various works in his possession, such as the watercolours of John Robert Cozens.

The Monro Academy would meet regularly on winter evenings at Dr Monro's town house at 8 Adelphi Terrace where he had moved in 1794. There are a number of references to the activities of the Monro Academy in the *Farington Diary*. The doctor had had double desks constructed facing each other so that one candle and one water pot and ink pot would serve for two artists face to face. In October 1798 Farington records that Turner and Girtin had said 'they had been employed by Dr Monro for three years to draw at his house. They went at six and stayed till ten. Girtin drew the outlines and Turner washed in the effects.'[10] They were chiefly employed in copying the watercolours by John Robert Cozens of which Dr Monro had temporarily obtained possession while he was treating Cozens's insanity. Dr Monro paid Turner 3*s*. 6*d*. each night. Girtin did not say what he was paid but it was likely to have been the same.

The first known reference to Dr Monro's patronage of Hunt is in 1806 when Hunt was sixteen and had just entered John Varley's studio. This reference occurs in the diaries of E. T. Monro (the Doctor's eldest son) where for April 1806, it is recorded 'Linnell, Hunt and Turner to draw'.[11] This must have been at Dr Monro's London house, 8 Adelphi Terrace. Hunt had already been engaged, while a pupil of Varley, in copying drawings by Canaletto in Dr Monro's collection. Another task which Hunt and Linnell, who often worked together at Dr Monro's house, performed for the Doctor was to make copies from his fine collection of Gainsborough drawings.

Linnell describes in his autobiographical notes, previously cited,[12] how:

Very often William Hunt and I went to draw for two or three hours at Dr. Monro's after the Academy – Dr. Monro had a large collection of the early drawings of Girtin and Turner both of whom he had been in the habit of taking out to draw from Nature for him and these drawings with compositions in charcoal by Gainsborough of which the Doctor had a great number William Hunt and I copied for the Doctor who paid us each one shilling and sixpence the hour. We sometimes had some supper also – some of these copies were afterwards, I have no doubt sold for originals.

Dr Monro had purchased *en bloc* about eighty drawings by Gainsborough from the artist's daughter Margaret Gainsborough in 1801[13] for which he paid 160 guineas, afterwards adding 20 guineas on her complaining that it was too little. Linnell's biographer Alfred T. Story confirms[14] Linnell was of the opinion that Monro would sell their copies for originals but he goes on to say that 'F. G. Stephens, who has made a careful enquiry into the matter, is convinced that this is a mistake and that the Doctor was actuated solely by his love of art'. 'A parcel of copies by Hunt' was Lot 14 on the fifth day of the Dr Monro Sale at Christie's on 2 July 1833, among other lots of copies from Gainsborough.

Dr Monro also owned a country house at Fetcham in Surrey, but he moved from there in 1805 and after spending a year or so looking for a house in the neighbourhood of Bushey in Hertfordshire he rented, in 1808, an agreeable house, Merry Hill, on the outskirts of Bushey. Here, in addition to his London Academy, he maintained a kind of rural academy, spending his summers at Bushey until in 1820 he retired permanently to Merry Hill and gave up 8 Adelphi Terrace. He continued, however, to carry on his practice from Merry Hill until after 1825 when he ceased to visit any patients. According to an unpublished biography of Dr Thomas Monro by Dr F. J. G. Jefferiss,[15] Monro, after his retirement,

occupied himself with working on his collection of drawings in an octagonal room in the middle of the house lit by a sky light, usually dressed in a loose wrapper or dressing gown and visited by his children and grandchildren in truly patriarchal style. He pasted drawings all over the walls of his room, nailing strips of wood between them to give the appearance of frames. In snowy weather he would have the garden paths swept and artificial flowers put in the flower beds as he disliked the lack of colour. He had many friends in and around Bushey including Lord Essex at Cassiobury Park whom he visited frequently. As he found difficulty in walking, he rode everywhere even in the churchyard.

Dr Monro died in 1833 in his seventy-third year and was buried in Bushey churchyard by the graves of his wife, his second son Henry and his old artist friends, Hearne and Edridge.

It is not known when Hunt first visited Dr Monro at Merry Hill. The first specific references to a visit of Hunt are contained in E. T. Monro's diaries:[16]

1815	17 Aug	– Mr. Hunt came to stay and draw [at Bushey].
	18 Aug	– Mr. Hunt coloured first sketch. F [father] went early.

	19 Aug	– Hunt drawing the stables this evening.
	21 Aug	– Sketched the house. Mr. Hunt drawing 'Bob'.
	3 Sept	– Church. Mr. R with us. Walked to Cassiobury with boys. . . . Mr. Hunt went to Harrow.
	10 Sept	– Mr. Hunt returned from Harrow.
1816	20 July	– Mr. Hunt at Bushey.
	29 Aug	– Dined at Bushey. Mr. Hunt still there.
	3 Sept	– Dined at Bushey. The Smiths and Mr. Hunt still there.
	5 Sept	– Dined at Bushey. The boys went to St. Albans with Mr. Hunt.

It is clear from these diary entries that Hunt's visits to Dr Monro were fairly prolonged and that he had become an intimate member of the Doctor's family. The diary entry of 19 August 1815 must refer to the drawing of Dr Monro on horseback inspecting his burnt-out stables (23, Plate 12). Other examples drawn with the reed pen at about this period are 'Dr Monro's Carpenter at Work' (234) and 'The Saw Mill, Bushey' (89, Colour Plate 2).

This use of the reed pen by Hunt is directly attributable to his early days in the Monro Academy. One of Hunt's tasks there was to copy some of the fine series of drawings by Canaletto owned by Dr Monro. At the sale at Christie's of the Doctor's collection shortly after his death in 1833, the sale catalogue included thirteen drawings 'attributed to Canaletti [sic]' and four drawings in two lots, lots 35 and 36, each entitled 'A Pair after Canaletti [sic] by Hunt'.[17] A number of such copies exist, of which 'A Scene in Venice' (134, Plate 4) is a typical example. It shows how well Hunt had absorbed the lively and nervous touch with the reed pen which Canaletto had perfected. That Dr Monro owned these copies by Hunt up to his death is a good indication of the value he placed on the copying skill of his young protégé.

Hunt continued most successfully the use of reed pen and ink for a number of years and particularly in his drawings of Bushey, Aldenham and Watford churches, as will shortly be described. In London also he continued with his series of Thames bridges, of which 'London Bridge with Pool of London Beyond' (31, Plate 11) and 'Rebuilding London Bridge' (58, Plate 9) are fine examples. He was also commissioned in 1822 by Dr Monro to do a drawing of St Martin-in-the-Fields which resulted in one of his greatest works in reed pen, of the portico of that church (141, Plate 24).

Hunt was one of the most active members of the Academy in Bushey, and would spend more than a month at a time with the Doctor at Merry Hill, being paid 7*s.* 6*d.* a day.[18] He was at first to a great extent under instruction from the Doctor. F. G. Stephens writes that 'at times it happened that the employer discovered the student not to be going on so steadily as he judged right or that he was tending to heedlessness in execution and he would then come behind Hunt, put him out of his chair and wipe out with a sponge the least satisfactory portions of a drawing.'[19] It must be remembered that in 1815 Hunt was only twenty-five years of age and very much in the early stages of his career.

Hunt may well have started to work at the Monro Academy in the neighbourhood of Bushey several years before 1815, the date referred to above in E. T. Monro's diary. There is, for example, a watercolour of 'Singer's Farm, Bushey', by Henry Edridge in the British Museum (1845. 8.18.7), of which Hunt made an almost identical copy (233). Edridge's drawing in the British Museum is not dated but there is an early inscription on the mount 'drawn October 17th 1811'. It seems reasonable to assume that Hunt's copy might have been made, perhaps at Bushey, a year or so prior to 1815.

There can be little doubt that Henry Edridge must have had a considerable influence on Hunt. Edridge, born in 1769, was Hunt's senior by twenty-one years and in 1811, when Hunt was still young and struggling, Edridge was a mature and successful artist in both portraiture and landscape. He was of the same generation as Dr Monro and they were close and intimate friends. Edridge was a frequent visitor to Bushey and stayed with the Doctor at Merry Hill on many occasions. He drew numerous cottage and farm scenes round Bushey. For example, 'View near Little Bushey with St Albans Abbey in the Distance' in the Victoria and Albert Museum [2938.1876] very closely resembles Hunt's work of this period and could well be confused with it. One can fairly assume that it was the young Hunt who was influenced by the older Edridge rather than vice versa.

Edridge, towards the end of his life, made three painting visits to France in 1817, 1819 and 1821, the year of his death, and drew both in pencil and in watercolour a number of large architectural works of towns and churches in Normandy such as Rouen and Abbeville. Hunt was subsequently to make copies of several of Edridge's Normandy scenes, such as 'Rouen' (Huntington Library, 96), 'Beauvais' (Yale Center, 254), and several others.

Whether Hunt ever crossed the Channel cannot be finally answered, though it is not improbable. Spending so many winters at Hastings he could well have done so from a little way down the coast, perhaps Folkestone or Dover. Two drawings, one in black chalk (212), the other in pencil (211), of the Castle of Arques, both so inscribed in Hunt's handwriting, strongly convey the impression of sketches done on the spot. Arques is just south of St Omer in the Pas-de-Calais and within twenty-five miles of Calais, Boulogne or Dunkerque, and within easy reach of English ports on the south coast.

As the years went on, Hunt, while still working as a pupil at the Academy, was commissioned by Dr Monro to draw specific views in the neighbourhood of Bushey. One of the most notable in the reed pen and watercolour technique is 'Bushey Churchyard' (252, Plate 25), with the tombs of his second son Henry, himself an artist of promise who died in 1814 at the early age of twenty-three, and of the Doctor's devoted artist friends Thomas Hearne (died in 1817) and Henry Edridge, and with Dr Monro himself on horseback. It is likely to have been drawn around 1822, the year following Edridge's death. There are many other fine reed pen and watercolour drawings by Hunt of church interiors and exteriors, not only of Bushey Church itself but of the neighbouring churches of Aldenham and Watford. 'The Nave, Bushey Church' (17, Plate 26) is a particularly fine example, and the following are notable works of the same kind: 'Bushey Church, South Side' (24, Plate 27), 'North Porch of Bushey Church' (138), 'The Nave, Aldenham Church' (95), and 'Side Chapel in an Old Church' (Aldenham Church, 173).

'Interior of the Belfry, Bushey Church' (197, Plate 28) is of particular interest. It is a preliminary drawing in reed pen and brown ink of the interior of the belfry, Bushey Church, squared for enlargement, the squares being numbered in pencil on the right-hand side of the drawing. The finished and larger version in reed pen, brown ink and watercolour is at the Yale Center (251, Plate 29).

In addition to his views of churches, Hunt worked extensively in the villages and countryside in the neighbourhood of Bushey, and produced a number of beautiful landscape drawings, sometimes with the reed pen and watercolour and sometimes in pure watercolour. These would, for the most part, have been done when Hunt was staying with Dr Monro at Merry Hill. There is a delightful view of the house (29, Colour Plate 5) with Mrs Monro looking down from the balcony and the Monro daughter Sally standing in the porch. Of works in pure watercolour, 'The Village in the Valley' (26, Plate 20), 'Village Street in St Albans' (247, Plate 18), 'View over Bushey' (90, Colour Plate 3), and 'Lecture House, Watford' (246, Plate 13) are outstanding examples.

It is a measure of the value which Dr Monro placed on Hunt's work that at his death he owned no less than 168 works by Hunt including many views of churches and landscapes in the neighbourhood of Bushey. These were included in the sale at Christie's by Dr Monro's Executors of his collection, starting on 26 June 1833 and lasting for five days. According to the sale catalogue the collection comprised works by:

> Wilson, Gainsborough, Hoppner, Loutherbourg, Bartolozzi, Marlow, Hearne, Wheatley, Edridge, Girtin, Cozens, Webber, Rooker, Sandby, Neale, Alexander, Havell, Munn, Bonington, Turner R.A., Reinagle, Barret, Varley and Hunt, also a collection of prints and drawings by Old Masters and a landscape by Salvator Rosa; an Historic Picture by Rembrandt and a Camera Obscura with Transparencies beautifully painted on glass by Gainsborough.

The last is now in the Victoria and Albert Museum.

It was during one of Hunt's sketching visits with Dr Monro in the neighbourhood of Watford and Bushey, and doubtless through his introduction and recommendation, that Hunt met one of his most important early patrons, the Fifth Earl of Essex (1757–1839) of Cassiobury Park, just outside Watford. The Earl, a close friend and neighbour of Dr Monro, was one of the most enlightened of the ennobled patrons of his age. He shared the Doctor's enthusiasm for helping young and virtually unknown artists at the outset of their careers. For example, the Earl continued the Doctor's patronage of Turner, who exhibited four large watercolours of Cassiobury in his own gallery in Harley Street which are likely to have been done in 1807–8.

Hunt was employed by the Earl of Essex in the early 1820s to make drawings of the interior of Cassiobury House and of views and cottages in Cassiobury Park. Two fine examples are 'The Dining Room' at Cassiobury (375, Plate 22), dated 1821 and exhibited at the Royal Academy in 1822, and 'The Drawing Room' at Cassiobury (376, Plate 23), dated 1823. 'The Dining Room' (Lot 194), together with other interiors at Cassiobury, 'The Anteroom' (Lot 195), and 'The Housekeeper's Room' (Lot 196), as well as 'A Cottage' at Cassiobury (Lot 199), were included in the sale of work from Hunt's studio sold by his Executors as directed by his Will on 16–17 May 1864 at Christie's. It seems surprising that these were still with Hunt when he died; one would have expected they would have been retained by the Earl. Reference is made throughout the Sale Catalogue to 'Cashiobury' rather than to 'Cassiobury'. A copy of the Sale Catalogue is contained in Appendix I.

Shortly before the Earl's death in 1839 he had commissioned John Britton to produce an illustrated *History and Description of Cassiobury Park*. This was published in 1837 with four illustrations by Turner, four by Edridge, seven by Pugin, and an elaborate view of 'The Essex Chantry, Watford Church' (248) and three woodcuts of cottages in the Park by Hunt.

It has been mentioned earlier that Hunt was since boyhood something of a cripple. F. G. Stephens records that 'about Bushey and in the woodlands of Cassiobury, William Hunt used to be trundled on a sort of barrow with a hood over it, which was drawn by a man or a donkey while he made sketches for that Earl of Essex who had married Miss Stephens, the present Dowager Countess of Essex, who is famous in the role of English singing.'[20]

In 1822 Hunt secured another important new client, the Sixth Duke of Devonshire. How this came about is not known and it appears there are no letters, bills or receipts to or from Hunt now surviving at Chatsworth recording this relationship. The Duke had succeeded to the dukedom in 1811 and was responsible for the rebuilding of large parts of Chatsworth, including the Library, particularly during the 1820s. There are a number of elaborately finished watercolours by Hunt in the Chatsworth Collection of interiors of the Duke's various houses at Chatsworth, Hardwick, Devonshire House and Chiswick. These are dated in various years between 1822 and 1828. There are eight interiors of Chatsworth, three of Hardwick, and three of Chiswick House, including one of the Park and one of Devonshire House. They are of the highest quality as illustrations of grand interiors and technically of great brilliance, as can be seen in 'The Library, Chatsworth' (341, Colour Plate 6), 'The Long Gallery, Hardwick' (351, Plate 46), 'The Saloon, Devonshire House' (332, Plate 47), and 'The Gallery, Chiswick House' (334, Plate 45). There are also a number of drawings of members of the staff at Chatsworth.

In 1822 Hunt returned to the Royal Academy, where he exhibited three watercolours, 'Sketch of the Porch of St Martin's Church' (141, Plate 24) and 'Sketch of the Dining Room at Cassiobury Park, the Seat of the Earl of Essex' (375, Plate 22), as well as a 'Sketch from Nature'. His address is given in the Royal Academy Catalogue as 36 Brownlow Street, Drury Lane, so although still living near to the

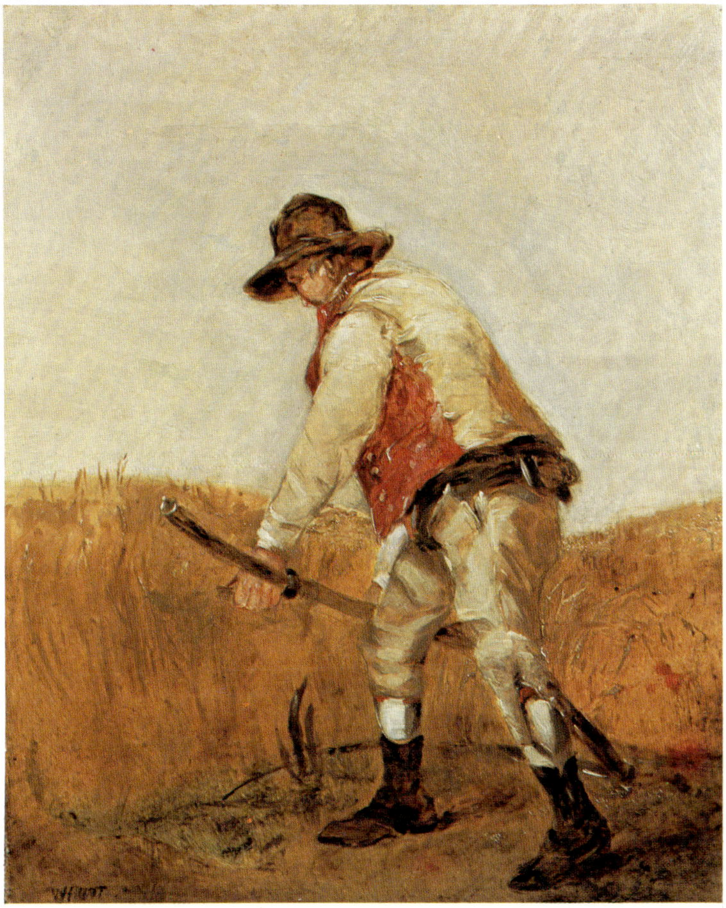

1 (361) The Reaper
Oil on canvas, 11½ × 9½ (292 × 241)
Fry Collection

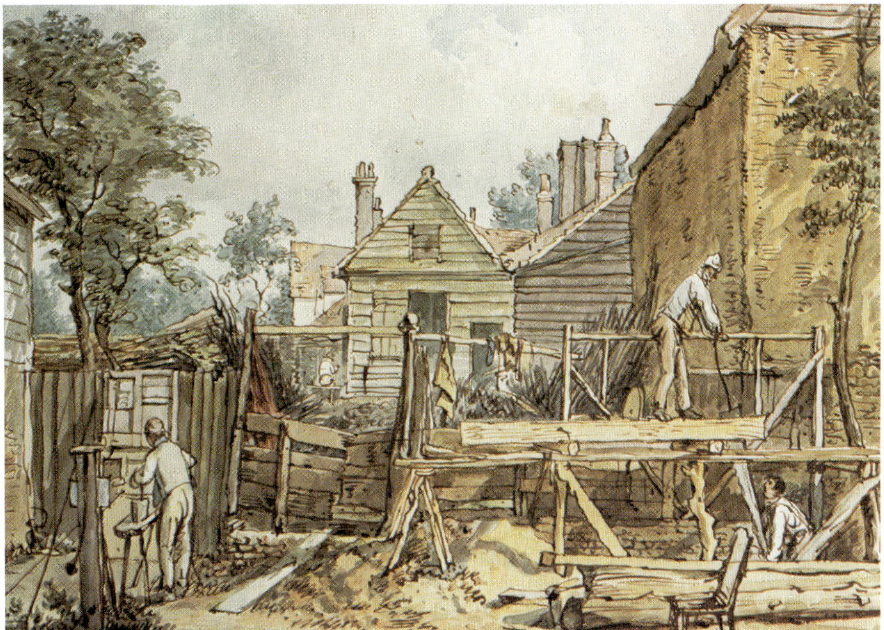

2 (89) Saw Mill, Bushey
Reed pen, brown ink and watercolour, 10⅛ × 14⅛ (257 × 358)
Huntington Library, San Marino

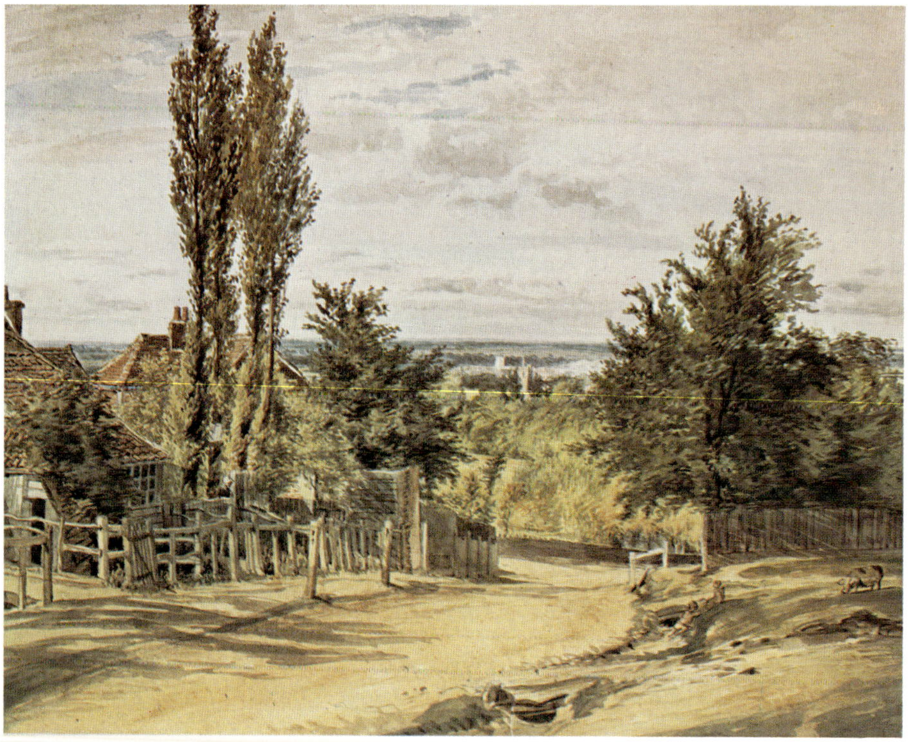

3 (90) View over Bushey with Bushey Church in the Distance
Watercolour, $10\frac{3}{8} \times 13$ (263 × 330)
Huntington Library, San Marino

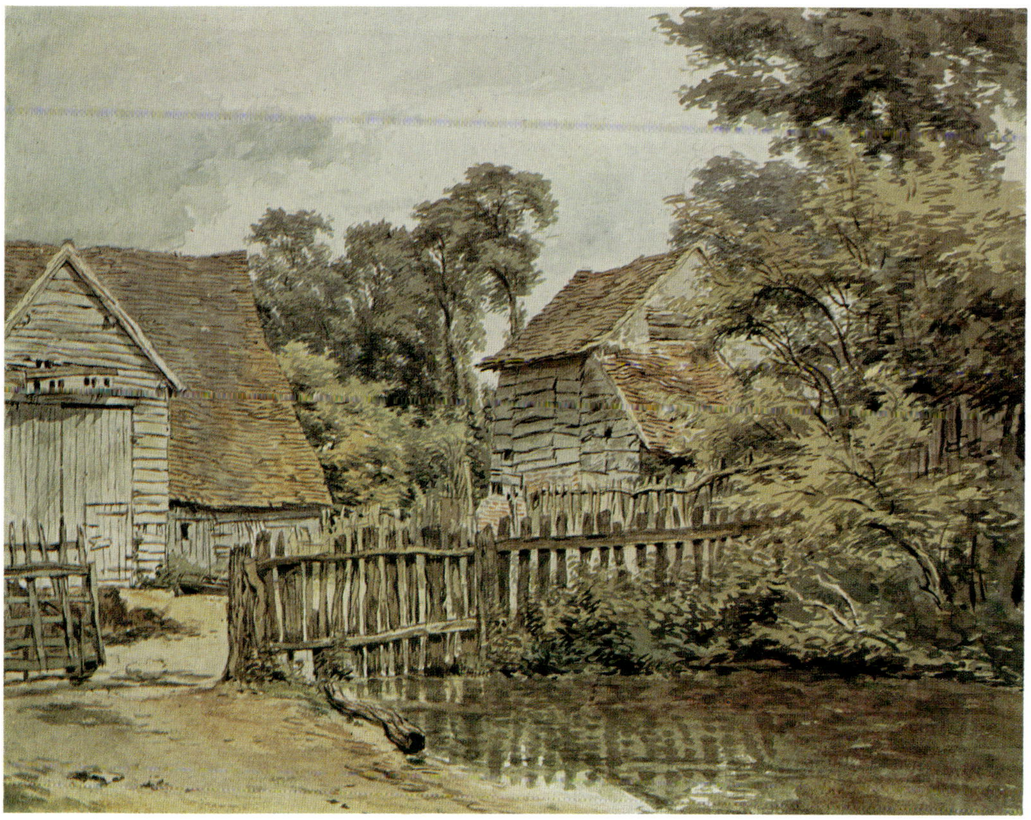

4 (169) Farmyard with a Pool
Pencil and watercolour, $13 \times 16\frac{5}{8}$ (330 × 423)
Victoria and Albert Museum, London

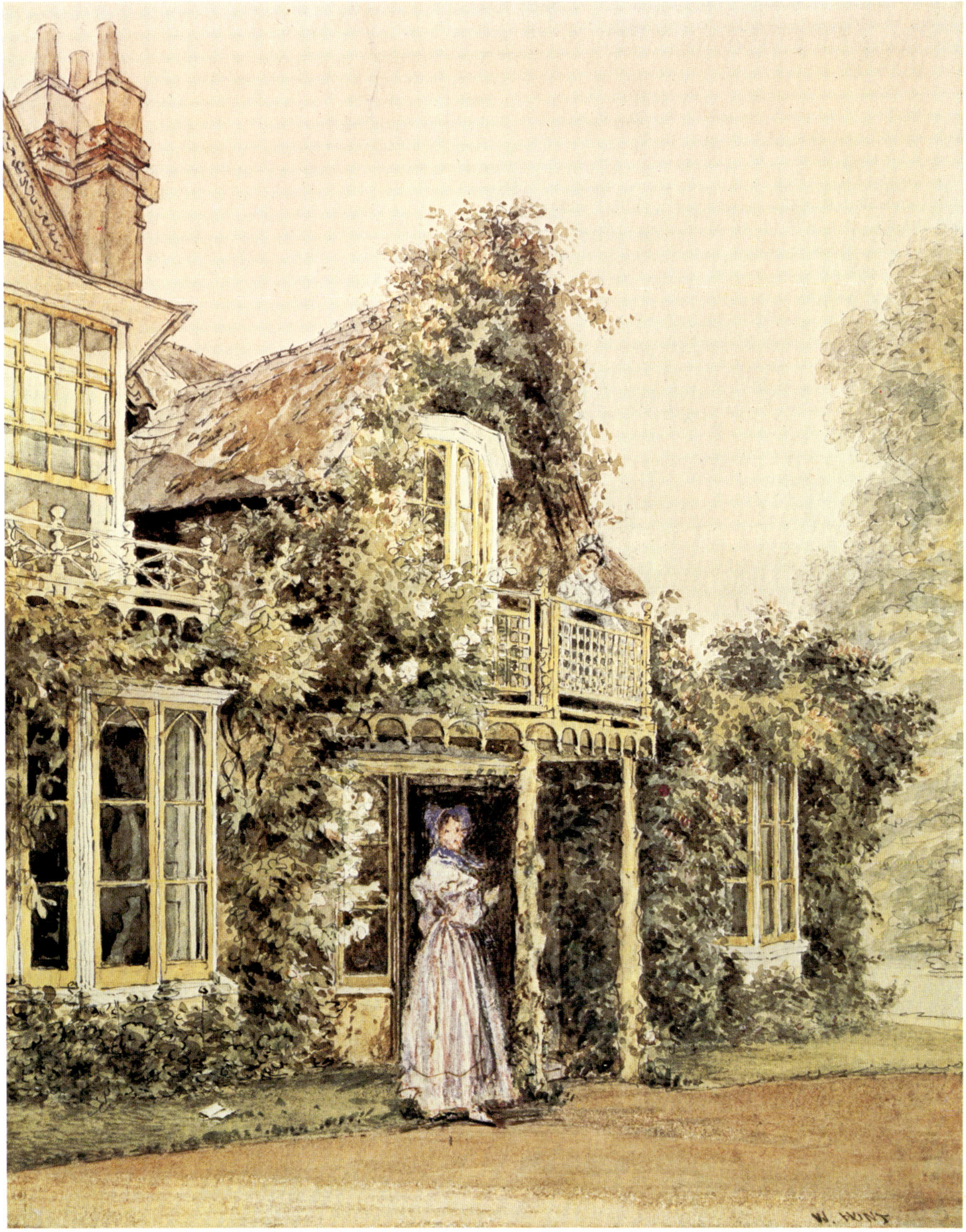

5 (29) Merry Hill, Bushey
Pencil and watercolour slightly heightened with white, $13\frac{1}{4} \times 10\frac{1}{2}$ (336×267)
British Museum, London

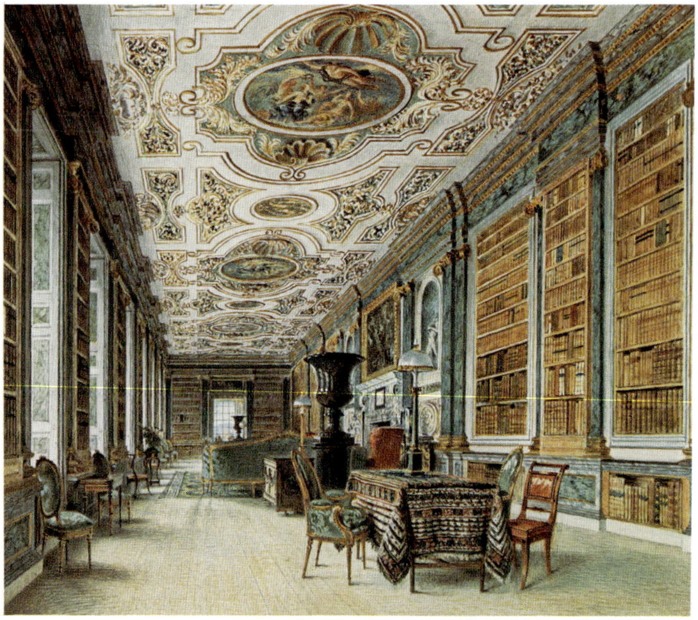

6 (341) The Library, Chatsworth
Watercolour, 10 × 11¼ (255 × 285)
Devonshire Collection, Chatsworth

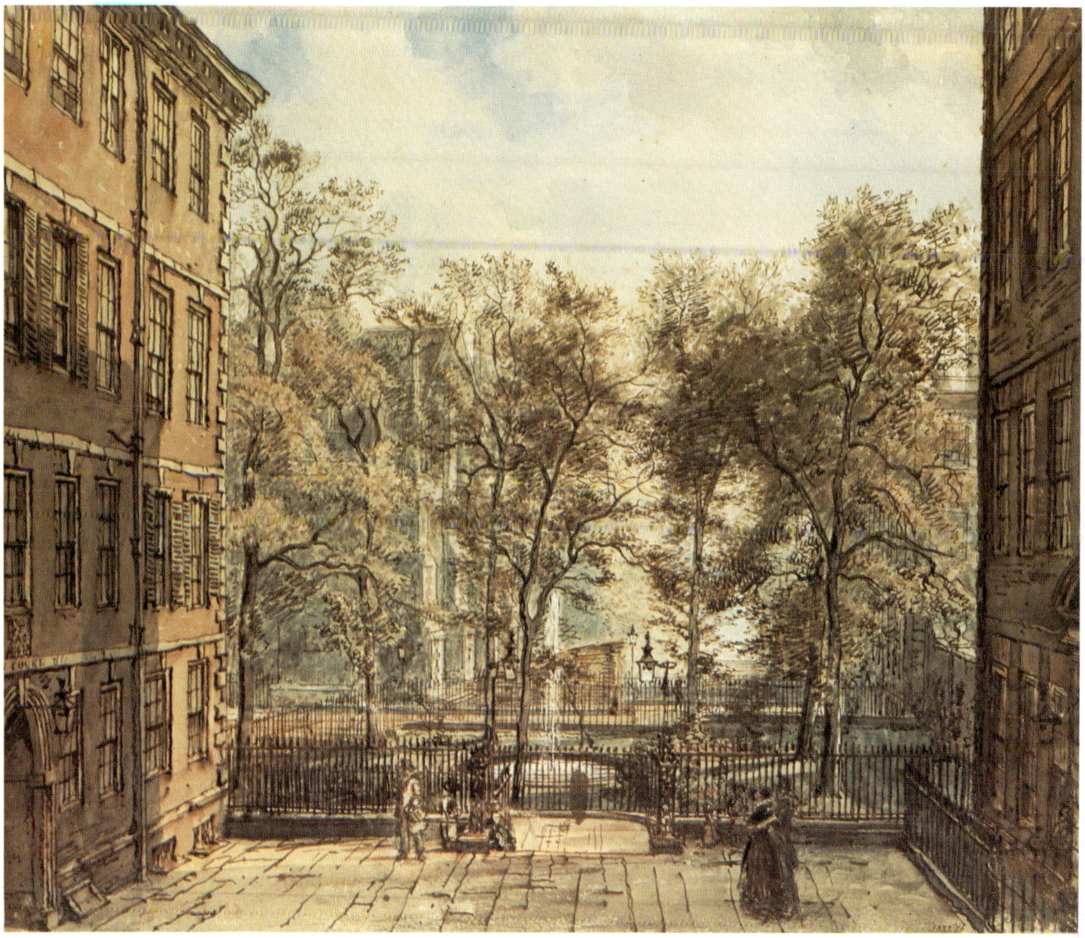

7 (174) New Court, The Temple, London
Reed pen, brown ink and watercolour, 16⅜ × 19¾ (416 × 502)
Victoria and Albert Museum, London

family home in Belton Street, he had by this time moved to an independent address. He did not, however, remain long in Brownlow Street for in the Royal Academy Catalogue of 1825 his address is given as 6 Marchmont Street, Brunswick Square. Here Hunt remained for many years until in 1842 he moved to 55 Burton Street, Burton Crescent, and finally in 1845 to his last home at 62 Stanhope Street, off the Hampstead Road, where he remained until his death.

In 1823 Hunt exhibited two further 'Sketches from Nature' at the Royal Academy, in 1824 'A Study from Nature', and in 1825 a 'Sketch from Nature in Cassiobury Park'. All these, which have not been identified, were presumably landscapes in watercolour. 1825 was the last year he exhibited at the Royal Academy. From then onwards he was to devote himself exclusively to watercolour. A list of the fourteen works exhibited by Hunt at the Royal Academy from 1807 to 1825 is contained in Part III, section 2.

In the meantime the Society of Painters in Oil and Water-Colours had not prospered. Notwithstanding the admission of painters in oil there was an increasing financial deficit and the Society became convinced that the experiment of 'pouring oil on the troubled waters' had failed. Accordingly, at a well-attended meeting of the Society in 1820, it was resolved after a full discussion 'that the Society shall henceforth be a Society of Painters in Water-Colours only and that no oil paintings be exhibited with the works'.[21] The name of the Society was formally changed to that assumed by the original body, namely The Society of Painters in Water-Colours (henceforth to be called the Old Water-Colour Society). The change was not carried without dissent and two members, Linnell and Cornelius Varley, announced their intention of resigning. However, there still remained of the original members John Varley, Joshua Cristall, Copley Fielding, George Barret, Warwick Smith and William Turner of Oxford. At the election of officers of the Society at the 1820 meeting Joshua Cristall was elected President and Copley Fielding Secretary, the presidency of Joshua Cristall lasting for the next eleven years to 1831.

Hunt had applied and been rejected as a candidate for the renamed Old Water-Colour Society in 1823, but was persuaded by a fellow artist, G. F. Robson, to try again. In this he was successful and was elected an Associate Exhibitor on 9 April 1824. Hitherto he had exhibited mainly landscapes but he now made his début in his new capacity as a painter of rustic figures, and exhibited in 1824 two watercolours, one of a 'Gamekeeper' (perhaps 377), a subject he was to repeat on several occasions, and the other of 'A Miller in his Mill' (272, Plate 36). 'Gamekeeper' received favourable press notice and in the following terms: 'Another happy effect of water-colours particularly engaged our attention, although by an artist whose modest talent has remained in obscurity. This is not a landscape but a coloured study of a gamekeeper in the service of the Earl of Essex. It is a very original and masterful example of richness and effect.'[22]

In 1825 Hunt exhibited at the Old Water-Colour Society twelve works, consisting of two 'Gamekeeper's, 'A Poacher' (268), 'The Gardener' – probably that at the Courtauld Institute now entitled 'The Vegetable Seller' (324, Plate 35) – five studies of game, one of which was entitled 'Woodcock' (686, Plate 53) and three landscapes, each entitled 'A Sketch from Nature', the last all done probably in the area of Cassiobury and Bushey. He also produced several outstanding still lifes including 'Study of Copper Pot and Horn Mug' (685, Plate 52), 'Still Life with Earthenware Pitcher, Coffee Pot and Basket' (684, Colour Plate 21), now both in the Ruskin Collection at the Ashmolean Museum, Oxford, and 'Still Life: Copper Jug and Blue Vase' (773, Plate 51). All these still lifes are of high quality and, as suggested in the Introduction, surely deserve comparison with those of Chardin in the preceding century, of which that shown at Colour Plate 20 is a splendid example.

In the following year, 1826, Hunt exhibited eight works of similar subjects. In June of that year, at a General Meeting of the Old Water-Colour Society at which sixteen members were present, he was unanimously elected to full membership of the Society. As a full member he was entitled to exhibit a greater number of works, a privilege of which he was quick to take advantage. Between the years 1824 and 1831 Hunt exhibited no less than 153 works, of which as many as 34 and 32 were exhibited in the years 1829 and 1831 respectively.

According to the sale catalogues and ledgers of sale prices of the Old Water-Colour Society from 1828 to 1862, now owned by the Royal Society of Painters in Water-Colours, Hunt's exhibited works from the earliest years of his membership of the Society sold well. The prices he charged ranged at the outset from five to twenty guineas with the majority of his works priced at or below ten guineas. Most of his exhibited works were sold and he quickly built up a number of titled purchasers from those visiting the Society's exhibitions.

In 1827 he exhibited sixteen works, including studies of flowers, vegetables, and his first exhibited study of grapes, the first of many: this was either 'White Grapes in a Basket' (759, Plate 54) or 'Black Grapes in a Basket' (654), both dated 1827. But the particular work which went far to establish his reputation[23] was that entitled 'Paper Lanthorn', of a paper lanthorn attached to a greengrocer's stall with the light of a candle shining through. Hunt was to repeat this lanthorn theme on many future occasions, as in 'The Turnip Lantern' (419, Plate 58).

In 1828, among twenty-two exhibited works – of which no fewer than twenty were sold at the Exhibition – were 'Westminster Schoolboy in Rowing Attire' (401, Colour Plate 8), a second study of grapes 'from Nature', the first example of fruit 'from Nature', a subject he was often to exhibit in later years, another 'Paper Lanthorn' and another 'Gamekeeper'. In 1829 he exhibited thirty-four works including two examples of 'A Lady Reading by Lamplight', a subject which he was to make particularly his own, and 'A Radish Stall' (430, Plate 42). He continued to exhibit landscapes and also interiors of cowsheds, smithies and cottages. Not until 1830 (twenty-eight works) did he exhibit his first bird's nest under the title of 'Bird's Nest and Lilac', and a second entitled 'Fruit and Bird's Nest'.

In addition to the figure studies already mentioned, Hunt produced during this First Period a number of fine studies which he did not exhibit at the Old Water-

Colour Society: for example, in reed pen, 'Old Man Fishing by a Lock Gate', dated 1822 (258, Plate 34), and in pure watercolour, 'Negro Boxer' (329, Colour Plate 10), 'James Holland' (526, Colour Plate 9), and 'Young Woman Standing' (470, Plate 38).

During much of this First Period, Hunt was accustomed to spend the winter months of each year at Hastings. Farington mentions in his diary entry of 11 May 1808 James Ward telling him that 'in consequence of Cristall's drawings made last summer having been much admired a Host of Artists are preparing to go to Hastings'.[24] At Hastings Hunt occupied lodgings in the Old Town adjacent to the fishing quarter. Here he did innumerable drawings, many simply slight pencil sketches of fishing boats being loaded or unloaded on the beach. Other pencil sketches of a similar lively character provided material for his numerous watercolours of seascapes, shore scenes, sunsets and fisher folk which he made over a number of years.

The year 1830 or 1831 could well be regarded as the end of the First Period of Hunt's career both stylistically and materially. By then, at the age of forty, he was accepted as a successful member of the Old Water-Colour Society. He had attracted important and influential patronage from three distinguished patrons, Dr Monro, the Earl of Essex and the Duke of Devonshire. He had become well-established.

F. G. Stephens divided Hunt's work stylistically into three periods, the first ending around 1825, the middle from about 1825 to 1840, and the last from 1840 to his death in 1864.[25] Any line to be drawn in the dating of Hunt's drawings must be a fine one. The present writer prefers to extend Hunt's early period a little further to around 1830, and his middle period to around 1845. Several dated or exhibited works in the late 1820s are typical of his early period, notably the fine 'Dead Hare and Cooked Lobster on a Bench' in reed pen and watercolour (774, Plate 55) exhibited in 1827 at the Old Water-Colour Society (No. 216), and the superb portrait of the artist James Holland in pure watercolour dated 1828 (526, Colour Plate 9).

In this First Period, and particularly at its beginning, Hunt followed the eighteenth-century tradition of pure watercolour over pen or pencil outlines as he had learned in his apprenticeship with John Varley. A little later on, when a member of the Monro Academy, he had learned from the Doctor how to copy the pen and ink outlines of John Robert Cozens and also the reed pen and ink drawings of Canaletto. Hunt extended this technique of reed pen and ink with merely sepia wash to a varied use of pure watercolour. His technique in this early period was appropriately described by F. G. Stephens as 'thin in handling, sober and delicate in colour, warm and grey according as the subject or even the motive of the theme required'.[26] It was, through his pupillage with John Varley, essentially a continuation of the eighteenth-century school of watercolour in the spirit of the Sandbys and of Rowlandson. Only right at the end of this early period did Hunt begin to make modest use of Chinese white to obtain certain highlights.

It is hard to fault Ruskin's estimate of Hunt's early drawings as depending 'for their peculiar charm on the most open and simple management of transparent colour'.[27]

2
Second Period: 1830-45

During Hunt's Second Period his technique became far more varied. For example, he began to develop the use of the knife for scratching out points and lines to provide patches of light from the paper. He also began to break up his washes into detached and separately defined touches and patches which can be described as a form of stippling. He also made increasing use of Chinese white as a means to obtain his highlights. These different methods, which Hunt sometimes combined in a single work, are more fully described in Part I, Chapter 4, 'Technique'.

In 1831 Hunt exhibited thirty-two works including a third bird's nest. This was the subject he was to repeat so often and so profitably in subsequent years and on which his reputation became largely and unfairly based, so that he was often referred to as 'Bird's Nest Hunt'. He also continued to exhibit many examples of peasant and fisher folk, but began to increase notably his studies of fruit and particularly of grapes.

It is interesting to speculate on the reasons for Hunt's interest in birds' nests as a subject, though no satisfactory explanation can be offered. So far as the present writer knows, Hunt was the first English watercolourist frequently and regularly to make use of that subject, of which chaffinch and hedge sparrow's nests and eggs were the most common examples. Certainly his birds' nests quickly found favour with his Victorian patrons and were the progenitors of the numerous birds' nest artists later in the century referred to in Part I, Chapter 5, 'Pupils, Followers and Imitators'.

Around 1831 Hunt added a new dimension to his art as a result of meeting a family during his winters at Hastings, the Swains, from whom three brothers were to serve him as invaluable models for a number of years. Roget vividly describes the gifts of one of these boys as a model:

At what precise date is uncertain, but it must have been near the end of Cristall's [in 1831] or the beginning of Fielding's reign [as presidents of the Old Water-Colour Society] when Hunt had the good fortune to meet with a model at Hastings who served him for many of his best known and most characteristic works for years to come. He was a healthy looking boy, a typical rustic in figure and face; and withal a remarkably clever lad, being a capital mimic, who could assume a variety of expressions and retain them long enough for the artist to fix them on his paper for all time. He was just the character for Hunt's pencil and fed his lively zest for fun. The youth was accordingly captured and brought to London where the painter kept him in his house to draw from. Many and varied are the characters in which this lad was made to figure, and many and varied his depicted occupations as shown on the walls of the Gallery in Pall Mall East, for a large series of years, during which 'Hunt's Boys' were always a stock feature of the Old Water-Colour Society Exhibitions. At one time he would be a sturdy young cricketer, handling his bat with nervous grasp and knitted brow, lips compressed, watchful and eager of eye, the whole body braced up for a hard hit. At another he would be fast asleep in placid unconsciousness. In one picture you might see him burning his mouth with hot porridge: in another red to the finger tips with the winter's cold. In course of time it was but natural that Hunt should be deprived of his clever boy model with the flexible face. Being a strong healthy lad, he in a few years outgrew his master's requirements. With his waning adolescence the series of portraits came to an end. 'What a pity', sighed Hunt. 'He ought never to have grown'. But the grateful painter did not forget him in after years and left him a small legacy.[1]

Another account of Hunt's young boy models is given by William Collingwood[2] in an article entitled 'Reminiscences: William Hunt' written in 1898.[3] Collingwood describes how in 1838, when himself a young man of nineteen, he first met Hunt at Hastings at the house of a Mr Maw, the senior partner in the firm of J. and S. Maw of Aldersgate, Surgical Instrument Makers, with whom Hunt was on very friendly terms. Mr Maw, 'loving art better than business', had retired at a relatively early age. He was a keen collector of the works of contemporary artists including Hunt and was himself an amateur artist. He was also a pupil of Hunt, as is shown by a letter[4] written from 6 Marchmont Street to him by Hunt dated 8 March 1839, in which Hunt writes: 'I still hope to visit Hastings in the Summer and shall certainly accept your offer of becoming my assistant'. Hunt decorates his letter with a watercolour of a bowl of fruit inscribed 'for Master George Maw, with Mr Hunt's Kind regards. 1839'.

Collingwood describes Hunt's boy models from the Swain family, and some of his working methods, as follows:

With old Hastings, Hunt had great sympathy, and from among these people he often took his models. One family supplied him for many years. He took the eldest of the lads into his service as his page and his model till he outgrew the office and was fit for other employment. Then the next brother came in for his place, and he in his turn made room for the younger of the three. If I remember right, Johnny, the second of the Swains, was with him when I first knew him, and afterwards was succeeded by his brother Bill. It was amusing sometimes, when a visitor called, to be received by a 'buttons' in anything but the approved livery – Johnny, dressed up in some strange style, coming straight from the studio to answer the door. But all this was in keeping with the man, whose life was one of consistent simplicity, and with one aim only. These were arch-lads, clever in their native way, and excellently suited to his purpose, willing to be all things to him, and who did their best to act their parts. His pictures taken from these models tell not only his skill in portraying rude character, but theirs in the help they gave him. It was not easy to keep his model always up to the mark. If he wanted to paint him crying, he was not satisfied with a pretence; he had to scold him, and pinch him, and use all the means he could devise to make the expression genuine. Then, again, for hours he wanted him to laugh. That he could well do. His fund of humour was at no loss for means of keeping him amused. But even this would fail, and he had to scold him into laughing till he cried. Then there was 'The Attack' – of a pie – and 'The Defeat,' or 'A Marine Effect' – of sea-sickness, in all which he needed to have the expression sustained for every touch of his pencil. He painted nothing but as he saw it, trusted nothing to his knowledge or his memory; would not add the smallest thing to what he saw before him. It was because he saw so much more than others saw, that his work transcended theirs. If he saw what struck him as a subject in the corner of a room, he would ask that it might be left untouched till he had finished the drawing of it. No profane touch of the housemaid's duster must be permitted; and this sometimes for weeks together. Or if he saw a dish at dessert or a pheasant or a fish newly arrived, worth painting, it was bodily removed to his room, to be immortalised on his paper, till it could be kept no longer. If he composed a picture – which he rarely did – such as a trooper sitting in a chair – he would not do a stroke till his subject was complete, the chair covered with brown paper to match the colour of oak, and the background as he required it to be; so much with him depended on the relation of all the parts to each other. Or if he painted a bank of primroses, or anything in his background, it must be there before his eyes, the piece of the bed dug out and brought to him in a barrow just as it stood. It was thus he obtained the wonderful truth and naturalness that so singularly marked his work.

In a letter dated November 1862, now in the possession of Mr Jeremy Maas, Hunt writes of the Swain brothers: 'I shall never meet such clever boys they never ought to have become men'. Under his will made in 1861, he left a legacy of £10 each to William and John Swain. Their faces appear in a number of his works during the 1830s.

'The Attack', originally entitled 'The Commencement' (499, Colour Plate 11), and 'The Defeat', originally entitled 'The Conclusion' (500, Colour Plate 12), were both exhibited in 1834 at the Old Water-Colour Society and were acquired shortly afterwards by the great collector of the works of Victorian artists, John Sheepshanks, who purchased them, and five other watercolours in which the boy models featured, direct from the artist. In all, John Sheepshanks owned thirteen splendid examples of Hunt's work, none of which he included in his great gift of the remainder of his collection of works by then contemporary or near-contemporary artists to the nation, preferring to retain them for his own enjoyment.[5] They are still owned by descent by the Sheepshanks family, together with fifteen letters from Hunt to his patron John Sheepshanks written from various addresses between 1835 and 1854. In one of these letters, Hunt expresses his concern and regret at a rumour which has reached him that Sheepshanks may have disposed of some of his Hunts. In another Hunt requests the loan of several of his works for the Exposition Universelle at the Paris Salon in 1855. This request was granted and both 'The Attack' – entitled 'L'Attaque du pâté', together with 'The Defeat' – entitled 'Le pendant de L'Attaque',[6] as well as 'The Flower Girl' – entitled 'Une jeune fille avec une corbeille de fleurs' (507, Colour Plate 19), were included in the eleven works which Hunt exhibited there. These were followed, among others in which the faces of the boy models appear, by 'A Shrimper' dated 1835 (437, Plate 57), 'The Turnip Lantern' dated 1838 (419, Plate 58), 'Puzzled' dated 1839 (420, Plate 60), and 'A Young Cricketer' (323, Plate 62), to give just a few examples. Hunt also used the boys' mobile faces to introduce a humorous element into his subject-matter, as in 'The Scrub' (434) and 'The Young Shaver' (270) exhibited in 1841 under the title of 'Giving Himself (H)Airs'. There are a number of other examples of this humorous tendency in Hunt's work which he started with his boy models and continued in later years.

The contemporary success and popularity of 'Hunt's Boys', particularly those with a humorous element, are confirmed by the publication in 1844 of a book of coloured lithographs entitled *Hunt's Comic Sketches, drawn on stone by Thomas Fairland from original drawings exhibited in the Water-Colour Society.*[7] This book contained a frontispiece and lithographs of thirty-three works, and a brief description of each giving a reasonably complete picture of the humorous element of 'Hunt's Boys' (see Part III, section 3).

Hunt was well aware of the importance of lithography for extending and widening his public. But for an artist in whose work colour was so vital an element, the discovery of the then new process of chromolithography was of crucial importance. This method of relatively cheap art printing was developed during the 1850s; Hunt himself approved of the process and was quick to take advantage of it. There are several chromolithographs of Hunt's work in the British Museum, of which 'Basket of Primroses and Orchids, Bird's Nest and Blossom' is a fine example. Christie's sale of Hunt's studio in 1864 contained a number of lithographs and chromolithographs of his works (Lots 388, 390, 391 and 392).

Hunt was also aware of the importance of photography, though still a relatively new medium, for publicising his works. The sale of his studio included a photographic portrait of himself and thirty photographs after his works (Lot 393), seventy-one photographs (various – Lot 394), and twenty-one photographs of the Crimea by Roger Fenton (Lot 395).

Ruskin in his Notes to the Hunt Exhibition of 1879–80 divides Hunt's work into six classes:

Class I. Drawings illustrative of rural life in its vivacity and purity, without the slightest endeavour at idealization, and still less with any wish either to caricature or deplore its imperfections. All the drawings belonging to this class are virtually faultless, and most of them very beautiful.

Class 2. Country life, with endeavour to add interest to it by passing sentiment. The drawings belonging to this class are almost always over-finished, and liable to many faults.

Class 3. Country life, with some expression of its degradation, either by gluttony, cowardice, or rudeness. The drawings of this class are usually very clever, and apt to be very popular; but they are, on the whole, dishonourable to the artist.

Class 4. Flower pieces. Fruit is often included in these; but they form a quite separate class, being necessarily less finished drawings – the flowers sooner changing their form.

Class 5. Fruit pieces, on which a great part of the artist's reputation very securely rests.

Class 6. Dead animals. Alas! if he could but have painted living ones, instead of those perpetual bunches of grapes. But it could not be. To a weakly, sensitive, nervous temperament, the perpetual changes of position, and perpetual suggestion of new beauty in an animal, are entirely ruinous: in ten minutes they put one in a fever. Only the very greatest portrait painters – Sir Joshua and Velasquez – can draw animals rightly.[8]

Some of Hunt's humorous drawings with his boy models, although highly popular both at the time and subsequently, can be justifiably brought within Ruskin's criticism of works in Class 3.

At the beginning of this Second Period a major event occurred which produced for Hunt a new and delightful female model. On 13 September 1830 he married his cousin Sarah Holloway, then aged eighteen, the daughter of his mother's sister. Her father was a miller and a farmer, and the family lived near Bramley in the neighbourhood of Basingstoke, Hampshire, where Hunt had previously stayed with her family and worked. 'A Miller in his Mill' (272, Plate 36) is probably a study of his future father-in-law. That he had not married earlier must have been largely due, apart from purely financial considerations, to his unattractive appearance. In height he was only about five feet, two inches, and F. G. Stephens recalls that as he remembered him when Hunt was past middle age he

was a little less than that probably about five foot. He was broad as well as round shouldered and his head was large beyond proportion to the rest of his figure of which the torso was that of a taller man. His large and long frock coats and loose trousers although favourable to him on other accounts, did not add to his outward graces.[9]

Stephens also writes[10] that Hunt had complained sadly that he could not get anyone to have him, and had added: 'What a sad thing it is to be so deformed and miserable looking'. Stephens further recalls that Hunt's personal disabilities

frequently made him reserved and not very easily accessible to strangers. At times, however, especially when his health was at its best and his spirits good there were few more boisterous gay and frolicsome men than little 'Billy' Hunt. He loved and was beloved by children, assisted at their games, 'was great in charades', and accompanied their songs by performing on the bones.[11]

Throughout his life Hunt was also passionately fond of the theatre.

It was very striking [writes F. G. Stephens] to see the white-haired eager-looking old man absorbed in the glitter of the stage. And strange to say, what charmed him most were productions of a melodramatic kind – a sensational piece was his delight. Fireworks fascinated him, blue and red fire had charms at the age of three score years and ten.[12]

Another reference to Hunt's sensitivity about his appearance is recorded in the Diaries of G. P. Boyce, himself an artist and close personal friend of Rossetti and his circle. In his diary entry for 8 April 1854, Boyce records:

Rossetti came in at 3 and stayed till 10. . . . He thought I painted a good deal like old Hunt – wish I had a little of his genius. . . . He [Rossetti] told me in conversation that W. H. Hunt had a morbid conviction of his own ugliness and desired that all record of him to the present in the way of portraits or letters should be destroyed.[13]

As if the rest of his appearance were not enough, Hunt had a long nose, and Stephens recalls that Hunt had said that 'When walking on the Parade at Hastings the small boys laughed at him because he was deformed and because his hair was long. "I turned round upon them after such an event", he recalled, "and shook my nose at them and they were afraid".'[14]

Hunt drew himself on a number of occasions. Two examples reproduced in this book (451, Plate 80, which shows him aged about forty-five, and 452, Plate 93, around sixty) are of head and shoulders only. Plate 1, showing a photograph at the National Portrait Gallery of Hunt in his late sixties or early seventies, is a full-length study and though he is seated gives some idea of his stunted appearance.

During this period Hunt used his wife Sarah as a model on a number of occasions and the works where she appears, when undated, can be dated at least approximately by reference to her being eighteen years old at the date of the marriage in 1830. She appears as the model in several studies of young women formerly in the J. P. Heseltine Collection, of which 'Love's Missive' (529) and 'An Interesting Letter' (539, Plate 66) are good examples. 'At the Cottage Door' (408, Plate 67) is dated 1835, when Sarah would have been twenty-three, and 'The Outhouse' (321, Colour Plate 15) is dated 1838. There are several undated works in which Sarah appears in her middle twenties: 'The Kitchen Maid' (460), 'The Orphan' (388, Plate 69), and 'Woman Reading by Candlelight' (490, Plate 68).

At the beginning of 1832 an important event took place in the Hunt household with the birth of his daughter Emma. She, like her mother, was a favourite model for her father from her early days. A charming example is inscribed 'Little Emma Reclining' (301) where she must be about five years old, and a year later she appears in 'Peasant Girl' dated 1838 (515). In 'Portrait of the Artist, his Daughter and Niece' (535, Plate 96) there is a reference inscribed on the mount to his daughter 'whom he was in the habit of dressing up on occasion'.

It was during the 1830s that Hunt produced his splendid series of bedroom interiors. There are three dated works: 'Girl Reading at a Window' dated 1832 (458, Plate 78), 'Sunday Morning' dated 1833 (407, Plate 74), and 'A Bedchamber' dated 1839 (439, Plate 79). There are also several undated works in the same series, including 'Girl at Prayer' (277) and 'Girl at her Toilet' (553, Colour Plate 16), both of which have the same patchwork bedspread as in 'Sunday Morning' and the same furniture which appears in 'Preparing for Sunday' (482). Other examples of the series are 'The Jewels' (409, Colour Plate 17) and 'Interior with a Young Girl' (516).

It should also be recorded that during the 1830s Hunt produced some outstanding works of unusual size. Three are landscapes, 'Pollard Elm and Village Pound at Hambledon, Hampshire' dated 1833 (144, Colour Plate 13), 'Rock on the Downs, near Hastings' (145, Plate 86), and 'Old Oak at Faversham, Kent' dated 1836 (146). Other fine large works of this period are 'Plucking the Fowl' dated 1832 (298, Colour Plate 14) and 'The Maid and the Magpie' (267, Plate 75). These are all superb examples of the Second Period of Hunt's career, and show the complete technical mastery he had by then attained.

3

Third Period: 1845-64

Although Hunt continued into the mid-1840s to use the Swain boys and his daughter Emma as models, the life studies became fewer. He went on exhibiting interiors and candle-light effects but virtually no landscapes; while fruit, bird's nest and flower subjects became increasingly numerous. 'Hearing Lessons' (536, Colour Plate 18) is a kitchen interior done while Hunt was living in Bloomsbury at 55 Burton Street; it shows his wife Sarah aged about thirty and Emma who looks about ten, which dates the work around 1842. He continued to use Emma as a model and there are a number of other drawings of her during her teens, for example 'The Artist's Daughter Holding a Jug' (518, Plate 95), aged about thirteen, and 'Portrait of his Daughter' aged about fifteen (557, Plate 94). 'What Shall I Sing?' – A Portrait of the Artist's Daughter (441), which was exhibited at the Old Water-Colour Society in 1848, shows Emma at sixteen. There is a typical Hunt watercolour of white grapes in a heavy gold frame hanging behind the piano.

Hunt had continued after his marriage to reside at 6 Marchmont Street, Brunswick Square where he had lived as a bachelor since 1825. His house must have been at the southern end of what is now the Brunswick shopping and residential complex. However, in 1842 with his daughter Emma growing up and occupying and perhaps demanding more room, the family moved a short distance away to 55 Burton Street, then a typical Bloomsbury street of narrow, three-storey brick houses. They stayed there only three years and in 1845 moved to 62 Stanhope Street just off the Hampstead Road where Hunt remained until his death in 1864. This again was a narrow, three-storey brick house, built perhaps in 1820 as a terrace house, and only a few hundred yards from Chester Gate, off Albany Street, leading into Regent's Park. A number of other watercolourists lived in the same district between Hampstead Road and Regent's Park, among them Joshua Cristall, James Holland, Frederick Nash, George Chambers and William Callow.

For several years after 1845 Hunt continued to exhibit extensively at the Old Water-Colour Society. However in 1851, when he had reached the age of sixty-one, the number of his yearly exhibits drops suddenly from twenty-one in 1850 to eleven, all of which are flower and fruit pieces. The year 1851 is the first in which he gives a country address in the Catalogue of the Old Water-Colour Society, namely Parkgate, Bramley, near Basingstoke, as well as his London address of Stanhope Street, Hampstead Road. Roget suggests, no doubt rightly, that Bramley in the summer had taken the place of his previous winter visits to Hastings. Probably he was beginning in his sixties to slow down a little.

From then on to his death in 1864, Hunt exhibited an annual average of only some eight works. Fruit, birds' nests and flower subjects are in the majority, doubtless as proving the most financially successful. Indeed, he was now looked upon almost exclusively as a painter of these subjects, and became as popular in this field as he had been with the humorous drawings of his boy models.

Hunt's fruit pieces display an amazing technical virtuosity. The bloom he produced on peach, plum or bunch of grapes has to be seen to be believed. According to Roget, 'those who had been most tickled with the fun of his boy pictures declared that his fruit made the mouth water'.[1] Hunt was only able to achieve this effect by his invention of a new technique of painting in pure watercolour on a hard ground composed of a mixture of Chinese white and gum. This method is more fully described and discussed in Part I, Chapter 4. 'Fruit' (626, Plate 99) is an excellent example of this method. The work is unfinished, and clearly shows the prepared ground on which Hunt would have completed the painting of the fruit by stippling on it in pure watercolour. 'Peach and Grapes' (599, Plate 104) was described by Ruskin as 'the most beautiful painting of fruit that Hunt ever did, and it hangs among the Turners like a brooch'.[2] During most of the time that Ruskin lived at Brantwood from 1871 till his death in 1900, the drawing hung over his bedroom fireplace surrounded by some of his Turner collection. An engraving of April 1900 by Arthur Severn (Plate 105) of Ruskin's bedroom at Brantwood[3] shows it so hanging.

Hunt's birds' nests again are marvels of technical skill. They are mainly of chaffinch nests with mottled brown and white eggs or hedge sparrow nests with bright blue eggs. Often, as in 'Roses and Bird's Nest' (771), or as in 'Spring Flowers and Birds' Nests' (658, Plate 108), they include a jar or mug containing flowers or a sprig of some flower or blossom, as in 'Bird's Nest and Blossom' (659, Plate 110). Perhaps the finest of all Hunt's birds' nests is 'Long-Tailed Tit's Nest', with holly leaves and red holly berries (606, Colour Plate 25).

Hunt was also a highly skilled flower painter. 'Roses' (657, Colour Plate 26) is a particularly fine example. 'Fruit and Tankard' (668, Plate 101) is a *tour de force* of technical skill but lacks the beauty of his simpler flower pieces such as 'Blossom' (728, Plate 98) which is dated 1860, when Hunt was seventy. Reference has already been made in the Introduction to James Holland's tribute, himself a flower painter in his early days. F. G. Stephens refers to Hunt as 'the man who painted flowers as they had never been painted before in England or elsewhere, and as (except by M. Fantin only) they have never been painted since'.[4] For the present writer, the comparison with Fantin Latour, one of the most restrained and elegant painters of flowers, seems fully justified.

John Ruskin's father, a rich wine merchant, was a collector of Hunt's work, and it was doubtless through his father that Ruskin's attention was first drawn to it. The first reference to Hunt in Ruskin's writings is in 1846, when Ruskin was thirty-seven. In the revised third edition of volume I of *Modern Painters* he refers to Hunt in the following terms: 'There are few men, for instance, more limited in subject than Hunt, and yet I do not think there is another man in the Old Water-Colour Society with so keen an eye for truth or with power so universal.'[5] Again, in the same work, Ruskin speaks of his landscapes: 'Hunt, I think, fails in foliage, and in foliage only; for foliage will not be imitated, it must be reasoned out and suggested: yet Hunt is the only man we have who can paint the real leaf-green under sunlight and in this respect his trees are delicious summer itself.'[6]

In 1879 Ruskin organised a retrospective loan exhibition at the Fine Art Society's Galleries in New Bond Street as a tribute to Samuel Prout and Hunt, both of whom he greatly admired. The exhibition comprised 103 works by Prout, sixty-five by Hunt, and thirteen by Ruskin himself. The Hunt section, of which seven were owned by Ruskin, contained a preponderance of his later works with a strong emphasis on fruit, flowers, and birds' nests, and his more elaborate figure studies, including several representing his boy models. There were only two landscapes, neither of the landscape and churches around Bushey. The full list of Hunt's works with titles and names of lenders is contained in Appendix II.

Ruskin's Notes to the Exhibition are of great interest as providing his general assessment of Hunt's qualities and his specific comments on a number of the works by Hunt exhibited; some of the latter, indeed, have already been quoted in this book.

In the Preface to his Notes, Ruskin contrasts the naturalism of Hunt's flower pieces with the artificial formality of Dutch flower painters such as Van Huysum, and the European tradition which 'never seems to perceive any conditions of beauty in the things themselves, which would make them worth regard for their own sake . . .'[7] No. 174 in his Exhibition ('An Interior of a Farm Shed', 286) Ruskin takes to epitomise what Hunt stands for.

> . . . the drawing of the interior, No. 174, may be taken as a final example of the confidence which the painter felt in his power of giving some kind of interest to the most homely objects, and rendering the transitions of ordinary light and shade impressive, though he had nothing more sacred to illuminate than a lettuce, and nothing more terrible to hide than a reaping-hook. The dim light from the flint-glass window, and the general disposition and scale of the objects it falls on, remind me sometimes, however unreasonably, of the little oratory into which the deeply-worn steps ascend from the Beauchamp Chapel at Warwick. But I know perfectly well, and partly acknowledge the rightness of his judgment, though I cannot analyze it, that Hunt would no more have painted that knightly interior instead of this, with helmets lying about instead of saucepans, and glowing heraldries staying the light instead of that sea-green lattice, than he would have gone for a walk round his farm in a court dress.[8]

In his detailed comments, Ruskin is as always strong in his preferences.

130. Grapes. Consummate. Can't be better anywhere . . .

129. Grapes. Perfect work, but wasted. Why he did so many grapes, and scarcely ever sloes, or finely russet apples, or *growing* strawberries, always mystified me.

Plums. Finest work, but a little dull. My own favourites of his plums were such variegated ones as 133 and 135; but I somehow never got any. This drawing, however, was the one of which Hunt said to me innocently – seeing it again after some ten years – 'It's very nice, isn't it?'[9]

The drawing belonged to Ruskin and on another occasion Ruskin expands the story as follows:

The last time my dear old friend William Hunt came to see me, I took down one of his early drawings for him to see (three blue plums and one amber one and two nuts). So he looked at it happily for a minute or two and then said, 'Well, it's very nice isn't it? I did not think I could have done so well.'[10]

Ruskin came to have his fill of Hunt's grapes, as is shown in his review of the Old Water-Colour Society Exhibition of 1856, in which he writes:

There are two or three pounds of grapes – those in 285 'Fruit' particularly good; but when not on the vine, grapes are precisely the dullest fruit that can be painted; and I can only advise, or beg, any reader who is inclined to attend to me, never in future to buy any of Hunt's grapes. He wastes an inconceivable quantity of time on them, and this is the fault of the public; for the grapes always sell.[11]

Ruskin concludes his remarks on Hunt in the Preface to his Notes in the following terms:

I therefore esteem Hunt's work all the more exemplary in acknowledging without disguise the restrictions imposed on the use of water-colour as a medium for vigorously realistic effects; and I have placed pieces of it in my Oxford School[12] as standards of imitative (as distinguished from decorative) colour, in the rightness and usefulness of which I have every day more confirmed trust. I am aware of no other pieces of art, in modern days, at once so sincere and so accomplished: only let it be noted that I use the term 'sincere' in this case, not as imputing culpable fallacy to pictures of more imaginative power, but only as implying the unbiassed directness of aim at the realisation of very simple facts, which is often impossible to the passions, or inconsistent with the plans, of greater designers.[13]

In 1856 Hunt received a commission from Ruskin for a work exhibited at the Old Water-Colour Society as No. 253 'A Bit of Mont Blanc (painted for J. Ruskin Esq.)'. William Collingwood writes of this work in the following terms:

One of his works, which never could be forgotten by those who saw it in the [Old Water-Colour Society's] Gallery, though all else may have faded from their recollection, was 'A Bit of Mont Blanc' – a piece of granite brought thence by Mr. Ruskin and painted for him. This he invested with such an interest, not by its staring reality, but by the wonderful beauty he there discerned and revealed. It was a lesson for all to learn, not only of what Nature is if we have eyes to see it, but of how art is dependent on the treatment rather than on the subject of the picture.[14]

Again in 1859 Hunt exhibited at the Old Water-Colour Society two works painted for Ruskin, 'Shells' (620, Plate 113) and 'An Oyster Shell and an Onion' (634, Colour Plate 27). In 1860 he exhibited the two works, 'Pilchards – Study of Gold' and 'Mushrooms – Study of Rose Grey', each described as 'One of a series painted for J. Ruskin Esq., to be presented to Schools of Art'; and in 1861 'A Chick' similarly described (653, Plate 111). 'Pilchards – Study of Gold', under the title 'Herring and Pilchard', and 'A Chick', under the title 'Dead Chicken', were both included in Ruskin's Hunt Exhibition of 1879–80. Ruskin, in his notes on the individual works in the Exhibition, refers to 'Herring and Pilchard' as 'Supreme painting again, and done with his best pains' and writes that it and 'Dead Chicken':

were done by the old man, in all kindness and care, at my own request, for me to give as types of work to country schools of art. Yet no kindness or care could altogether enable him to work rightly under the direction of another mind; and the project was ultimately given up by me, the chicken, finished as it is, having been one of my chief disappointments.[15]

Roget states[16] that when painting 'An Oyster Shell and an Onion' (634, Colour Plate 27) Hunt would cry out 'How difficult it is to paint this Oyster shell', and after completing 'Pilchards – Study of Gold' Hunt wrote to a friend, 'if you want studies of colour, fish is the sort of thing to look at'.

Hunt had on another occasion experienced difficulty in working to commission when he had been asked by Ruskin to draw his wife Effie (subsequently Lady Millais). Roget records[17] that Hunt wrote in a letter to an intimate friend:

I do not wish it to be known what I had to do for Mr. Ruskin, but have no other objection to tell *you*, only to say that I am ashamed to say that I broke down; it was to make a drawing of Mrs. R—. I think I could have made a nice drawing of her if she had been one of my tramp girls. I think her very beautiful.

In another letter Hunt writes:

I wish I could get a very beautiful face to paint from, so that I might by taking a long time try if I could not, though I broke down with Mrs. R— still do something that way. It is a different thing to have a lady to sit, to a model that you pay, and can have at your command at any time.

Ruskin was clearly aware of Hunt's problem in this respect when he wrote 'Turner, Bewick, Hunt and Prout, all four agree that they can draw the poor but not the rich'.[18]

Another example of Hunt's difficulty of working to commission occurred in 1852 over 'Wood Pigeon etc.' belonging to Ruskin, exhibited at the Old Water-Colour Society in 1852 and as 'A Pigeon' (either No. 141 or 145) in Ruskin's Hunt Exhibition of 1879–80. Ruskin's note reads: 'of highest quality. I must be pardoned for saying so of my own drawing; but of course, after long and affectionate relations with the painter, it would be strange if I had not some of his best works.'[19]

Ruskin must have inherited this drawing from his father John James Ruskin who wrote to his son in 1852: 'I got a piece of advice from Hunt never to commission a picture. He could not have done my pigeon so well had he felt he was doing it for anybody.' Ruskin, on hearing of the purchase, wrote to his father from Venice:

> 10th Jan [1852] I forgot – my head being full of Turner and Tintoret yesterday – to thank you for your kindness both to Hunt and me in buying the Ringdove – no subject could possibly be better fitted to show his powers. I would – if I had given him a commission which he says I ought not – have commissioned him just for that.[20]

Hunt was an indefatigable worker, beginning early in the morning, dining about one o'clock, and resuming his work until dusk. He was not a fast worker, and Stephens writes that 'it appears from a previous record of my own that, taking an average drawing and granting fine weather and long days, a fortnight or eighteen days is represented by it.'[21]

Stephens rightly believes that the real reason for Hunt's preference for his fruit and birds' nest subjects was economic and financial, and was to be found in the greatly increased prices he was able to obtain for this class of work.[22] Roget[23] states that in October 1863 Hunt had written to a friend: 'I was in hopes of trying my hand at figures, but have so many persons' promises to do fruit and flowers for them that I can get no time to do anything else.' In September 1858 Hunt writes: 'I have now thirty five guineas for the same size that I used to have twenty-five, perhaps somewhat more finished.' On 8 March 1862 he writes: 'Friend Brown – I am still painting fruit. You will be glad to hear a drawing of mine of a bird's nest was sold at Christies yesterday for £117 size 11 by 10 inches.'

Stephens[24] says that when Hunt was a young man he was quite satisfied with two or three pounds for a small drawing and thought ten pounds a large sum for a more important work. Hunt himself noted with care the prices which his works fetched at public sales and was delighted when they were higher than those he had originally received. Several of his letters describe the increase of his prices from five to ten, to fifteen, to twenty, to thirty guineas and in some special cases to much larger sums. Stephens also writes that 'Hunt was unable to resist the crackle of crisp bank notes, a sound which mastered his strongest reluctance to part with a drawing he was loath to sell.'[25] Roget confirms this feature of Hunt's character when describing Hunt's studio in Marchmont Street as 'an untidy place with a flight of ladder steps by which to climb into it and a dirty floor full of holes'.[26] He goes on to relate an event which the artist James Holland recalled:

> how the dealer Roberts (nicknamed 'Spectacles') who had a keen eye to business, once paid Hunt a visit there and glancing round at the dirt, scraps of paper, drawings and sketches, remarked that 'it was no use working in such a sty as that' and advised him as a friend 'to have a clear out and sell the whole, muck and all, in a lot'. 'But who would be the buyer?' said Hunt. 'I will', replied the dealer flourishing a handful of new bank notes, amounting in value to £200. The bargain was struck. Hunt took the notes; and Roberts, after having the drawings 'shaved pared clipped and mounted' made a good thing of the transaction; while the artist found that he had been too precipitate in the matter.

Ruskin also confirms the humble nature of Hunt's studio when he refers to him as 'the modest painter whose only studio was his little back parlour, commanding a partial view of the scullery steps and the water-butt.'[27]

W. R. Sickert, writing in 1910, gives a similar description of what had once been Hunt's studio:

I never shall forget my pleasure and 'attendrissement' about twelve or thirteen years ago at an accident which brought me sharply into contact with a great and reverend memory. I was looking for a studio in Stanhope Street. I need not say N.W. Guided by an advertisement, I went into a house on the east side of the road, and asked to be shown the studio. To my surprise, I was shown into a little box lit from above that cannot have measured more than seven foot square. I swallowed my amusement, and after a while I hazarded to the landlady: 'Isn't it rather small for a studio?' 'Well, you see, sir, the gentleman that used to work here only painted birds' nests, so there was plenty of room for him.' You have guessed that I was in William Hunt's studio![28]

Stephens, again, writes: 'I do not know what Hunt obtained for one of the many versions of the famous "Too Hot", when it came from his hands [but] the present possessor gave three hundred guineas for it, an immense price for a repetition by an artist who was then still living'.[29] This drawing, or a replica – Lot 227 – fetched 750 guineas at the sale at Christie's on 8 April 1875 of the William Quilter Collection which comprised thirty-nine works by Hunt.

Hunt's works were extensively collected both during his lifetime and afterwards. Some of his patrons gave or bequeathed their collections of watercolours to their native cities or towns. Others continued to enjoy them on their walls during their lifetimes and their collections were sold on their deaths. (A list of the chief past collectors of Hunt's works, with the location, date of sale, and number of works sold is contained in Appendix III.)

An important collector of Hunt's works during the artist's lifetime was his friend and doctor Dr Wade, who lived in Dean Street, Soho, and who owned a number of his works, particularly his later fruit and flower pieces. Dr Wade's collection was sold by his Executors in 1872 when 'Roses in a Jar and Mossy Bank' fetched 500 gns.

Richard Newsham (1798–1883), a native of Preston who practised as a solicitor there and became Deputy Lieutenant of the county, was another important collector of Hunt's work. Newsham formed a magnificent collection of nineteenth-century pictures and watercolours including twenty extremely fine works by Hunt, and bequeathed his whole collection to his native city; they are now in the Harris Museum and Art Gallery, Preston.

Yet another important collector of Hunt's works during the latter's lifetime was his friend the artist James Orrock (1829–1913), a member of the Royal Institute of Painters in Watercolours. The sale of Orrock's collection took place at Christie's on 4 June 1904, and comprised fourteen important works, including 'Jim Crow' and 'The Blessing' which fetched respectively 180 and 500 guineas. It also included 'An Oyster Shell and an Onion' (634, Colour Plate 27), referred to earlier.

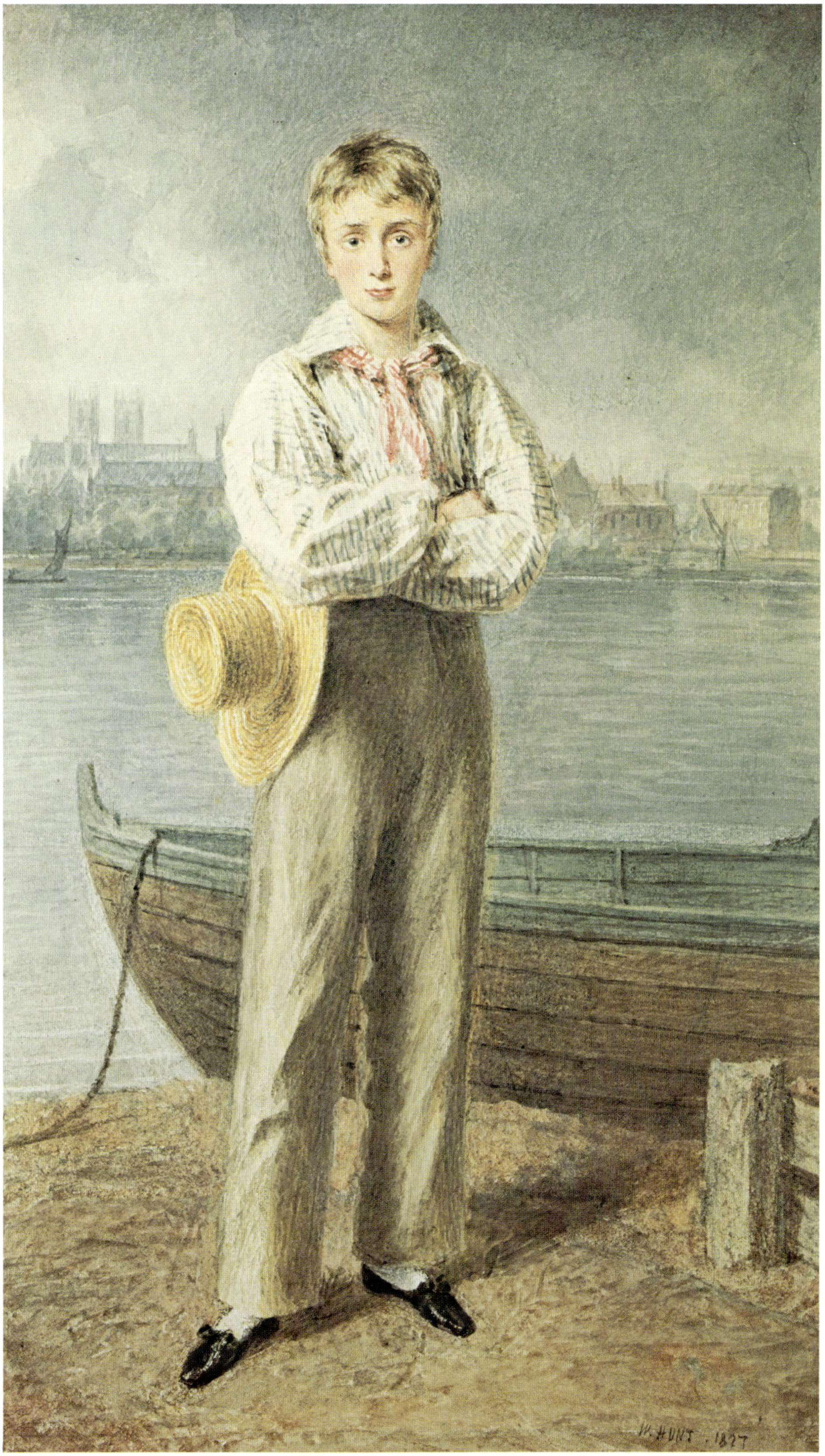

8 (401) Westminster Schoolboy in Rowing Attire
Watercolour, 13 × 7¾ (330 × 197); dated 1827
Huntington Library, San Marino

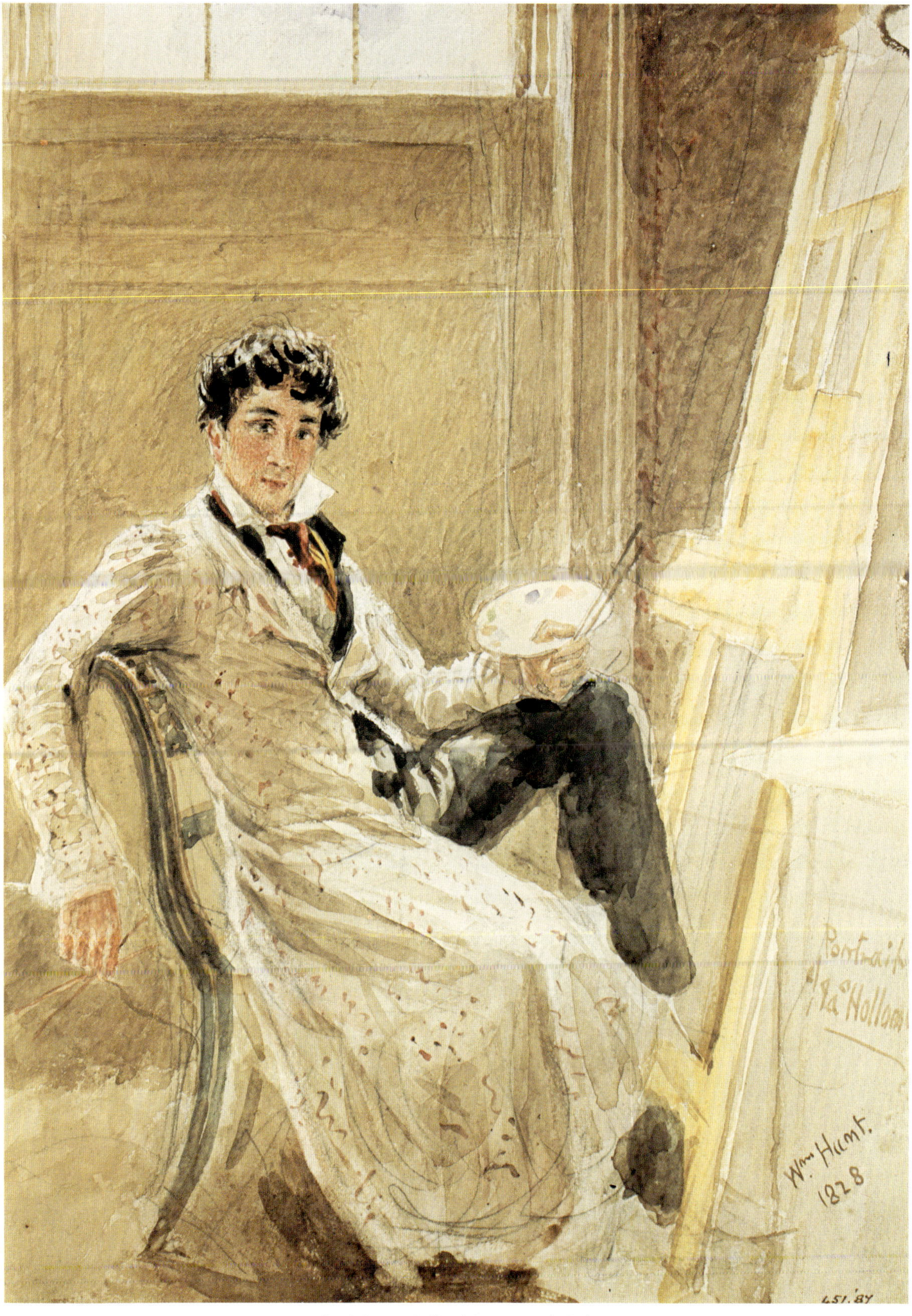

9 (526) James Holland (1799–1870), Painter
Watercolour, $12\frac{1}{4} \times 8\frac{3}{4}$ (311 × 223); dated 1828
Victoria and Albert Museum, London

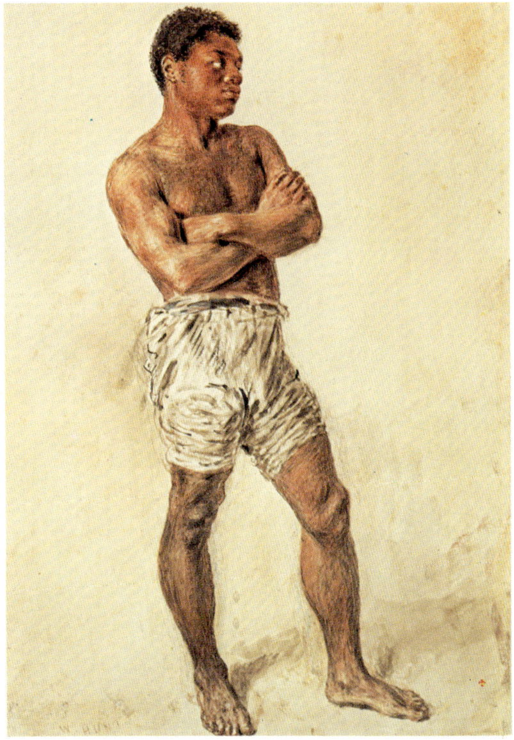

10 (329) Negro Boxer
Watercolour heightened with white, 14 × 9½ (355 × 242)
Mr David Daniels, New York City

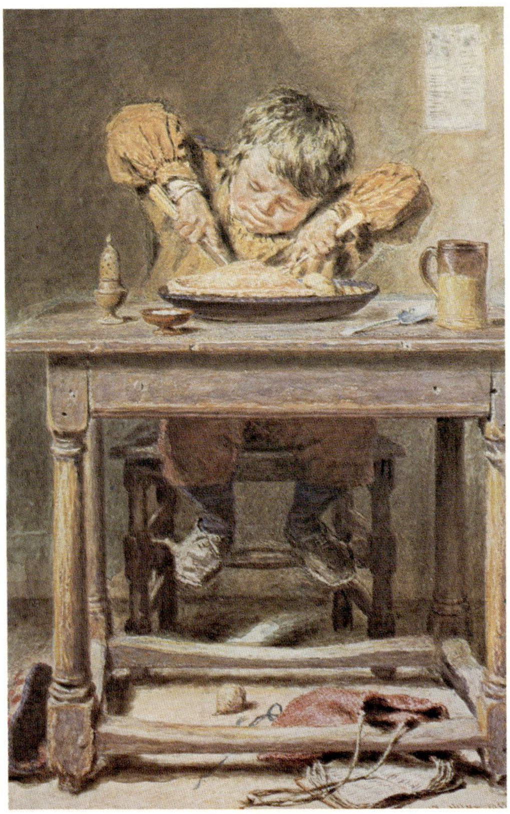

11 (499) The Attack
Watercolour, 16½ × 11 (419 × 280)
Captain R. Sheepshanks, Suffolk

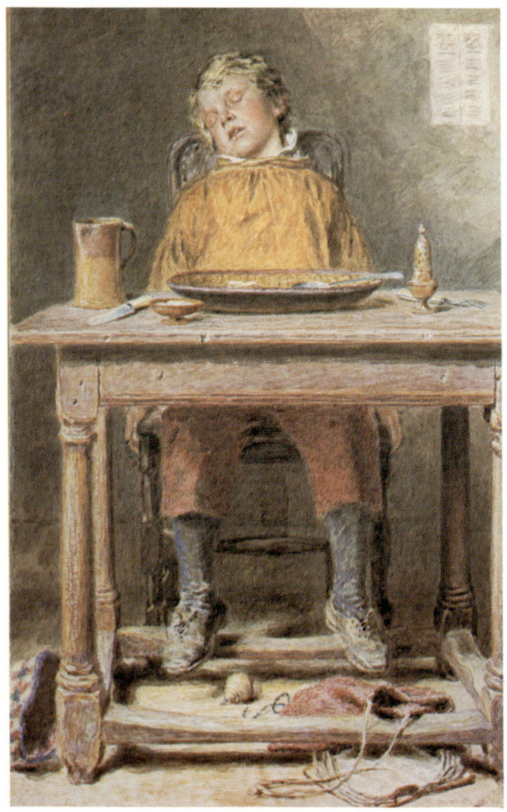

12 (500) The Defeat
Watercolour, 16¾ × 11 (426 × 280)
Captain R. Sheepshanks, Suffolk

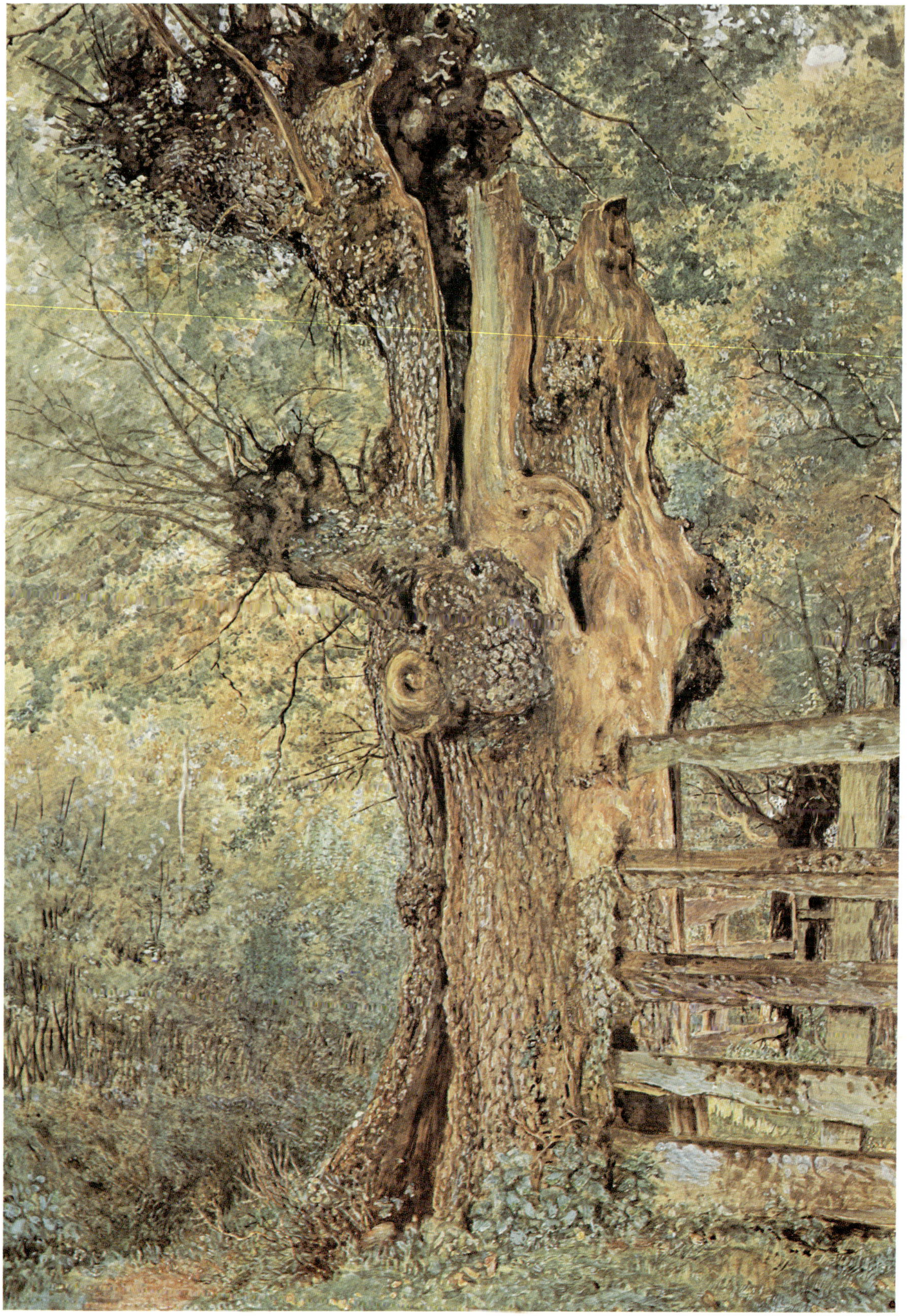

13 (144) Pollard Elm and Village Pound at Hambledon
Watercolour heightened with white, 30 × 22 (762 × 558); dated 1833
Preston, Harris Museum and Art Gallery

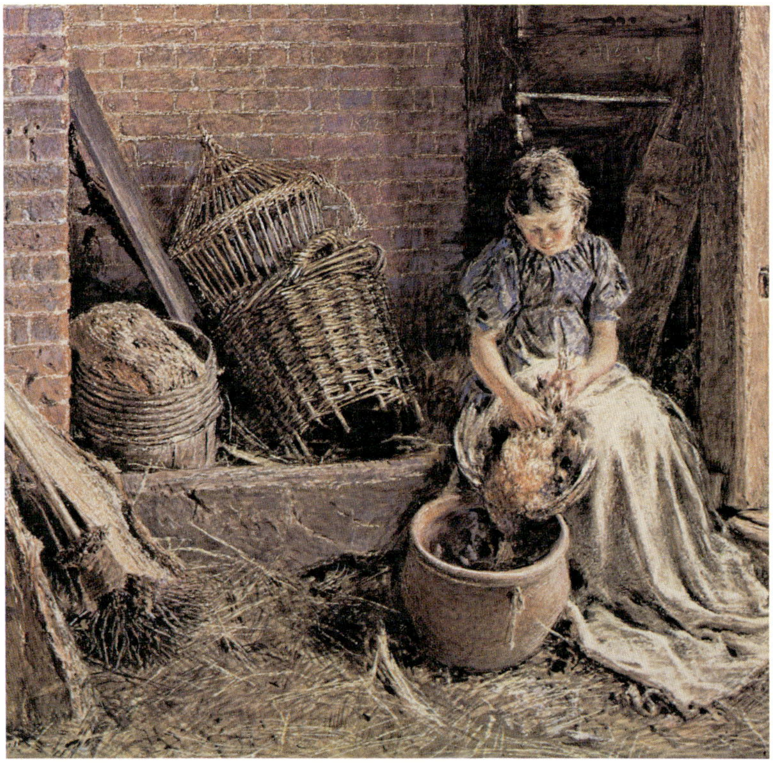

14 (298) Plucking the Fowl
Watercolour with much scratching, $13\frac{5}{8} \times 14\frac{1}{4}$ (346 × 362); dated 1832
British Museum, London

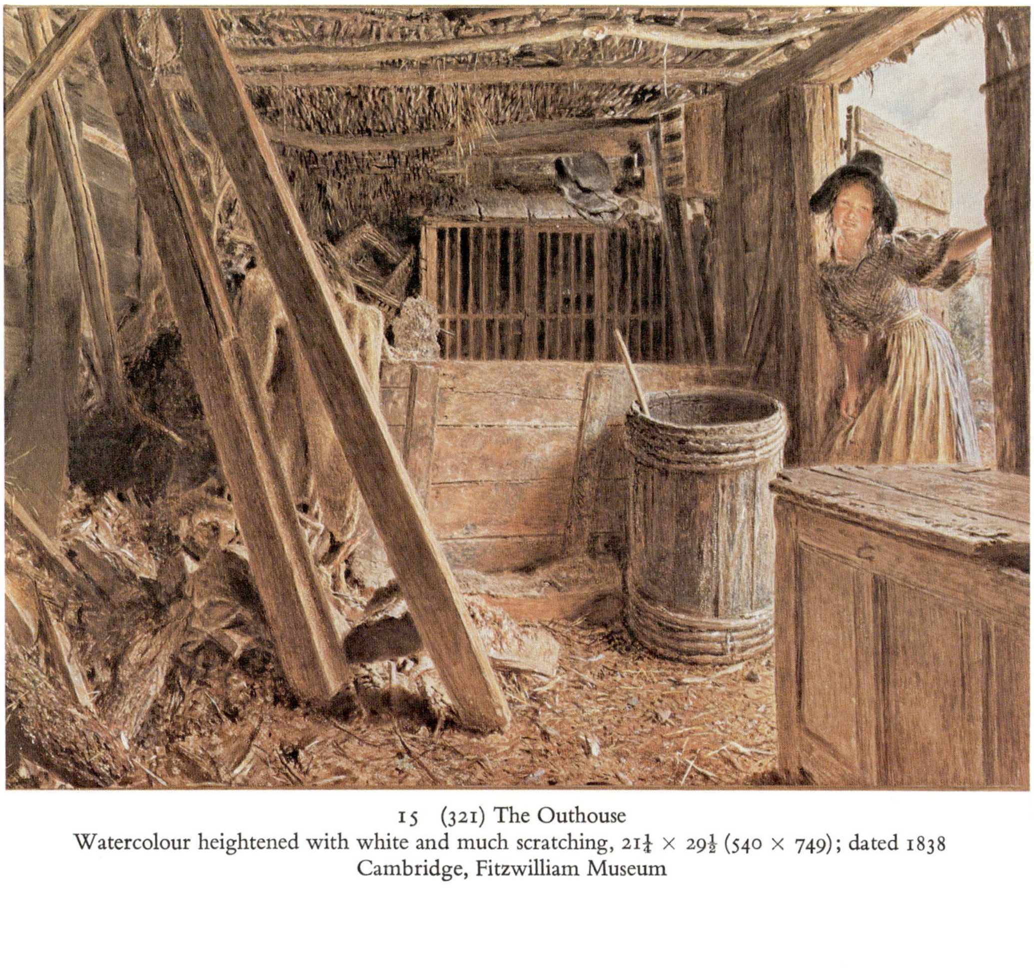

15 (321) The Outhouse
Watercolour heightened with white and much scratching, $21\frac{1}{4} \times 29\frac{1}{2}$ (540 × 749); dated 1838
Cambridge, Fitzwilliam Museum

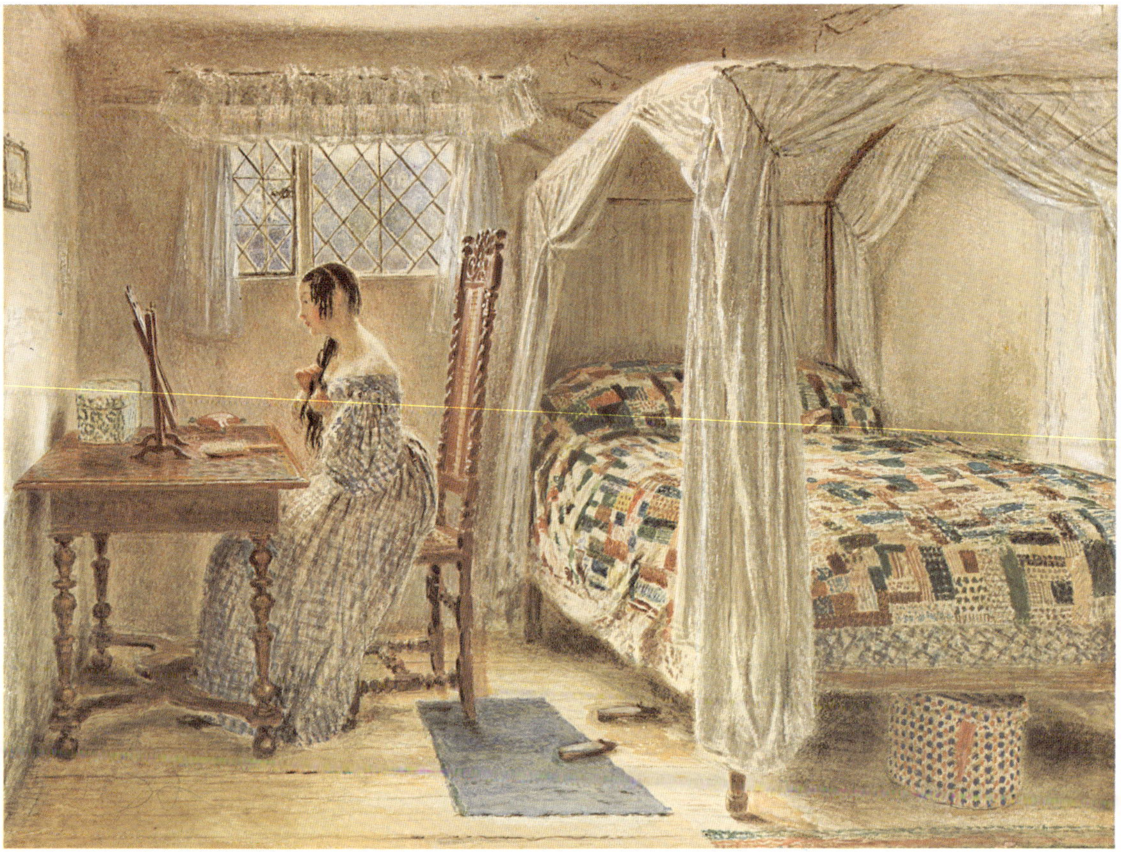

16 (553) Girl at her Toilet
Watercolour, 12¼ × 16½ (312 × 420)
Witt Collection

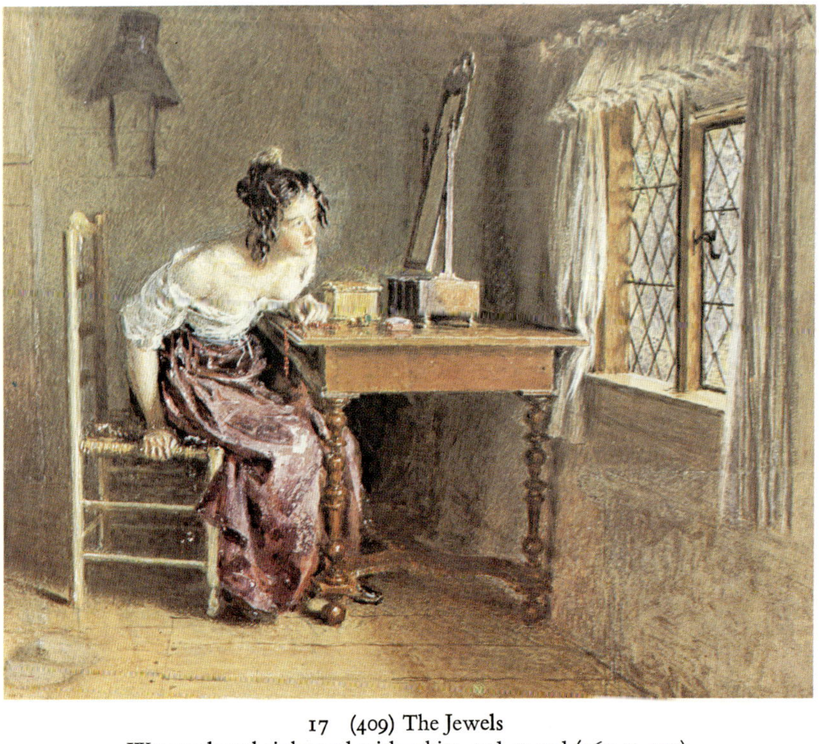

17 (409) The Jewels
Watercolour heightened with white, 10½ × 12½ (267 × 317)
Huntington Library, San Marino

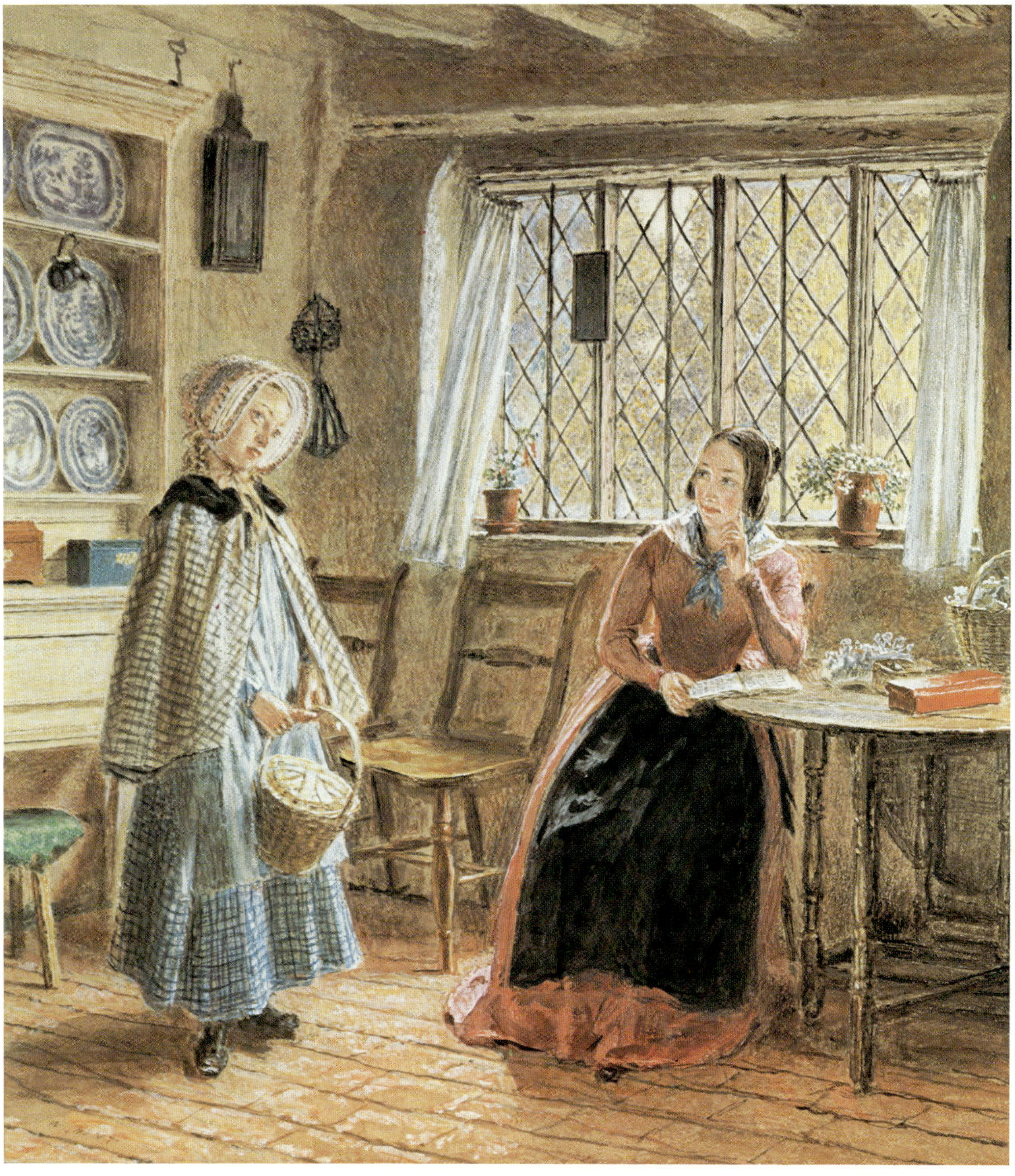

18 (536) Hearing Lessons
Watercolour, 14½ × 13½ (368 × 344)
Victoria and Albert Museum, London

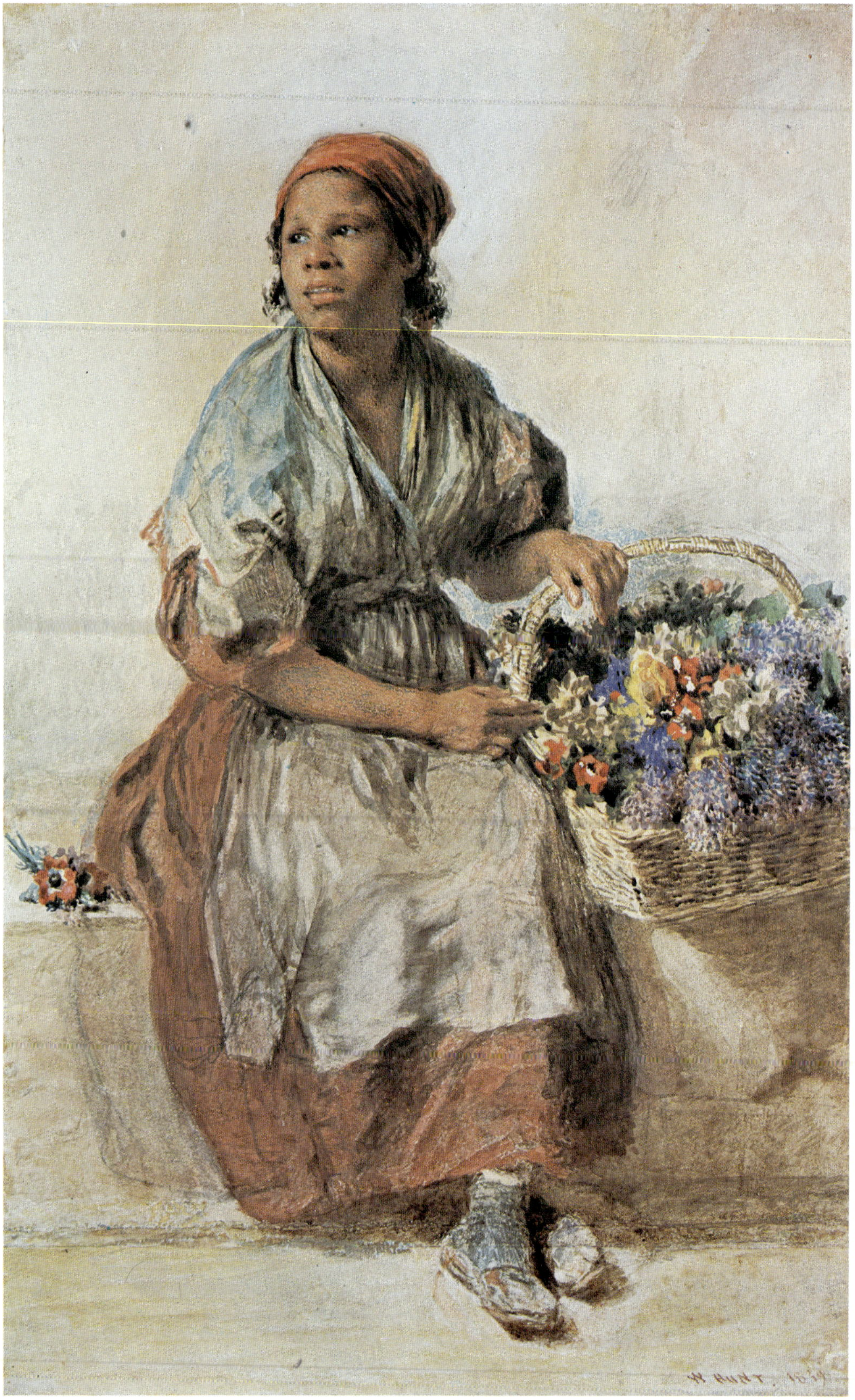

19 (507) The Flower Girl
Watercolour heightened with white, $19\frac{1}{4} \times 12\frac{1}{2}$ (488 × 317); dated 1839
Captain R. Sheepshanks, Suffolk

Orrock was only thirty-five years of age at Hunt's death, and a considerable number of Hunt's works in his collection must have been acquired after Hunt's death. Orrock's biographer Byron Webber records that:

Mr. Orrock saw Mr. Hunt paint in the small bare and plainly furnished back room which commanded a view of a dismal regular back yard or garden. Orrock remembers the bunches of grapes and other newly gathered fruit on the table and also recalls a prepared background of crumpled brown paper upon which had been deposited and roughly built up patches of earth, and over these in ordered irregularity a distribution of lichens and mosses. There were amongst the painter's 'properties', handfuls of grass and sprigs of ivy.[30]

Orrock also gives a detailed description of Hunt's use of body-colour (quoted in Part I, Chapter 4, 'Technique').

Hunt, like so many artists throughout the ages, would supplement his income by giving drawing lessons to pupils. But he would not have been a conventional drawing master: he disliked the then recognised system of teaching. He wrote to a prospective pupil,

I cannot tell what to recommend you to do. I should say paint your pictures from nature; and if you did that there are some of the members [presumably of the Old Water-Colour Society], Mr. Harding[31] in particular, who is strong against that, and says if that is Art he knows nothing about art. Perhaps he cannot paint from nature, at all events only in his mannered way. I like some of the Preraphaelites' works which looks like the thing they represent, not as if they had been taught in a conventional manner like Harding and lots of his school.[32]

Hunt had also been known to say, on looking at a picture, 'I like that because it is not like a drawing-master's drawing'.[33]

Ruskin formed a practical view of Hunt's inability to impart instruction to a pupil. He writes in January 1861 to William Ward, a pupil of his own: 'I've got leave from Mr Hunt for you to see him paint. I'll give you six lessons, that is to say, six hours to sit by him (for you'll find he can't *tell* you anything), as soon as he comes back to town in two or three weeks.'[34]

Brief reference was made in the Introduction to two important exhibitions held during Hunt's lifetime. The first was the Exposition Universelle at the Paris Salon, 'Palais des Beaux-Arts', in May 1855 where Hunt had eleven works in the 'Aquarelle' section including several of the boy model such as 'The Attack' (499, Colour Plate 11) and 'The Defeat' (500, Colour Plate 12). Hunt's works shown in this exhibition are listed in Part III, section 4. Hunt was awarded a certificate of Merit, 3rd Class. George Cattermole was awarded 1st Class with eleven works and Louis Haghe 2nd Class with two. William Callow, William Dyce, Copley Fielding, John Frederick Lewis and Samuel Palmer also exhibited in the Aquarelle section. In the oil painting section, Charles Leslie was awarded 1st Class. Edwin Landseer, John Linnell, James Holland and William Holman Hunt also exhibited.

Doubtless as a result of his success at this exhibition, and coupled with the favourable comments on his exhibits, particularly by Baudelaire in the French Press (previously referred to in the Introduction), Hunt was in 1856 awarded the honorary title of Member of the Royal Academy of Amsterdam.

Hunt was extremely proud of these honours, and under his Will, dated 29 November 1861, directed that one of his Executors, Robert Galloway (the husband of one of his nieces), should:

take and have the possession of the gold medal presented to me in consequence of the Exhibition of my works at the Paris Universal Exhibition of 1855 and of my diploma as a member of the Royal Academy of Fine Arts at Amsterdam until one of the sons of my daughter Emma Robinson shall attain the age of 21 years and on the attainment of that age by the first son who shall attain that age such medal and diploma shall thereupon be given up by the said Robert Galloway to such son and I bequeath the same to him in the hope that he will appreciate preserve and keep the same as memorials of the honour conferred on me thereby.

Roget records[35] that the Robinsons did have several children but how many and of what sex has not been ascertained.

The second of the two important exhibitions held in Hunt's lifetime was the Exhibition of Art Treasures of the United Kingdom held at Manchester in 1857. This was an exhibition of great size and scope, embracing Old Master paintings as well as British. Manchester was chosen as the venue since that city, outside London, was one of the most important and prosperous as the centre of the cotton trade. In its review of the exhibition, the *Manchester Guardian* noted: 'What in the world do you want with Art in Manchester? Why can't you stick to your cotton spinning? So a noble Duke is said to have inquired when applied to for a [loan] contribution from his Gallery to the Manchester Exhibition.' The section of 'Drawings in Watercolours' alone contained 965 works. Of these Hunt contributed thirty – a mixed bag, including figure studies in which the boy models were again prominent, grapes, plums, birds' nests, and so forth, but no landscapes. Hunt's exhibited works are listed in Part III section 5. Among other living artists represented were George Cattermole also with thirty works, David Roberts with thirty-seven, David Cox with seventeen, and Clarkson Stanfield also with seventeen. Several artists then dead were included in the exhibition, notably Turner with eighty-five works, Girtin with seventeen, Peter de Wint with fifteen, and John Varley with eleven.

The following extract from the *Manchester Guardian*'s notice of this exhibition shows the esteem in which Hunt was then held:

Back to the homesteads, and streets, and waysides of dear Old England with William Hunt, the truest delineator of the British country boy through all the phases of his joy and sorrow, his shiverings in the winter frost, his warm snooze by the chimney-corner, his terrible onslaught on the meat-pie, his heavy happy sleep after clearance of the enormous dish, in his school sufferings and school sports; – with William Hunt, the most pathetic painter of the devotion of the English village church or Irish village chapel; the truest delineator of the weariness of vagrant life, not dressed up in attractively-cast drapery and glowing studio tatters, but given in its own grey, dusty, draggled garb, only with such beauty of youth as survives even in the midst of the sins and sadness of a wandering life; – with William Hunt, painter of still life, which competes for minute truth with Gerard Dow [Dou] or Teniers, – the fruit and flower painter, whose bunches of blossom and wayside flower, whose glowing piles of plums and peaches surpass immeasurably all that has ever been put upon canvas by Ruisch or Van Huysum, by Snyders or Leghers. No fewer than thirty of this admirable painter's works (518–547) are here. Painter we may call him, for his work is rather painting than drawing. It is executed entirely in body colour, in a manner which Hunt has invented for himself, applied entirely with the point, and in touches of pure primitive colour, making up by their various combinations every shade of secondary and tertiary colour, and all tones of grey that are required in this whole range of representation. Hunt is with reason one of the most popular of our water-colour masters; and he takes the very highest rank amongst the English painters of humble life.[36]

A circumstance which gave Hunt much pleasure towards the end of his life was the resumption of his old friendship with John Linnell. They exchanged letters and photographs of each other which culminated in a letter from Hunt written from 62 Stanhope Street, Hampstead Road, NW, and dated and postmarked 9 December 1863.[37] The letter, which is wholly devoid of punctuation, is reproduced in facsimile on page 60.

Hunt was a man of great modesty and simplicity. Ruskin confirms this, writing in 1854 to his friend Lady Trevelyan about Hunt, one of whose drawings he had encouraged her to acquire: 'He is so modest that he never knows whether what he does is his own doing, I believe. I think he has a vague idea that it comes on the paper by accident.'[38] Hunt was also always ready to bestow praise when he felt praise was due, as he showed in a letter of April 1862 to his friend Philip Brown when he wrote: 'I think I have learnt much from seeing Birket Foster's and some other drawings and intend to try to take advantage of the knowledge as soon as I get into the country', 'for', as the letter charmingly and modestly concludes, 'I think it never too late to try to do better.'[39] Hunt was then seventy-two, and one is reminded of Renoir's remark towards the end of his life some fifty years later, 'I begin to show promise.'

In the last few years of his life, Hunt had become increasingly accident-prone. Thus on 17 May 1861 he writes 'with a sprained hand, having tumbled out of a cab a fortnight back'. In May 1863 he had written to his 'friend Brown':

I am glad to say I can still amuse myself by making drawings. Of course you will still be in town before long to see the Exhibitions. I fear I shall not be able to see them. If you or your son Charles are in Town before I leave, which will not be yet awhile, perhaps you would help my nephew get me up the steps and the stairs of the Royal Academy. I should very much like to go there.[40]

The nephew referred to was Hunt's namesake William Henry Hunt, the son of his younger brother Thomas James Hunt. This nephew was by this time living in Hunt's house at 62 Stanhope Street and would often help his uncle in various ways when he began to get old and infirm. Hunt appointed him one of his Executors and left him

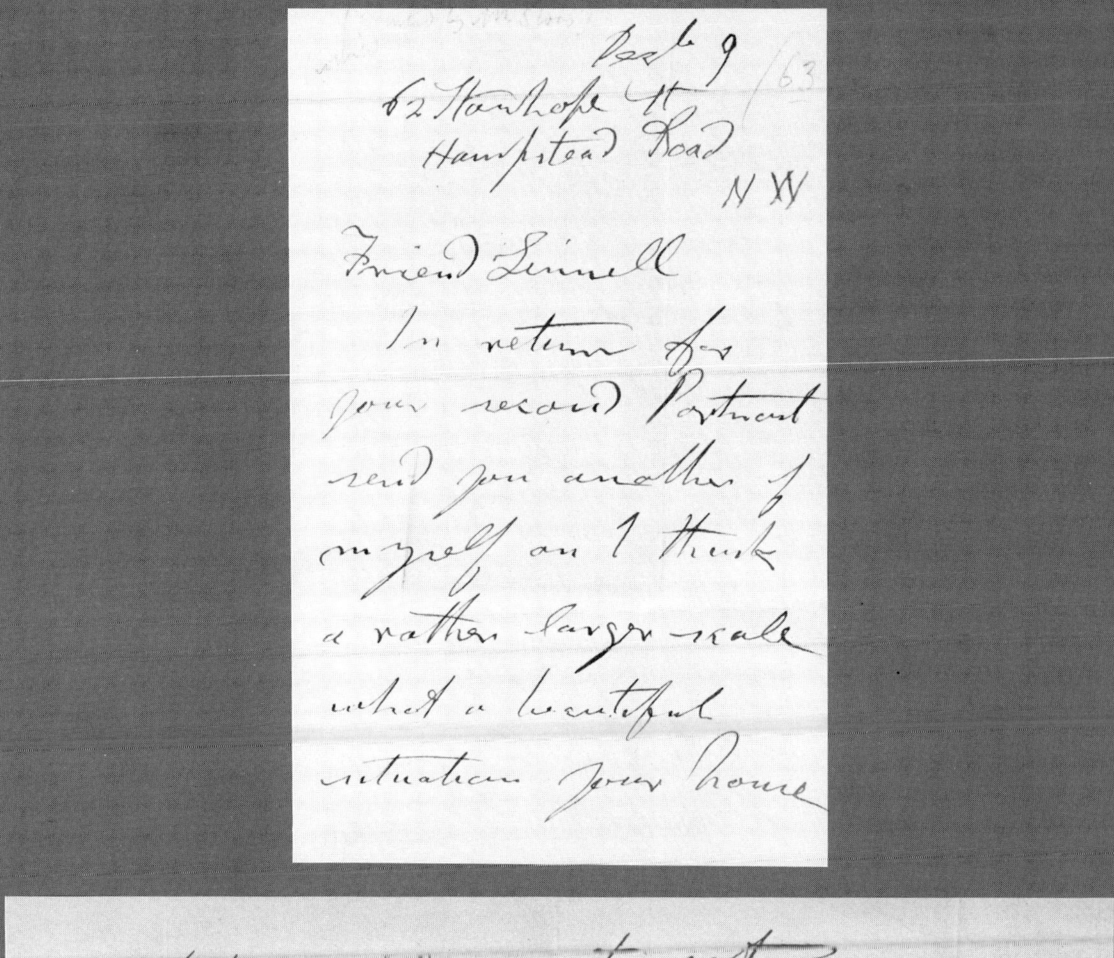

Decr 9
62 Stanhope St
Hampstead Road
NW

Friend Linnell
In return for
your second Portrait
send you another of
myself on I think
a rather larger scale
what a beautiful
situation your house
must be my Country
retreat is an old
farm house near
Basingstoke Hants
and that I rent
I still work very hard
at grapes and apples
but I wish persons
would like the drawings
as bits of colour instead
of something nice
to eat
With best Respects to
Mrs Linnell and
family
I am Yours truly
W Hunt

J Linnell Esq

Letter from Hunt to John Linnell, 9 December 1863

his house, 62 Stanhope Street, all his household furniture and effects, and an annuity of £50 tax free for life. The nephew's sister Maria Madison Hunt (Hunt's niece) was an amateur artist, and two signed drawings by her are in the British Museum.[41] One of fishing boats on the beach at Hastings, apart from being greatly inferior in execution, closely resembles Hunt's own beach scenes at Hastings.

Later in the summer of 1863 when he was living at his country place at Bramley, Hunt suffered a severe accident by the breaking of a rope which he used instead of a rail to haul himself up to his bedroom. It broke as he was descending the stairs and, to use his own expression, he 'tumbled down to the first landing all of a heap'. Soon afterwards he had another accident owing to having mistaken the position of his chair. 'Of course', he writes in August 1863, 'I fell to the ground all my weight and hurt the opposite side to that which was hurt before and now I am quite unable to walk at all.' In October 1863 he writes to the same friend,

I am tolerable myself – except that I am very feeble. How I do wish that I were thirty years younger! How I would paint out of doors! I suppose it is that I must not sit out of doors that makes me think I never saw the country looking half so beautiful as it does at present. . . . One sees so much more might be done when we are about being obliged to leave it off altogether. . . . You must fag away and do better and better.[42]

The last acts of Hunt's life were concerned with the selection of candidates for admission as associates to the Old Water-Colour Society. The members were to meet for this purpose at the Society's gallery in Suffolk Street on Saturday, 6 February 1864. Hunt had sent on his invalid chair, and after spending the morning at his easel, was carried up to the room where the probationary drawings were on view. On the next day he wrote to the secretary: 'will you have the kindness to give my vote for Watson, Walker, Lundgren and Solomon. The drawings by Shields and Johnson are very good, do you not think so? If you elect more than four, I should give my vote to Johnson.' Frederick Walker (1840–75) recalls that he submitted three finished drawings, one of which he took to 'dear old William Hunt who seemed greatly pleased with it which gratified me very much'.[43] Walker was duly elected a member of the Old Water-Colour Society, and writes that at the private view 'his work was most favourably compared with that of the lately lost William Hunt'.

The letter from Hunt just quoted was the last he was destined to write. The effort in attending the meeting was too great, and soon after returning home he suffered a stroke. On the Monday shortly after his letter about the candidates had arrived at Spring Gardens, a further message was received that Hunt was speechless. He died on the following Wednesday, 10 February 1864.

His daughter Emma must have sent a letter by hand to Ruskin informing him of her father's death for Ruskin replied that same evening.

DENMARK HILL, 10th Feb., 1864, evening

I thank you for your letter: no one living of your father's friends will mourn him more deeply than I: – it was my pride, that I could recognize his unrivalled powers in art – and one of my chief happinesses that I could sometimes hope he took pleasure in my sympathy and admiration.[44]

Emma must have written again with the date and time of her father's funeral, to which Ruskin replied:

DENMARK HILL, 14th Feb., 1864

I have your kind letter, and I entreat you not to think that because I cannot come to you to-morrow I am wanting in respect or regard for your father. I am naturally of sad disposition, and I simply *cannot* go to funerals – I was not at *Turner's*. I differ from every one nearly in my dealings with the living and dead. Most people thwart, malign, distress and dishonour the living – and then build fine tombs for the dead. I try to honour the living as best I may. Once lost it is a matter of indifference to me how many plumes are at the grave.[45]

Hunt was buried in Highgate Cemetary on the following Monday, 15 February 1864. A number of artists attended the funeral, including a representative group from the Old Water-Colour Society. Among the obituary notices, F. G. Stephens, in the *Athenaeum* of 20 February 1864, referred to Hunt's success at the Exposition Universelle in Paris of 1855 and followed with a biographical account of his career. The *Reader* of 27 February 1864 contained a reference to the recent deaths of Hunt and William Dyce and concluded: 'we were but faintly beginning to appreciate and understand his [Hunt's] genius when he was taken from us – one of the greatest artists of the Century.'

In the Summer Exhibition in 1864 of the Old Water-Colour Society, a marble bust of Hunt by the sculptor Alexander Munro was placed in the middle of the gallery.[46] This bust belonged to Madame Bodichon, a friend of Hunt's, who presented it to the Society in 1889, to whom it still belongs, and where for many years it occupied a recess on the staircase. The bust is illustrated as Plate IX in F. G. Stephens's article of 1865.

By his will dated 29 November 1861 and codicil dated 4 July 1862, Hunt left a number of legacies mainly to members of his family: his leasehold house at 62 Stanhope Street and contents (other than his works of art) to his nephew William Henry, and annuities to his daughter Emma, his son-in-law and other relatives, and the residue to his daughter's children. His total estate amounted to about £20,000.[47]

Hunt further directed that 'all my drawings sketches prints pictures and frames articles and things belonging to or connected with my profession of an artist should be sold by my Executors by public auction.' The sale occupied two days at Christie's on 16 and 17 May 1864. The Catalogue heading is:

The Whole of the Remaining Works of that highly-talented Artist, William Henry Hunt, Deceased: Comprising a large number of Sketches in Pencil and Water-Colours; highly interesting finished Studies and Drawings; Also, a Few Pictures and Water-Colour Drawings by other Artists; Engravings and Artistic Accessories, Frames, Painting Materials, etc.

The first day's sale (16 May 1864) comprised 199 lots (Lots 1–199), of which Lots 1 to 25 inclusive were each of 'Twenty-five slight studies of figures, shipping etc.' Lots 56–74 were 'Sketches in Chalk' and the remaining lots 'Water-Colours'. Many of these were of scenes at Hastings, for example 'Houses at Hastings', 'The fish-market, Hastings', 'The beach at Hastings', 'Boats and figures, Hastings'. Lot 159, 'Portico of St Martin-in-the-Fields with Figures' (256) was described by F. G. Stephens[48] as 'A recent copy made by Hunt' from a work of the same subject now in the Ashmolean Museum, Oxford (141, Plate 24).

Lot 162 was 'Bushey Churchyard, Herts, with the Tombs of Hearne, Edridge, and Alexander [it should be Henry] Monro' (252, Plate 25). Lot 184 was 'A View in the Isle of Wight, After Linnell'.

In the last fourteen lots – Lots 186 to 199 – the titles were printed in large capitals and were clearly to be regarded as the most important items:

186	'The Mishap.' *Very fine*
187	The Dwarf at Hastings
188	'The Connoisseur'
189	Black and White Grapes and a Basket
190	A Girl in Fancy Costume Sleeping – lamplight
191	The Bedroom at Hardwick, with a Female
192	The Music Lesson – candlelight
193	In the Garden at Chiswick [now at the Rijksmuseum, Amsterdam (148)]
194	The Dining-Room at Cashiobury [now in the Fry Collection (375, Plate 22)]
195	The Anteroom, Cashiobury
196	The Housekeeper's Room, Cashiobury
197	A Girl Seated Reading a Letter
198	A Girl at her Devotions
199	A Cottage at Cashiobury [probably 'A Lodge at Cassiobury', Yale Center (245, Plate 19)]

('Cashiobury' was the spelling always used at this time.)

The first day's sale produced a total of £1,154.

The second day's sale (17 May 1864) comprised 196 lots (Lots 200 to 395), of which Lots 200 to 223 inclusive were each of 'Twenty-five slight studies of figures, shipping etc.' As on the first day's sale, there were numerous scenes at Hastings, Bushey and Cassiobury Park. Lot 262 was 'The shepherd, after Cristall'. Lot 275 was 'Mountebanks in St Mark's Place. *A capital copy after Canaletti*' [sic] (134, Plate 4). Lot 305, 'Old London Bridge – Boats, etc., in the Foreground', was the later copy by Hunt, View of London Bridge (32) of one of the two versions, both dated 1825, 'London Bridge with Pool of London Beyond' (31, Plate 11) and 'View of Old London Bridge' (253).

In the following lots the titles were printed in large capitals and, similarly to those on the first day, were to be regarded as the most important items. They were:

290 A Negro's Head – *oval*
308 A Study of a Pollard, near a pond [it should read pound]
[Dated 1833; now at the Harris Museum, Preston (144, Colour Plate 13)]
310 Old London Bridge, boats and a sailing barge in the foreground
[This is the version either at the British Museum (31, Plate 11) or at the Yale Center (253), both being dated 1825.]
311 Farmyard, with Figures, Bramley, Hants
312 Southwark and Blackfriars Bridges, from the Thames

Lots 313 to 348 inclusive were designated 'Drawings in Water-Colours' and were by artists other than Hunt. They provide an interesting picture of his personal taste for other artists. They included 'The extravagant wife' and twelve other works by Rowlandson; 'A lake scene', and another work by Turner; three sketches in pen by Wilkie; an illustration to a novel by Stothard; 'A canal scene, Amsterdam', 'Gravesend', and 'Dutch boats in a stiff breeze' by G. Chambers; two landscapes by de Wint; 'Hampstead Heath, with cattle', 'Windsor Castle', a river scene, and four landscapes by Varley; 'A snow-scene', and four other works by Prout; 'Figures on a road under a rocky height' by Clarkson Stanfield, RA; two illustrations to Shakespeare by Massey Wright; 'London from the Thames' by Vickers; two female figures – *in red chalk*', 'A woman sleeping', and three others by Bega; and 'A view in Venice, with figures – *in Indian ink*' by Canaletti [sic]. There was a picture of 'A combat' by T. Stothard, RA, and various 'Artistic Accessories', which included a number of brown jugs, a brown 'ginger-jar', two metal pots, and a two-handled jar with initials W.H., a camera-lucida, four mahogany boxes with paints, a box of brushes, and a pallet. The pallet is likely to have been the pallet of the artist now owned by the Royal Society of Painters in Water-Colours.

The second day's sale produced a total of £1,180, making a grand total of £2,334 for both days.

4
Technique

In the art of pure watercolour the pigments used require some binding material to hold them together. A number of different substances have been used for this purpose. Of these, several varieties of gum are the most common and gum arabic the most widely employed. This is a vegetable gum, obtained from the acacia, and is soluble in water. The colour resulting from the combination of pigment and gum arabic is then dissolved in water and applied by the artist to the surface of the paper. This is commonly a white surface which remains throughout as the lighting surface of the work. 'Never lose your paper' has always been a golden rule for the pure watercolourist.

This was the basic method employed by John Varley, to whom Hunt was apprenticed, and by Varley's predecessors, the Sandbys, John Robert Cozens, Francis Towne and the early topographers such as Thomas Malton, Edward Dayes and Thomas Hearne. It certainly formed the method by which Varley gave instruction to his numerous pupils such as Hunt and John Linnell. As a result, most of Hunt's early work (apart from his work in oils which he was to discontinue in 1825) was done in even washes of pure watercolour, in which he achieved, in Ruskin's words already quoted, 'the most open and simple management of transparent colour'. Notable examples in this method are 'Saltwood Castle, Kent' (179, Plate 5), with its strong Varley influence, 'View of Hastings' (137, Plate 6), and 'The Flagstaff, Margate' (250, Plate 7).

Hunt also combined the use of these even washes with his lively and sensitive handling of the reed pen. Typical examples are 'London Bridge with Pool of London Beyond' (31, Plate 11), 'The Portico of St Martin-in-the-Fields' (141, Plate 24), and the various views of Bushey, Aldenham and other Hertfordshire churches illustrated in this book. A little later on, in the early 1830s, Hunt began on occasions to discard the even wash and instead to break up his washes into detached and separately defined touches and patches which could be described as a kind of stippling. 'The Turnip Lantern' (419, Plate 58), other studies of the boy models, and 'An Old Man's Head' (514, Plate 64) are examples.

He also began to develop the use of the knife[1] in scratching out points and lines to provide patches of light from the paper which he would either leave untouched or would modify by dotting with pure watercolour. Good examples of this knifing or scratching technique are found in 'Boy and Goat' (530, Plate 59), 'Slumber' (274, Plate 77), 'Plucking the Fowl' (298, Colour Plate 14), 'The Gleaner' (318), and 'In Val Crucis Abbey' (472, Plate 76). William Collingwood gives a good description of Hunt's knifing method:

As an example of his perception of colour, I remember his bringing a drawing of a kingfisher, just finished, which startled us all by the brilliancy of its emerald green. When asked what new colour he had been using, he said, 'Put on your spectacles.' On applying a lens we saw that he had obtained the colour by picking out points with a knife and letting in vermillion – a practice which may be often detected in his work. And to his realising the value of complementary colour his pictures largely owe their power.[2]

The drawing referred to is probably 'Dead Kingfisher and Fishing Tackle' (635) which was exhibited at the Old Water-Colour Society in 1840 (No. 280).

As has been suggested in the Introduction, there are strong grounds for asserting that Hunt's stippling technique had a strong and direct influence on the Pointillism of Seurat and Signac and the so-called Neo-Impressionist French artists of the end of the nineteenth century.

The essential link is *The Elements of Drawing* which Ruskin wrote towards the end of 1856 and which was published in the middle of 1857. This was an immediate success and went into a number of editions. Ruskin and Hunt had been in close touch in 1853 and 1854[3] and *The Elements of Drawing* contains laudatory references to Hunt particularly in relation to his stippling technique in Letter III 'On Colour'. The following is an example:

When you have time, practise the production of mixed tints by interlaced touches of the pure colours out of which they are formed, and use the process at the parts of your sketches where you wish to get rich and luscious effects. Study the works of William Hunt, of the Old Water-Colour Society, in this respect, continually, and make frequent memoranda of the variegations in flowers; not painting the flower completely, but laying the ground colour of one petal, and painting the spots on it with studious precision: a series of single petals of lilies, geraniums, tulips, etc., numbered with proper reference to their position in the flower, will be interesting to you on many grounds besides those of art. Be careful to get the gradated distribution of the spots well followed in the calceolarias, fox-gloves, and the like; and work out the odd, indefinite hues of the spots themselves with minute grains of pure interlaced colour, otherwise you will never get their richness or bloom. You will be surprised to find as you do this, first, the universality of the law of gradation we have so much insisted upon; secondly, that Nature is just as economical of *her* fine colours as I have told you to be of yours.[4]

In 1879, Ogden N. Rood, a noted American authority on colour, published *Modern Chromatics*.[5] In it he quoted passages from *The Elements of Drawing* where Ruskin's references to Hunt's stippling technique are mentioned. A French translation of *Modern Chromatics* appeared in 1881.[6] This work must have been known to Seurat. W. I. Homer, in *Seurat and the Science of Painting* (1964), asks:

'What were the sources of the "petit point" employed by Seurat?' and answers, 'Of great consequence were Rood's citations of Dr Jean Mile and John Ruskin both of whom suggested the use of a stippled technique in painting.'[7]

In 1899 (eight years after Seurat's death) Paul Signac published his belated manifesto in support of Seurat and the Neo-Impressionists entitled *D'Eugène Delacroix au néo-impressionisme*. The work contains quotations from Rood and Ruskin about stippling and Pointillism and concludes:

Ainsi, un peintre comme Delacroix, un esthéticien comme Ruskin, un savant comme Rood ont prévu ou indiqué les différents procédés qui constituent l'apport novateur des néo-impressionnistes et semblent même recommander spécialement la partie de leur technique qui est la plus attaquée aujourd'hui, celle que l'on trouve si fâcheuse: l'emploi de touches d'éléments purs.[8]

Hunt also made use of the medium which is often generically described as 'body-colour'. The term body-colour in fact comprises three quite different methods, all of which involve the use, in some form, of an opaque white pigment often called Chinese white. The first method is to apply this opaque white pigment as a means of providing the highlights in a drawing. The second method involves the mixing of this opaque white pigment with transparent watercolour. The third method involves using the opaque white pigment as a ground on which the artist then places his transparent watercolour. These three different methods must now be described in greater detail.

The first method was used by a number of Old Masters, particularly by artists of the Italian School, notably the Bolognese School of the seventeenth century. Claude also used this method extensively in his more finished drawings. In the eighteenth century, Richard Wilson adopted the same method of highlighting many of his drawings done in black chalk and stump on grey paper. Often this white pigment, over the years, turned almost black by oxidisation and came to provide the opposite effect to what the artist intended; it can, however, usually be revived, by appropriate treatment, to its original whiteness. Hunt frequently used this method during his career both before and after he ceased to paint in pure transparent watercolour. An early example is 'The Jewels' (409, Colour Plate 17), painted in the mid-1830s, where the girl's nose and blouse are highlighted with this opaque white. 'Light and Shade' (399, Plate 91), and many flower pieces such as 'Roses' (657, Colour Plate 26), are good examples of Hunt using this method in his later works.

The second method (the mixing of the opaque white pigment with transparent watercolour) can be regarded as the antithesis of pure watercolour, since it consists of a pigment containing enough 'body' to make it opaque instead of transparent. Chinese white is the description normally given to the substance which provides the element of body, and all watercolours, when mixed with Chinese white, become opaque and semi-liquid. In consequence, the white surface of the paper disappears and ceases to provide the lighting element as it does in pure watercolour painting. The term 'body-colour' as defined in this method is synonymous with the term 'gouache'. Body-colour was extensively used in the seventeenth century by artists such as Gaspard Poussin in France, and Jordaens and Van Huysum in the Netherlands. In the eighteenth century its use was extensively practised by Marco Ricci and Zucharelli, both of whom visited England. It was a special favourite of Paul Sandby, who was well acquainted with Zucharelli, both having been founder members of the Royal Academy. Painting by this method could be a quick and showy method of producing popular landscapes, but one that degenerated later on the Continent into a tourist traffic of lurid views of Vesuvius and the Bay of Naples for those returning from the Grand Tour. In England from 1830 onwards it grew in popularity, and Turner used it freely in his drawings by mixing some white in his water-bottle, thus giving the water a milky appearance and consistency.

The term 'Chinese white' as a form of body-colour did not, however, occur until 1834 when Messrs Winsor and Newton, even then a well-known firm of suppliers of artists' materials, put on the market an opaque white pigment under the title of 'Chinese White'. It was specially prepared for use with watercolour, and had a base of oxide of zinc. This was a great improvement on previous forms of body-colour which had had a basis of lead, and were easily blackened by the sulphuretted hydrogen which existed particularly in the smoky atmosphere of crowded cities; whereas Chinese white, with its base of oxide of zinc, was relatively immune to this blackening process.

The third method of body-colour consists of using an opaque white pigment, Chinese white, as a ground on which the artist then places his transparent watercolour. This principle was already in use by nineteenth-century painters in oil, such as Turner, Etty and Mulready, to obtain greater brilliance of colour. But its use in watercolour painting was by an essentially new and original method of which Hunt can be regarded as the inventor. It was used extensively by him in his later work, particularly in his fruit paintings of grapes and plums. It is well described by Hunt's fellow watercolourist James Orrock (1829–1913), who actually saw Hunt at work.

In early life, Hunt painted without the use of any body colour and it was not until the middle period that he used it. It is quite certain however, that as no luminous sky can be represented with body colour, so no still life of the highest excellence can be produced without it. Hunt found this out and left off an extensive use of transparent colour when he painted his wondrous still-life pictures. He never however, at any time used body colour in his figure painting. Body colour painting in the ordinary sense means mixing pigment [i.e. pure watercolour] with body colour [i.e. the second method described above]. Hunt never did this; he painted *on* body colour which was laid on the objects thick and then left to dry to hardness. He would, for instance, roughly pencil out a group of plums or grapes and thickly coat each one with Chinese-white which he would leave to harden. On this brilliant china-like ground he would put his colours [i.e. pure watercolour], not in washes, but solid and sure so as not to disturb the ground which he had prepared. By this process the utmost value for obtaining strength and brilliancy was secured for the colours were made to 'bear out' and almost rival Nature herself. Hunt's backgrounds were painted to a great extent with transparent colours, with the exception of portions of them such as lichens, mossy grasses etc. which were first prepared with white like the chief objects in the drawing.

I have stated that Hunt rarely used body colour even in minute quantities in his figure work. He used the knife! Rather than have its background monotonous and flat, he would scrape up portions here and there and drop colours into the scrapes like mosaic work.[9]

Martin Hardie, himself a watercolour artist of distinction, describes, in *Water-colour Painting in Britain*,[10] certain interesting and valuable experiments which he himself made to discover the nature of Hunt's main use of Chinese white. Martin Hardie suggests that the method of working on a prepared white ground may well have been adapted from the practice of wood engravers. He refers to the statement of John Jackson in his treatise on wood engraving published in 1839 that 'some artists, previous to beginning to draw on the block, are in the habit of washing over the surface with a mixture of flake white and gum-water.' Martin Hardie continues:

Though Jackson did not entirely approve of this practice, it was in general use by the middle of the century. His reference to gum-water gives a clue, I think, to Hunt's method. My own experiments in trying to elucidate the manner in which Hunt painted his fruit or birds' nests showed that, when the paper was coated with pure Chinese White, the white being somewhat powdery in texture, became disturbed by the application of colour [i.e. watercolour] and tended to blur the edges and made the colour mat. One could understand the effect produced by this means in a water-colour by Arthur Melville, but not in the stippled method used by Hunt with its pure colour and compact detail. But on laying a ground made of Chinese White mixed with plentiful gum, I found that the surface of the paper became in Orrock's words, much 'more brilliant and china-like', with an almost enamel quality. The white was less liable to be 'lifted', and pure colour could be applied much more readily in stipple or in wash. I would suggest that Hunt and others, when laying their surface ground, used a free admixture of gum.

Hunt, fifteen years older than J. F. Lewis and three years his senior as a member of the Water-Colour Society, influenced his younger colleague considerably: to some extent in subject matter and to a large extent in the actual use of the body-colour method.

I have quoted and written so fully about Hunt's method of working upon a hard priming of Chinese White, because I believe that this particular method (the mixing of colour with Chinese White before applying it to paper was an old process), can be credited to Hunt as his own invention. And I have described it fully because it was the method adopted by his successors; by Lewis, Birket Foster, the whole Pre-Raphaelite group, and many others who were striving for exactness of meticulous detail.

This claim by Martin Hardie for Hunt to be considered the inventor of this special method of using Chinese white seems wholly convincing, and emphasises Hunt's importance as an inventor and discoverer of a new technical process of great value not only to himself but to his successors.

Hunt himself confirms Orrock's description of his method of using Chinese white when he describes the technique he used for his later works 'as pure colour over pure colour'.[11] Of body-colour (Chinese white) he says, 'I always glaze it over with pure colour'. Here he is distinguishing his own method of using body-colour (the third method described above) from the traditional method (the second method described above) of actually mixing body-colour with pure watercolour before it is applied to the paper. He writes with disfavour of the use of this second method by Lewis in one of Lewis's later works (probably 'The Harem' exhibited in 1850): 'I think it is much inferior to his former work. It is most painfully made out. It is painted in Body-colour [i.e. mixed with Watercolour] which will never do for flesh.'[12]

Ruskin justly points out that Hunt's later drawings 'depended for their highest attainments on the flexibility of a pigment which yielded to the slightest touch and softest motion of a hand always more sensitive than firm'.[13] Hunt's technical mastery of his various methods of working was so complete that he might use them all in the same work, depending on their suitability for its different parts. Thus he would work in pure watercolour, stipple or use the knife, heighten with white, or paint in pure watercolour on his specially prepared ground, as seemed appropriate to him for the task on which he was then engaged. This practice, incidentally, adds considerably to the difficulty of dating some of his works.

William Collingwood emphasises Hunt's technical mastery when describing how he and Hunt were working together on an elaborate interior of a room in the house at Hastings of their mutual friend Mr Maw. Collingwood writes:

The ceiling was elaborate, from his designs. It was a treasure-house of the picturesque and the beautiful in wood and porcelain. In this room we painted together. Hunt's was a piece of intense colour and harmony. But the ceiling bothered him, and he handed his picture over to Mr Maw, asking him to work it out. When Mr Maw objected that he should spoil his work, he said 'Do so, by all means; that is what I want.' Our friend took it in hand and elaborated various parts, which Hunt soon brought round to his own feeling. Sometimes when I said I had spoiled my work, he laughed at me, saying 'it was impossible to spoil a water-colour drawing, it could always be made right again.' And so it could – at least under his hands.[14]

How far Hunt was conscious of his different methods is open to doubt as is shown by the story of the reply, vouched for by Samuel Palmer and quoted in Roget, which Hunt gave to a question about the principles and methods by which he worked.

A lady of very superior taste and acquirement, who painted fruit objects, was anxious to be introduced to Hunt, not doubting that he would communicate some important principle or scientific information as to process, conduct of a picture or the like. To her astonishment, Hunt told her that he did not know anything of that kind. 'The only thing you can do is to *fudge it out.*' She then asked him if he knew Mr. —— (an artist). 'Yes to be sure I do. Of course I do. Well, he has fudged it out. We must all fudge it out. There is no other way than fudging it out.'[15]

By the expression 'fudging it out', Hunt in no way sought to imply that the labour involved in producing the drawing should be scamped or that corners should be lazily cut. In fact Hunt was himself an indefatigable worker as has been previously described, and he preached to young students the doctrine of hard work which he himself practised. Several letters which Hunt wrote in 1862 to his friend Philip Brown about Brown's son, who was studying to become an artist, are illustrations of his philosophy in this respect. He wrote:

Friend Brown, I am glad your son has sold a drawing at the Exhibition. . . . It will stimulate him to fag. But he must bear in mind there is something more to accomplish than he will ever do. As soon as he thinks he has become perfect he is *done for*. I should advise him to *see* all he can in the way of art, and to *draw* as much as he can from *nature*; and be very particular *not to copy* anyone's manner. . . . Never mind what others do; paint as *you* see nature, and try to get all other persons' ways of doing it out of your head.

Again:

I gave him [Brown's son] all the good advice I could, such as not to think anything of gaining a medal except that it gave one a great lift in the estimation of the public, but to *paint away for the pure love of the art.*

And again:

He must have a *greater love for his art than for anything else* and try and screw himself up to doing *whatever he does better than anyone else who has done the same sort of thing. . . . But do not copy any one.*

And yet again:

The way I suggest to do all this will be to *paint nature with your own eyes and feeling.*[16]

The sale of Hunt's studio in 1864 contained one unusual item of particular interest, 'A camera-lucida' (Lot 374). Hunt would have known of this device from his early days as a pupil in John Varley's studio. The camera-lucida was patented by Dr W. Hyde Wolleston in 1807 and, though working on the same principles, was an improvement on the camera obscura, being small, portable and cheap. John Varley's brother Cornelius, three years his junior, was a fellow pupil of Hunt at the Royal Academy and had in addition to his artistic interests a strong scientific bent. In 1811 he patented an improvement on the camera-lucida which he called 'Cornelius Varley's Graphic Telescope'.

These mechanical devices enabled an artist to make drawings, particularly of a topographical or architectural nature, with a speed and exactness of perspective which could not possibly be achieved without their aid. Hunt would have known also of Gainsborough's camera obscura from Dr Monro who owned it and in whose sale it was included on his death in 1833. The camera is now in the Victoria and Albert Museum.

Although no specific evidence of Hunt's use of a camera-lucida can be adduced, it is tempting to think that some of his early landscapes and of his later fruit arrangements may have been produced with the aid of this device. For Hunt, with his physical disabilities, it would have the advantage that he could work sitting down. However, whether or not Hunt in fact used such a device must remain a matter of speculation.

5

Pupils, Followers and Imitators

Hunt, like so many artists, supplemented his income by taking pupils. When working at Cassiobury in his early days for the Earl of Essex, he gave drawing lessons to the Earl's niece.[1] A Miss Moore who lived in Cheyne Walk was another of his pupils. There is a drawing of Miss Moore in her bedroom (439, Plate 79) for which 386 is a preliminary and smaller version. Also 82 comprises a series of twelve original letters written by Hunt to Miss Moore about times of lessons and so forth, each letter decorated with a small watercolour by Hunt mainly of flowers and fruit.

Ruskin was also one of Hunt's pupils, taking lessons from him, first in 1854 and again in 1861 as described in the Introduction. In April 1853, on Ruskin's recommendation his friend Lady Trevelyan applied to Hunt for some drawing lessons. On 21 April she went for her first lesson to learn 'his method of painting and came back delighted'. On 25 April she paid another visit to Hunt 'to see him draw': the next day 'drawing lessons, Birds' nests and eggs on mossy banks'. The cost of a lesson paid for by Sir Walter Trevelyan was three guineas.[2]

John Sherrin (1819–96) was another of Hunt's pupils.[3] Sherrin started as a jeweller and subsequently became a professional artist specialising in fruit and flowers. He began exhibiting at the Royal Academy in 1859 where he exhibited some forty-one works. He became an Associate Member of the New Water-Colour Society (subsequently the Royal Institute) in 1866 and a Member in 1879. During his membership he exhibited there 151 works. Many of his works, though of good quality, are somewhat hard in execution. A few are capable of being taken to be the work of Hunt, though Sherrin fortunately signed most of his works, so confusion can generally be avoided. There are three good examples of his work in the Victoria and Albert Museum: 'Branch of Plums and an Apple', signed (1175 1886 BGM), 'Primroses and Violets', unsigned (1206 1886 BGM), and 'Rabbits',[4] signed (169 1901).

Stephens issues a warning to collectors of Hunt's drawings to beware of copyists or imitators. So successful were they, he writes, that 'the very man himself was not able to decide in every case whether a picture sent to him for examination was the one he wrought or a copy from it.'[5] For the most part it was his later drawings that were

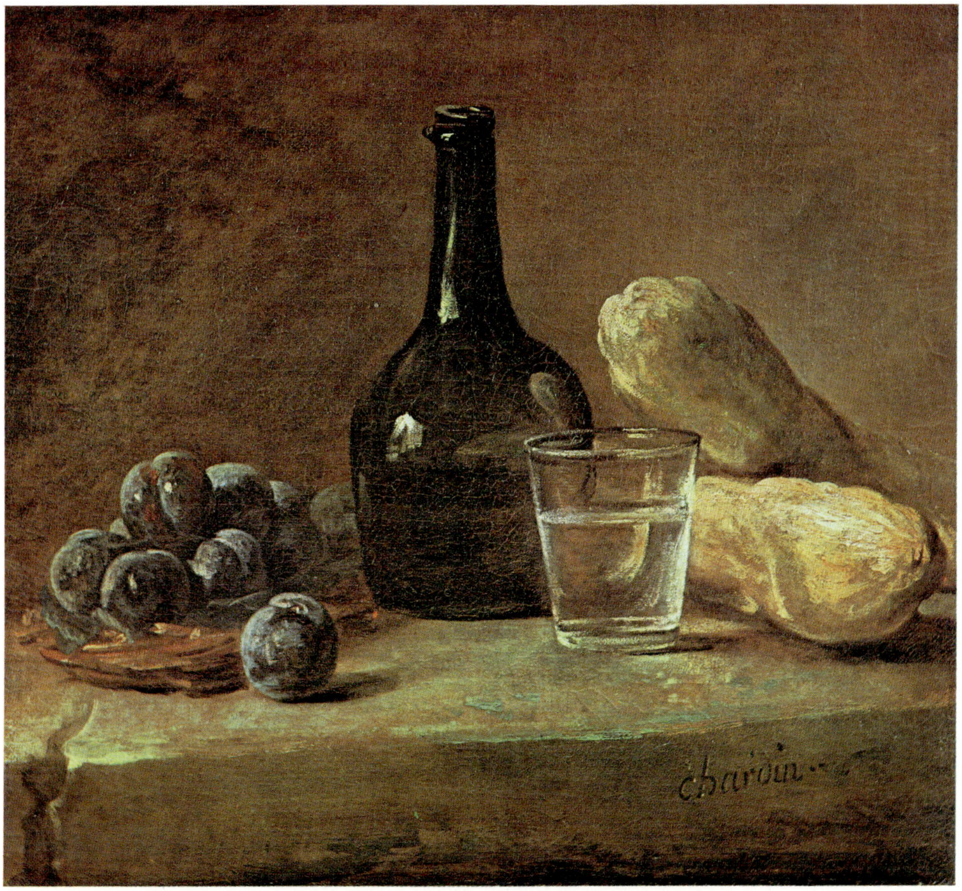

20 Still Life with Plums by J. B. S. Chardin
Oil on canvas
New York, The Frick Collection

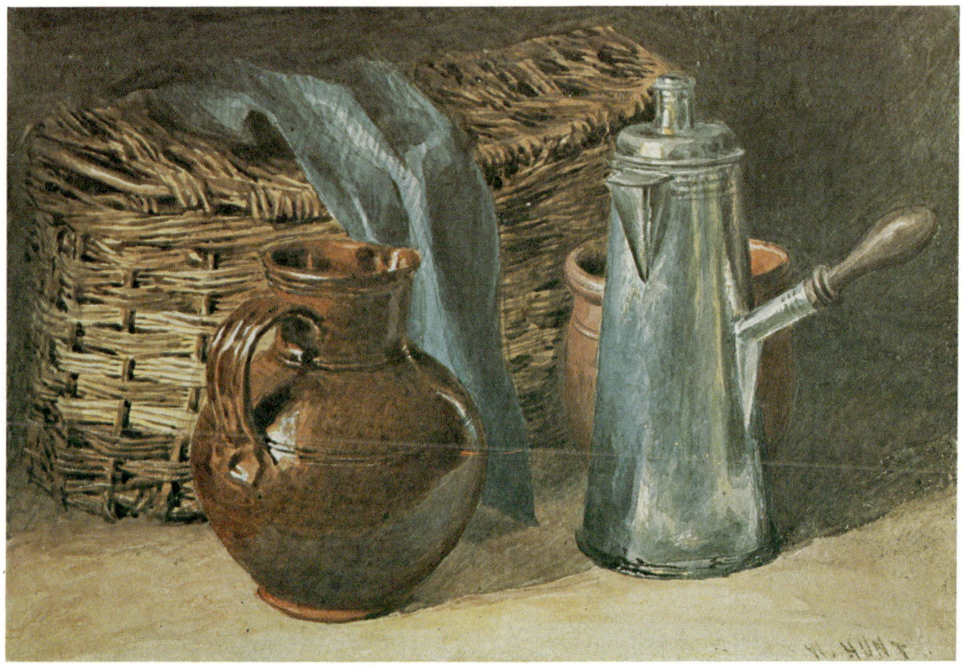

21 (684) Still Life with Earthenware Pitcher, Coffee Pot and Basket
Pencil and watercolour slightly heightened with white, $6\frac{3}{4} \times 9\frac{7}{8}$ (170 × 250)
Oxford, Ashmolean Museum

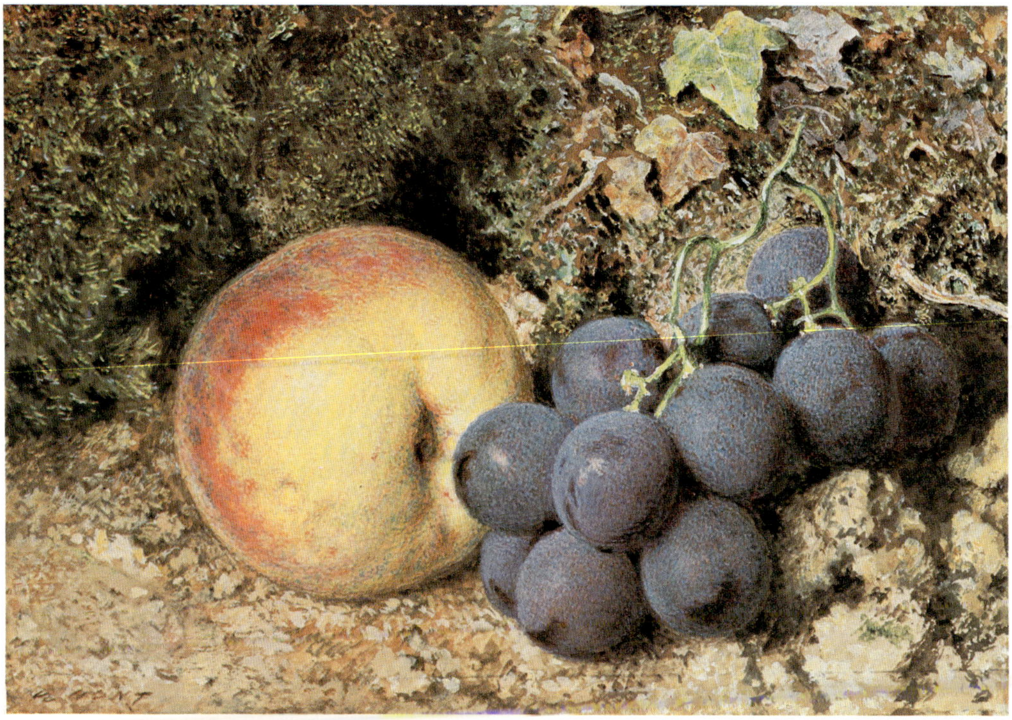

22 (689) Grapes and a Peach
Watercolour on prepared ground slightly heightened with white, $4\frac{1}{2} \times 6\frac{1}{2}$ (114 × 165)
Oxford, Ashmolean Museum

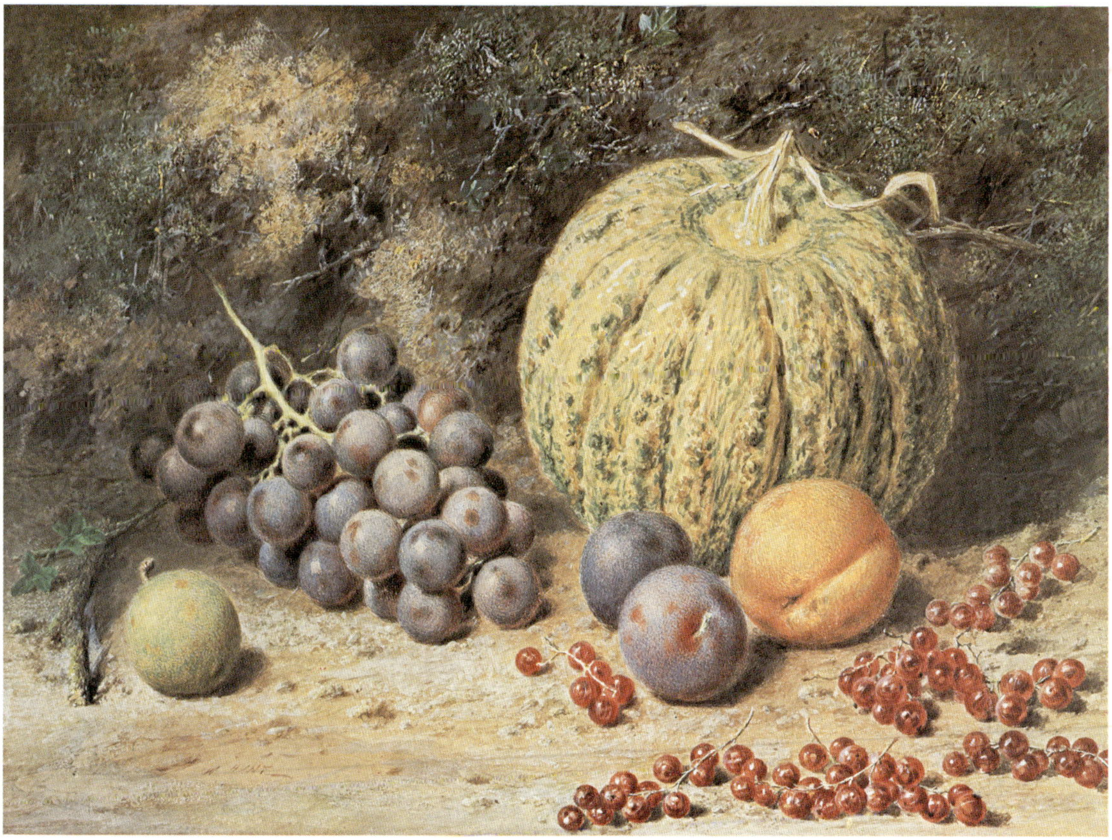

23 (615) Fruit (Melon, Black Grapes, Plums and Red Currants)
Watercolour on prepared ground, $10\frac{1}{8} \times 14\frac{1}{4}$ (257 × 362)
Cambridge, Fitzwilliam Museum

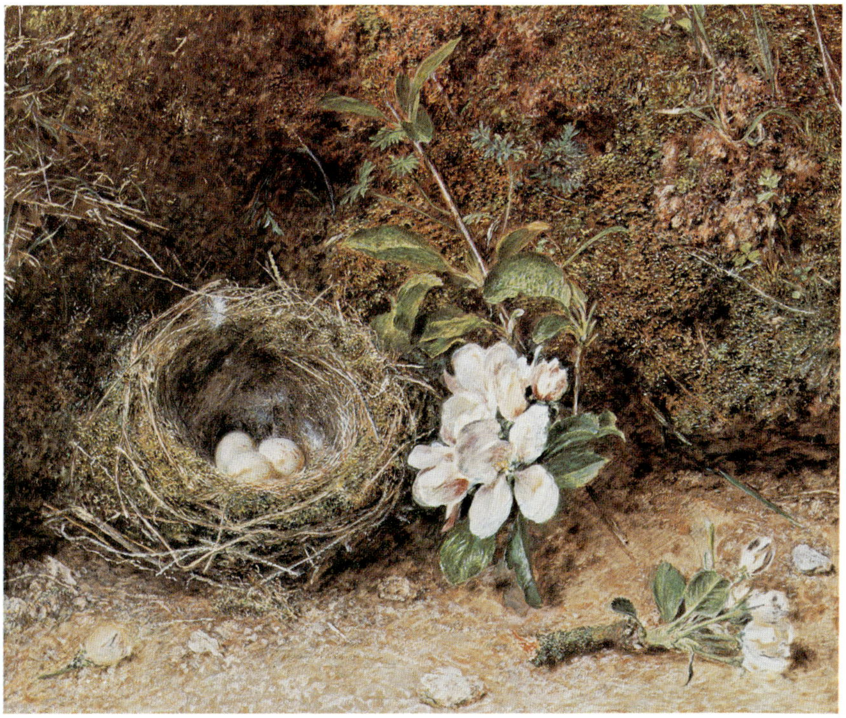

24 (775) Bird's Nest with Sprays of Apple Blossom
Watercolour heightened with white, 10 × 12⅛ (255 × 307)
Yale Center for British Art

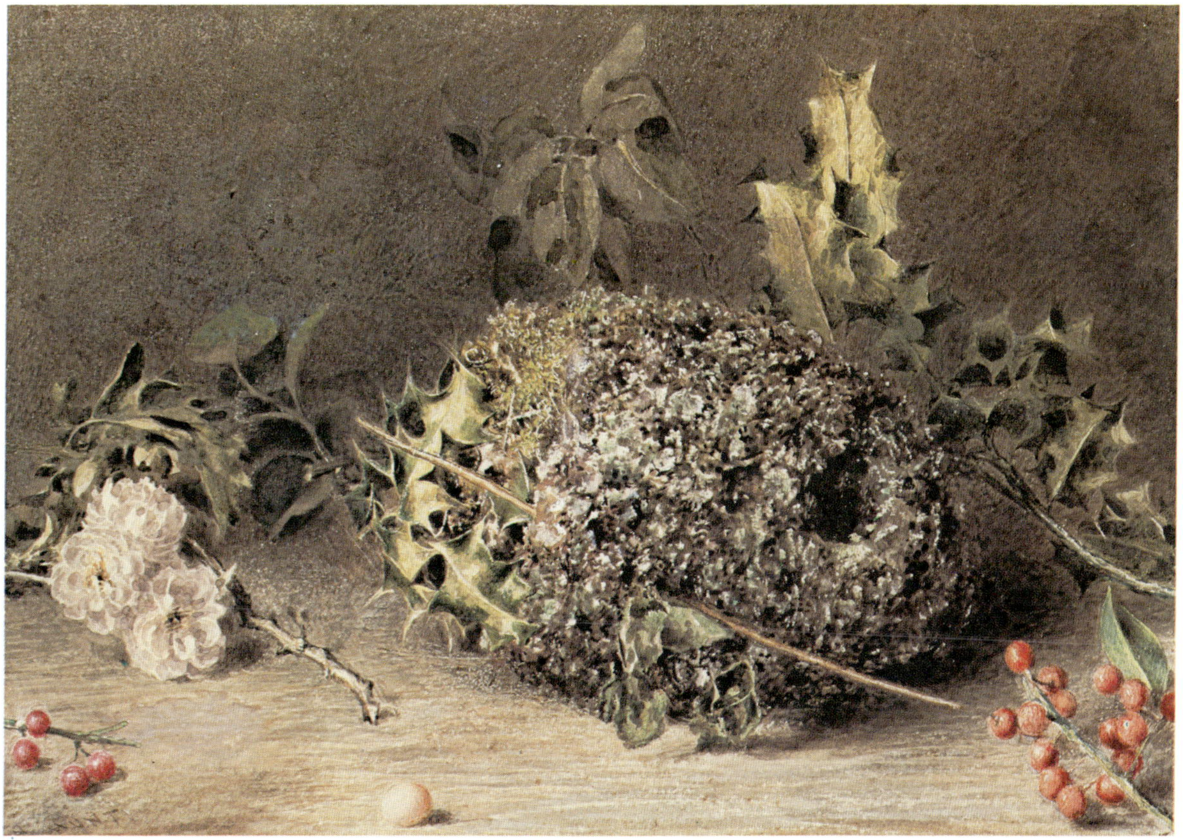

25 (606) Long Tailed Tit's Nest
Watercolour heightened with white, 13 × 9 (330 × 228)
British Museum, London

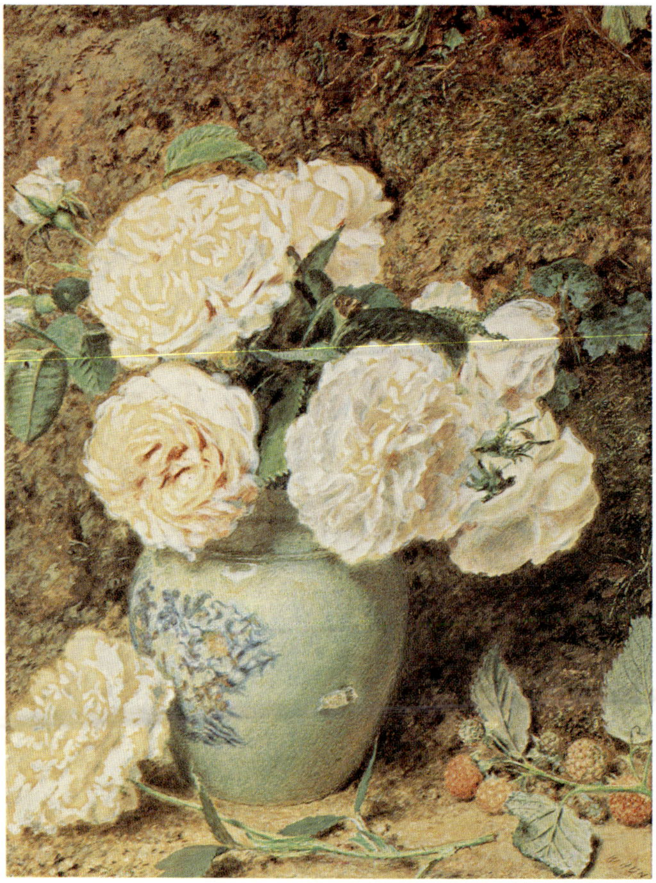

26 (657) Roses
Watercolour heightened with white, $11\frac{1}{2} \times 8\frac{1}{2}$ (292 × 217)
Manchester, City Art Gallery

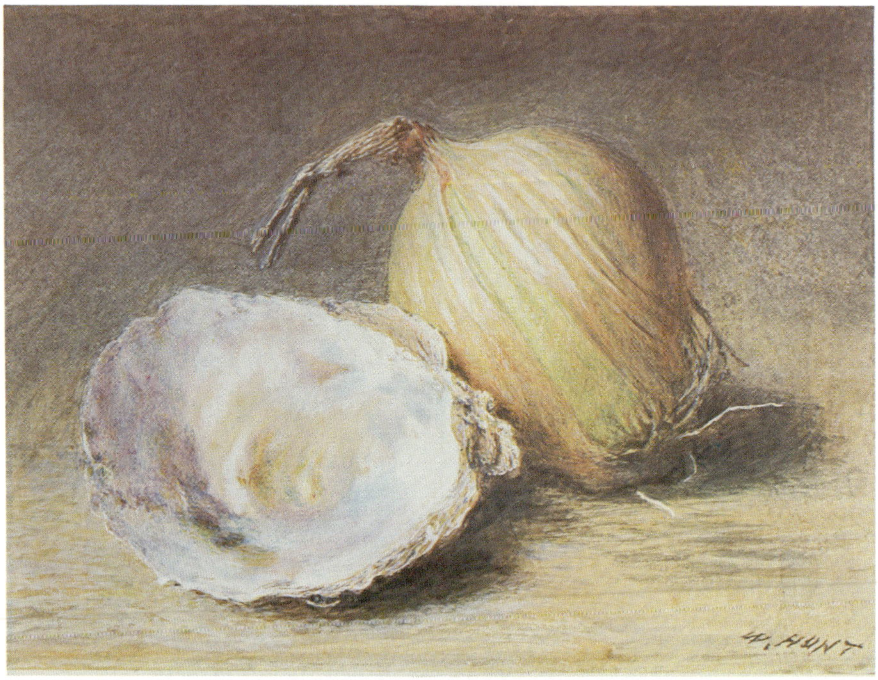

27 (634) An Oyster Shell and an Onion
Watercolour heightened with white, $4\frac{3}{4} \times 6\frac{1}{2}$ (123 × 165)
Fry Collection

imitated, partly because it was these that fetched the highest prices; but also because his earlier, freer drawings were more difficult to imitate.

The following is a selected list of artists in alphabetical order – not necessarily deliberate imitators – specialising in still lifes whose work could be confused with that of Hunt. Sherrin is the only one of them known to have been a pupil of Hunt.

Frederick T. Baynes exhibited between 1833 and 1864, mainly at the Royal Academy and the Society for British Artists, Suffolk Street. A typical example is 'Red and White Grapes', signed, Victoria and Albert Museum (1178 1886 BGM).[6] His work is of good quality.

George Clare exhibited between 1844 and 1899 at the Royal Academy, the British Institution, and the Society for British Artists, Suffolk Street. His work is of fair quality and might be mistaken for Hunt's.

Oliver Clare (brother of George) occasionally exhibited between 1873 and 1883. He is well represented at the Old Hall Gallery, Iden, Rye, Kent. Many of his works are signed but his work is on the whole hard and ugly and it should be easy to differentiate from Hunt's.

William Cruickshank exhibited between 1866 and 1886 at the Royal Academy and the Society for British Artists, Suffolk Street. He is well represented at the Old Hall Gallery, Iden, Rye, Kent. He frequently worked on ivory and the result is usually hard and metallic. He signed many of his works, but those unsigned are probably the best and most dangerous imitations, though not necessarily deliberate, of Hunt.[7]

John Jessup Hardwick (1831–1917) exhibited at the Royal Academy, the Society for British Artists, Suffolk Street, and extensively at the Old Water-Colour Society. His work is of good quality and might be mistaken for Hunt's.

William Hough exhibited between 1857 and 1894 at the Royal Academy and the Society for British Artists, Suffolk Street. He originally worked in Coventry, later coming to London. His work is well represented at the Herbert Art Gallery, Coventry. A good example is 'Fruit: Pineapple, Plums and Grapes' in the Victoria and Albert Museum (1191 1886 BGM).[8] A signed example is shown at Plate 107. Hough usually signed his works, which for the most part are sensitive and of good quality.

Edward Ladell, a native of Colchester, exhibited between 1856 and 1886 twenty-one works at the Royal Academy and five at the British Institution. His work is elaborate and painstaking and closer in spirit to the Dutch flower painters of the seventeenth century than to Hunt.[9]

John Sherrin was a pupil of Hunt, and his work is discussed above.

None of the works of these artists can really bear comparison with those of Hunt, but could, at their best and when seen in isolation, sometimes mislead the unwary.

Notes

See Bibliography for full details of publications cited.

Introduction

1 M. H. Spielmann, *The Royal Society of Painters in Water-Colour, A Retrospect, 1804–1904*.
2 Quoted J. L. Roget, *A History of the Old Water-Colour Society*, Vol. II, p. 192.
3 Charles Baudelaire, *Art in Paris, 1845–1862*, pp. 128 and 145.
4 Edmond About, 'Voyage à travers l'Exposition des Beaux-Arts', p. 32; quoted Roget, Vol. II, p. 201.
5 A. H. Palmer, *Life and Letters of Samuel Palmer*, p. 336.
6 H. M. Cundall, *Birket Foster*, 1906.
7 Ruskin, *Works*, Vol. XIV, *Notes on Samuel Prout and William Hunt*, p. 377.
8 *Ibid.*, Vol. XXXV, *Præterita*, p. 380.
9 *Ibid.*, Vol. XV, *The Elements of Drawing*, p. 220.
10 *Ibid.*, Vol. XIV, p. 373.
11 *Ibid.*, Vol. XIX, *The Unity of Art*, p. 315.
12 *Ibid.*, p. 316.
13 Virginia Surtees (edited), *Reflections of a Friendship: John Ruskin's Letters to Pauline Trevelyan, 1848–1866*, p. 76.
14 Virginia Surtees (edited), *The Diaries of George Price Boyce, 1851–1875*, p. 32.
15 W. R. Sickert, 'Fathers and Sons', *Art News*, 7 April 1910.

1. *First Period: to 1830*

1 Roget, Vol. II, p. 191, note 2.
2 Ruskin, *Works*, Vol. XIX, *The Cestus of Aglaia*, p. 55.
3 Roget, Vol. I, p. 390.
4 *Ibid.*
5 F. G. Stephens, 'W. H. Hunt', *The Portfolio*, 1891, p. 12.
6 Unpublished material in the possession of Mrs Joan Linnell Burton, great-granddaughter of John Linnell.
7 Stephens's whole article, 'William Henry Hunt', was reprinted in the Old Water-Colour Society Club, Vol. XII, 1934–35 with a note by the Editor, Randall Davies.
8 *Ibid.*, p. 23.
9 Waterloo Bridge was opened on 18 June 1817 by the Prince Regent on the second anniversary of the Battle of Waterloo.
10 *The Farington Diary*, 24 October 1798, ed. Greig, Vol. I, p. 243.
11 *Dr Thomas Monro and the Monro Academy*, Victoria and Albert Museum, 1976.
12 See note 6 above.
13 *The Farington Diary*, 11 April 1801, ed. Garlick and Macintyre, p. 1944.
14 Alfred T. Story, *The Life of John Linnell*, Vol. I, p. 41.
15 Extracts are included in the catalogue referred to in note 11 above.
16 Unpublished diaries of E. T. Monro in the possession of F. J .G. Jefferiss.
17 Dr Monro's sale, Christie's, 26 June 1833.
18 Stephens, 1934–35, p. 24.
19 *Ibid.*
20 Stephens, 'Henry Edridge', *The Portfolio*, 1880, pp. 198–99; Roget, Vol. I, p. 393.
21 Roget, Vol. I, p. 400.
22 *Somerset House Gazette*, 1824, II, p. 46.
23 Roget, Vol. I, p. 468.
24 *The Farington Diary*, 11 May 1808, ed. Greig, Vol. V, p. 60.
25 Stephens, 1934–35, p. 30.

26 *Ibid.*, p. 31.
27 Ruskin, *Works*, Vol. XIV, *Notes on Samuel Prout and William Hunt*, p. 376.

2. *Second Period: 1830–45*

1 Roget, Vol. II, pp. 191–92.
2 William Collingwood (1819–1903), a pupil of Hunt and J. D. Harding.
3 Collingwood, *Magazine of Art*, Vol. XXI, 1898, p. 504.
4 Owned by Hastings Museum and Art Gallery.
5 John Sheepshanks was born in 1789 (a year earlier than Hunt) and died in 1863, the year preceding Hunt's death. He gave his collection to the nation in 1857, intending it to become the nucleus of a National Gallery of British Art. The collection is now at the Victoria and Albert Museum.
6 Versions of both these works belonging to G. W. Moss were exhibited (Nos 526 and 527) at the Manchester Exhibition, 1857 and subsequently formed part of the F. J. Nettlefold Collection in 1935. Present ownership is unknown.
7 Published December 1844 by Henry Graves & Co. (Print Sellers to Her Majesty).
8 Ruskin, *Works*, Vol. XIV, pp. 442–43.
9 Stephens, 1891, p. 10.
10 *Ibid.*
11 Stephens, 1934–35, p. 28; Roget, Vol. II, p. 191.
12 Quoted *Roget*, Vol. II, p. 197.
13 Virginia Surtees (edited), *The Diaries of George Price Boyce*, p. 13.
14 Quoted Roget, Vol. II, p. 191.

3. *Third Period: 1845–64*

1 Roget, Vol. II, p. 195.
2 Ruskin, *Works*, Vol. XXXIV, *Conversations*, p. 670 recalling a conversation Ruskin had with M. H. Spielmann at Brantwood in 1884.
3 Reproduced in Ruskin, *Works*, Vol. XXXV, Pl. B (facing p. xliv).
4 Stephens, 1891, p. 10.
5 Ruskin, *Works*, Vol. III, *Modern Painters*, pp. 615–16.
6 *Ibid.*, pp. 603–4.
7 *Ibid.*, Vol. XIV, p. 377.
8 *Ibid.*, p. 378.
9 *Ibid.*, pp. 444–45.
10 Ruskin, *Works*, Vol. XIX, *The Cestus of Aglaia*, p. 53.
11 Ruskin, *Works*, Vol. XIV, pp. 79–80.
12 Ruskin is referring to the School which he founded in 1872 when he was Slade Professor at Oxford for the purpose of giving instruction in the art of drawing. See comment in Catalogue preceding entry No. 684.
13 Ruskin, *Works*, Vol. XIV, p. 384.
14 Collingwood, p. 504.
15 Ruskin, *Works*, Vol. XIV, p. 441.
16 Roget, Vol. II, p. 196.
17 *Ibid.*, p. 190.
18 Ruskin, *Works*, Vol. XIV, *Notes on Samuel Prout and William Hunt*, p. 401.
19 *Ibid.*, p. 443–44.
20 *Ibid.*, p. 441.
21 Stephens, 1891, p. 14.
22 Stephens, 1934–35, p. 53.
23 Roget, Vol. II, p. 201.
24 Stephens, 1934–35, pp. 35–36.
25 Stephens, 1891, p. 16.
26 Roget, Vol. II, p. 194.
27 Ruskin, *Works*, Vol. XIV, *Notes on Samuel Prout and William* Hunt, p. 375.
28 Sickert, 1910.
29 Stephens, 1934–35, p. 36.
30 Byron Webber, *James Orrock, R.I., Painter, Connoisseur, Collector*, p. 164.
31 James Duffield Harding (1797–1863), a landscape artist.
32 Quoted Roget, Vol. II, p. 198.
33 *Ibid.*
34 Ruskin, *Works*, Vol. XXXVII, *Biographical Appendix with Minor Letters*, p. 704.
35 Roget, Vol. II, p. 200.
36 *Handbook to the Gallery of British Painters in the Art Treasures Exhibition*, 1857, p. 25.
37 Now in the possession of Mrs Joan Linnell Burton.
38 Virginia Surtees (edited), *Reflections of a Friendship*, p. 83.
39 Quoted Roget, Vol. II, p. 197.
40 Quoted *ibid.*, p. 199.
41 British Museum Album (A.7) (1934. 9.22), Nos 125 and 126.
42 Quoted Roget, Vol. II, p. 199.
43 J. G. Marks, *Life and Letters of Frederick Walker*, pp. 45–48.
44 Ruskin, *Works*, Vol. XXXVI, *Letters of Ruskin*, Vol. I, pp. 466–67.
45 *Ibid.*
46 Roget, Vol. II, p. 201.
47 *Ibid.*, p. 200.
48 Stephens, 1934–35, p. 32.

4. *Technique*

1 Roget, Vol. I, p. 469.
2 Collingwood, p. 505.

3 Virginia Surtees (edited), *Reflections of a Friendship*, pp. 42–43.
4 Ruskin, *Works*, Vol. XV, pp. 152–53.
5 Ogden N. Rood, *Modern Chromatics with Applications to Art and Industry*, 1879 (2nd edition, 1883, pp. 278–9). The present writer is indebted to Mr Tom Jones, author of the Catalogue to the Hunt Exhibition at Wolverhampton, Preston and Hastings, 1981 for this and the succeeding three references.
6 Ogden N. Rood, *Théorie scientifique des couleurs et leurs applications à l'art et l'industrie*, 1881.
7 William I. Homer, *Seurat and the Science of Painting*, p. 144.
8 Paul Signac, *D'Eugène Delacroix au néo-impressionisme*, p. 125.
9 Webber, p. 149.
10 Martin Hardie, Vol. III, p. 108.
11 Quoted Roget, Vol. II, p. 197.
12 Letter to Philip Brown, quoted Roget, *ibid.*
13 Ruskin, *Works*, Vol. XIV, *Notes on Samuel Prout and William Hunt*, p. 376.
14 Collingwood, p. 504.
15 Roget, Vol. I, p. 469.
16 Quoted Roget, Vol. I, p. 470.

5. *Pupils, Followers and Imitators*

1 Andrew Wilton, *British Watercolours 1750–1850*, p. 52.
2 Virginia Surtees (edited), extracts from Sir Walter Trevelyan's diaries quoted in *Reflections of a Friendship*, pp. 42–44.
3 Roget, Vol. II, p. 198 note 2.
4 Reproduced in *British Watercolours in the Victoria and Albert Museum*, p. 348.
5 Stephens, 1934–35, p. 29.
6 Reproduced in *British Watercolours in the Victoria and Albert Museum*, p. 23.
7 A typical example, 'Still life with Bird, Bird's Nest and Blossom', is illustrated in Jeremy Maas, *Victorian Painters*, p. 172.
8 Reproduced in *British Watercolours in the Victoria and Albert Museum*, p. 194.
9 A typical example is illustrated in Maas, *Victorian Painters*, p. 174.

Bibliography

BASKETT, John and SNELGROVE, Dudley. *English Drawings and Watercolours 1550–1850 in the Collection of Mr and Mrs Paul Mellon*, Pierpont Morgan Library, Harper & Row, New York, 1972.

BAUDELAIRE, Charles. *Art in Paris, 1845–1862. Reviews of Salons and other Exhibitions by Charles Baudelaire.* Translated and edited by Jonathan Mayne, Phaidon, London, 1965.

BINYON, Laurence. *English Watercolours* (Library of English Art), A. & C. Black, London, 1933.

BRITISH MUSEUM, Department of Prints and Drawings. *Catalogue of drawings by British artists and artists of foreign origin working in Great Britain.* Compiled by L. Binyon, 4 vols, London, 1898–1907.

BRITTON, John. *The History and Description of Cassiobury Park, Hertfordshire*, published by the author, London, 1837.

CALLOW, William. *William Callow, an Autobiography.* Edited by H. M. Cundall, A. & C. Black, London, 1908.

CHRISTIE, MANSON & WOODS. Sale Catalogue, *The Remaining Works of Hunt's Studio*, London, 16–17 May 1864.

COLLINGWOOD, William. 'Reminiscences: William Hunt', *Magazine of Art*, Vol. XXI, 1898.

CUNDALL, H. M. *Birket Foster*, A. & C. Black, London, 1906.

EMMON, Robert. *Life and Opinions of Walter Richard Sickert*, Faber & Faber, London, 1941.

FAIRLAND, Thomas. *Hunt's Comic Sketches, Drawn on Stone from Original Drawings exhibited in the Water-Colour Society*, Henry Graves, London, December 1844.

FARINGTON, Joseph. *The Farington Diary.* (1) Edited by James Greig, 8 vols, Hutchinson, London, 1922–28. (2) Edited by Kenneth Garlick and Angus Macintyre, Vols I to VI (to be continued), Yale University Press, New Haven and London, 1978–79.

FRY, C. & S. *Catalogue of Watercolours and Drawings from the Collection of Mr and Mrs Cyril Fry, exhibited Castle Museum, Norwich and J. S. Maas Gallery, London, 1967*, Frowde (Printers), London, 1967.

GRANT, M. H. *A Chronological History of the Old English Landscape Painters (in oil) from the XVIth to the XIXth Century*, Vols I, II, the author, London, 1926; III, Lewis, Leigh-on-Sea, 1947.

GRANT LONGMAN, E. *Bushey Then and Now*, Booklet No. 4, The Hillberry Press, Sutton, Surrey, 1968.

HALL, S. C. *A Book of Memories of Great Men and Women of the Age*, Virtue, London, 1877.

HARDIE, Martin. *Water-colour Painting in Britain.* Edited by Dudley Snelgrove with Jonathan Mayne and Basil Taylor, 3 vols, B. T. Batsford, London, 1966–68.

HELENIAK, Kathryn Moore. *William Mulready*, Yale University Press, New Haven and London, 1980.

HESELTINE, J. P. *John Varley and His Pupils, W. Mulready, J. Linnell and W. Hunt. Original Drawings in the Collection of J. P. H.*, privately printed, reproduced by J. J. Waddington, London, 1918.

HOMER, William Innes. *Seurat and the Science of Painting*, Massachusetts Institute of Technology Press, Cambridge, Mass., 1964.

JONES, Tom. *William Henry Hunt. Catalogue of Wolverhampton, Preston and Hastings Exhibition*, Kenmore Printing (1972), Wolverhampton, 1981.

MAAS, Jeremy. *Victorian Painters*, Barrie & Rockliff, The Cresset Press, London, 1969 (reprinted with revised bibliography, Barrie & Jenkins, London, 1978).

MANCHESTER, Art Treasures Exhibition, 1857. *Handbook to the Gallery of British Painters in the Art Treasures Exhibition, being a reprint of Critical Notices originally published in the 'Manchester Guardian'*, Bradbury and Evans, London, 1857.

MARKS, J. G. *Life and Letters of Frederick Walker*, Macmillan, London, 1896.

MELLON, Paul. *See* BASKETT, John and SNELGROVE, Dudley.

PALMER, A. H. *The Life & Letters of Samuel Palmer*, Seeley, London, 1892.

QUILTER, Harry. *Preferences in Art, Life and Literature*, Sonnenschein, London, 1892.

REDGRAVE, R. & S. *A Century of Painters of the English School*, Longmans Green, London, 1866.

REDGRAVE, S. *A Dictionary of Artists of the English School*, Longmans Green, London, 1874.

REYNOLDS, Graham. *An Introduction to English Water-Colour Painting*, Country Life, London, 1950.

ROGET, J. L. *A History of the Old Water-Colour Society*, 2 vols, Longmans Green, London, 1891.

ROOD, Ogden N. *Modern Chromatics with Application to Art and Industry*, Kegan Paul, Trench, London, 1879. (Translated as *Théorie scientifique des couleurs et leurs applications à l'art et l'industrie*, 1881).

RUSKIN, John. *The Works of John Ruskin*. Library Edition, edited by Sir E. T. Cook and A. Wedderburn, 39 vols, George Allen, London, 1903–12.

SICKERT, W. R. 'Fathers & Sons', *Art News*, April 1910. Reprinted in full in *A Free House or the Artist as Craftsman. Being the writings of Walter Richard Sickert*. Edited by Osbert Sitwell (*q.v.*), pp. 306–7.

SIGNAC, Paul. *D'Eugène Delacroix au néo-impressionisme*. Edited by Françoise Cachin, Hermann, Paris, 1964.

SITWELL, Osbert (edited). *A Free House or the Artist as Craftsman. Being the writings of Walter Richard Sickert*. Edited by Osbert Sitwell, Macmillan, London, 1947.

SNELGROVE, Dudley. *See* BASKETT, John and SNELGROVE, Dudley.

SPIELMANN, M. H. *The Royal Society of Painters in Water-Colour, A Retrospect, 1804–1904*, Women's Printing Society, London, no date.

STEPHENS, F. G. 'William Henry Hunt', *Fraser's Magazine*, November 1865. Reprinted Old Water-Colour Society Club, Vol. XII, London, 1934–35.
'Henry Edridge', *Portfolio*, 1880.
'W. H. Hunt', *Portfolio*, 1891.

STORY, Alfred T. *The Life of John Linnell*, 2 vols, Richard Bentley, London, 1892.

SURTEES, Virginia (edited). *The Diaries of George Price Boyce 1851–1875*, Real World, Norwich, 1980.

SURTEES, Virginia (edited). *Reflections of a Friendship: John Ruskin's Letters to Pauline Trevelyan, 1848–1866*, Allen & Unwin, London, 1979.

THOMPSON, Francis. *History of Chatsworth, Being a Supplement to the 6th Duke of Devonshire's Handbook*, Country Life, London, 1949.

VICTORIA AND ALBERT MUSEUM. *British Watercolours in the Victoria and Albert Museum. An Illustrated Summary Catalogue of the National Collection*. Compiled by Lionel Lambourne and Jean Hamilton, Sotheby Parke Bernet and published in association with the Victoria and Albert Museum, London, 1980.
Dr Thomas Monro and the Monro Academy, Catalogue of Exhibition, Prints and Drawings Gallery, February–May 1976, with an Introduction with Extracts from a Biography of Dr Thomas Monro by Dr F. J. G. Jefferiss in preparation for publication.

WEBBER, Byron. *James Orrock, R. I., Painter, Connoisseur, Collector*, 2 vols, Chatto and Windus, London, 1903.

WILTON, Andrew. *British Watercolours 1750–1850*, Phaidon, Oxford, 1977.

Plates in Monochrome

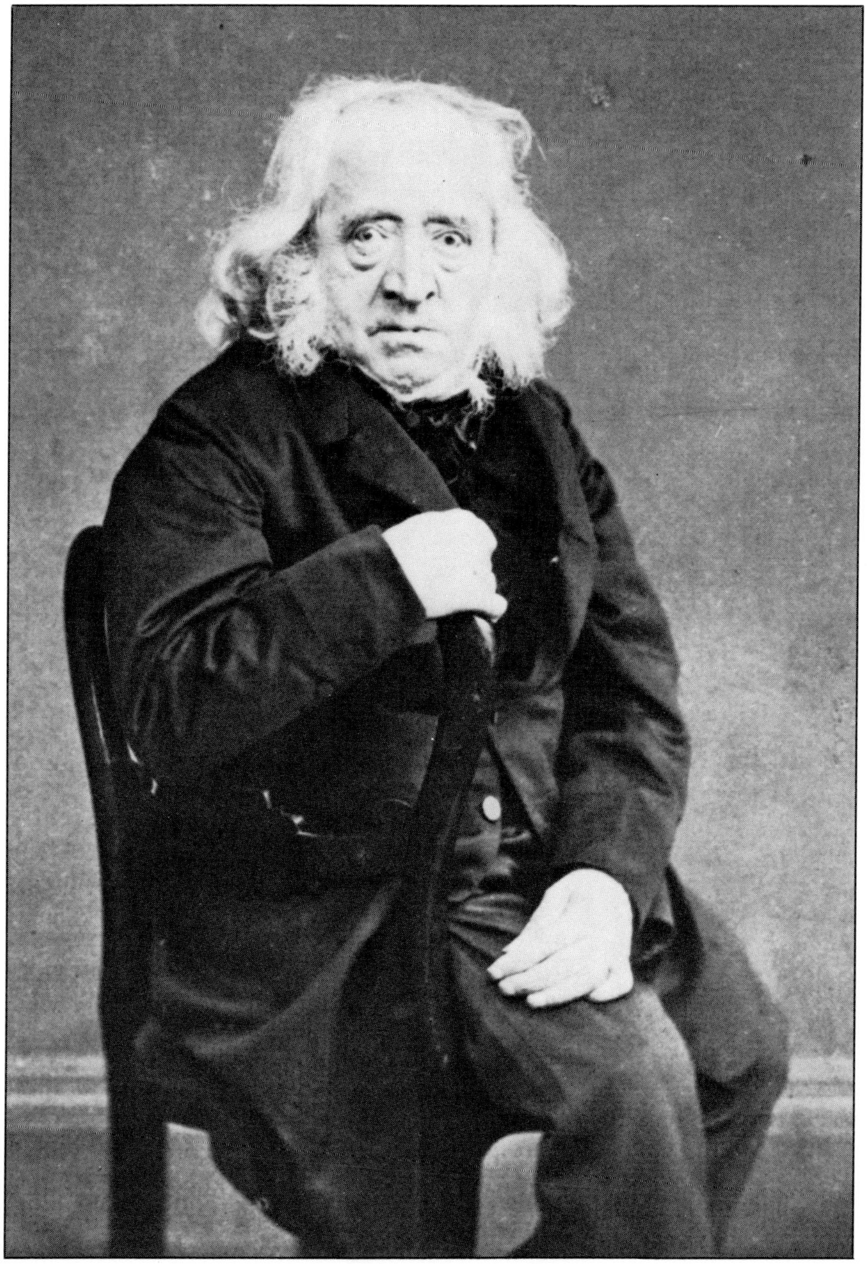

1 Photograph of W. H. Hunt
National Portrait Gallery, London

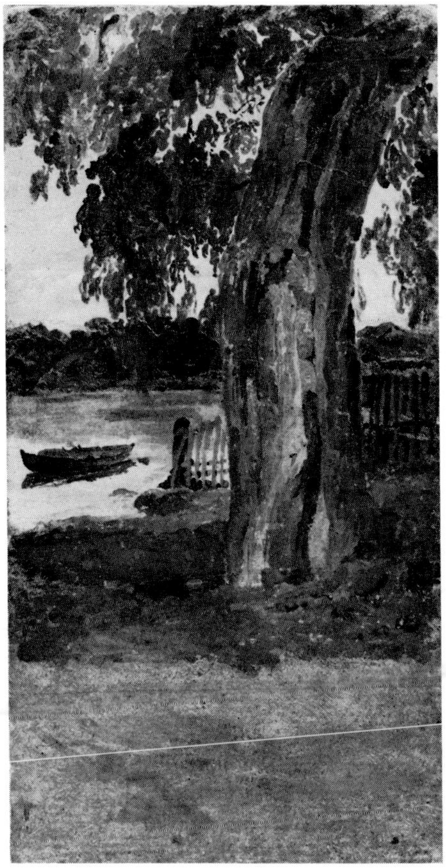

2 (158) Twickenham
Oil on millboard, $12\frac{3}{4} \times 6\frac{1}{2}$ (329×168)
Tate Gallery, London

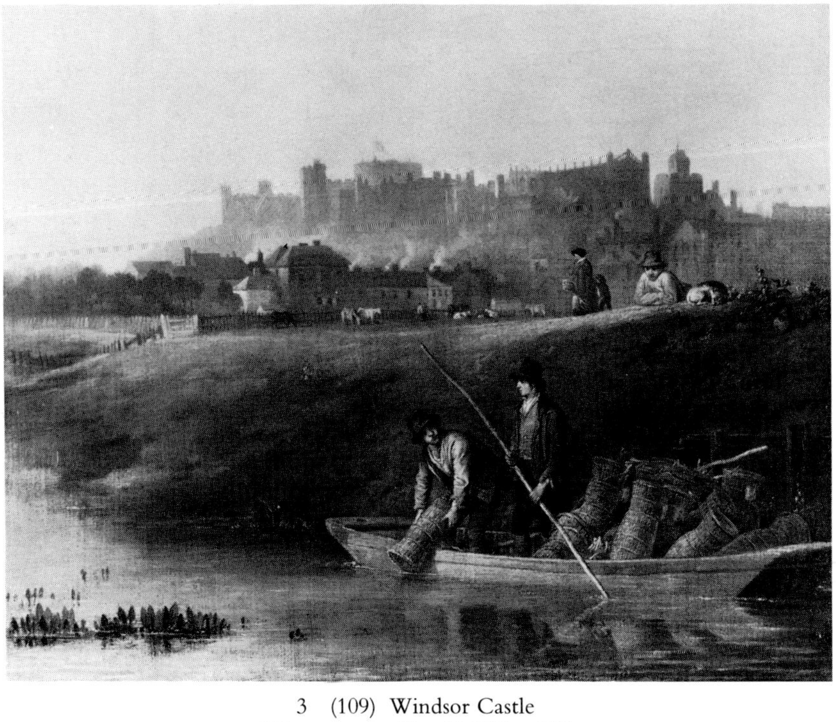

3 (109) Windsor Castle
Oil on canvas, 20×26 (508×660)
National Trust – Anglesey Abbey, Cambridgeshire, Fairhaven Collection

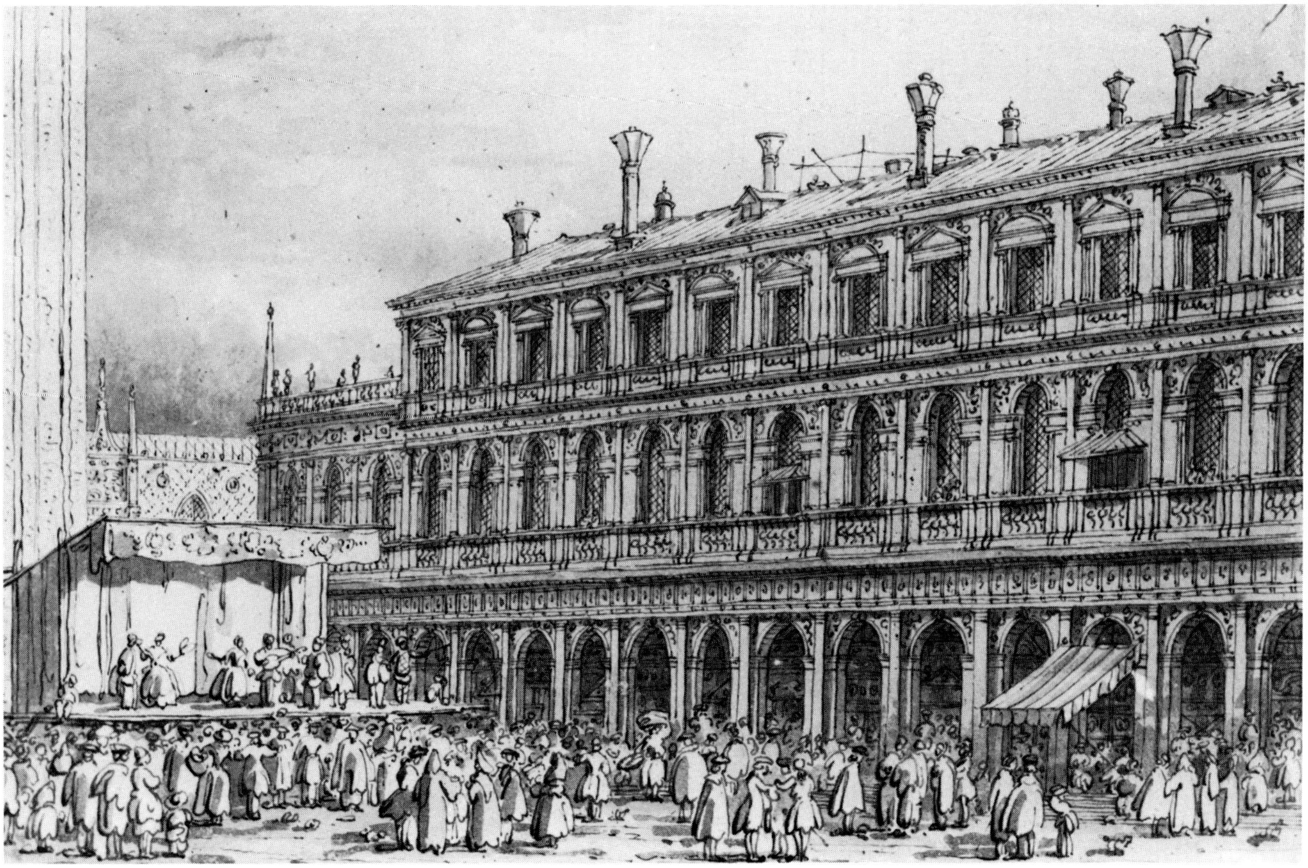

4 (134) A Scene in Venice – Crowds Watching the Comedy Players
Reed pen, brown ink and grey wash, $8\frac{1}{8} \times 12\frac{1}{2}$ (206 × 319)
Oxford, Ashmolean Museum

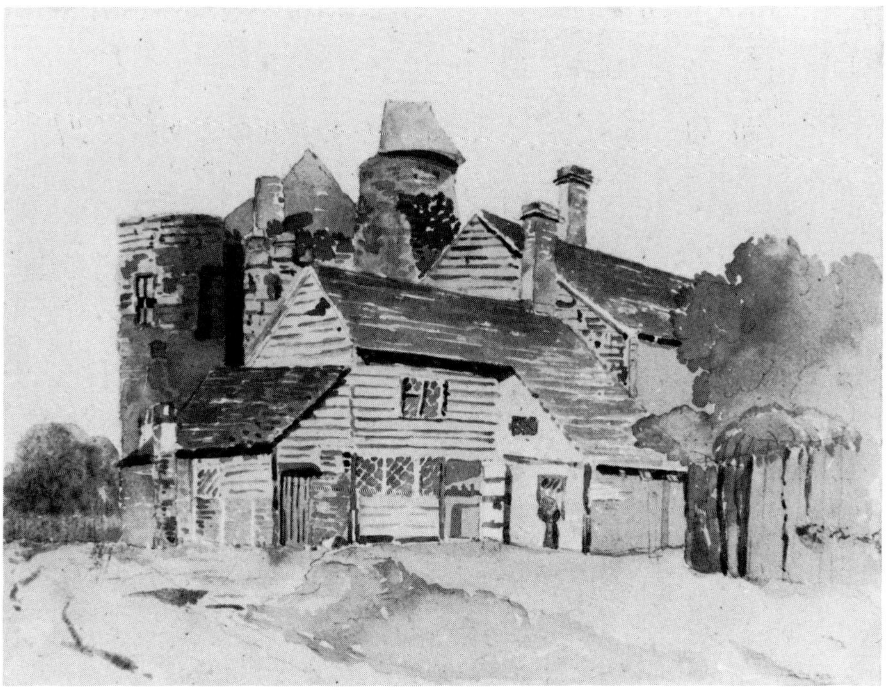

5 (179) Saltwood Castle, Kent
Pencil and watercolour, $5\frac{7}{8} \times 8$ (148 × 206)
Witt Collection

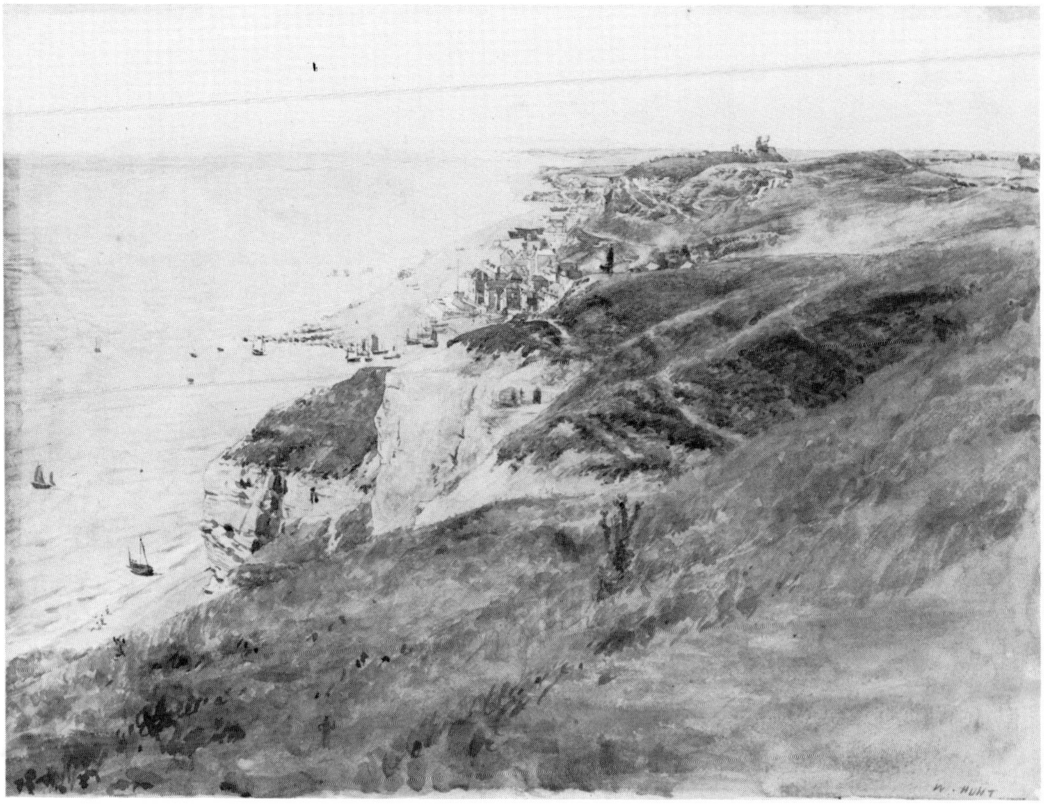

6 (137) View of Hastings
Pencil and watercolour, $11\frac{1}{2} \times 15\frac{1}{4}$ (291×393)
Oxford, Ashmolean Museum

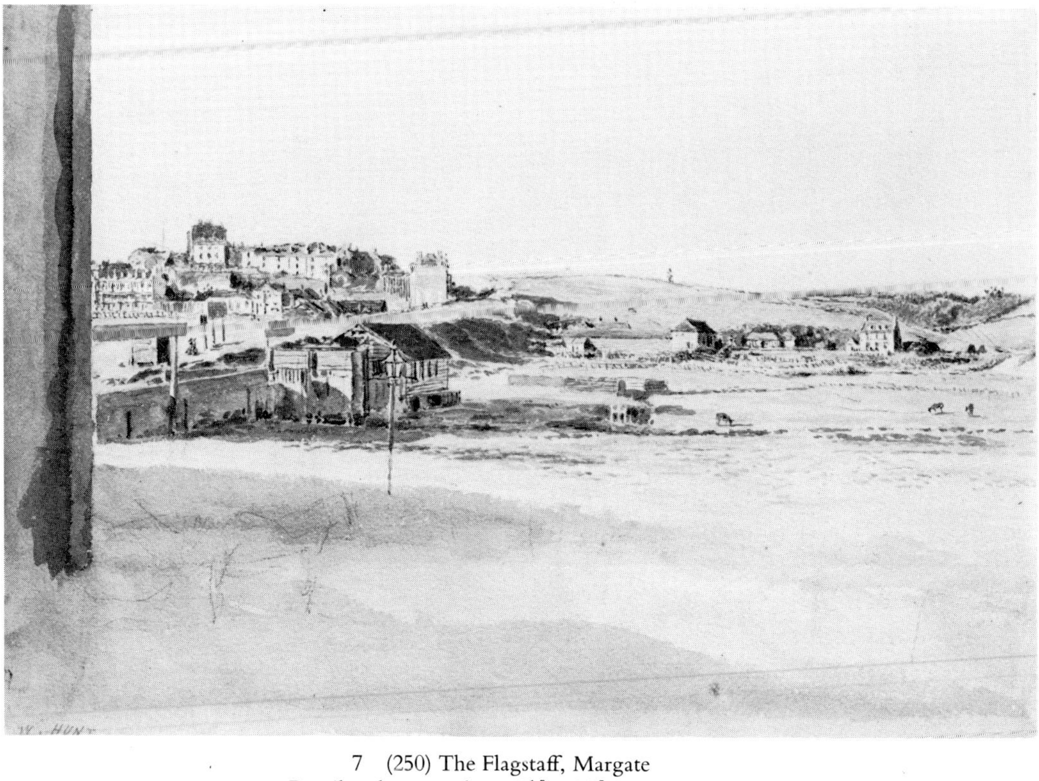

7 (250) The Flagstaff, Margate
Pencil and watercolour, $7\frac{15}{16} \times 11\frac{5}{8}$ (201×295)
Yale Center for British Art, Paul Mellon Collection

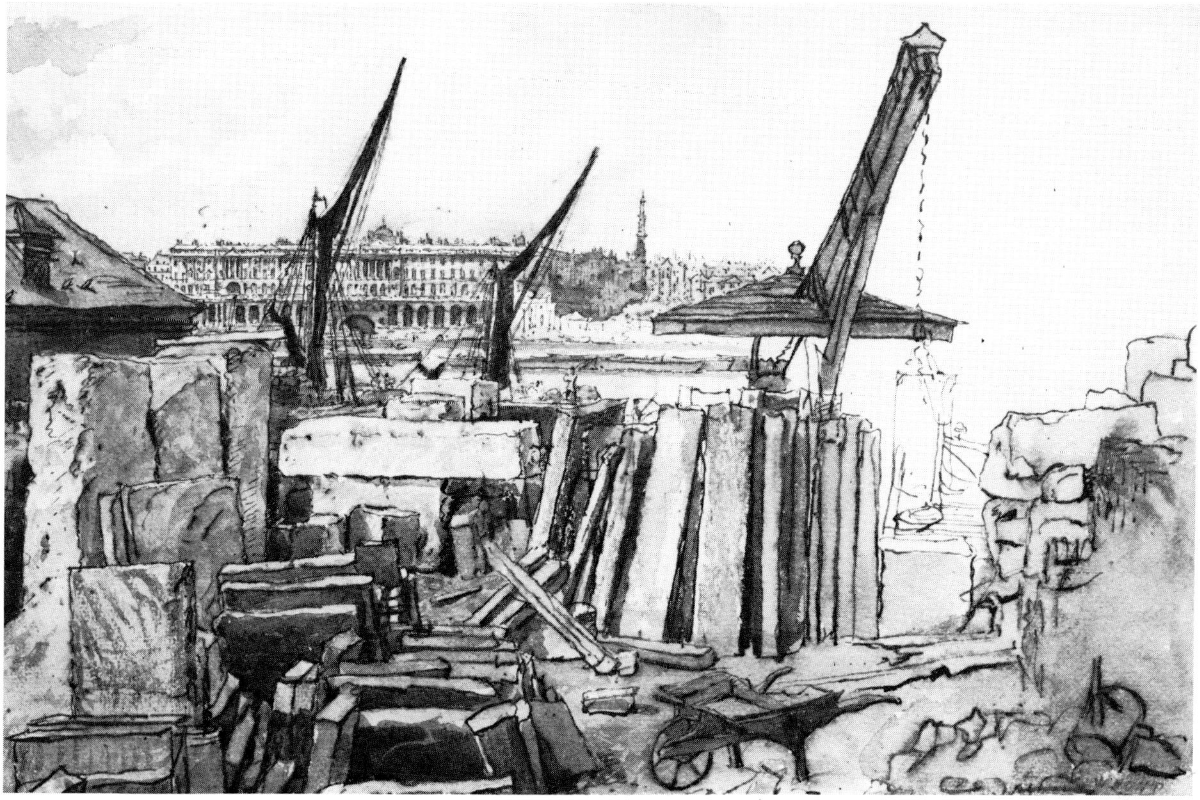

8 (239) Building Waterloo Bridge
Reed pen and brown ink with brown and grey wash, $9\frac{7}{16} \times 15\frac{5}{8}$ (252 × 396)
Yale Center for British Art, Paul Mellon Collection

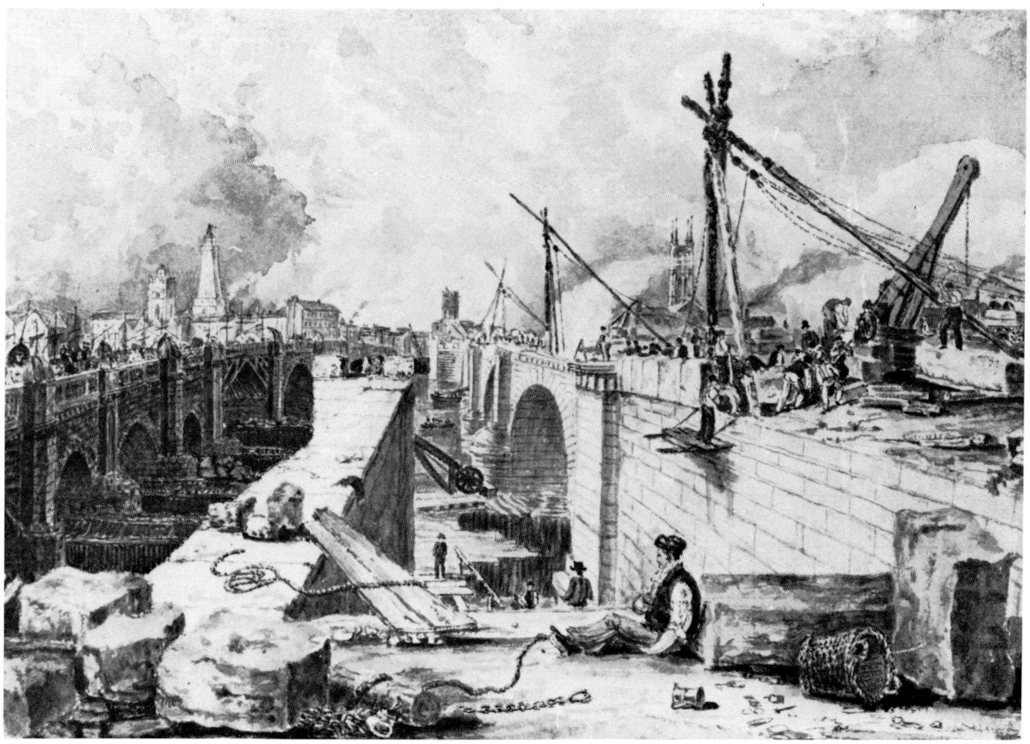

9 (58) Rebuilding London Bridge
Watercolour, $6\frac{3}{4} \times 9\frac{1}{8}$ (160 × 233)
Eton College, Windsor

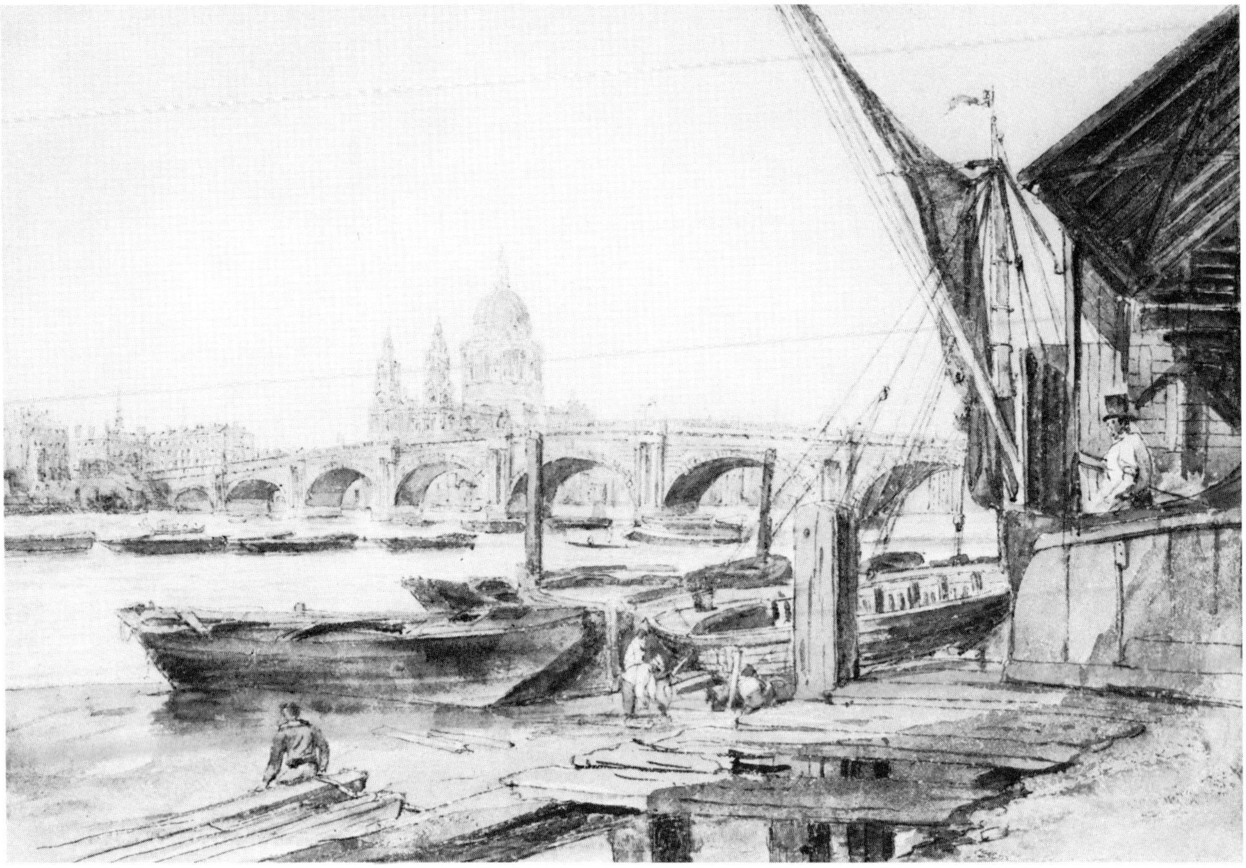

10 (244) St Paul's Cathedral and Blackfriars Bridge
Reed pen, brown ink and watercolour, 9 × 13⅜ (228 × 340)
Yale Center for British Art, Paul Mellon Collection

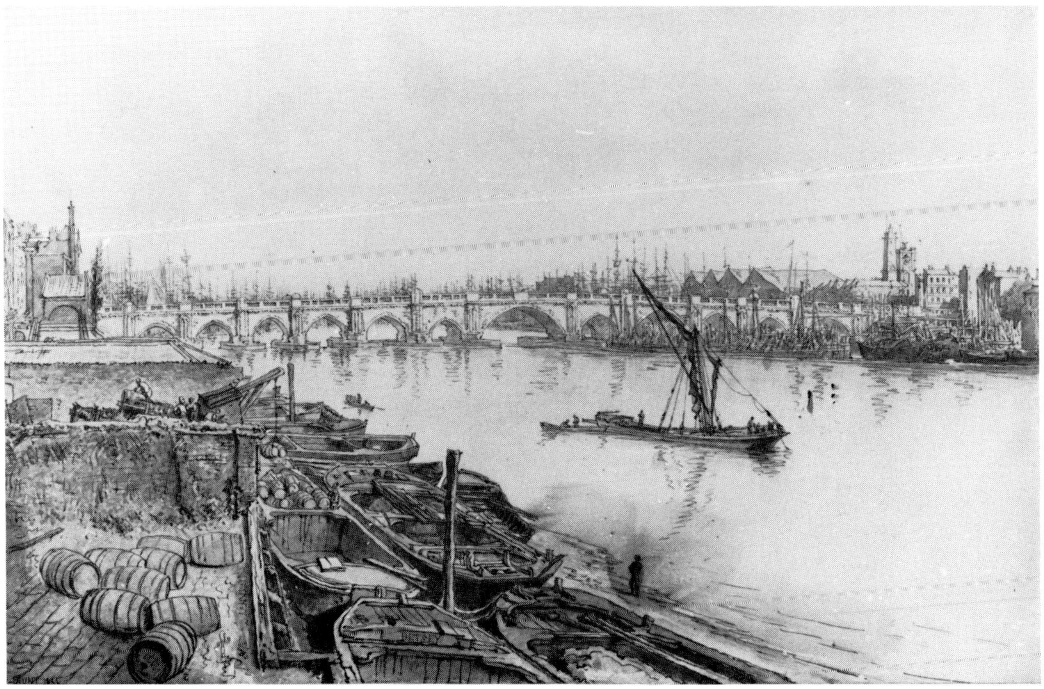

11 (31) London Bridge with Pool of London Beyond
Reed pen, brown ink and watercolour, 13⅜ × 21⅜ (342 × 544); dated 1825
British Museum, London

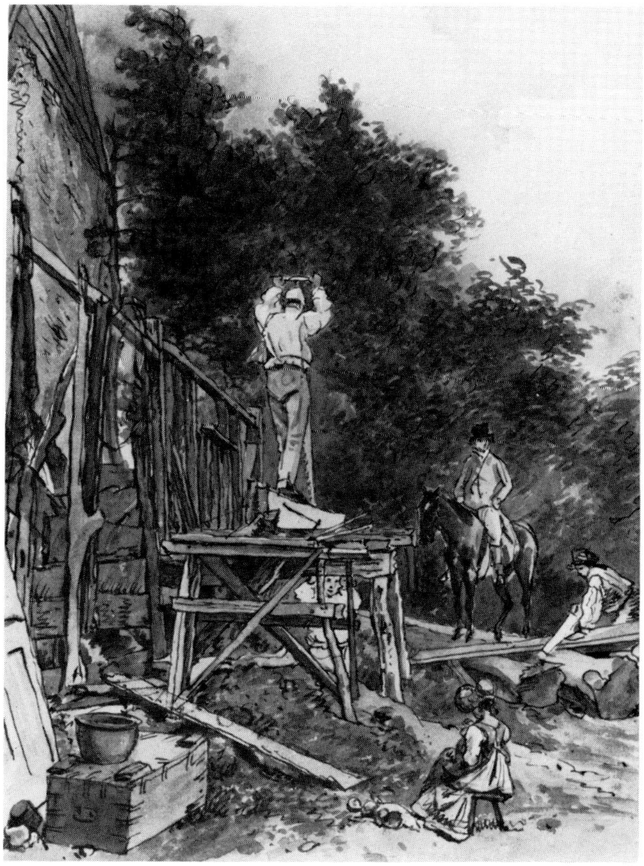

12 (23) Dr Monro Inspecting his Burnt-out Stables at Bushey
Reed pen, brown ink and watercolour, $13\frac{7}{8} \times 10\frac{1}{4}$ (354 × 262)
British Museum, London

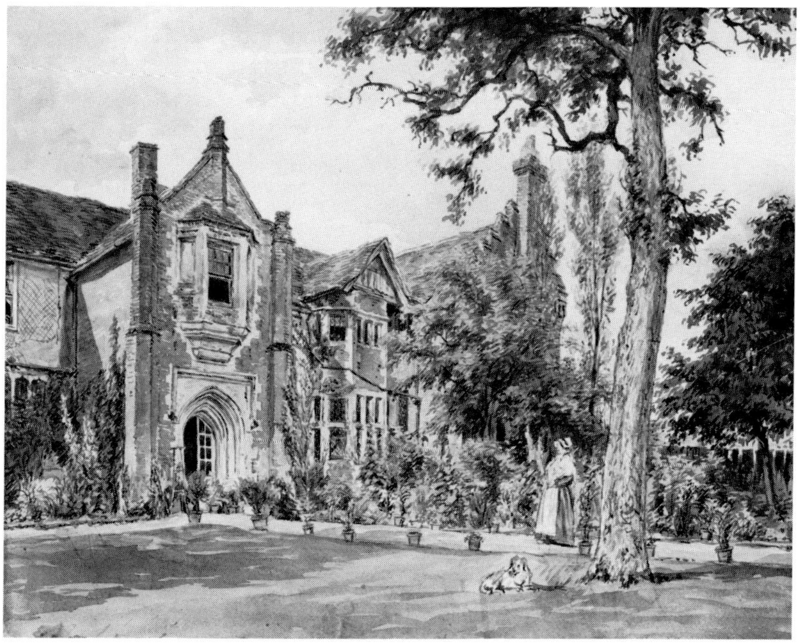

13 (246) The Lecture House, Watford
Watercolour, $12\frac{7}{8} \times 16\frac{13}{16}$ (327 × 427)
Yale Center for British Art, Paul Mellon Collection

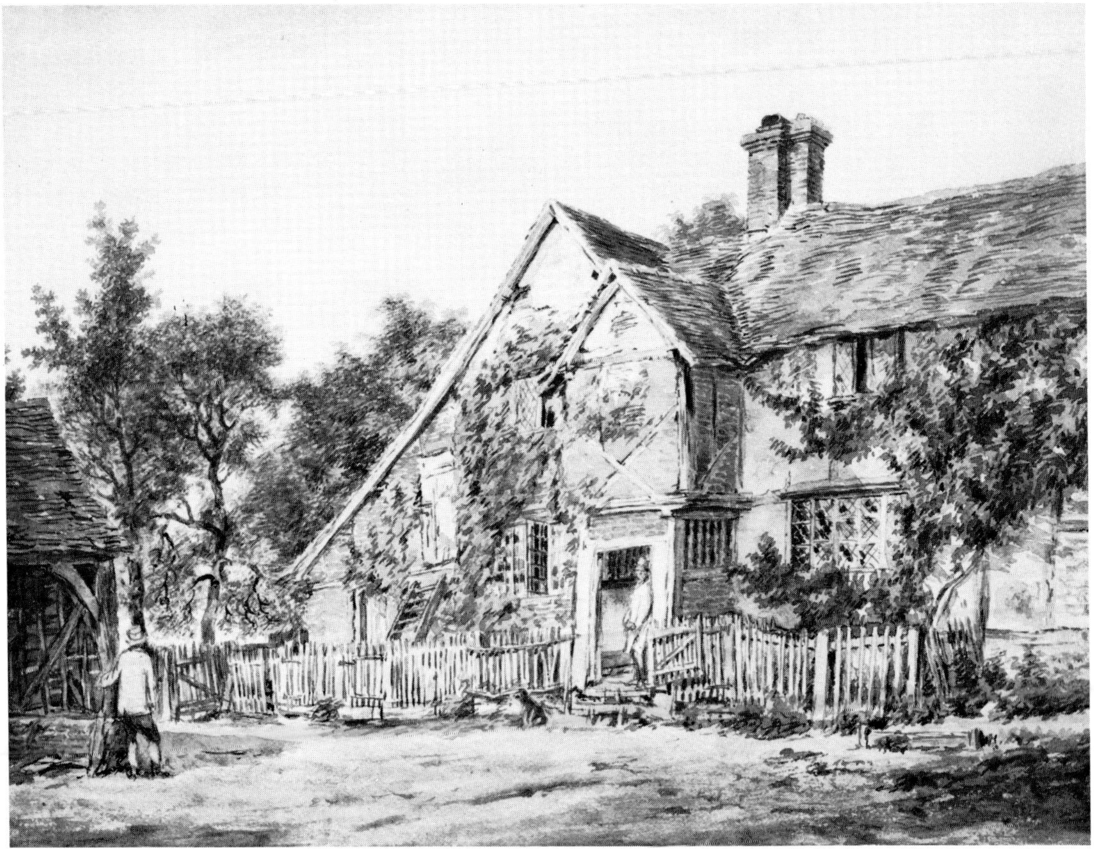

14 (243) A Farm House
Pencil and watercolour, $11\frac{13}{16} \times 15\frac{3}{4}$ (300 × 400)
Yale Center for British Art, Paul Mellon Collection

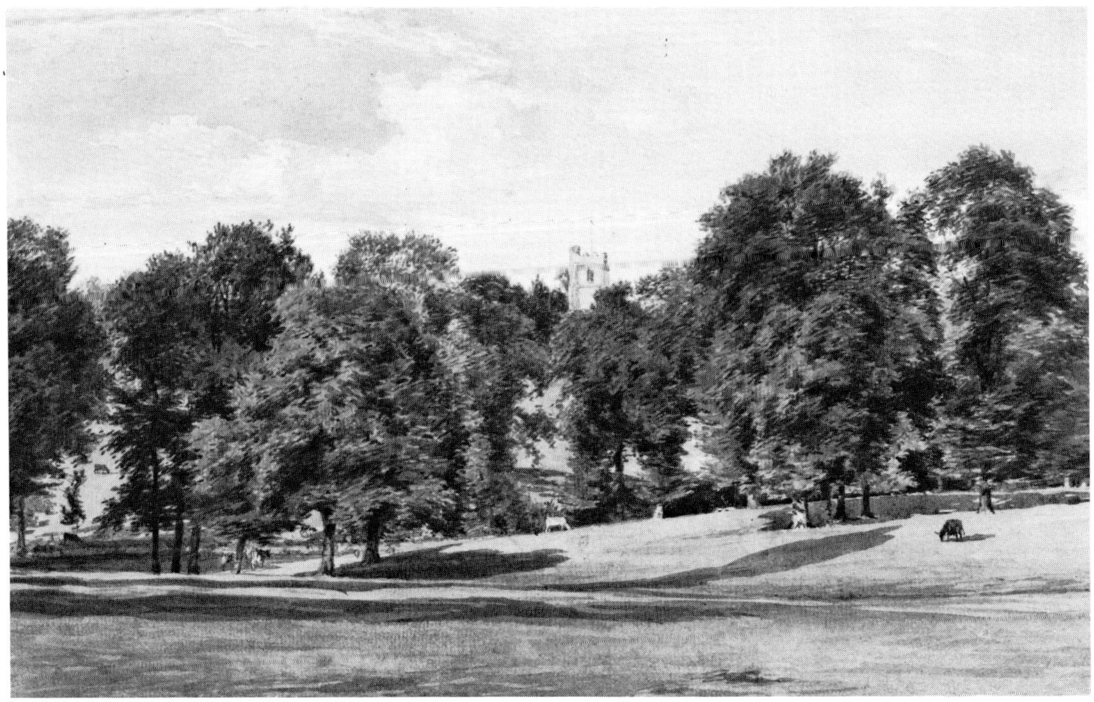

15 (240) Bushey Church from the South-West
Pencil and watercolour, $7\frac{1}{4} \times 10\frac{1}{8}$ (183 × 251)
Yale Center for British Art, Paul Mellon Collection

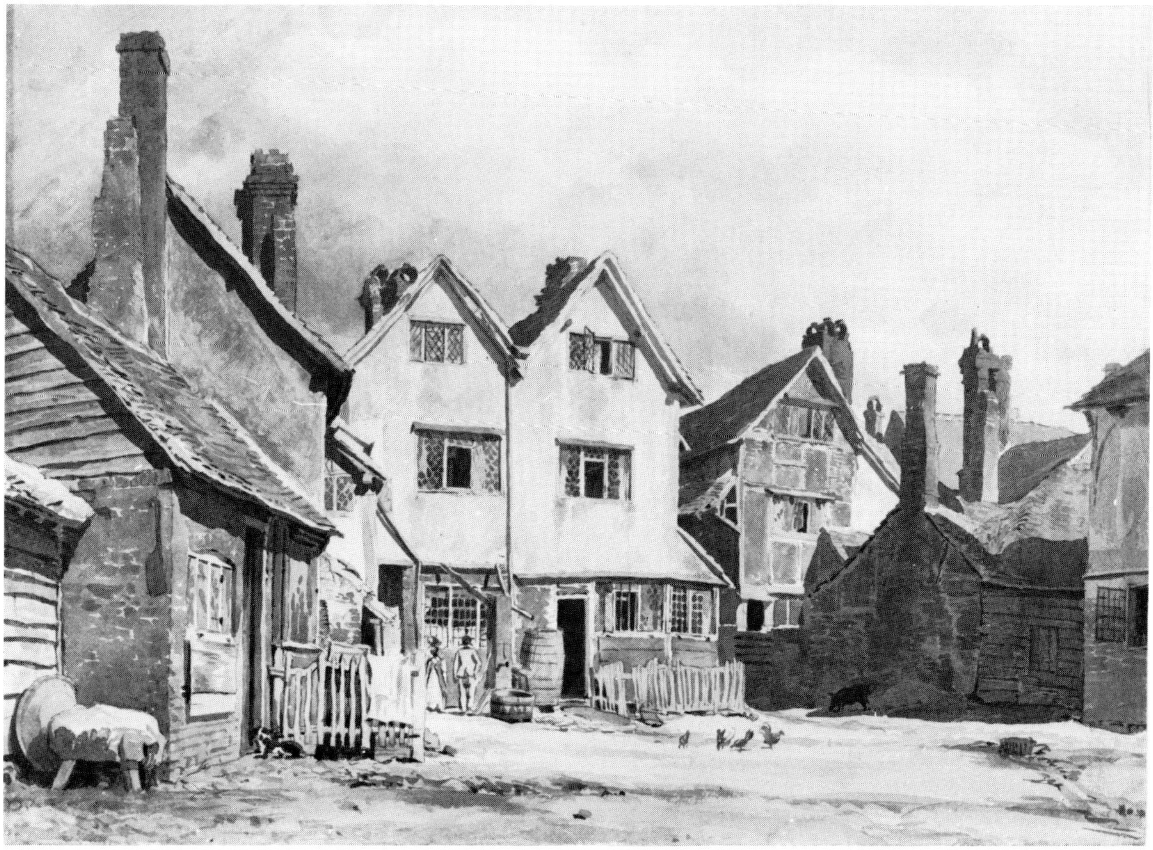

16 (47) Houses at Watford
Watercolour, $10\frac{1}{2} \times 14\frac{13}{16}$ (267 × 376)
Courtauld Institute of Art, London

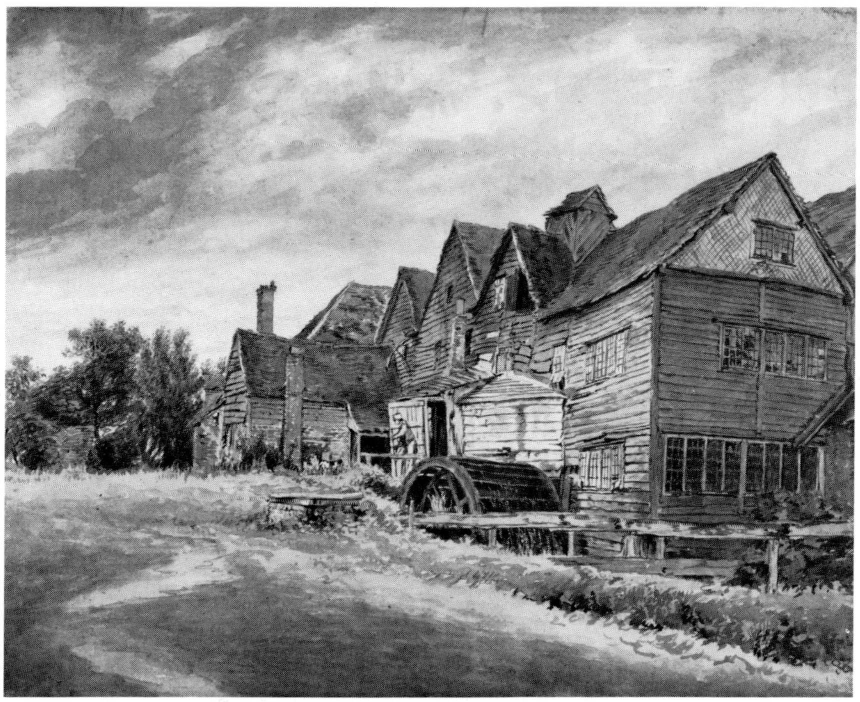

17 (8) The Water Mill, Bushey
Reed pen, ink and watercolour, $13\frac{1}{4} \times 16\frac{7}{8}$ (335 × 427)
Bedford, Cecil Higgins Art Gallery

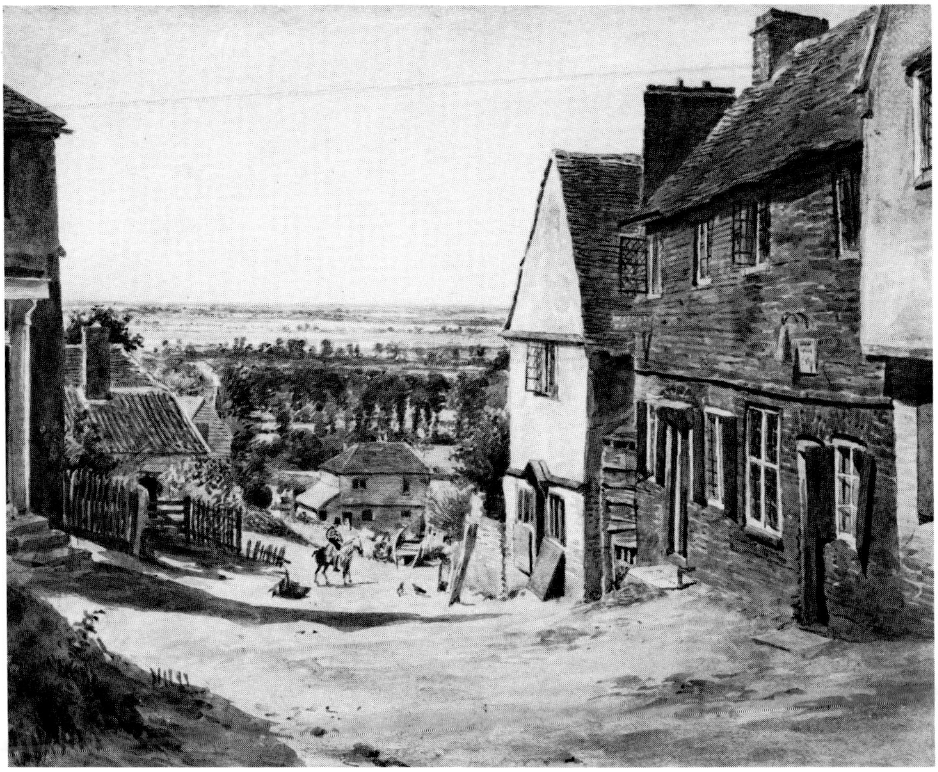

18 (247) Village Street in St Albans
Pencil and watercolour, $9\frac{3}{8} \times 11\frac{3}{4}$ (237 × 297)
Yale Center for British Art, Paul Mellon Collection

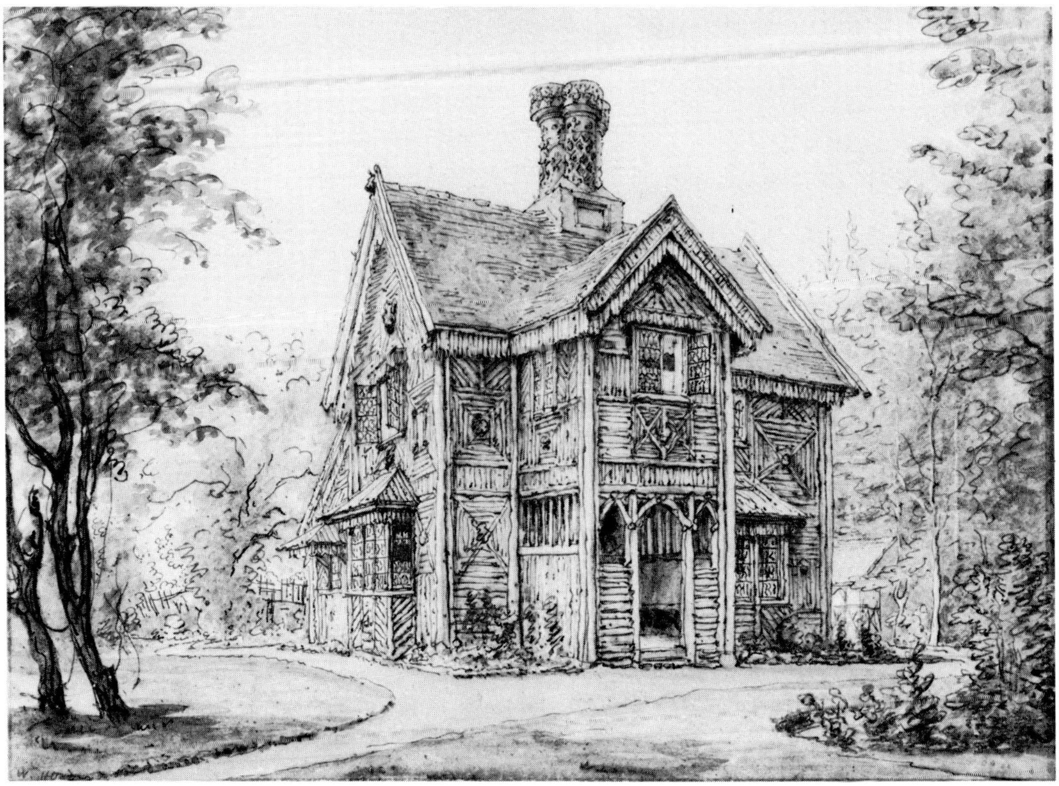

19 (245) A Lodge at Cassiobury
Reed pen, ink and watercolour, $10\frac{5}{8} \times 15$ (271 × 381)
Yale Center for British Art, Paul Mellon Collection

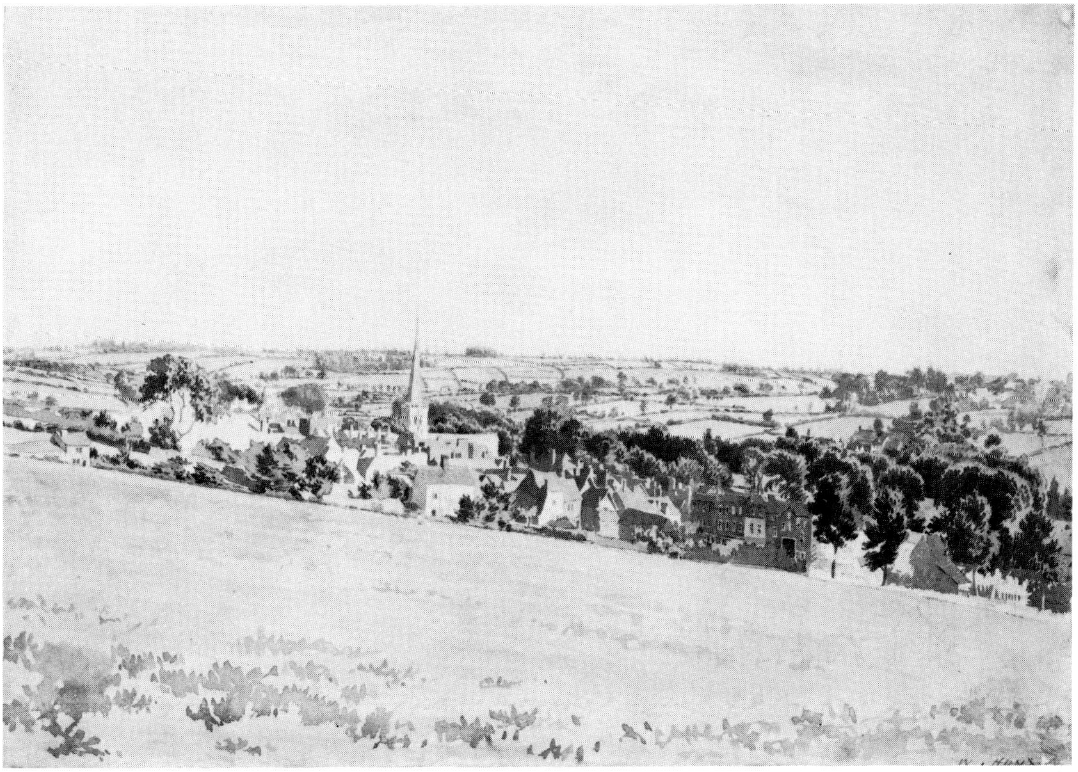

20 (26) The Village in the Valley
Watercolour, $10\frac{1}{2} \times 14\frac{3}{4}$ (267×375)
British Museum, London

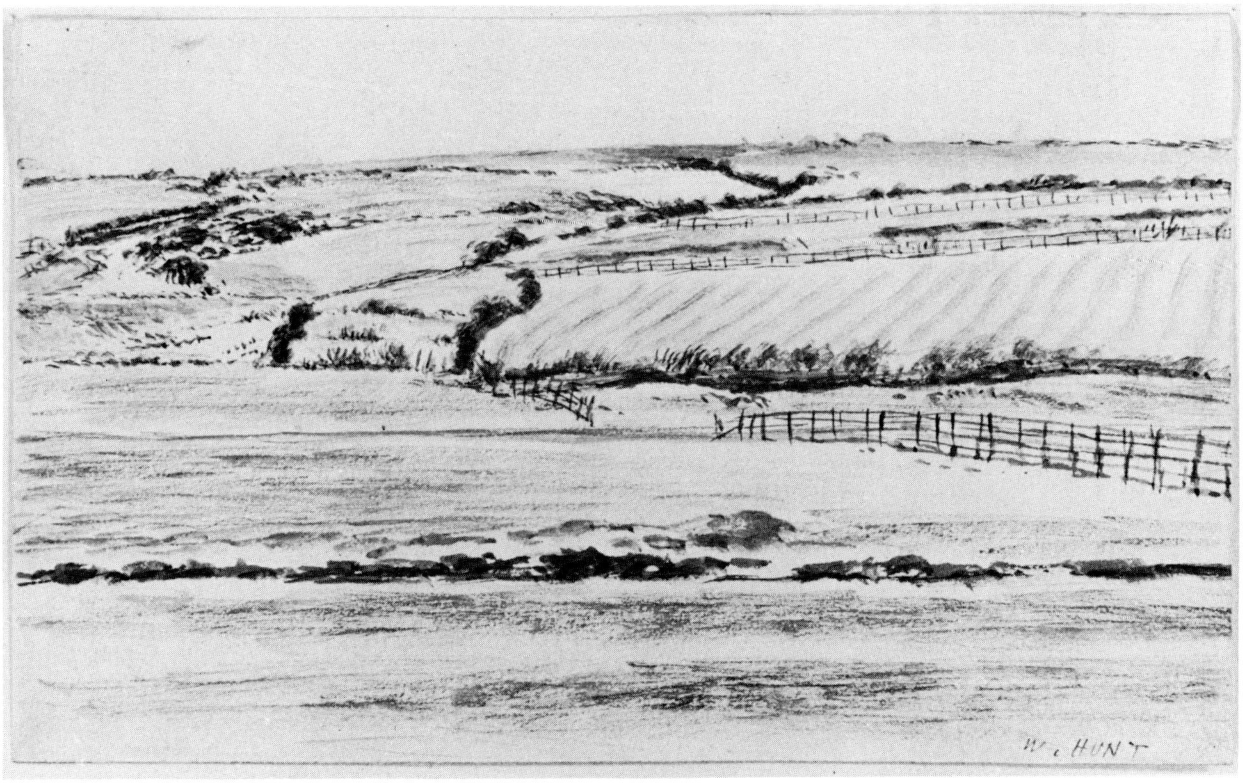

21 (210) Snow Scene (*actual size*)
Watercolour, $4 \times 6\frac{1}{2}$ (102×166)
Witt Collection

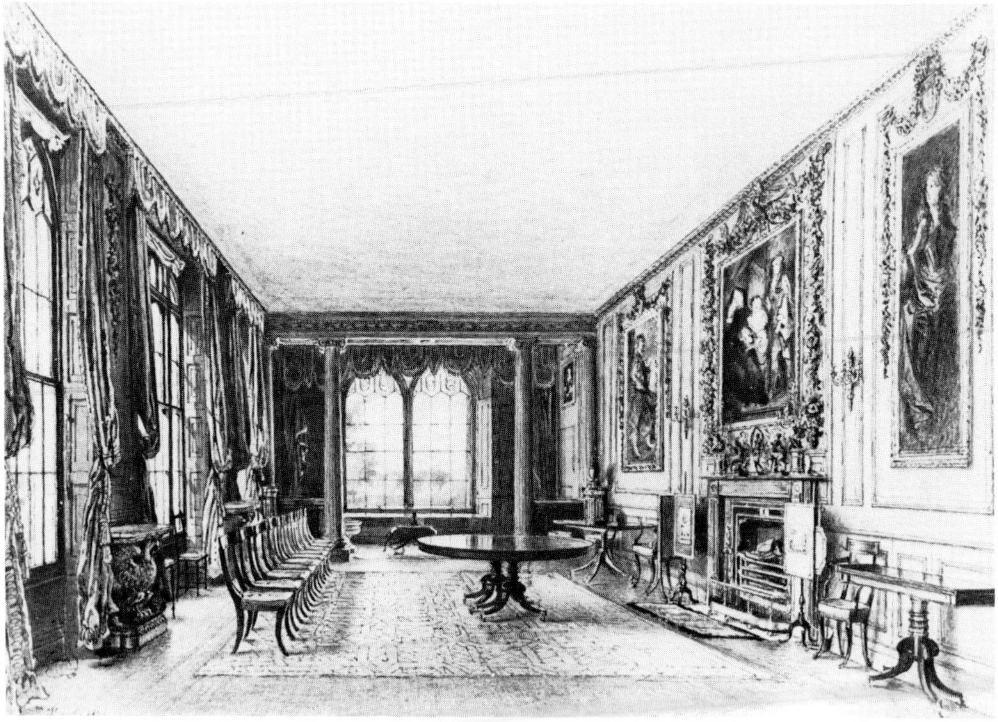

22 (375) The Dining Room at Cassiobury Park
Watercolour, $9\frac{5}{8} \times 13\frac{1}{4}$ (245 × 336); dated 1821
Fry Collection

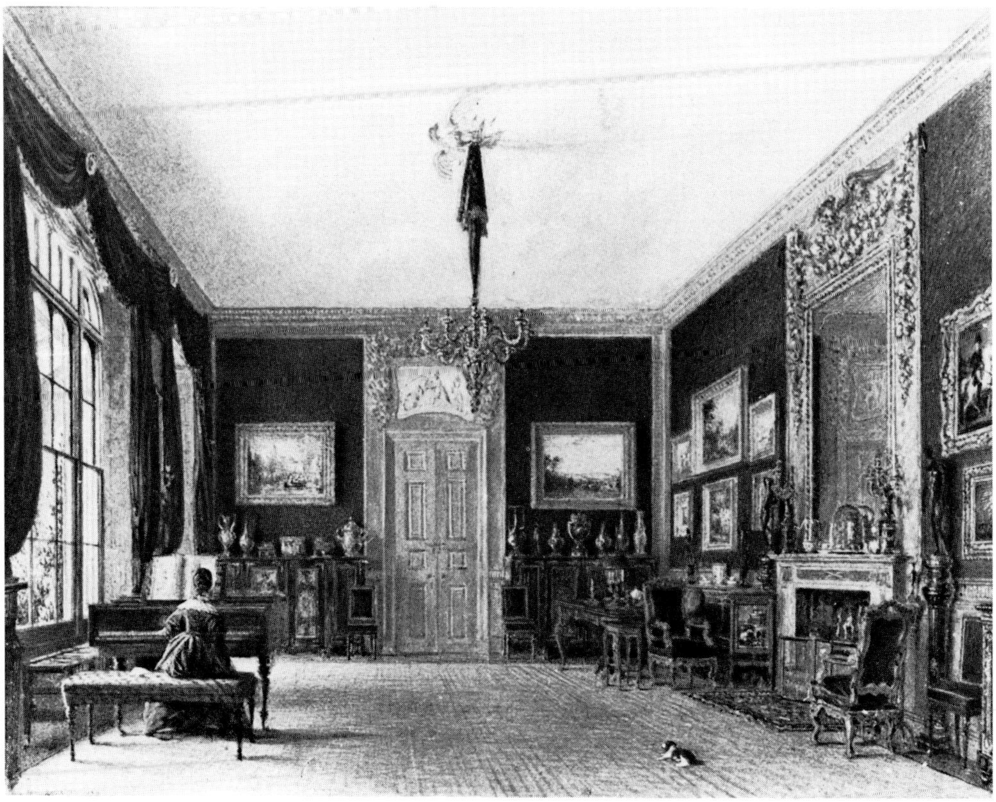

23 (376) The Drawing Room at Cassiobury Park
Watercolour, $8\frac{3}{8} \times 10\frac{3}{4}$ (211 × 270); dated 1823
Fry Collection

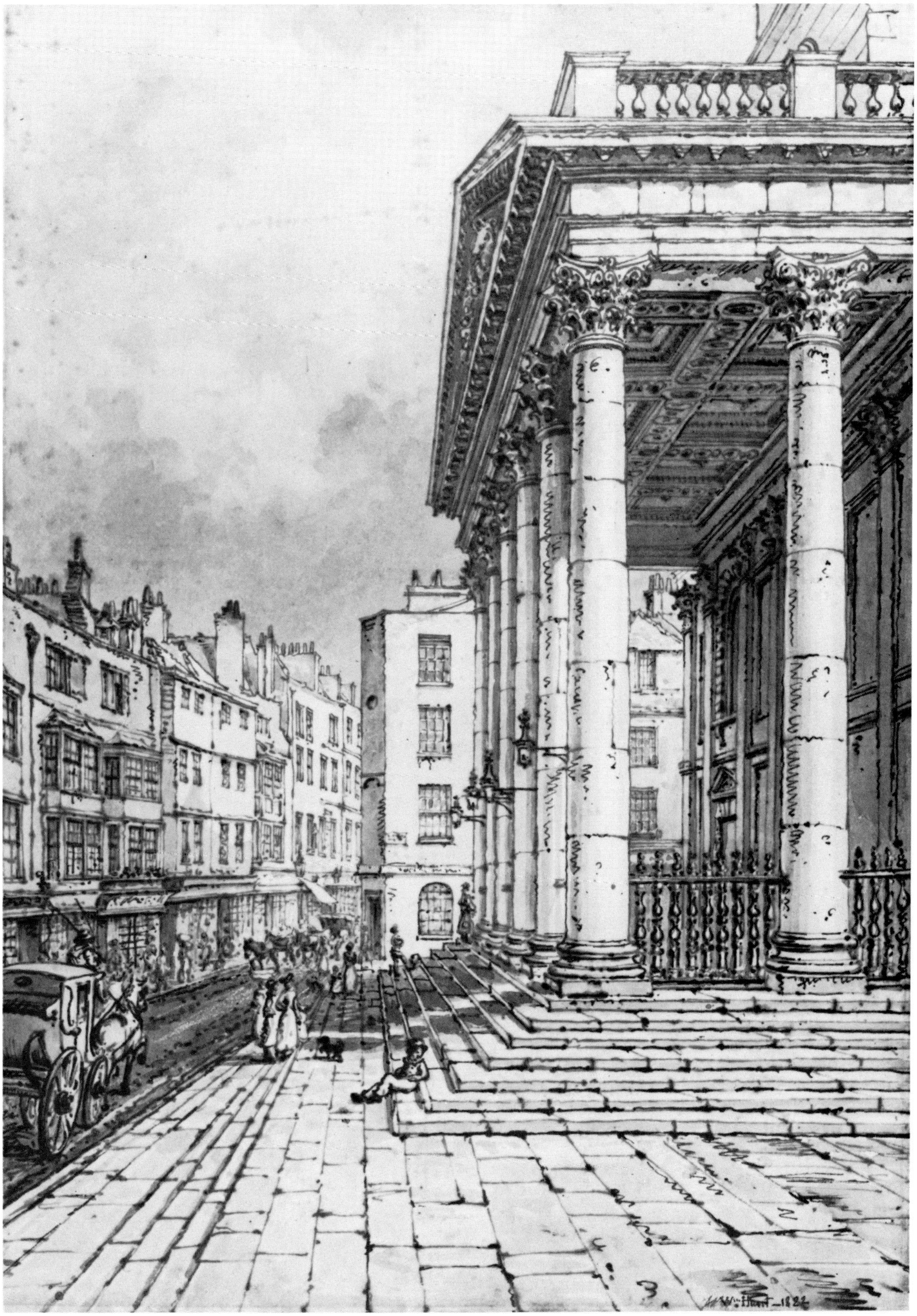

24 (141) The Portico of St Martin-in-the-Fields
Reed pen, brown ink and sepia wash, $19\frac{1}{2} \times 13\frac{7}{8}$ (494 × 353); dated 1822
Oxford, Ashmolean Museum

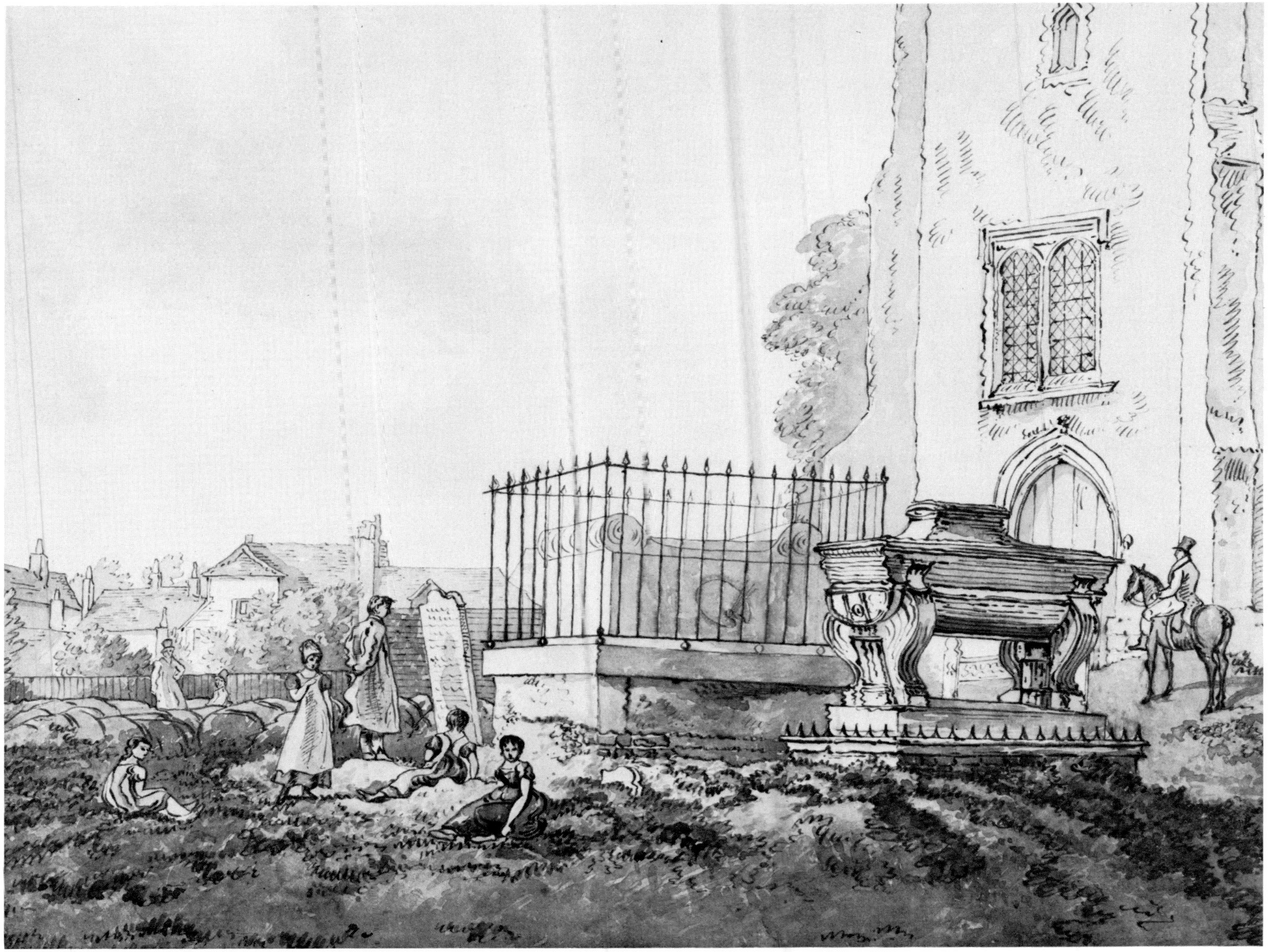

25 (252) Bushey Churchyard
Reed pen, brown ink and watercolour, $12\frac{1}{4} \times 16\frac{1}{4}$ (312 × 413)
Yale Center for British Art, Paul Mellon Collection

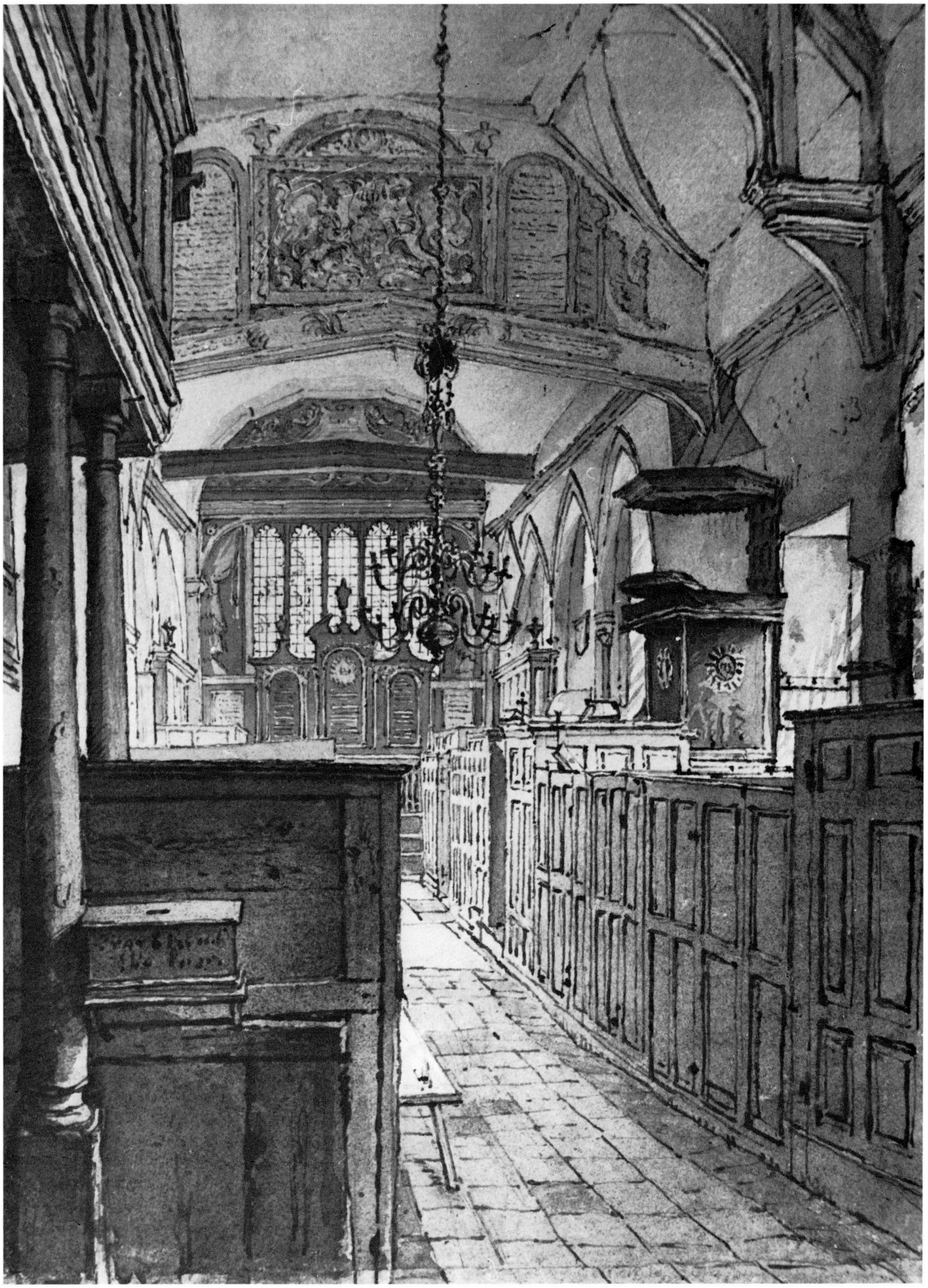

26 (17) The Nave, Bushey Church
Reed pen, ink and watercolour, $16\frac{5}{8} \times 12\frac{1}{2}$ (423 × 317)
Bradford, Art Galleries and Museums

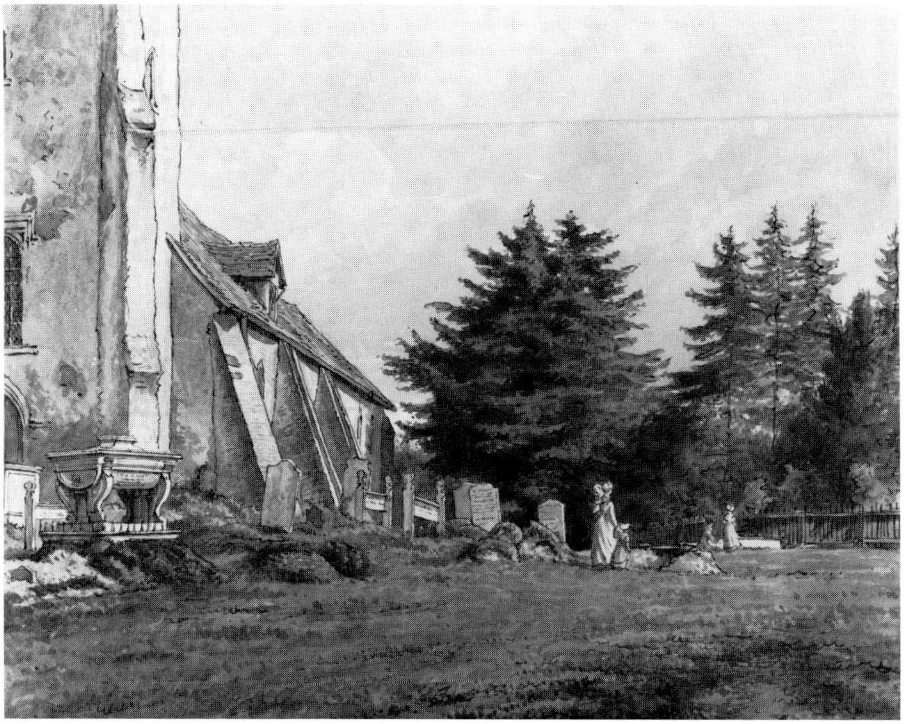

27 (24) Bushey Church, South Side
Reed pen, ink and watercolour, $12\frac{5}{8} \times 16\frac{1}{2}$ (322 × 420)
British Museum, London

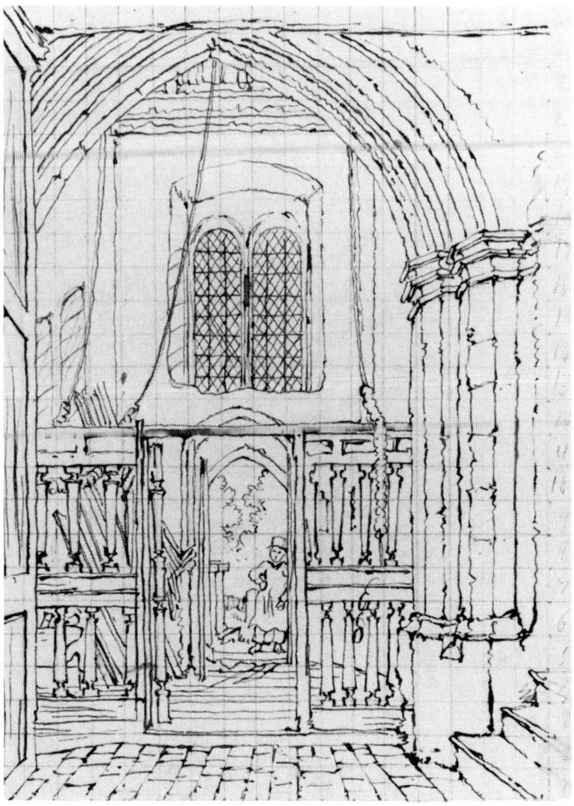

28 (197) Interior of the Belfry, Bushey Church
Reed pen and brown ink, $10\frac{7}{8} \times 8$ (277 × 203)
Witt Collection

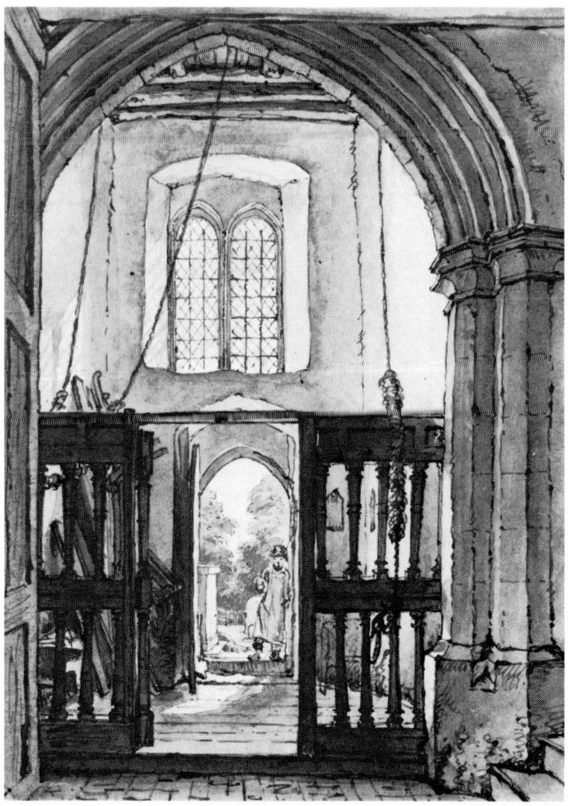

29 (251) Interior of the Belfry, Bushey Church
Pencil, reed pen, brown ink and watercolour, $14\frac{7}{16} \times 10\frac{5}{16}$ (366 × 266)
Yale Center for British Art, Paul Mellon Collection

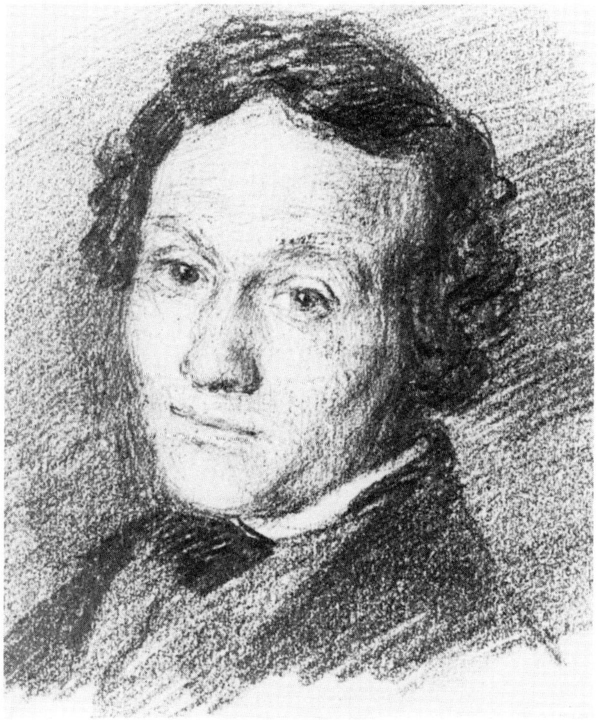

30 (362) Self Portrait Aged 25 Years (*actual size*)
Pencil and watercolour, $3\frac{3}{4} \times 3\frac{1}{8}$ (95 × 80)
Fry Collection

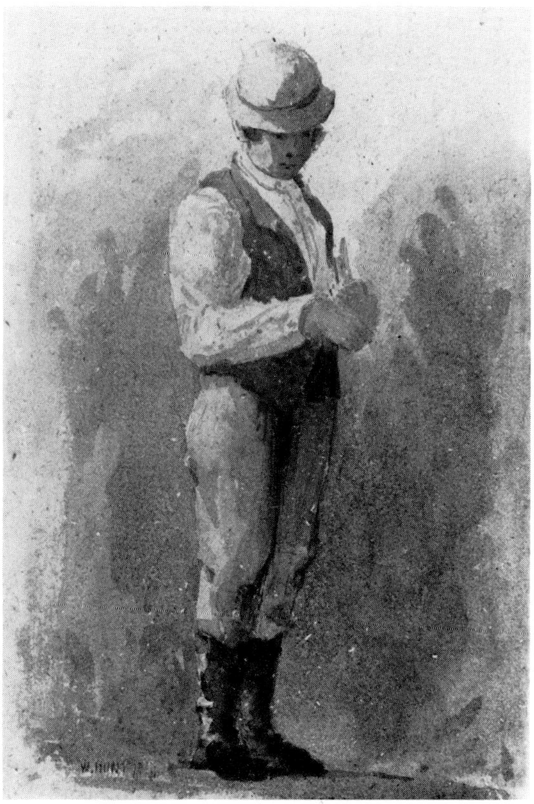

31 (540) Stable Boy
Watercolour, $10\frac{7}{8} \times 7\frac{1}{4}$ (276 × 184); dated 1815
Witt Collection

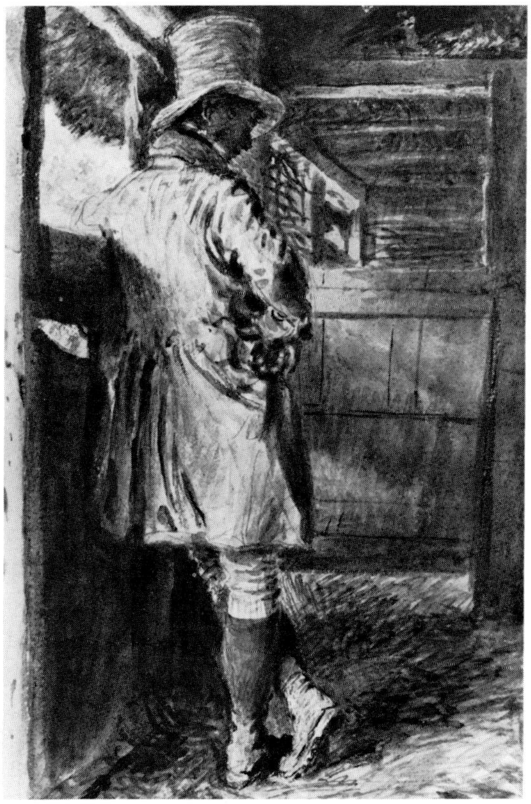

32 (271) Farmer in a Barn
Watercolour heightened with white, $10\frac{3}{4} \times 7\frac{1}{8}$ (274 × 182)
Birmingham, City Museum and Art Gallery

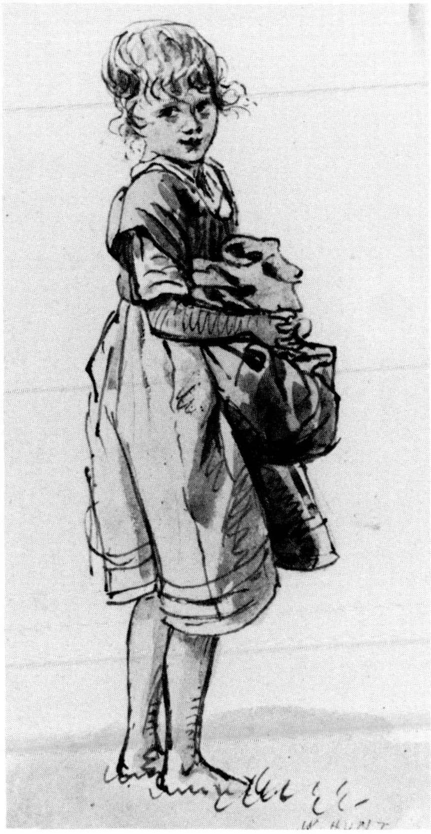

33 (544) Young Girl Standing Barefoot
Reed pen, ink and watercolour, $7\frac{1}{2} \times 3\frac{7}{8}$ (190 × 97)
Witt Collection

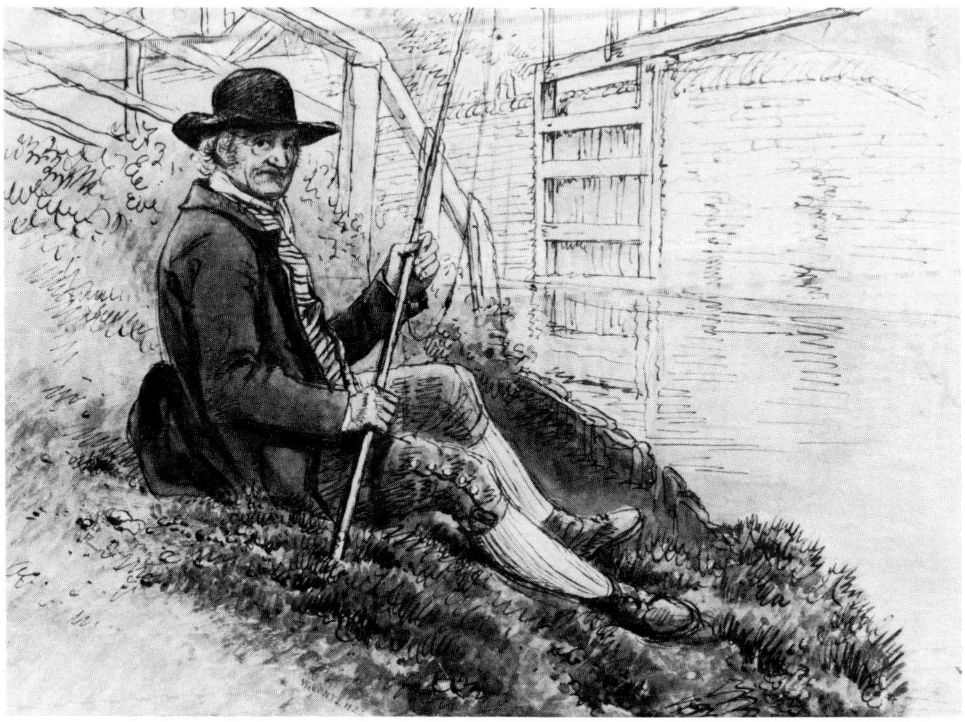

34 (258) Old Man Fishing by a Lock Gate
Reed pen, brown ink and watercolour, 11 × 15 (280 × 382); dated 1822
Mrs B. Asprey, London

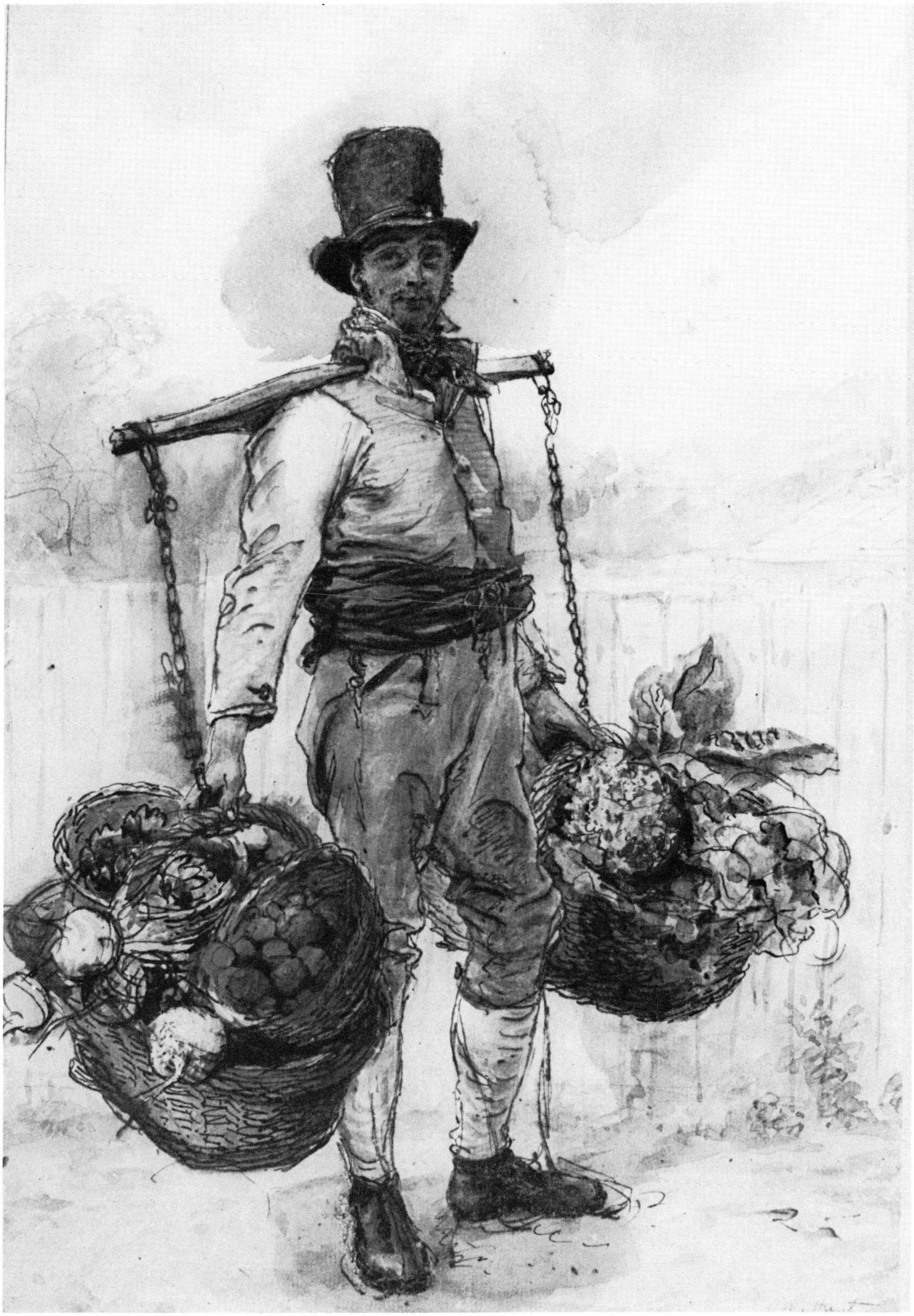

35 (324) The Vegetable Seller
Reed pen, ink and watercolour, $15 \times 10\frac{3}{8}$ (381×264)
Courtauld Institute of Art, London

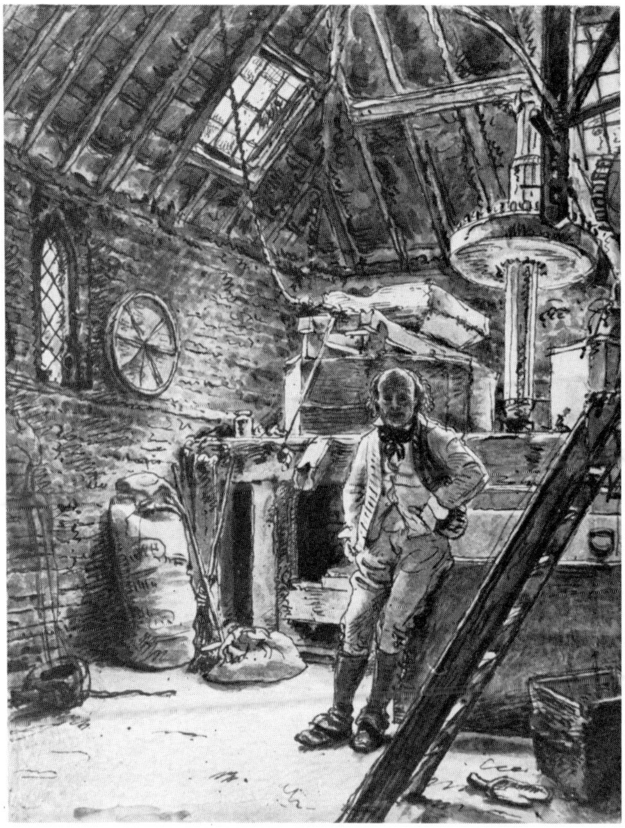

36 (272) A Miller in his Mill
Reed pen, ink and watercolour, $15\frac{1}{4} \times 11\frac{7}{8}$ (387 × 303)
Birmingham, City Museum and Art Gallery

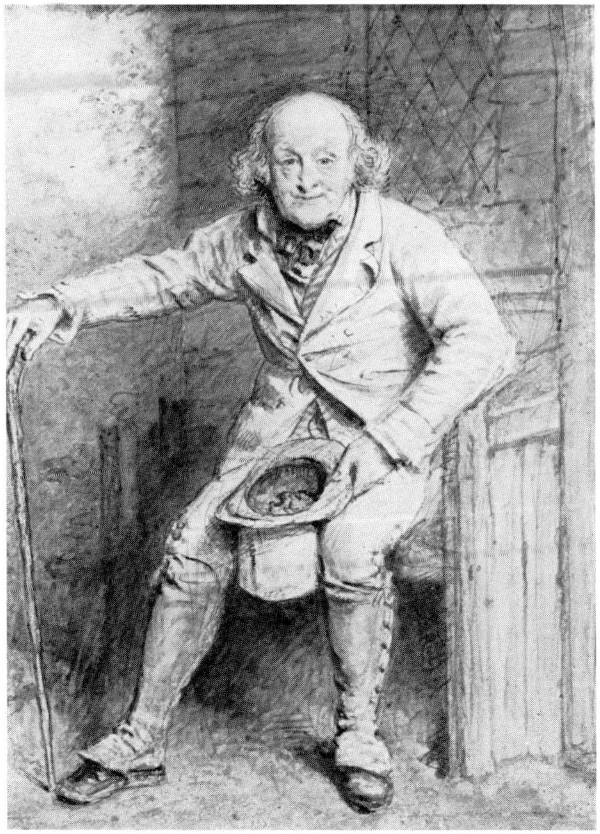

37 (473) Portrait of a Man
Pencil, reed pen, brown ink and watercolour, $15\frac{1}{2} \times 11\frac{1}{2}$ (394 × 293)
Port Sunlight, The Lady Lever Art Gallery

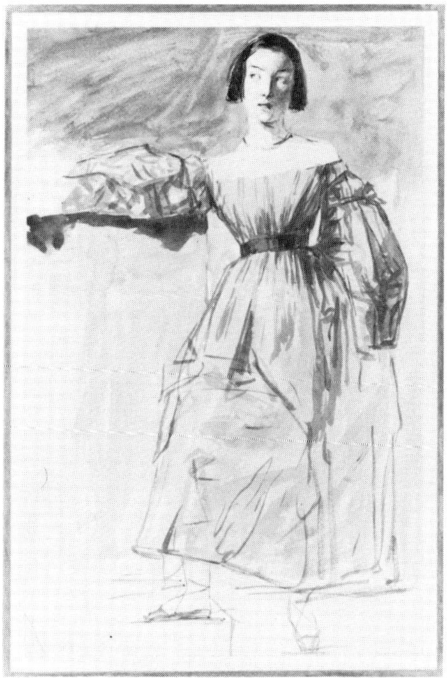

38 (470) Young Woman Standing
Watercolour, $10\frac{7}{8} \times 7\frac{1}{8}$ (276 × 180)
Oxford, Ashmolean Museum

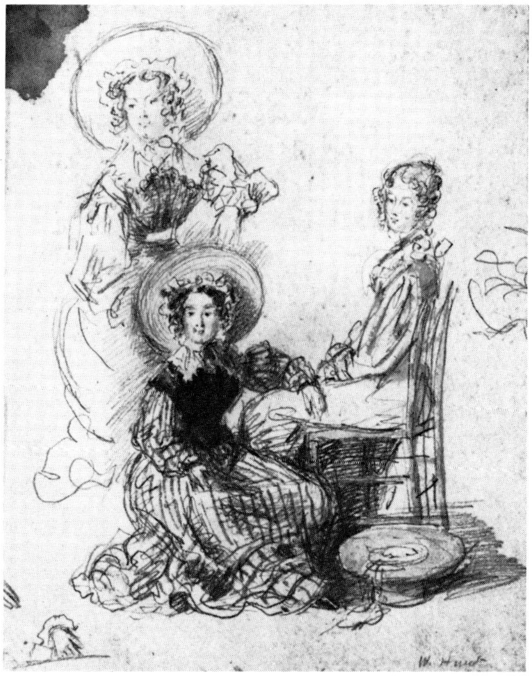

39 (293) Group of Three Women
Pencil and watercolour, $7\frac{1}{8} \times 5\frac{5}{8}$ (180 × 142)
British Museum, London

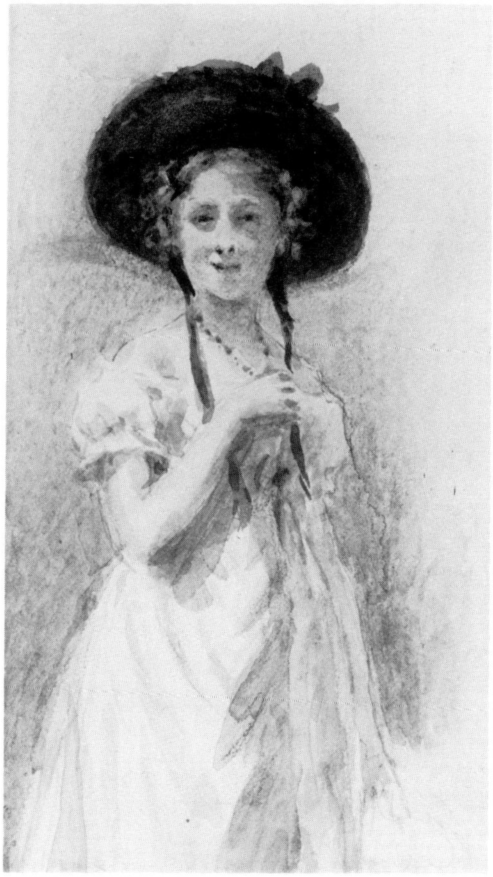

40 (391) Portrait of a Girl
Watercolour, 7 × 4 (177 × 100)
Halifax, Bankfield Museum

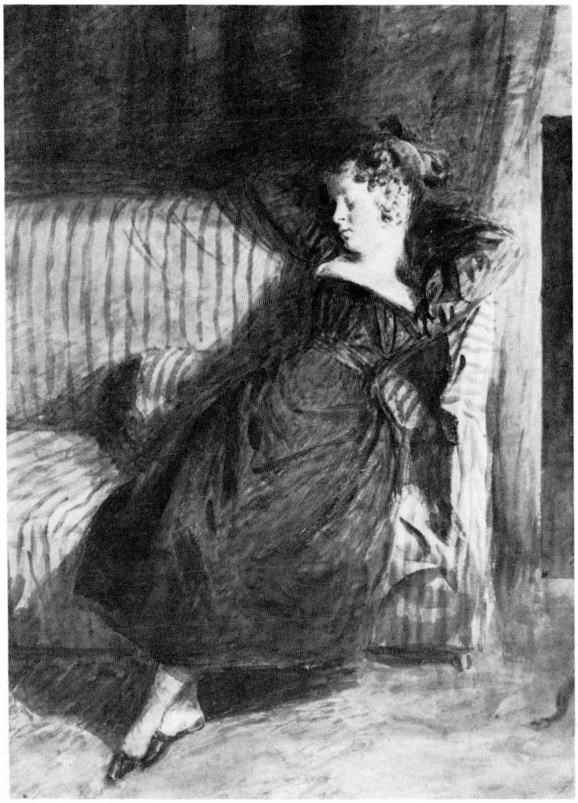

41 (266) Young Girl Reclining on a Couch
Watercolour, $14 \times 10\frac{1}{4}$ (354×260)
Bedford, Cecil Higgins Art Gallery

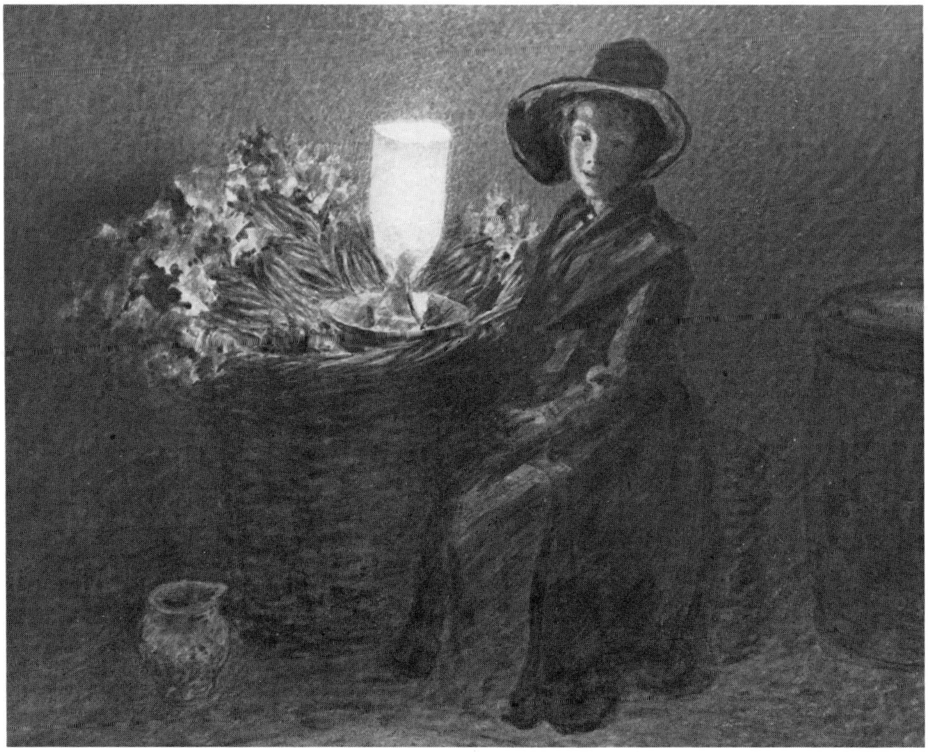

42 (430) A Radish Stall
Watercolour heightened with white, $8\frac{3}{4} \times 10\frac{7}{8}$ (223×277); dated 1829
Manchester, City Art Gallery

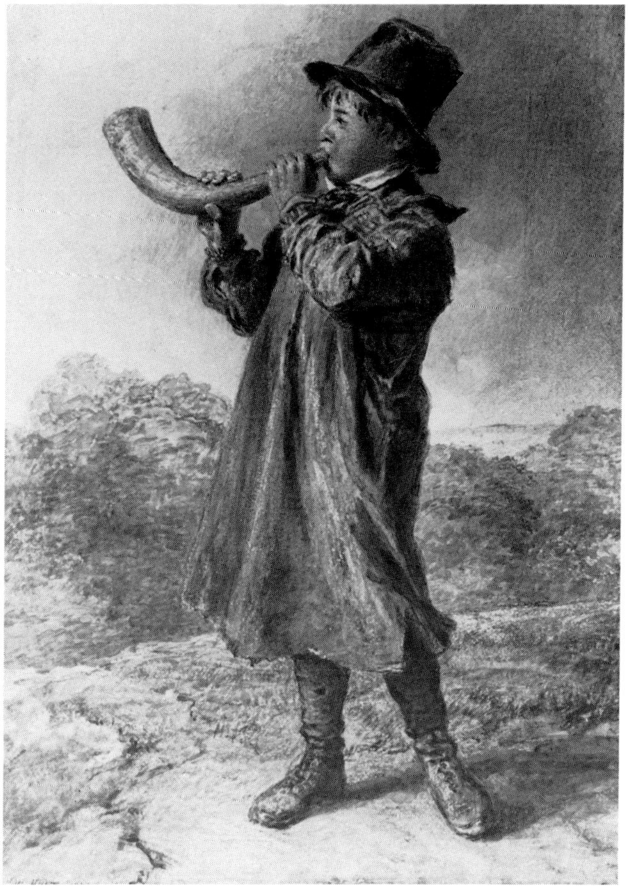

44 (429) Boy Blowing a Horn
Watercolour, 14 × 10¼ (356 × 262); dated 1829
Manchester, City Art Gallery

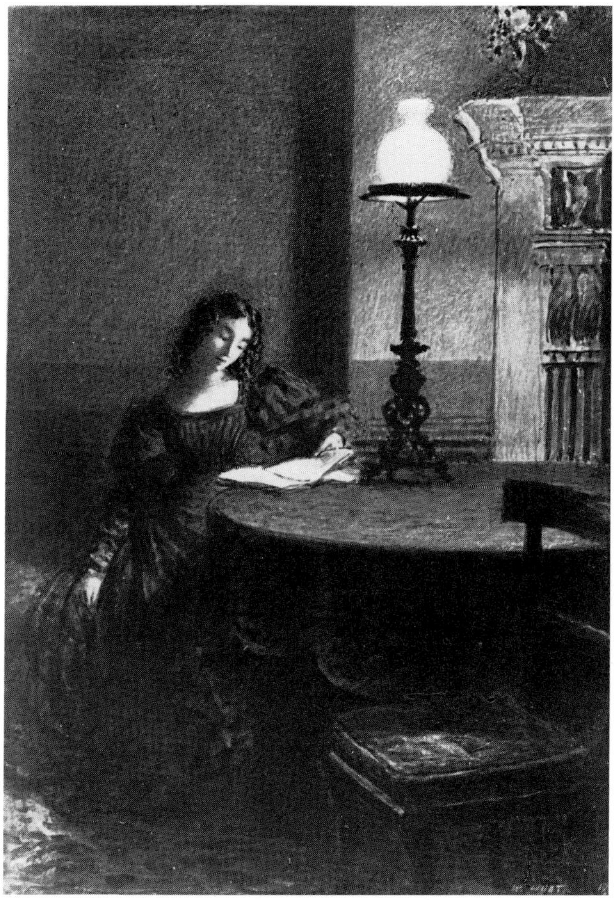

43 (379) Girl Reading by Lamplight
Watercolour, 12¼ × 8½ (312 × 220)
Fry Collection

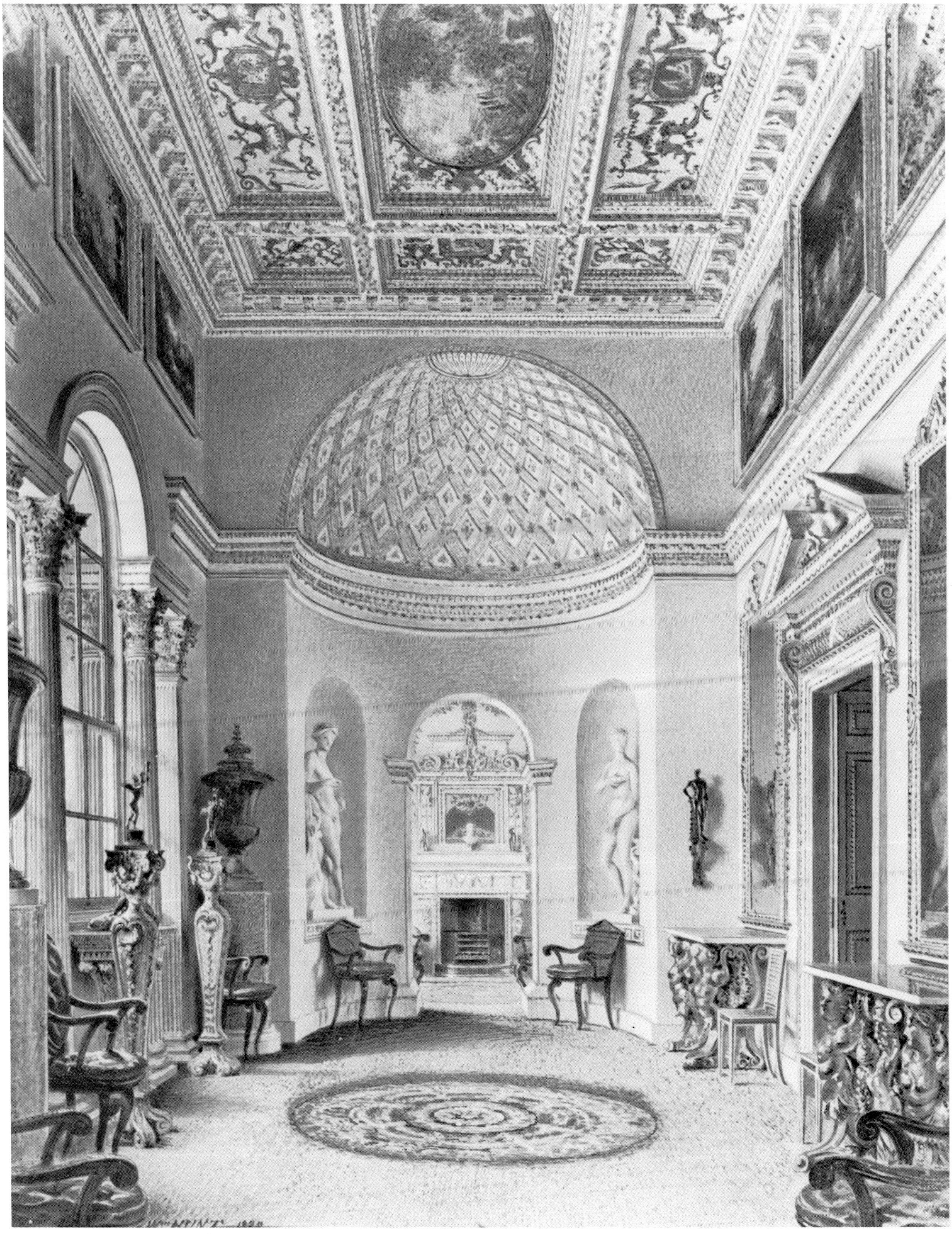

45 (334) The Gallery, Chiswick House
Watercolour, $12\frac{3}{4} \times 10$ (325×255); dated 1822
Devonshire Collection Chatsworth

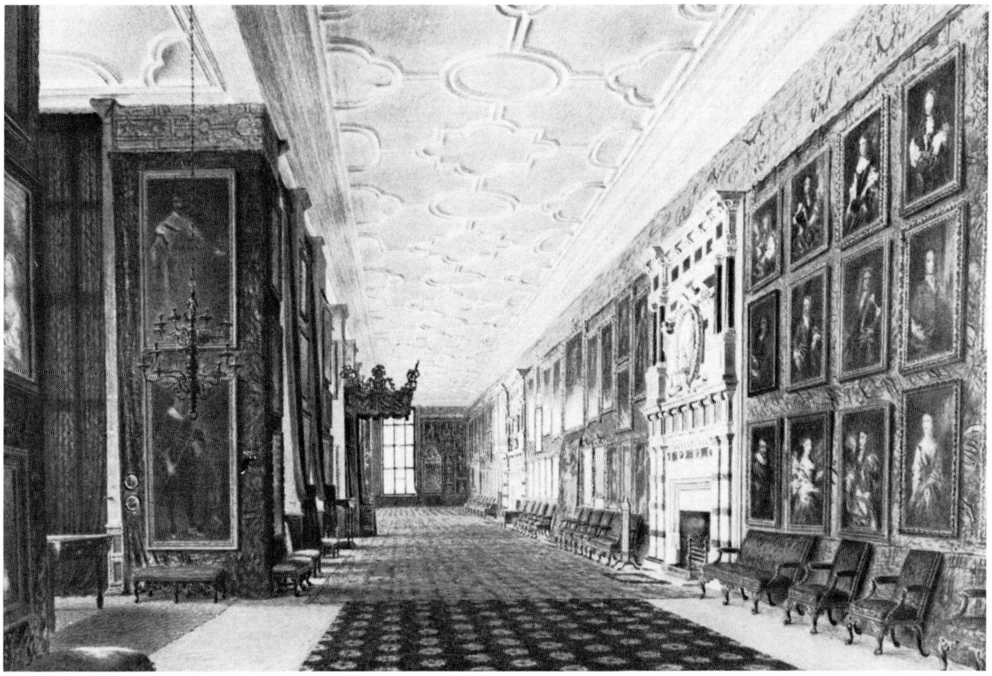

46 (351) The Long Gallery, Hardwick
Watercolour, $11\frac{1}{4} \times 16\frac{3}{4}$ (286 × 427); dated 1828
Devonshire Collection Chatsworth

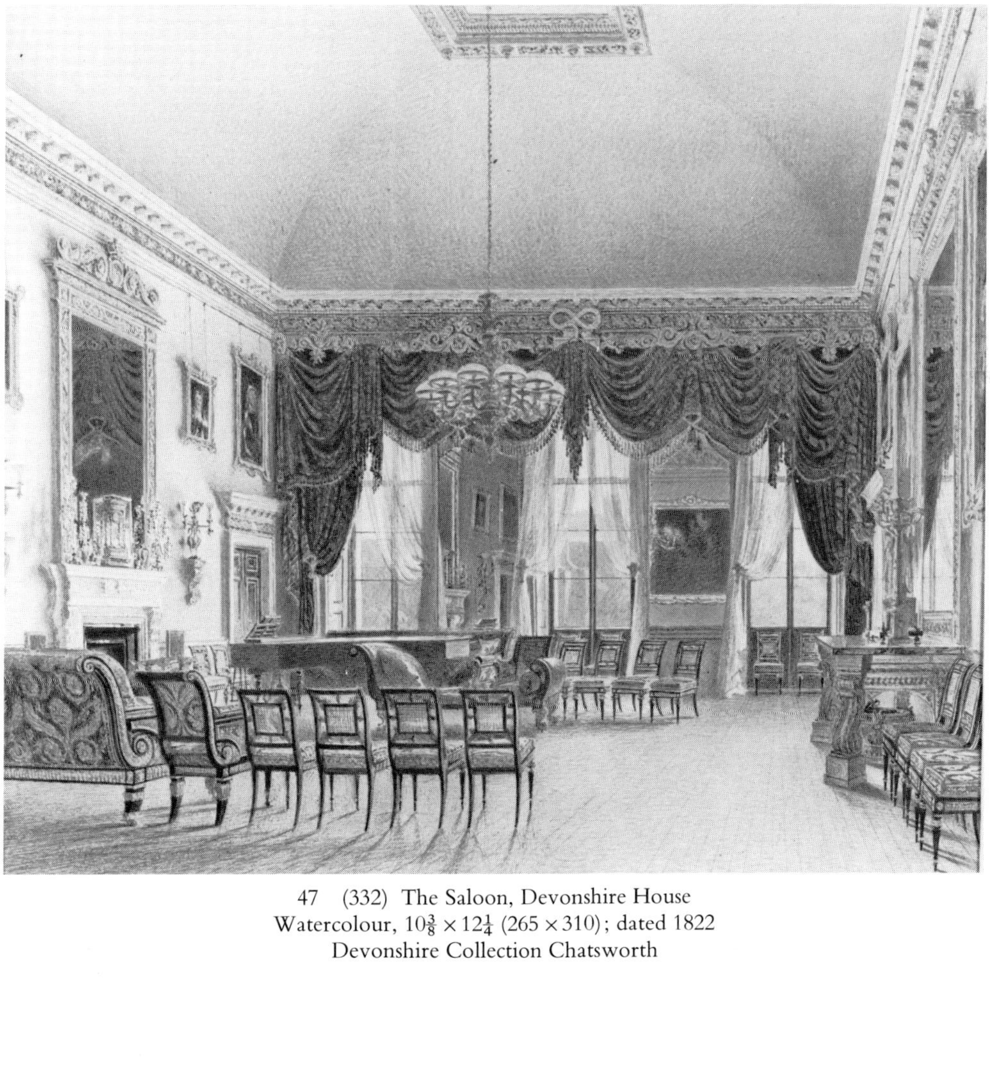

47 (332) The Saloon, Devonshire House
Watercolour, $10\frac{3}{8} \times 12\frac{1}{4}$ (265 × 310); dated 1822
Devonshire Collection Chatsworth

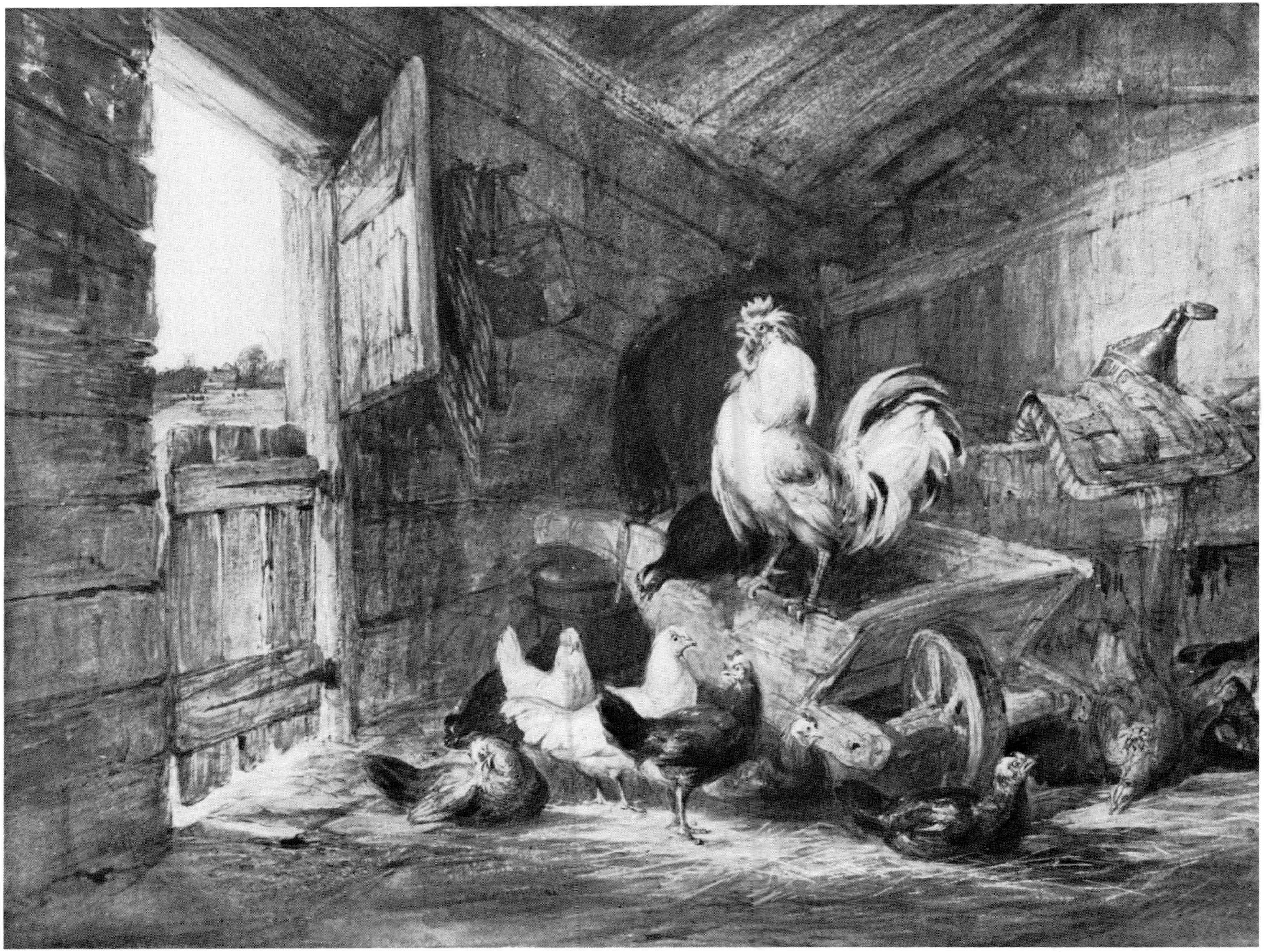

48 (748) Cock and Hens in a Barn
Watercolour heightened with white, $12\frac{1}{8} \times 16$ (307 × 408)
Mr C. W. Witt, Bucks.

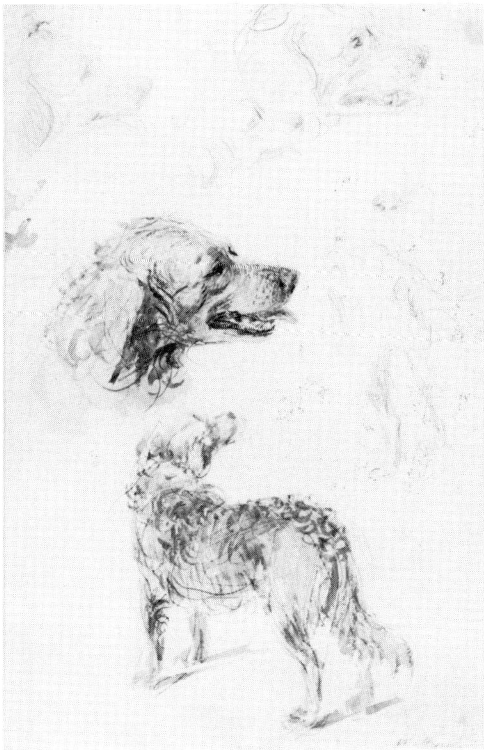

49 (642) Dog Studies
Pencil and brown wash, $10\frac{3}{4} \times 7\frac{1}{4}$ (274×184)
Huntington Library, San Marino

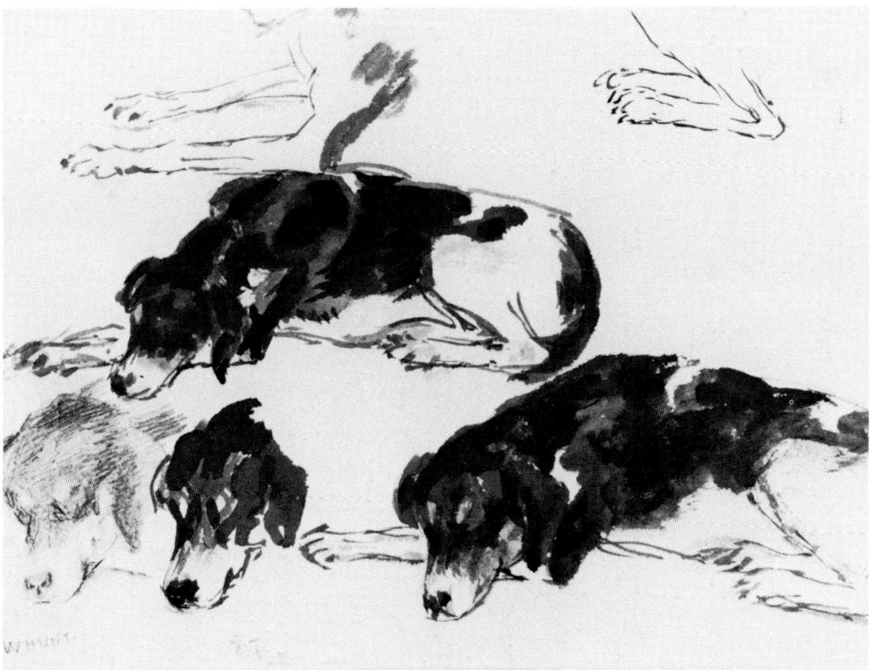

50 (736) Studies of a Dog
Pencil and watercolour, $5\frac{7}{8} \times 8\frac{1}{4}$ (148×210)
Mrs G. M. Tuff, London

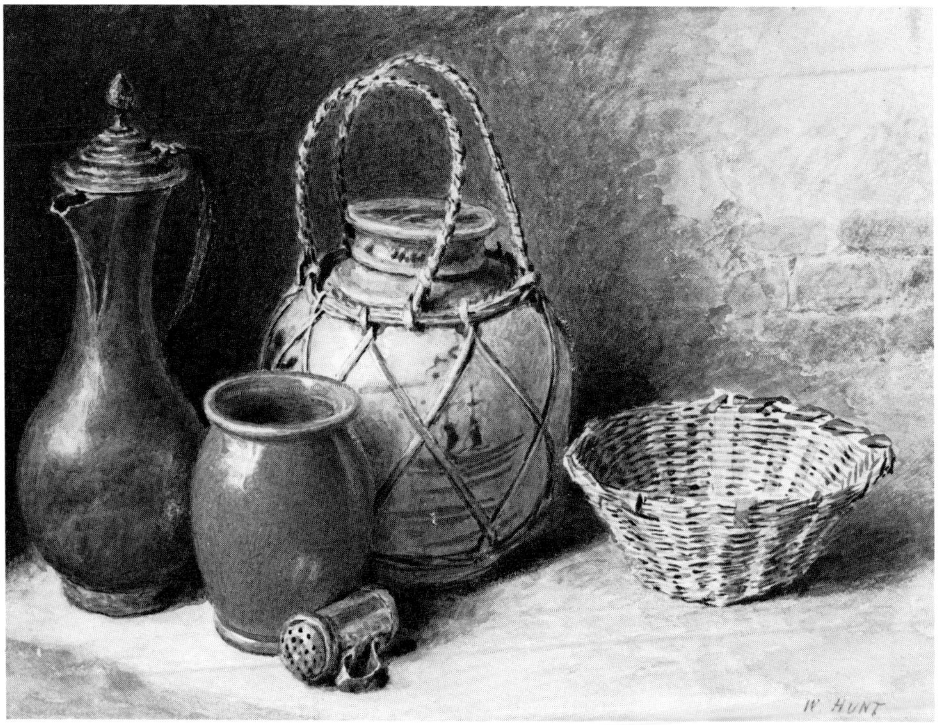

51 (773) Still Life: Copper Jug, Blue Vase,
Blue and White Ginger Jar, Pepper Pot and Basket
Pencil and watercolour, $7\frac{1}{2} \times 10$ (190 × 255)
Yale Center for British Art, Paul Mellon Collection

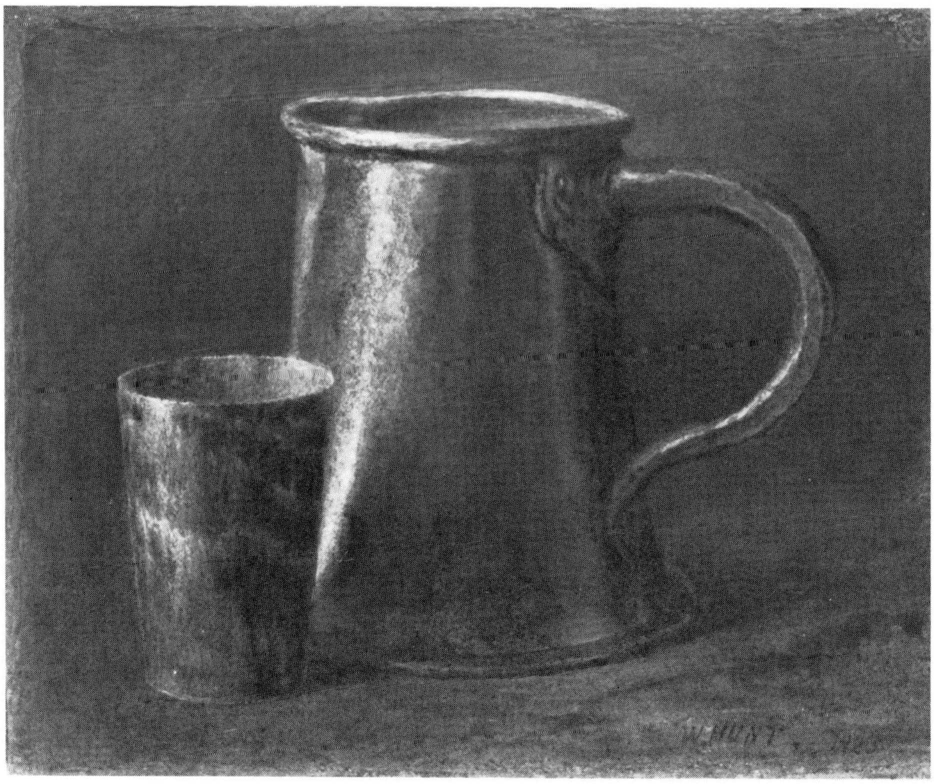

52 (685) Study of Copper Pot and Horn Mug
Watercolour heightened with white, $4\frac{1}{2} \times 5\frac{1}{4}$ (116 × 133); dated 1825
Oxford, Ashmolean Museum

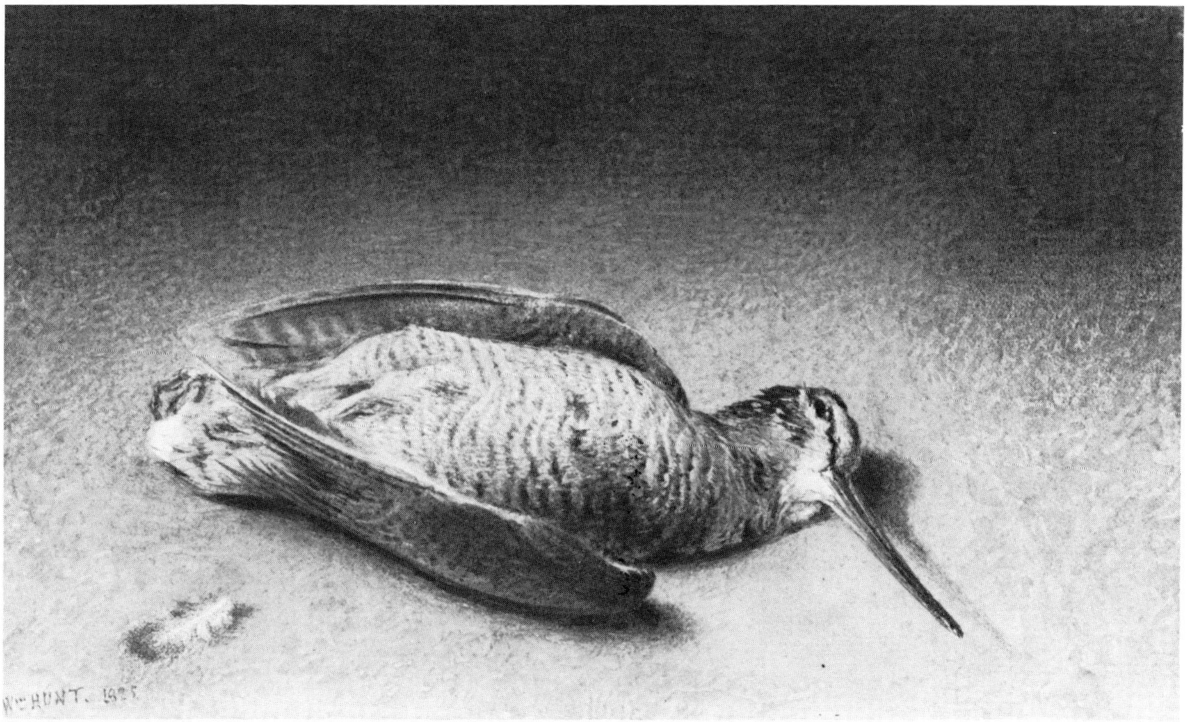

53 (686) Study of a Woodcock
Watercolour, brown and yellow, heightened with white, $5\frac{1}{8} \times 8\frac{5}{8}$ (129 × 220); dated 1825
Oxford, Ashmolean Museum

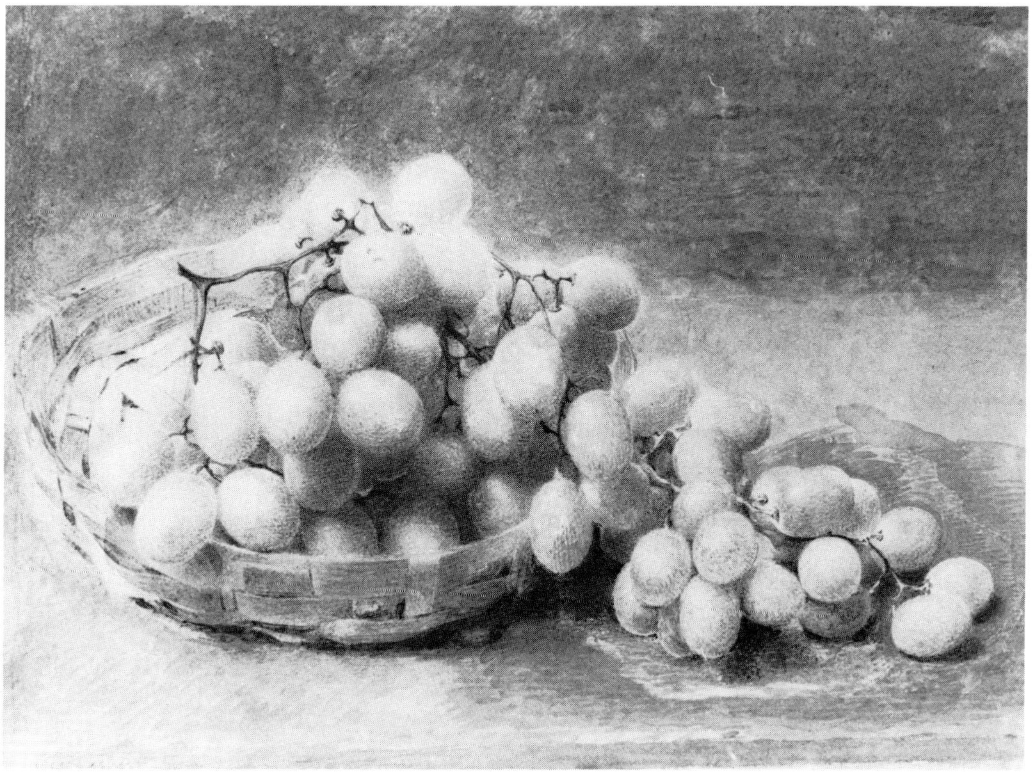

54 (759) White Grapes in a Basket
Watercolour heightened with white, $7\frac{7}{8} \times 11\frac{1}{4}$ (198 × 287); dated 1827
Witt Collection

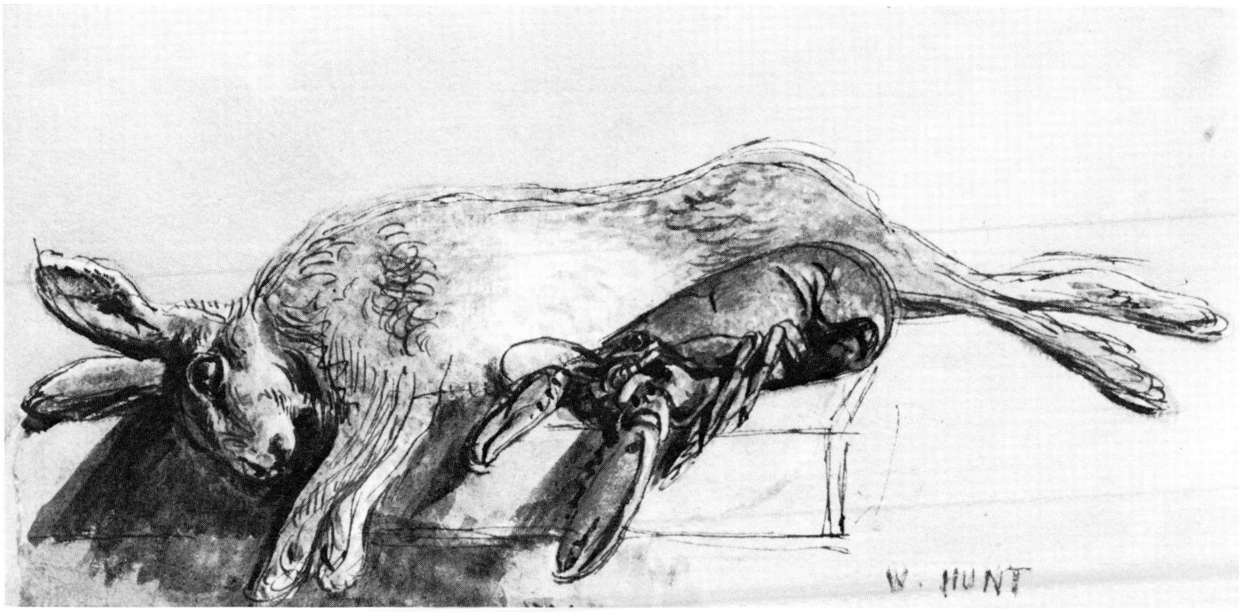

55 (774) A Dead Hare and a Cooked Lobster on a Bench
Pencil, reed pen, brown ink and watercolour, $4\frac{1}{4} \times 8\frac{15}{16}$ (108×227)
Yale Center for British Art, Paul Mellon Collection

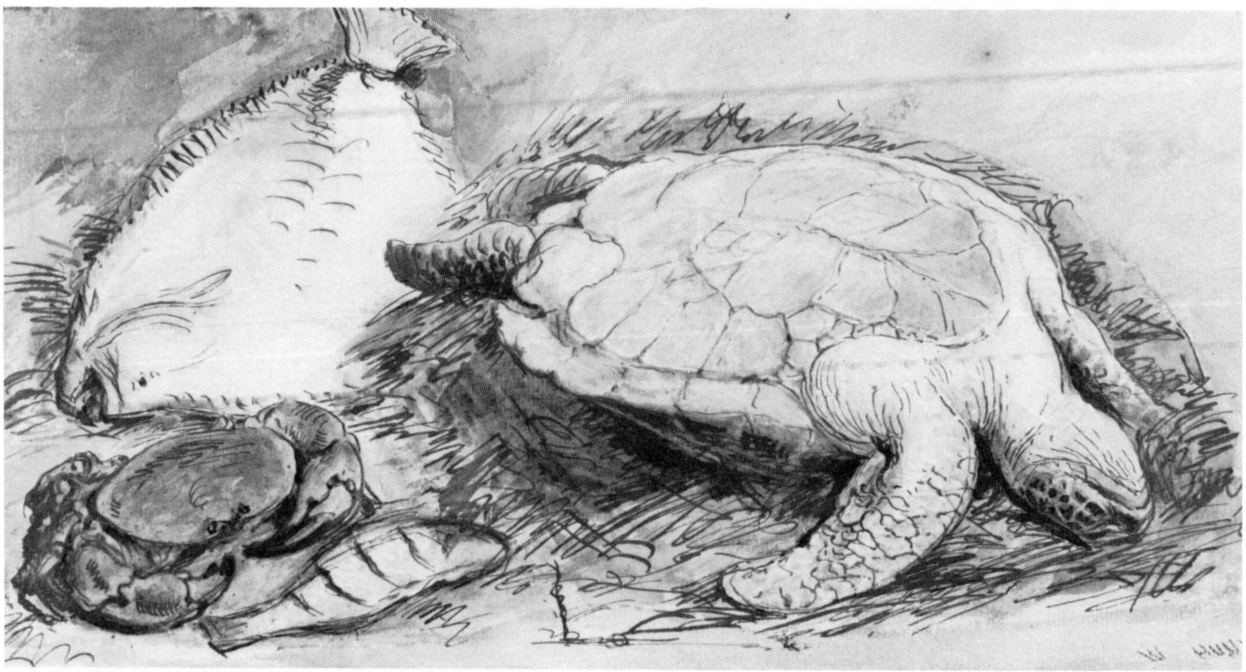

56 (665) Still Life: Turtle, Crab and Fish
Reed pen, brown ink and watercolour, $7 \times 13\frac{3}{4}$ (177×348)
Manchester, Whitworth Art Gallery

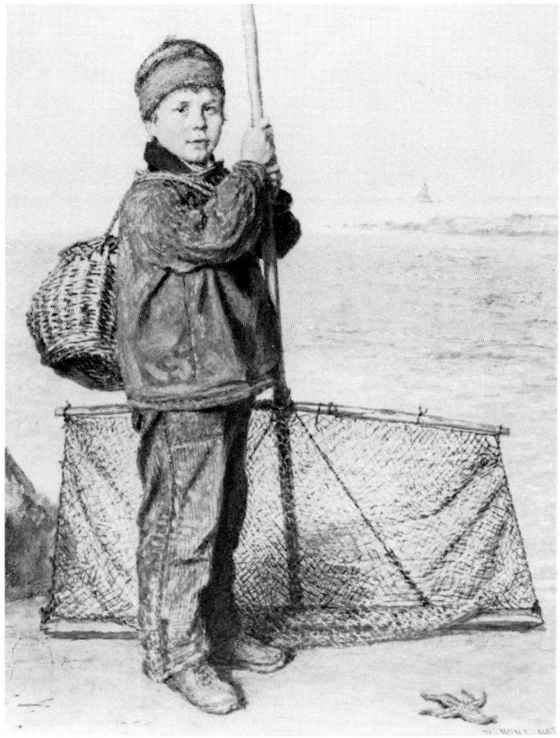

57 (437) A Shrimper
Watercolour, $15\frac{1}{8} \times 12\frac{1}{8}$ (384×307); dated 1835
Manchester, Whitworth Art Gallery

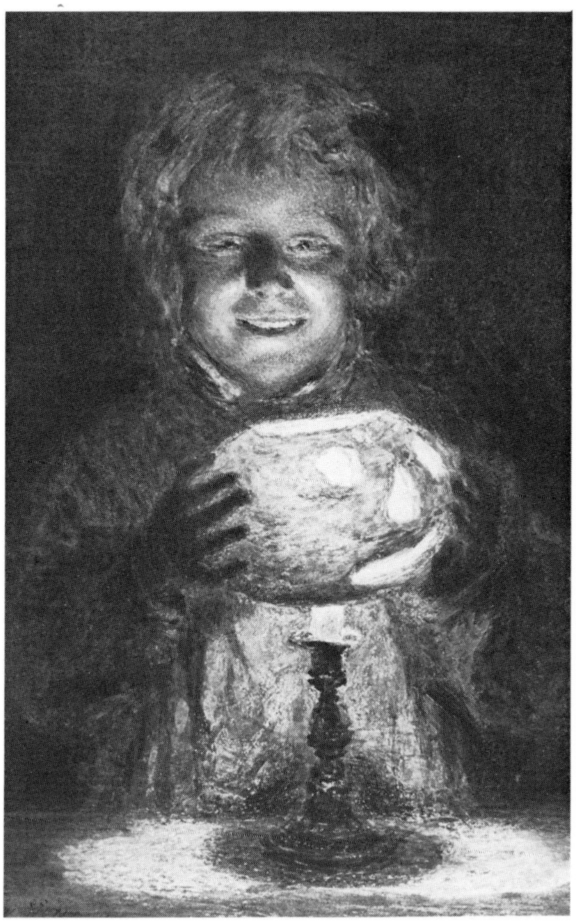

58 (419) The Turnip Lantern
Watercolour heightened with white, $13\frac{1}{8} \times 8\frac{7}{8}$ (336×225); dated 1838
Leicester, Museums and Art Galleries

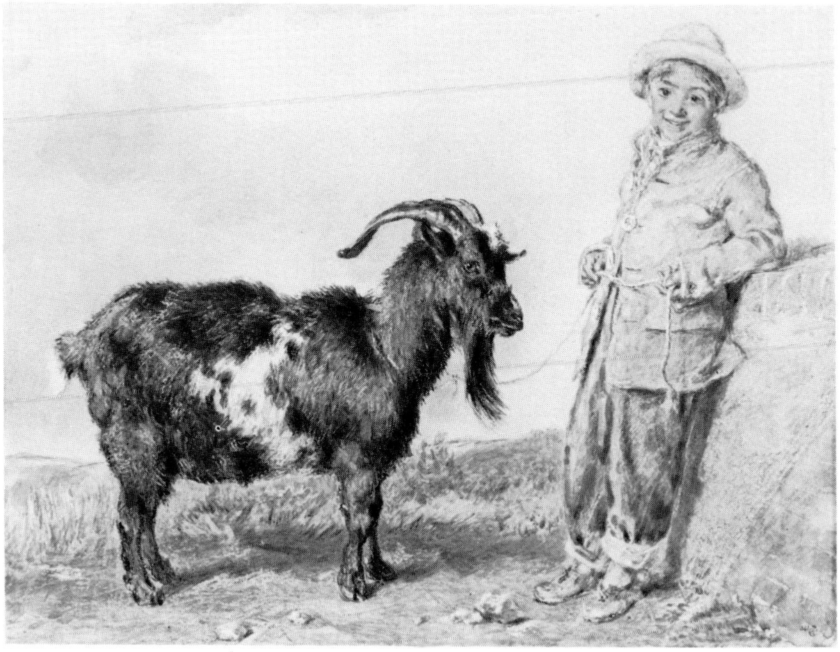

59 (530) Boy and Goat
Watercolour heightened with white and surface scratching, $12\frac{1}{4} \times 16$ (312×407); dated 1836
Victoria and Albert Museum, London

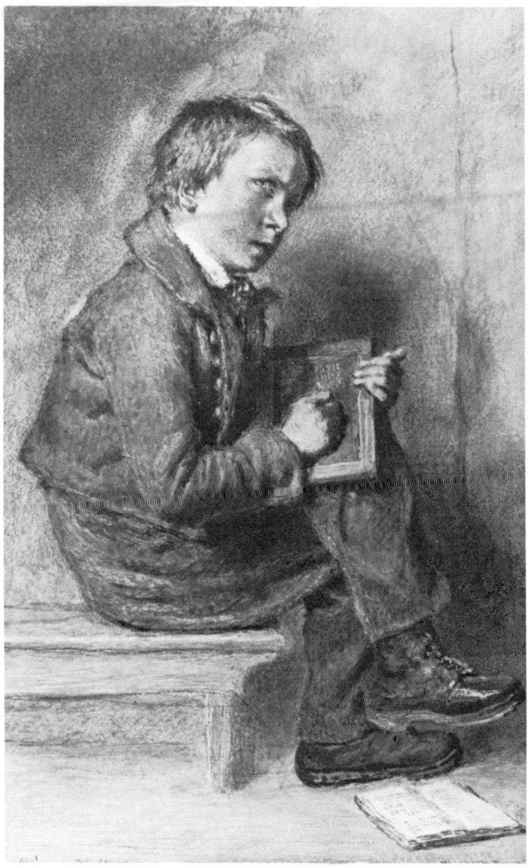

60 (420) Puzzled
Pencil and watercolour slightly heightened with white, $13\frac{1}{8} \times 8\frac{3}{4}$ (333×223); dated 1839
Leicester, Museums and Art Galleries

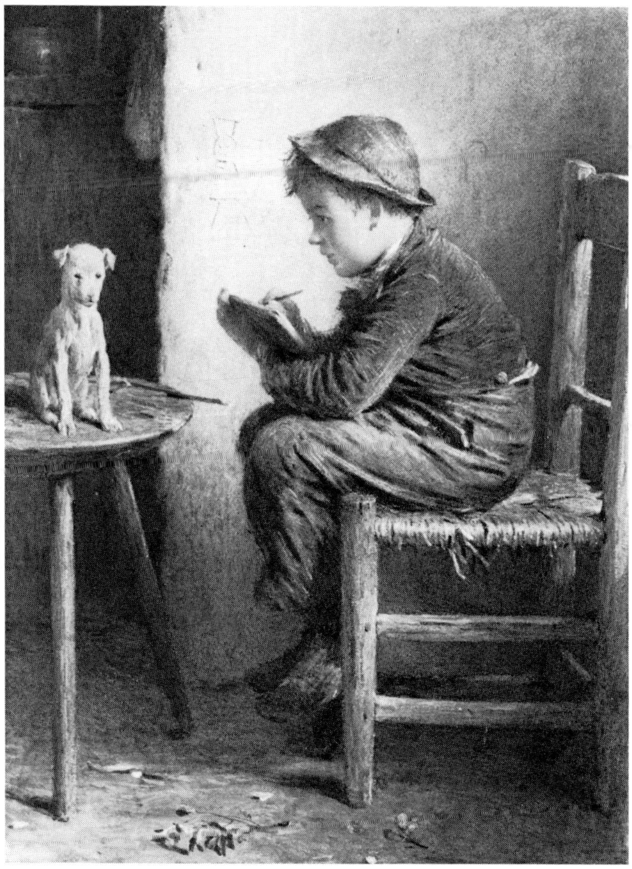

61 (410) The Young Artist
Watercolour heightened with white, $17\frac{7}{8} \times 12\frac{3}{4}$ (456×324)
Huntington Library, San Marino

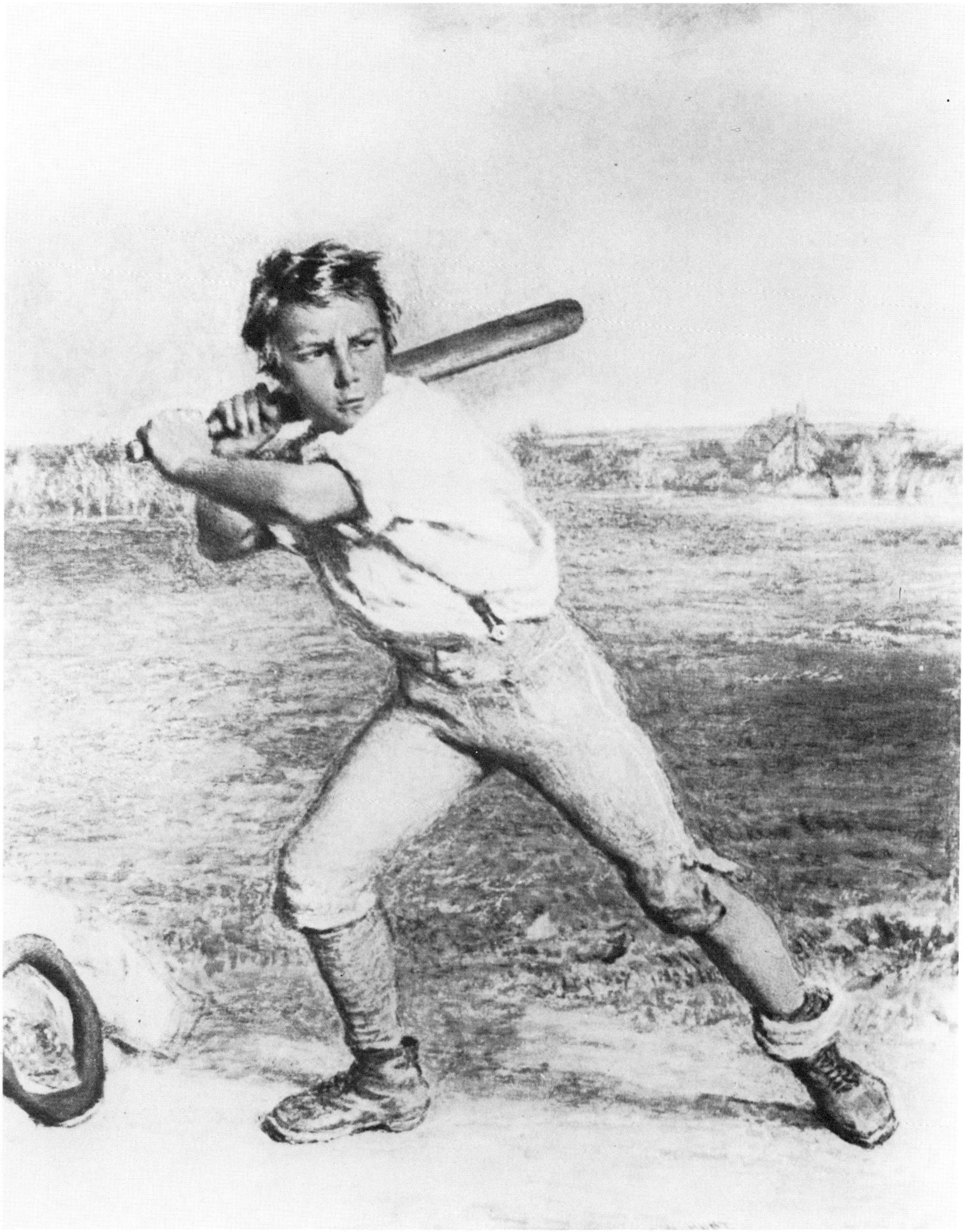

62 (323) A Young Cricketer
Watercolour, $18\frac{1}{8} \times 14\frac{1}{8}$ (462 × 360)
The late Sir Jeremiah Colman, Bt

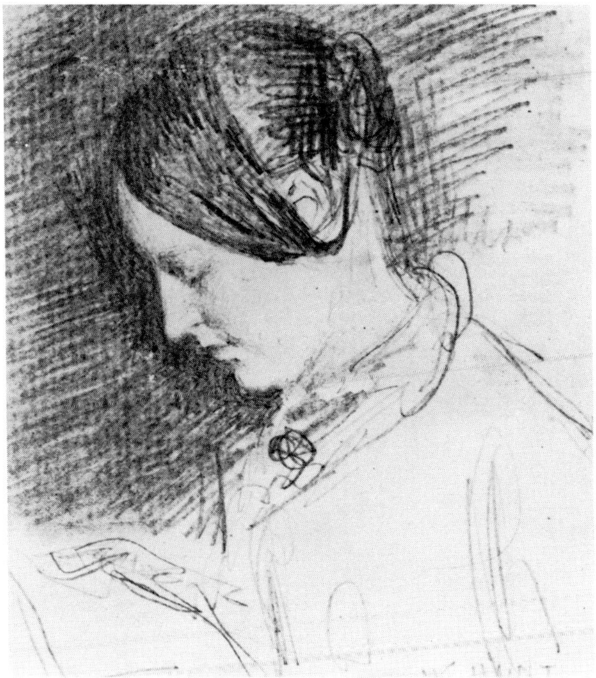

63 (510) The Artist's Wife
Pencil, $3\frac{7}{8} \times 3\frac{1}{2}$ (98×90)
Sheffield, Graves Art Gallery

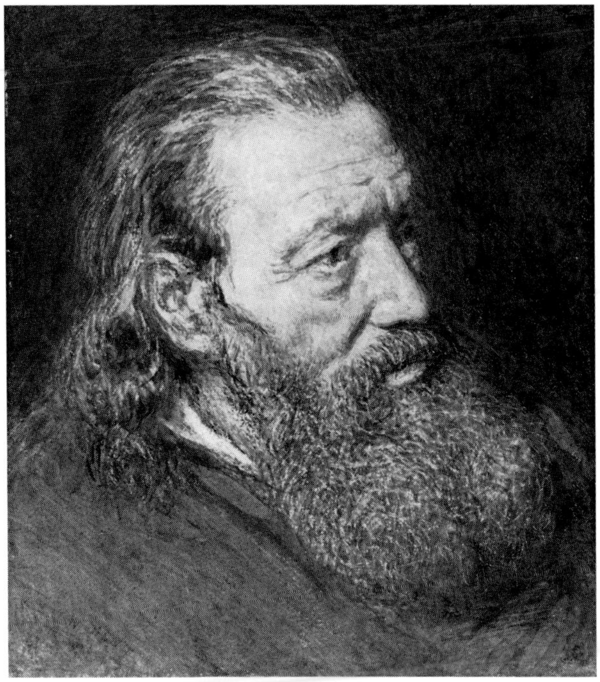

64 (514) An Old Man's Head
Watercolour, $9\frac{1}{4} \times 8$ (235×203)
Tate Gallery, London

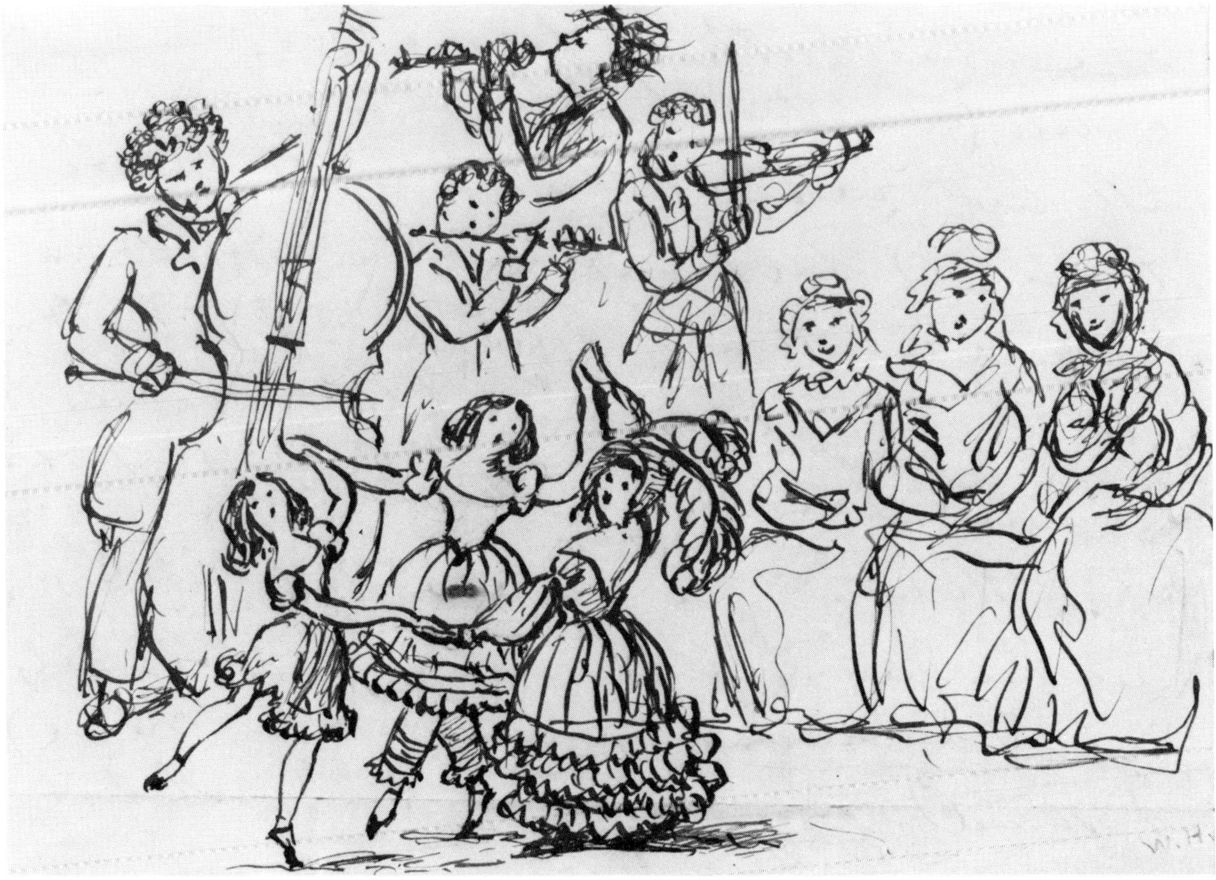

65 (387) Musical Party with Three Young Girls Dancing
Pen, $5\frac{1}{8} \times 7\frac{1}{4}$ (130×184)
Fry Collection

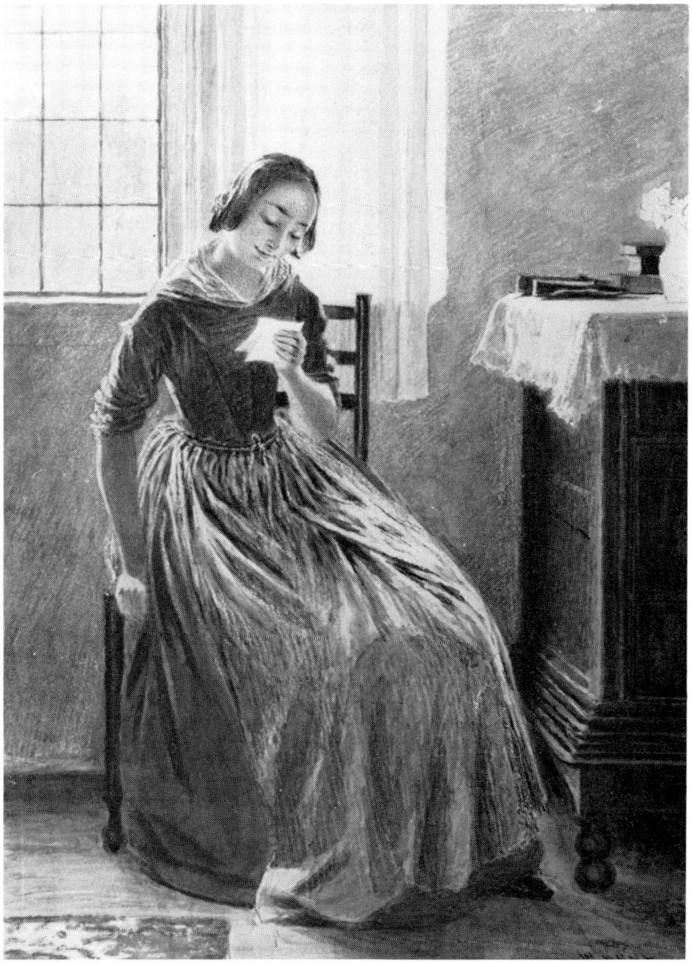

66 (539) An Interesting Letter
Watercolour, $13\frac{1}{4} \times 9\frac{3}{4}$ (337 × 246)
Mr C. W. Witt, Bucks.

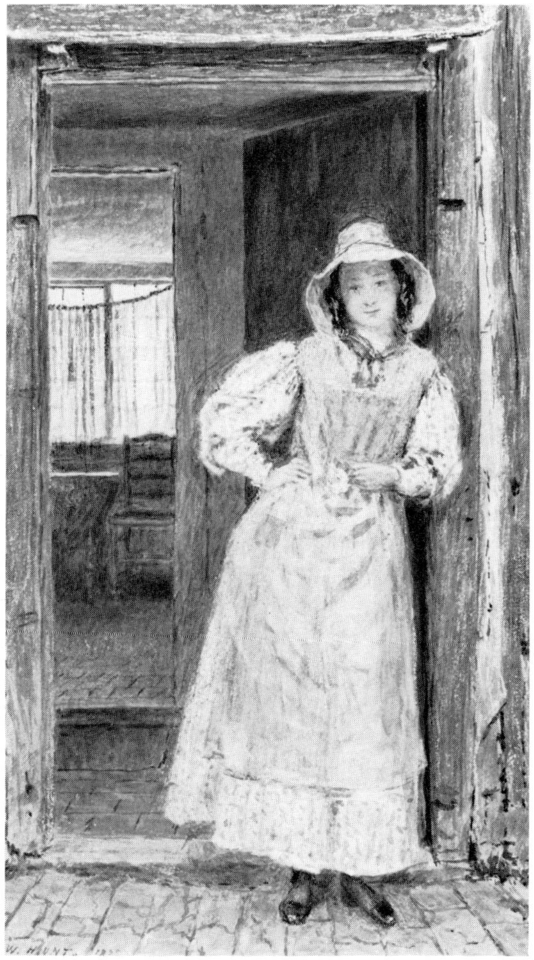

67 (408) At the Cottage Door
Watercolour, $12\frac{1}{2} \times 7\frac{1}{4}$ (324 × 184); dated 1835
Huntington Library, San Marino

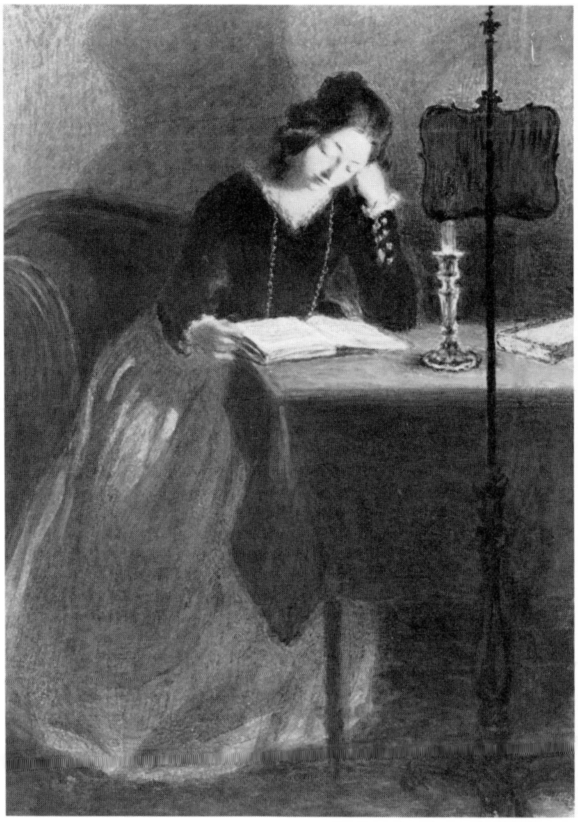

68 (490) Woman Reading by Candlelight
Pencil and watercolour, $13\frac{3}{8} \times 9\frac{1}{2}$ (340 × 242)
Mrs A. Reed, London

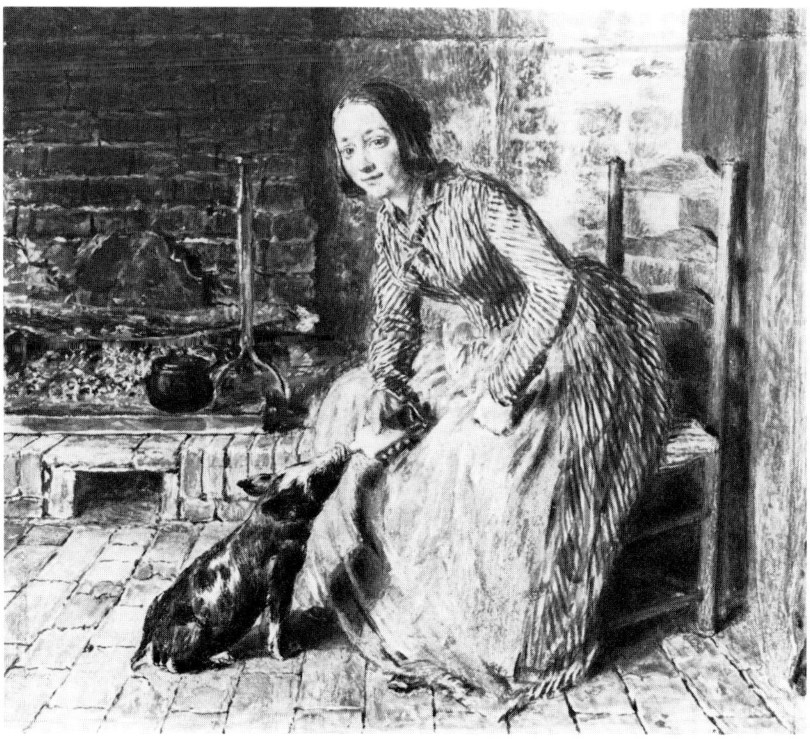

69 (388) The Orphan
Watercolour heightened with white, $11\frac{1}{2} \times 13\frac{1}{4}$ (297 × 355)
Fry Collection

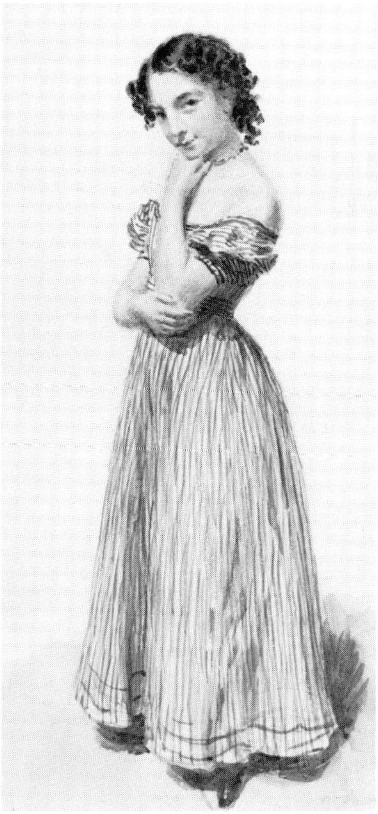

70 (400) Portrait of a Young Lady
Watercolour, $10\frac{3}{8} \times 5$ (263 × 127)
Huntington Library, San Marino

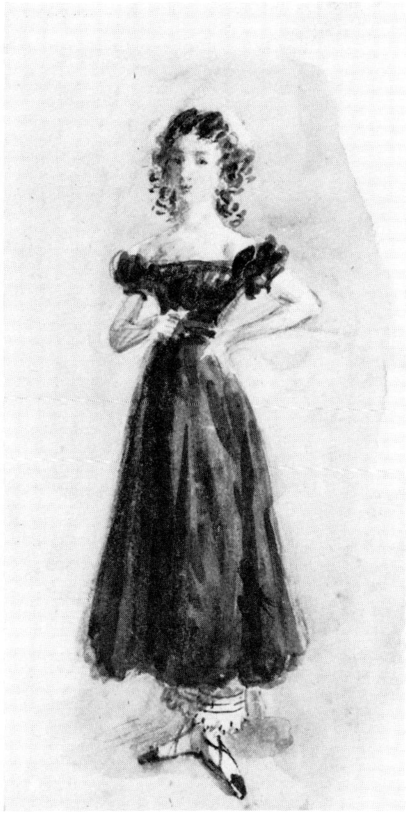

71 (571) Girl with a Black Dress
Watercolour, $7\frac{11}{16} \times 3\frac{7}{8}$ (195 × 98)
Yale Center for British Art,
Paul Mellon Collection

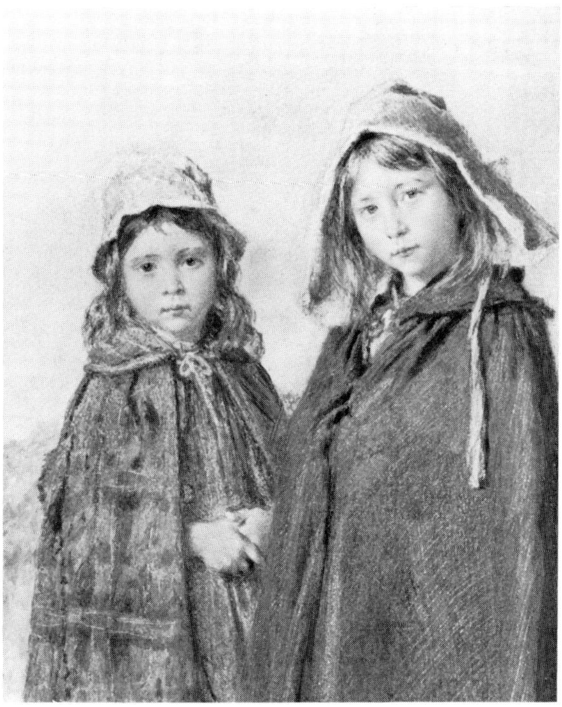

72 (411) The Sisters
Watercolour, $12\frac{1}{8} \times 9\frac{1}{4}$ (308 × 235)
Huntington Library, San Marino

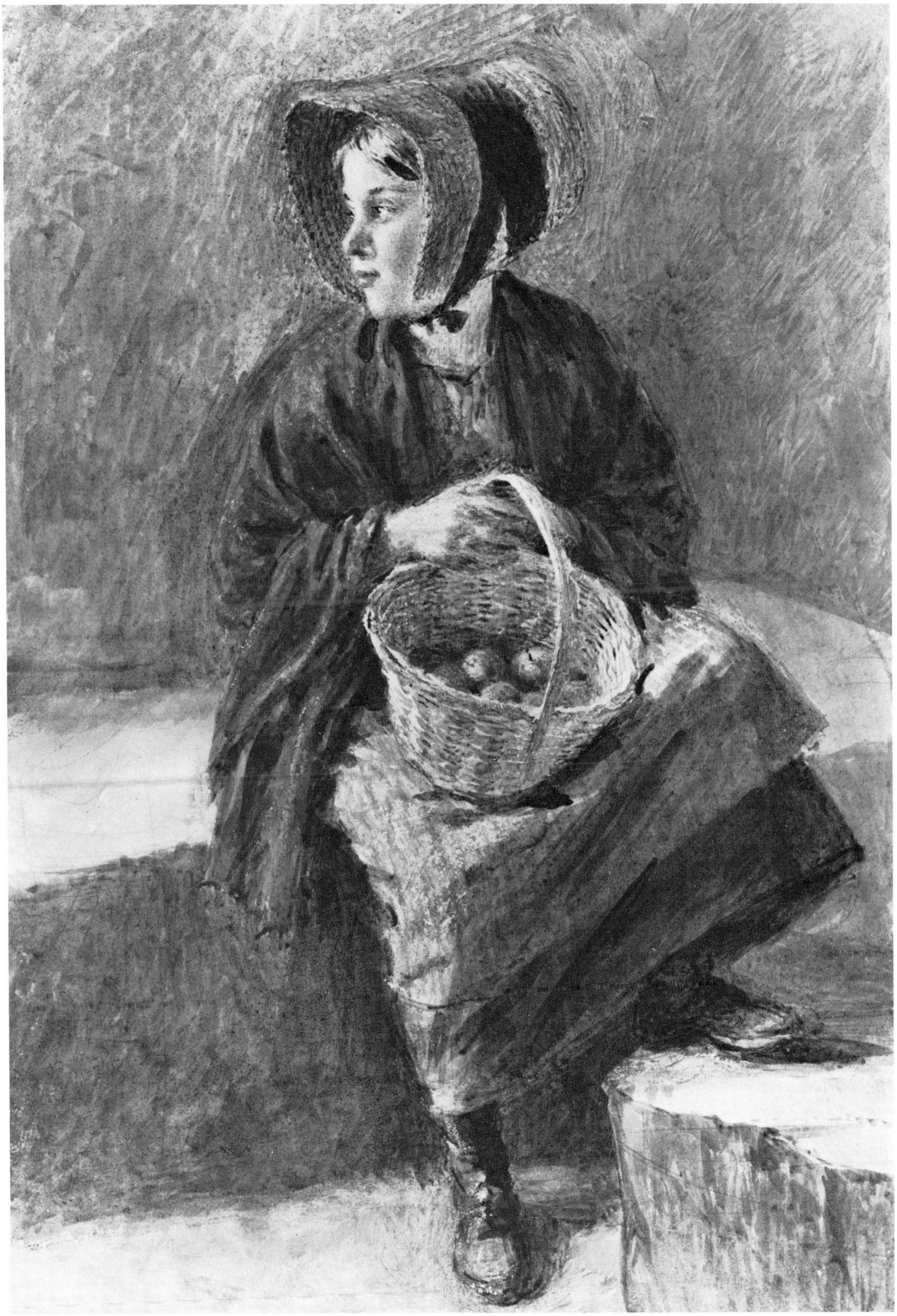

73 (328) The Young Apple Seller
Watercolour, $13\frac{5}{8} \times 9\frac{1}{2}$ (346 × 242)
Mr A. Cuthbertson, London

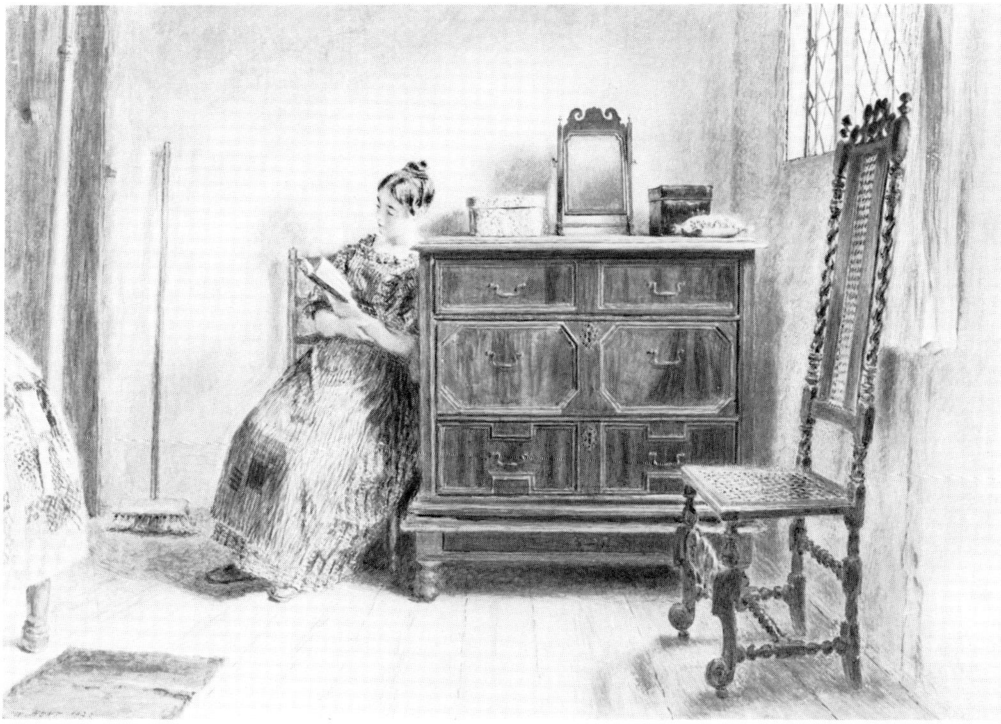

74 (407) Sunday Morning
Watercolour, $15\frac{3}{8} \times 21\frac{7}{8}$ (391 × 556); dated 1833
Huntington Library, San Marino

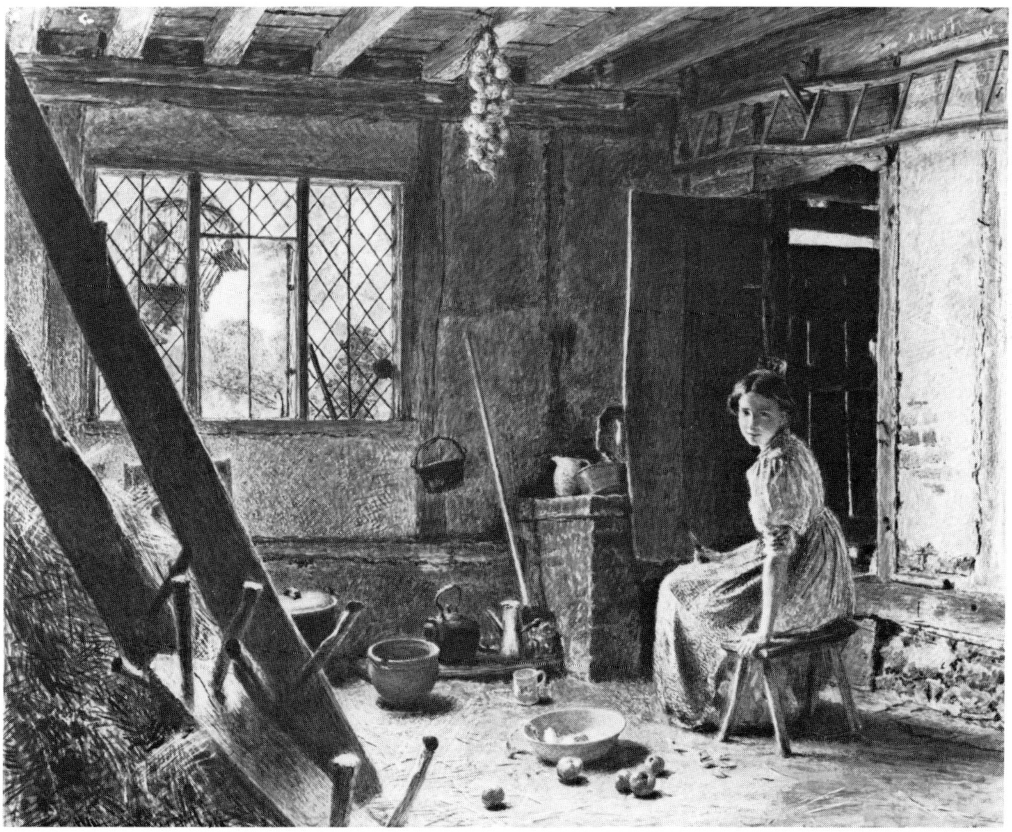

75 (267) The Maid and the Magpie
Watercolour slightly heightened with white, $17\frac{3}{8} \times 22\frac{3}{8}$ (441 × 569)
Bedford, Cecil Higgins Art Gallery

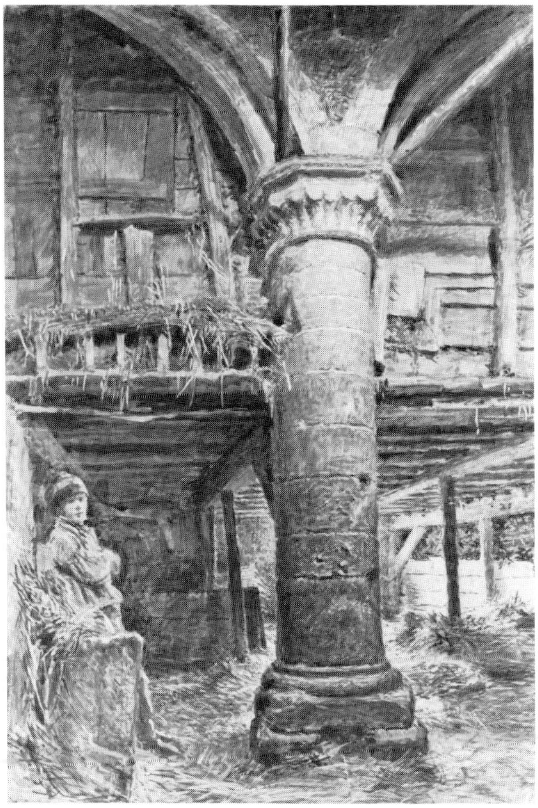

76 (472) In Val Crucis Abbey: The Interior used as a Barn
Pencil and watercolour heightened with white with
surface scratching, $23\frac{3}{8} \times 15\frac{3}{4}$ (593 × 402); dated 1836
Oxford, Ashmolean Museum

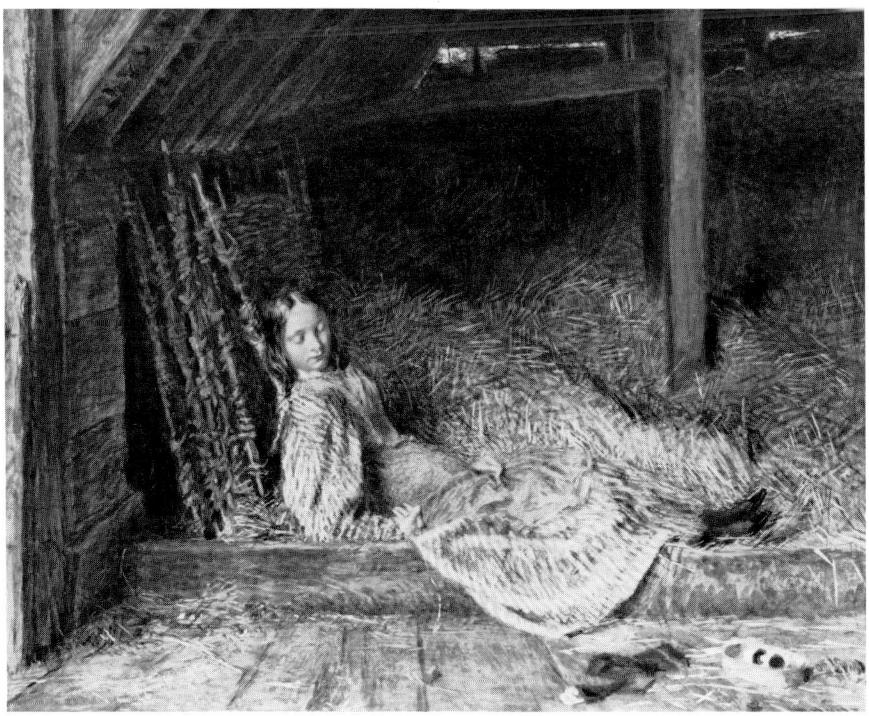

77 (274) Slumber
Watercolour, $13\frac{5}{8} \times 16\frac{7}{8}$ (342 × 428)
Birmingham, City Museum and Art Gallery

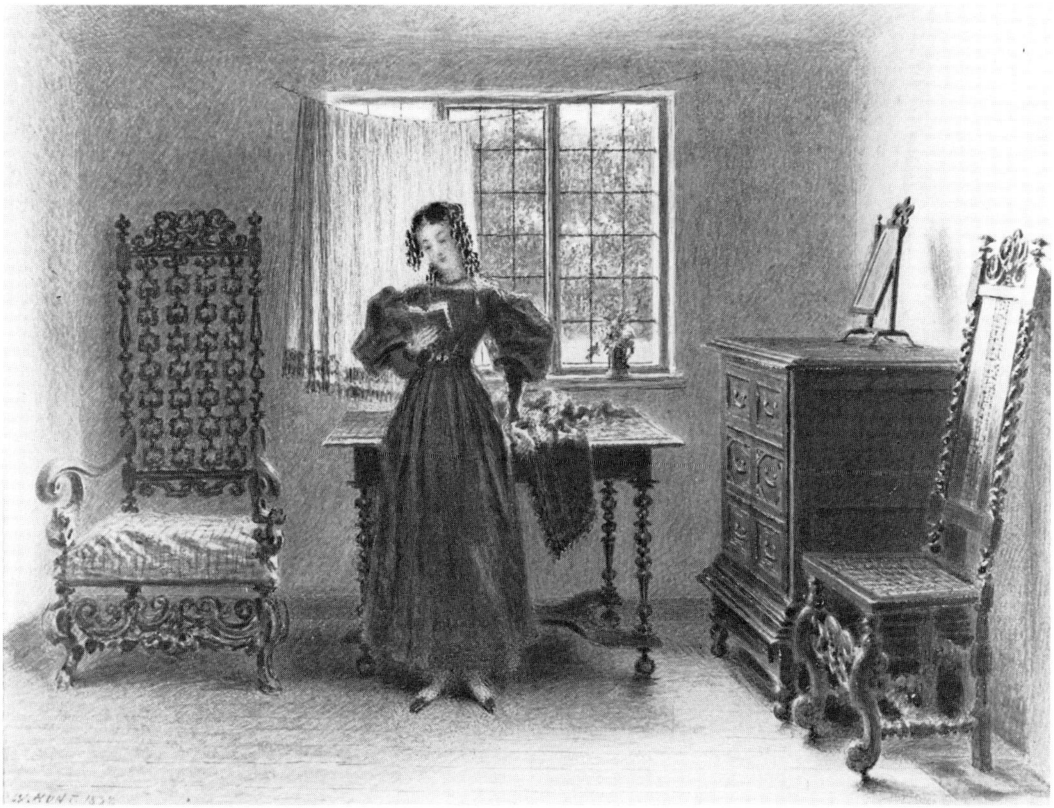

78 (458) Girl Reading at a Window
Watercolour, 8 × 10½ (203 × 267); dated 1832
The Duke of Norfolk, Arundel Castle

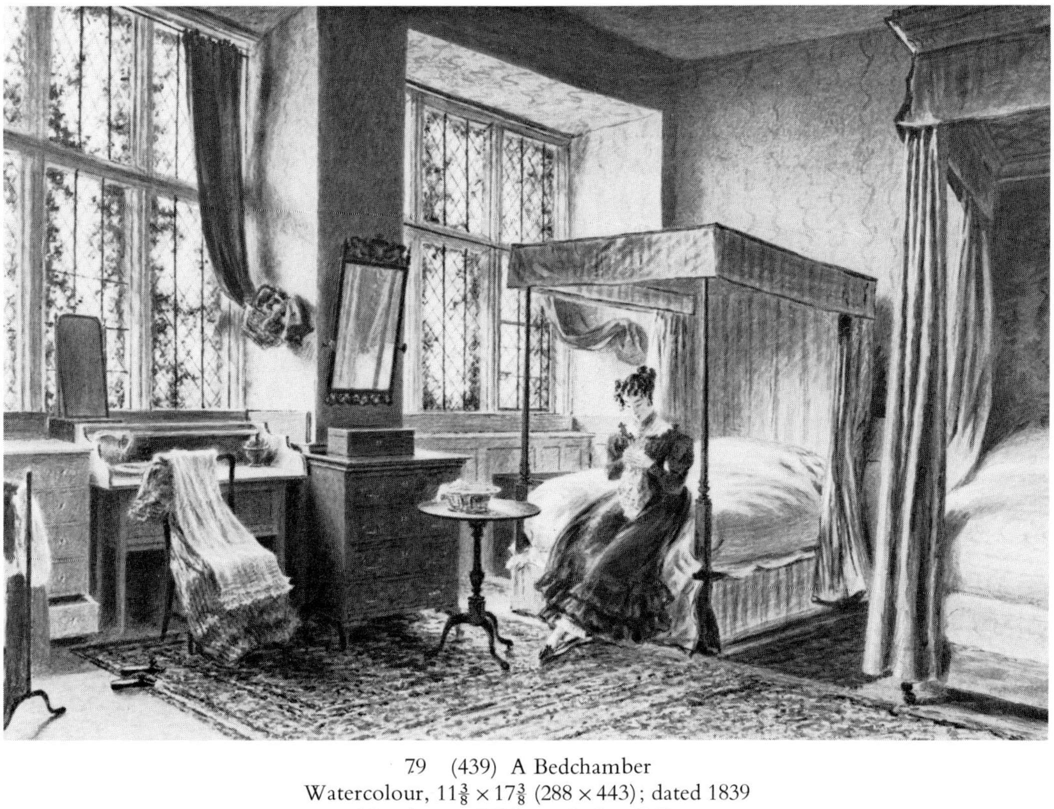

79 (439) A Bedchamber
Watercolour, 11⅜ × 17⅜ (288 × 443); dated 1839
Manchester, Whitworth Art Gallery

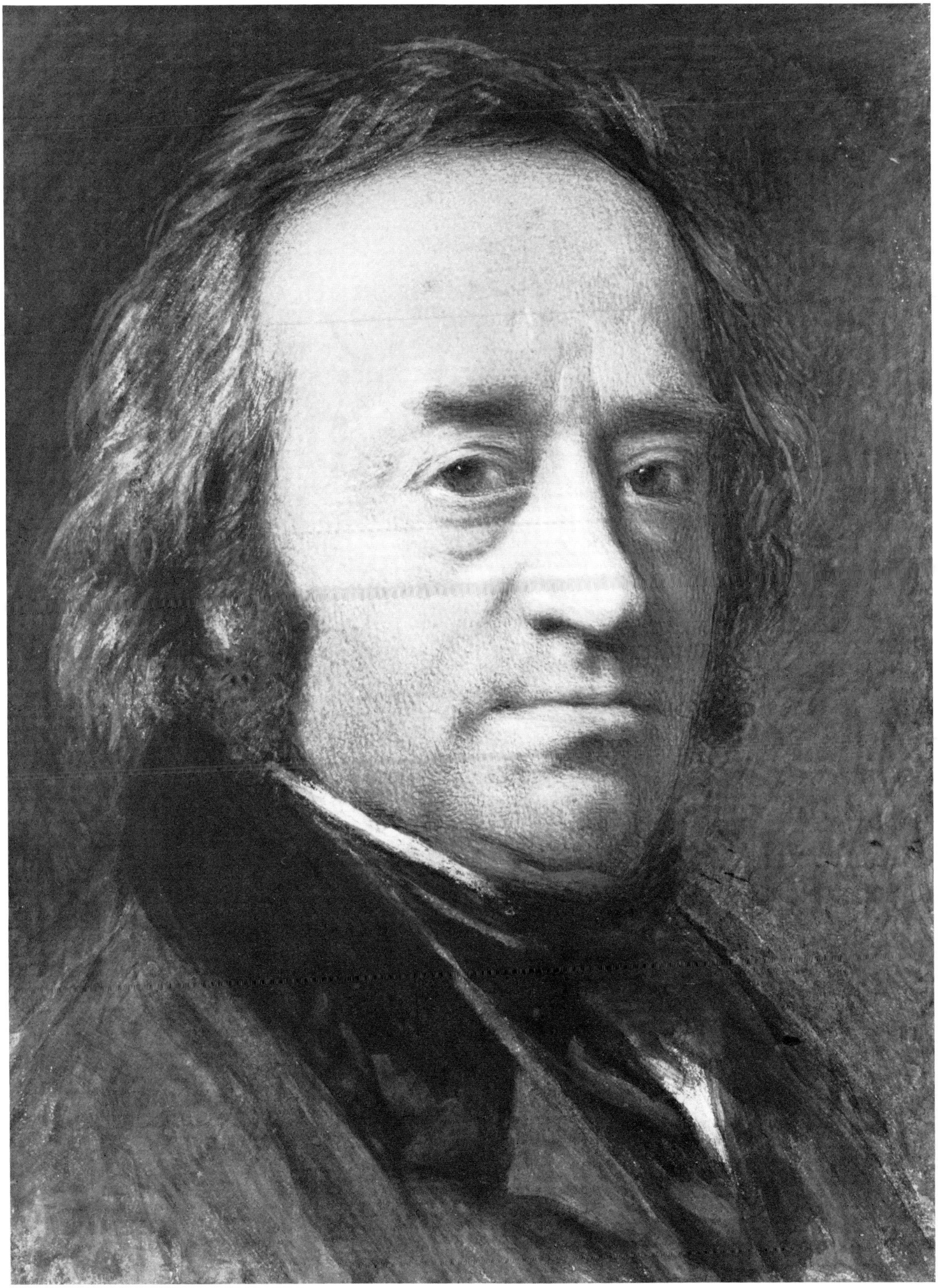

80 (451) Self Portrait
Watercolour, $14\frac{3}{4} \times 11$ (374×279)
National Portrait Gallery, London

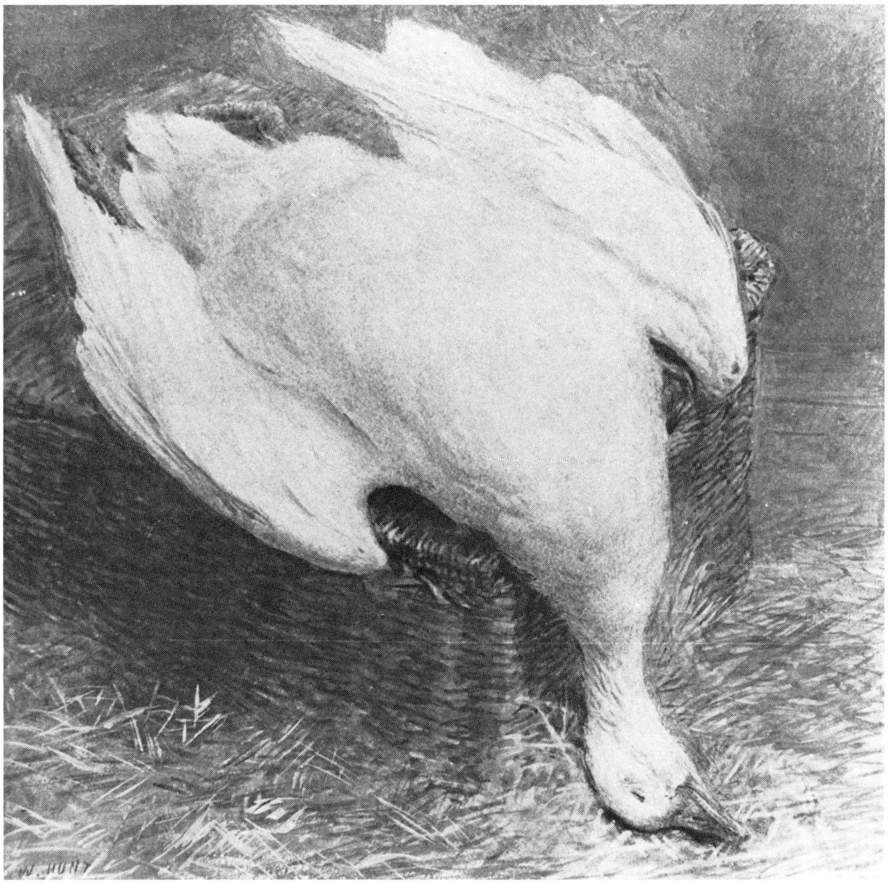

81 (593) Still Life of Slaughtered Goose and Basket
Watercolour heightened with white, $10\frac{1}{4} \times 10\frac{1}{4}$ (261×261)
Bolton, Museum and Art Gallery

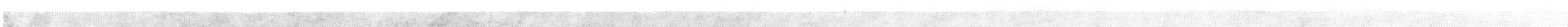

82 (763) Carrots, Celery, Mushrooms, Cheese and a Jug
Watercolour slightly heightened with white, $6\frac{3}{4} \times 12\frac{1}{2}$ (173×318)
Witt Collection

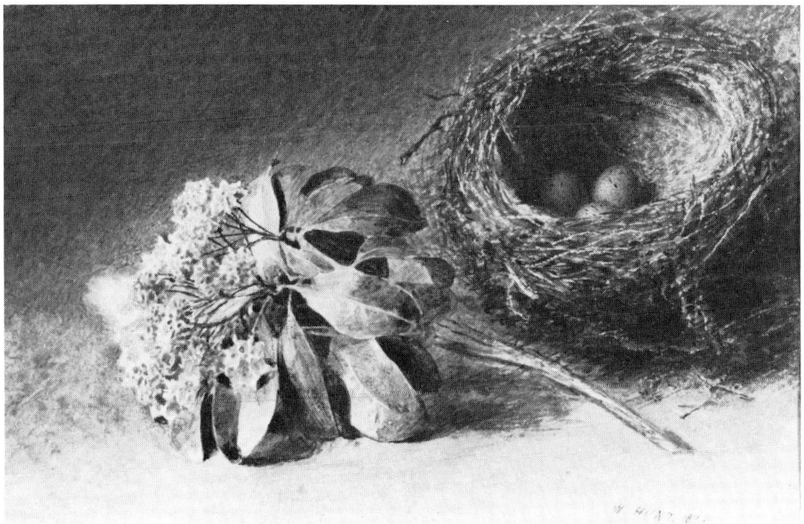

83 (675) Bird's Nest with Blossom
Watercolour heightened with white, $7\frac{1}{2} \times 12$ (191 × 305); dated 1831
Newcastle-upon-Tyne, Laing Art Gallery

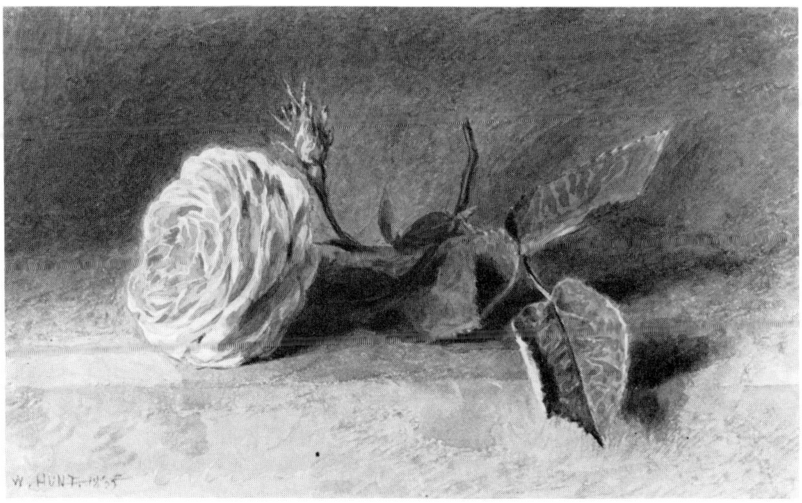

84 (614) Study of a Rose
Watercolour heightened with white, $5\frac{3}{8} \times 9\frac{1}{4}$ (138 × 235); dated 1835
Cambridge, Fitzwilliam Museum

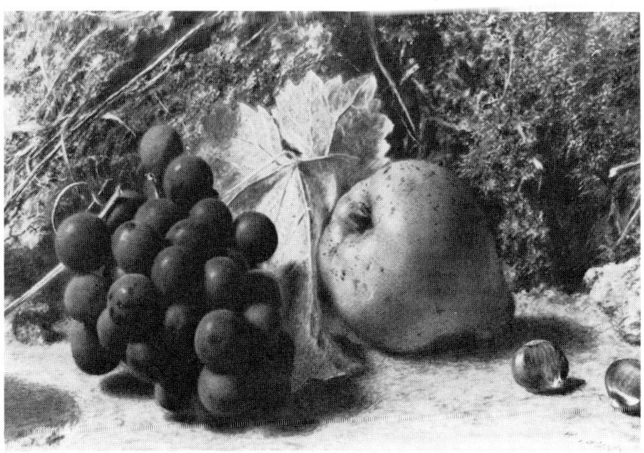

85 (586) Black Grapes and Pear
Watercolour on prepared ground, $7\frac{3}{4} \times 11$ (197 × 280)
Birmingham, City Museums and Art Gallery

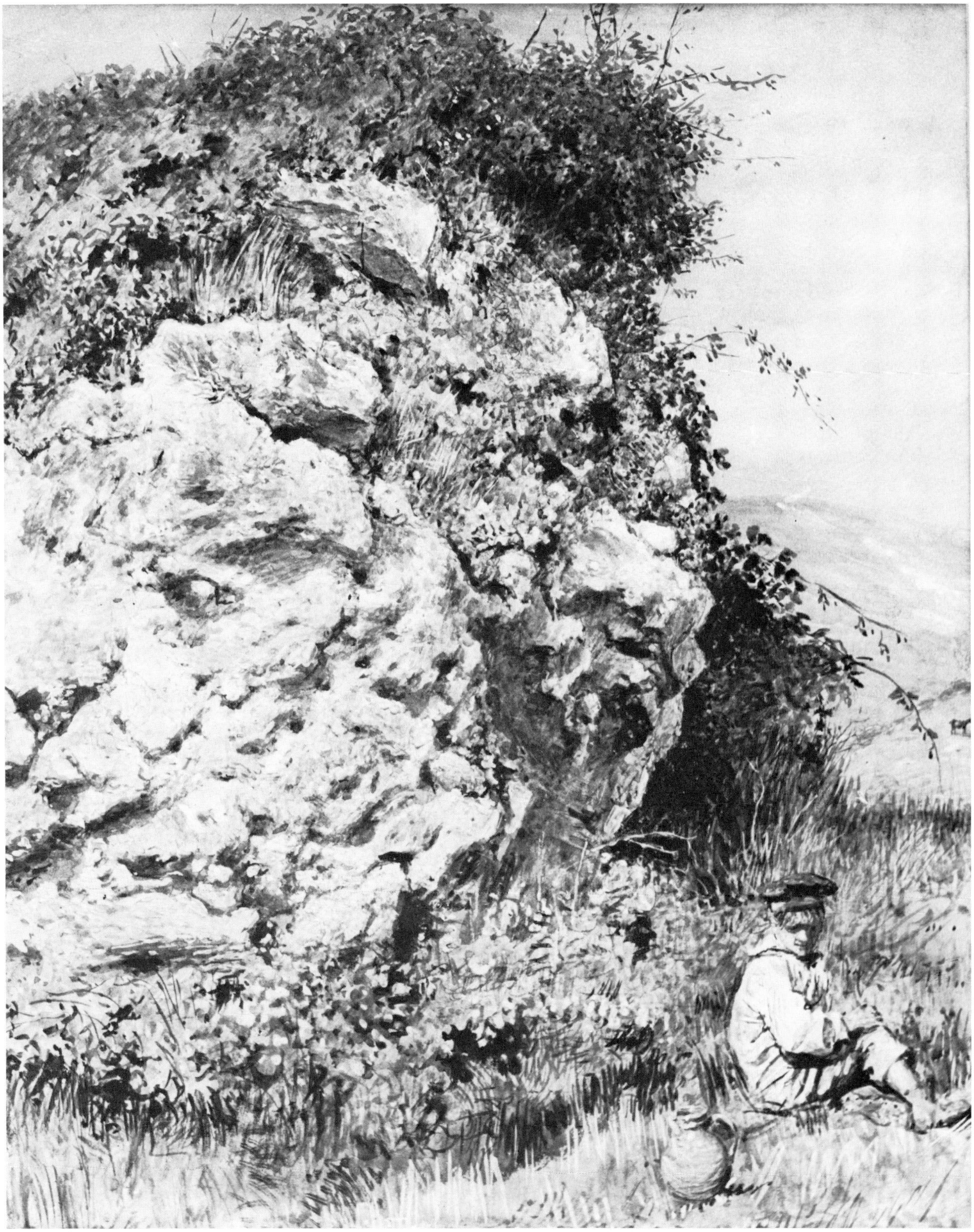

86 (145) Rock on the Downs near Hastings
Watercolour, $24\frac{1}{2} \times 20$ (622 × 508)
Preston, Harris Museum and Art Gallery

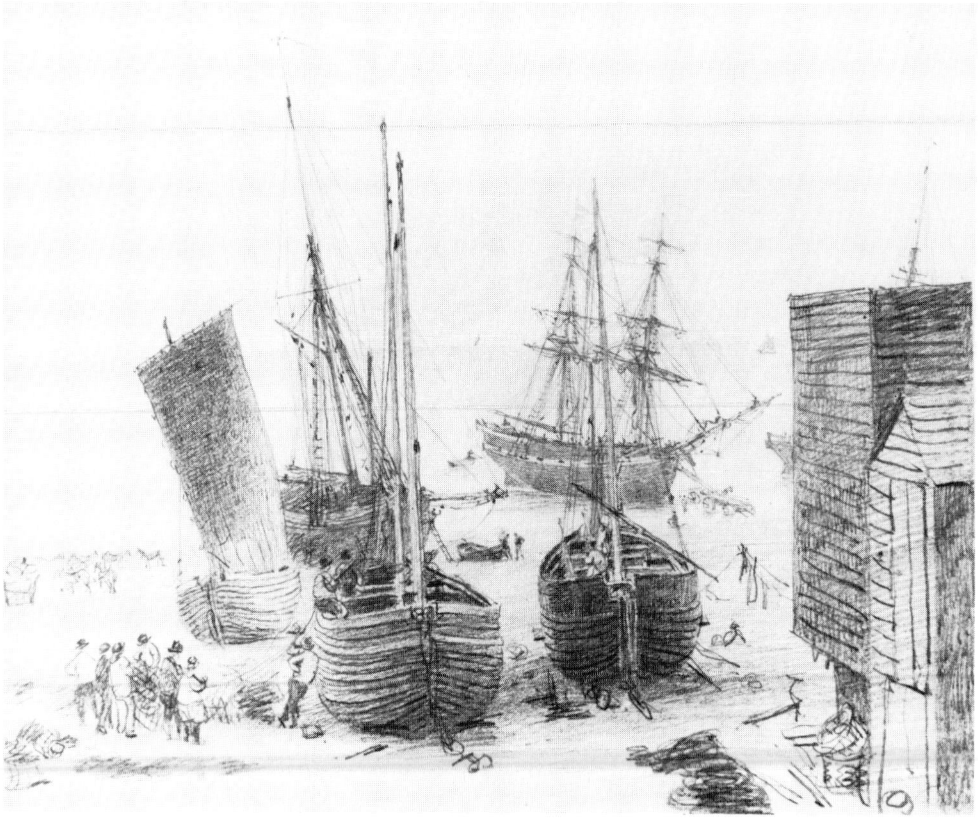

87 (219) Fishing Boats on the Beach at Hastings
Pencil, $8\frac{1}{8} \times 10$ (206 × 254)
Witt Collection

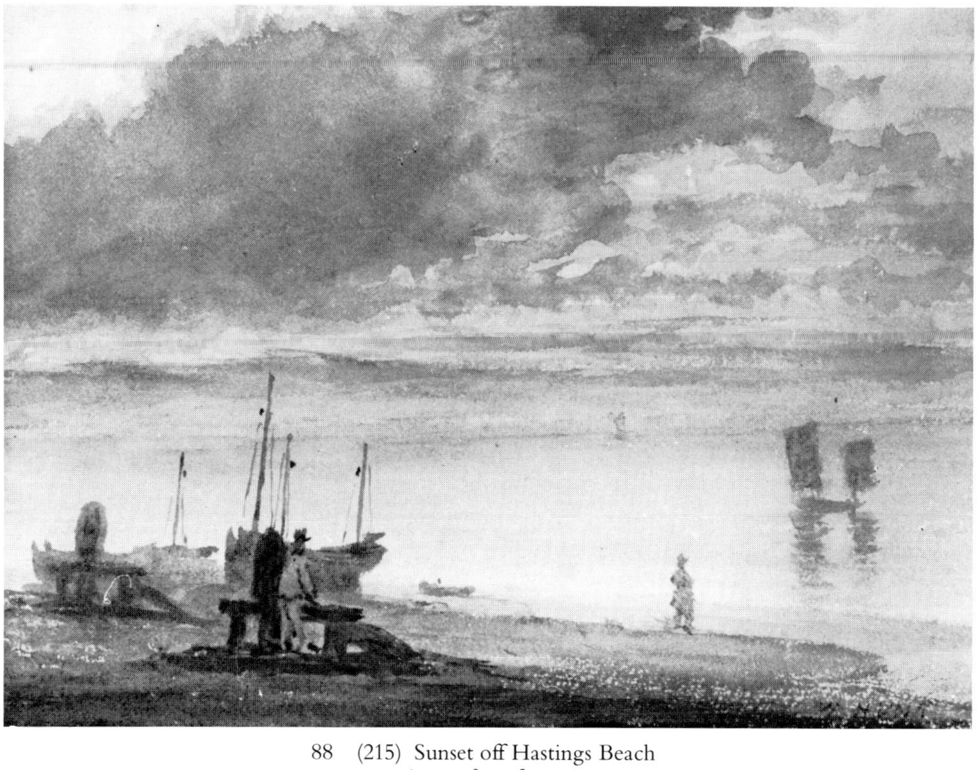

88 (215) Sunset off Hastings Beach
Watercolour, $4\frac{3}{4} \times 6\frac{5}{8}$ (121 × 167)
Witt Collection

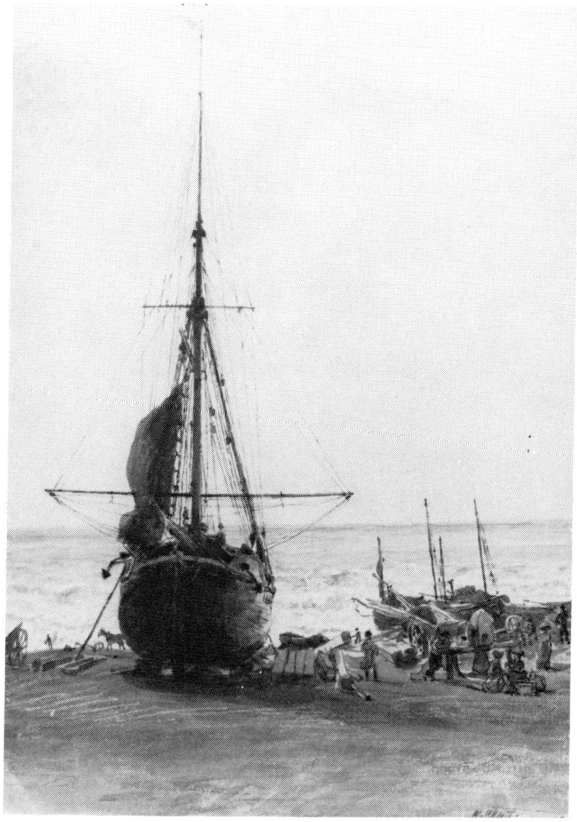

89 (105) Fishing Smack
Pencil, pen, ink and watercolour, $14\frac{5}{8} \times 10\frac{1}{4}$ (377 × 261)
Leeds, City Art Gallery

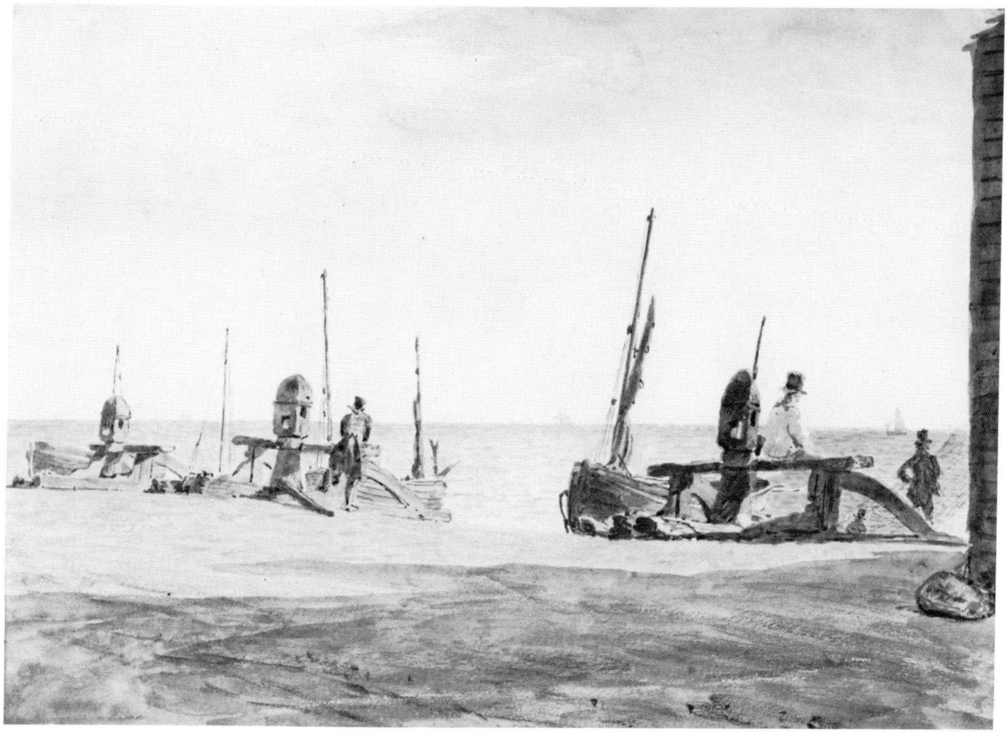

90 (99) Hastings Beach
Watercolour, $9\frac{1}{4} \times 12\frac{3}{4}$ (235 × 323)
Huntington Library, San Marino

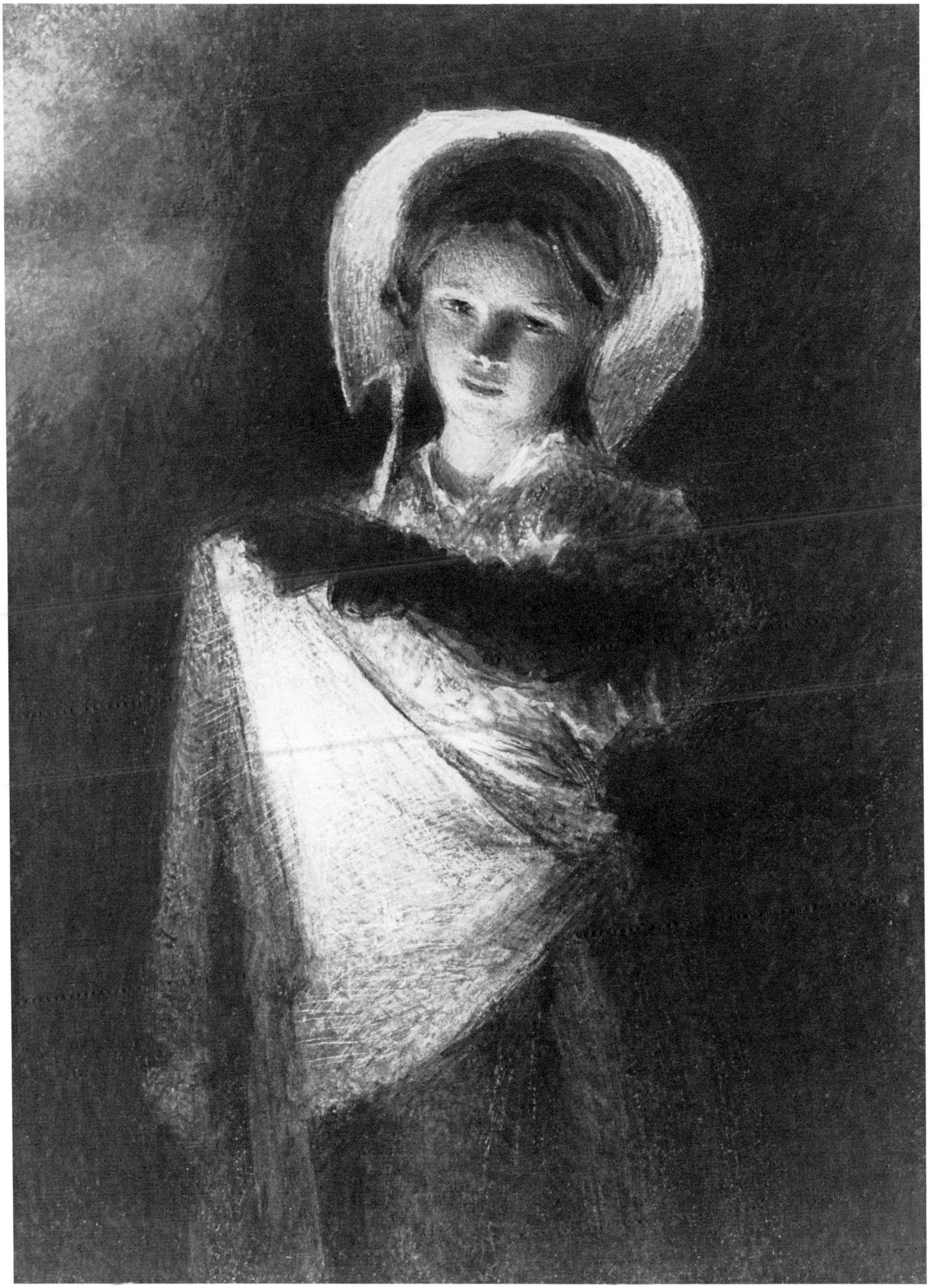

91 (399) Light and Shade
Watercolour heightened with white, 13 × 9½ (330 × 242)
Huddersfield, Libraries and Museum

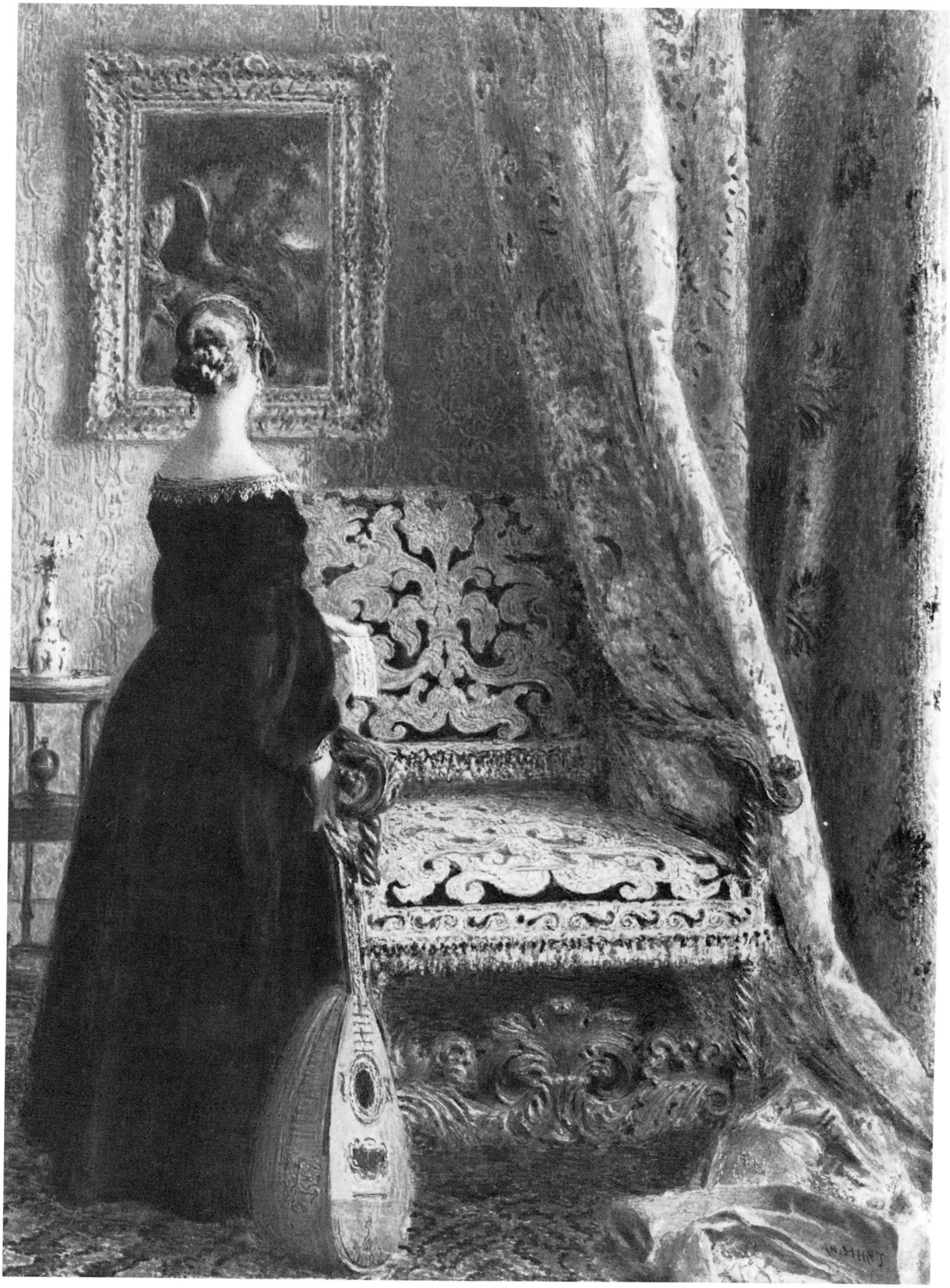

92 (390) Interior
Watercolour heightened with white, $17\frac{1}{8} \times 12\frac{3}{4}$ (434 × 323)
Glasgow, Art Gallery and Museum

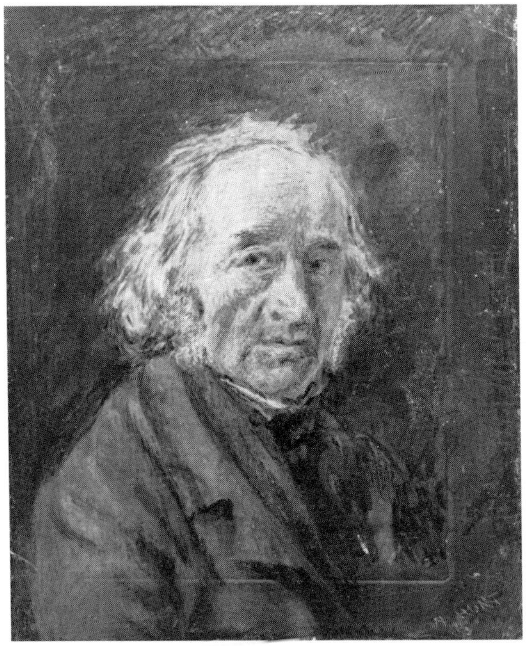

93 (452) Self Portrait
Oil on paper stuck on card, $5\frac{1}{4} \times 4\frac{1}{4}$ (135 × 110)
National Portrait Gallery, London

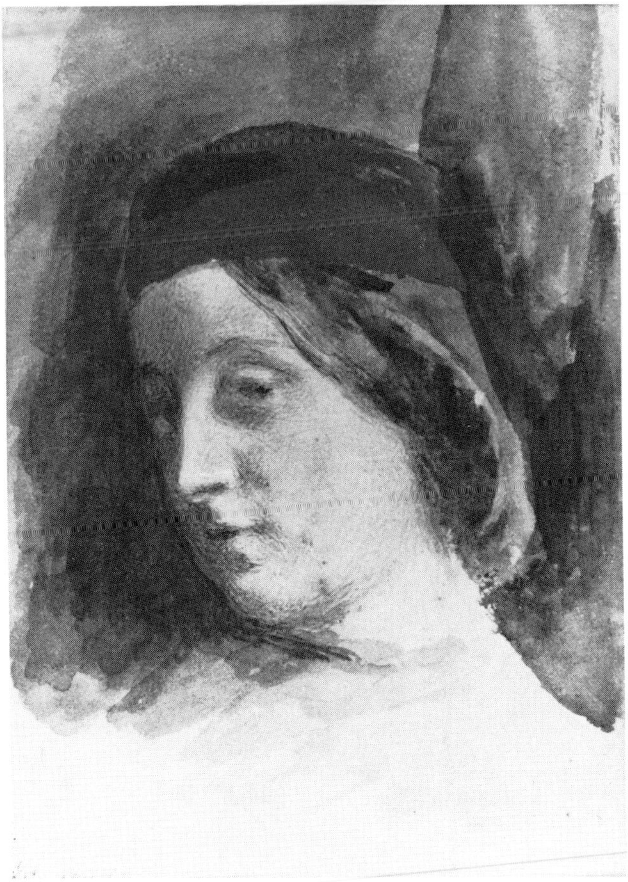

94 (557) Portrait of his Daughter
Watercolour heightened with white, $5\frac{1}{8} \times 3\frac{3}{8}$ (130 × 86)
Witt Collection

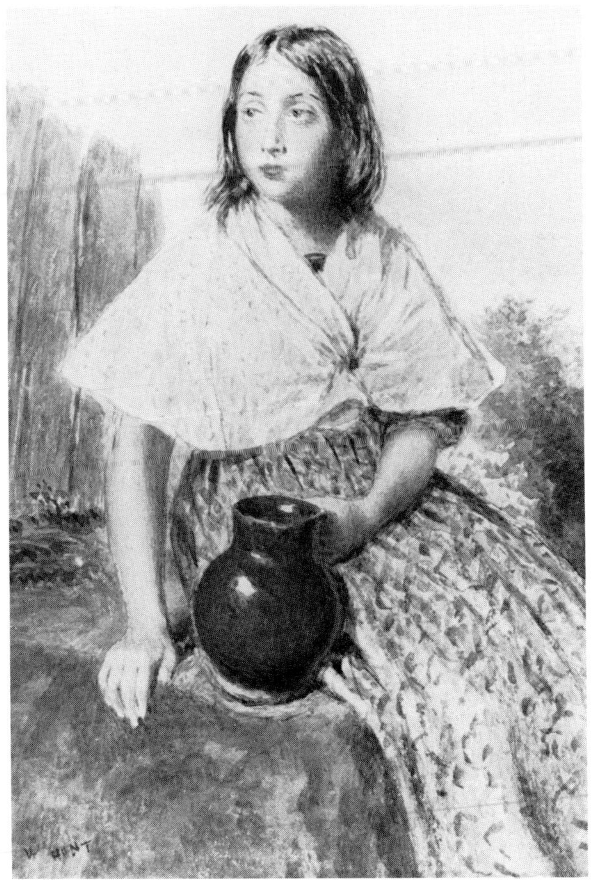

95 (518) The Artist's Daughter Holding a Jug
Watercolour, $10\frac{1}{2} \times 7\frac{1}{8}$ (267 × 182)
Mrs G. M. Tuff, London

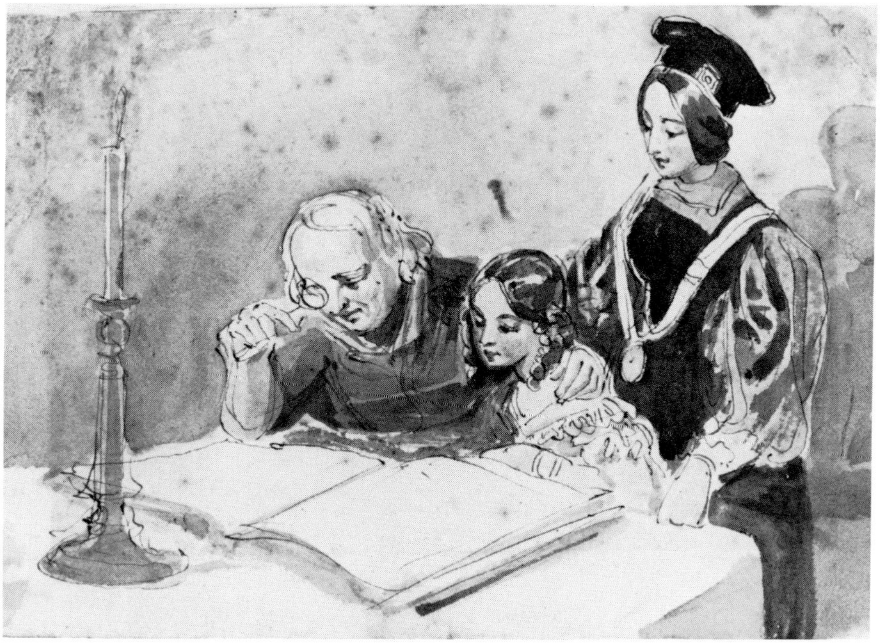

96 (535) Portrait of the Artist, his Daughter and Niece
Pen, ink and watercolour, $4 \times 5\frac{5}{8}$ (102×143)
Victoria and Albert Museum, London

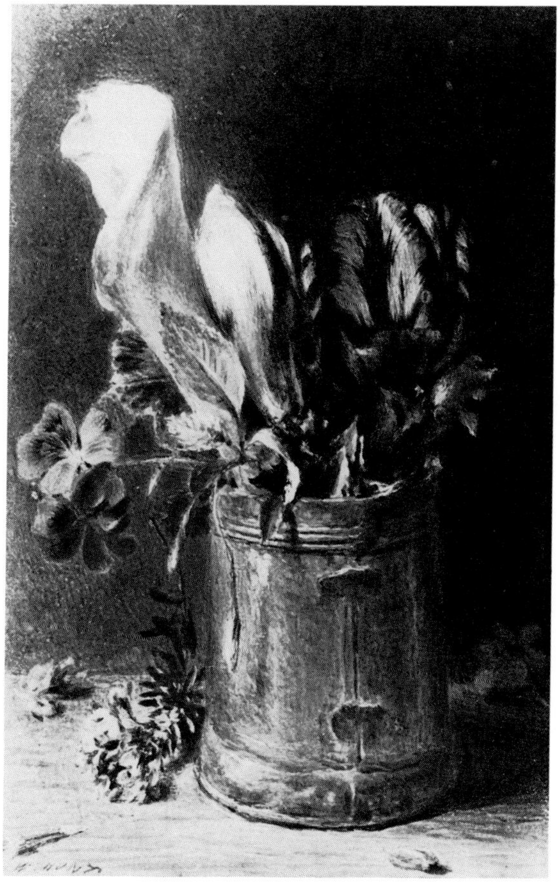

97 (633) Flowers in a Pewter Mug
Watercolour heightened with white,
$10\frac{5}{8} \times 6\frac{7}{8}$ (270×175)
Fry Collection

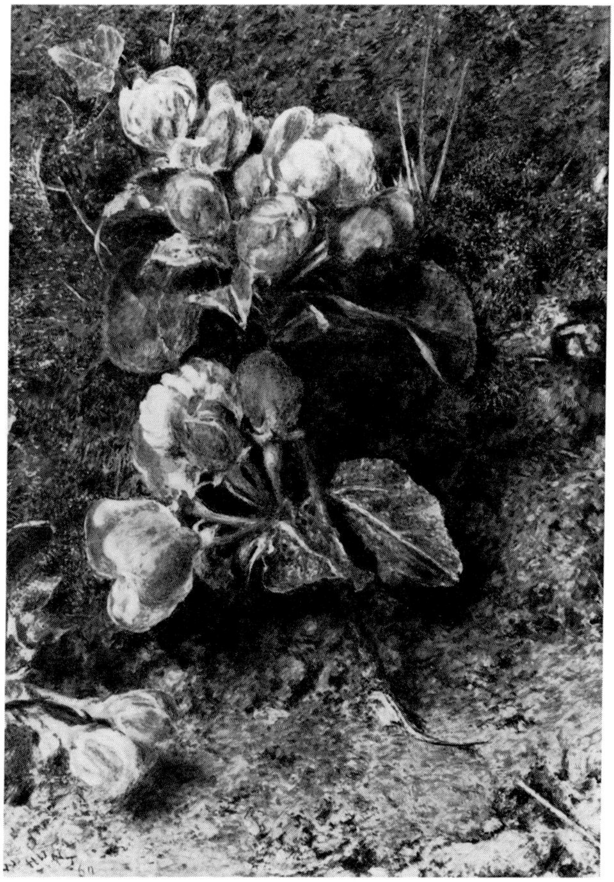

98 (728) Blossom
Watercolour heightened with white, $7\frac{3}{4} \times 5\frac{1}{2}$ (197×140);
dated 1860
Sheffield, Graves Art Gallery

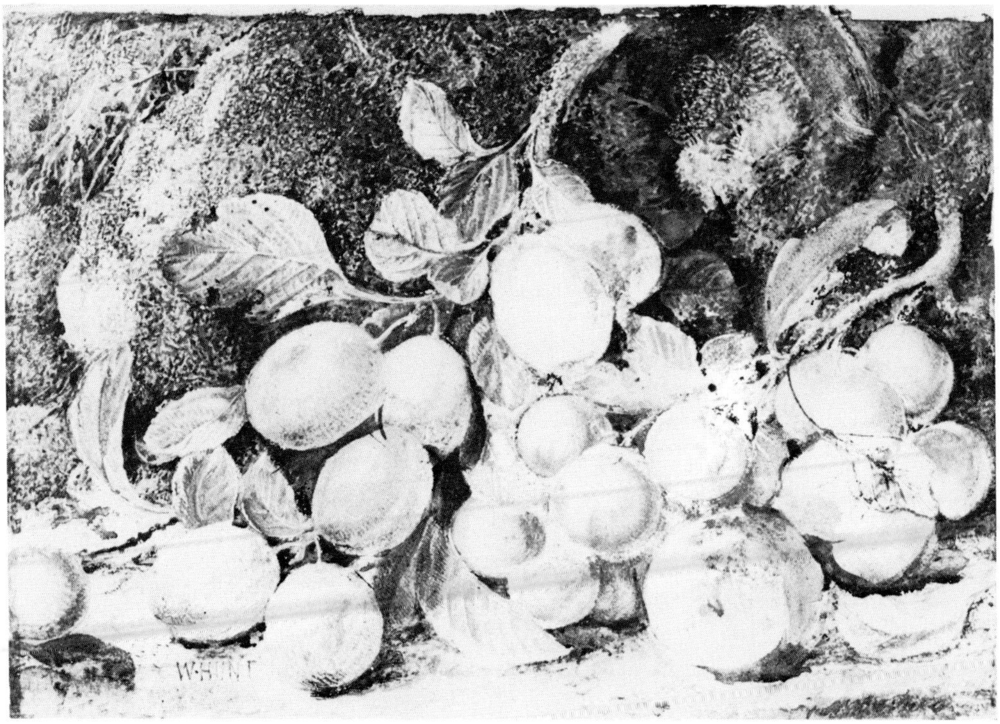

99 (626) Fruit
Watercolour on prepared ground, 9½ × 13 (242 × 330); unfinished
Dudley, Art Gallery

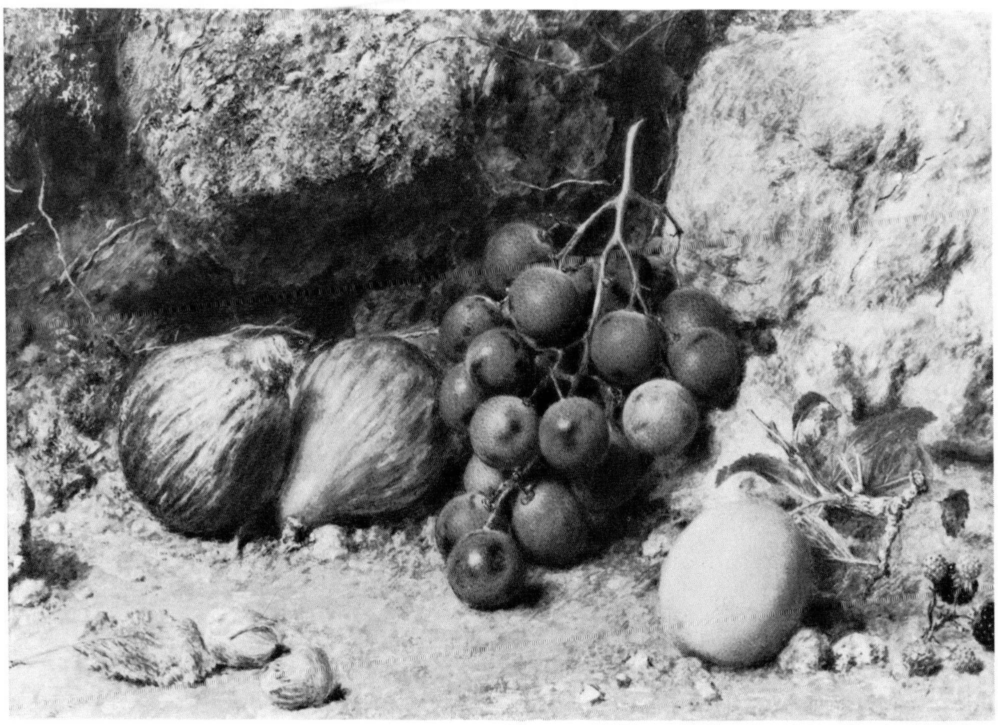

100 (616) Study of Fruit
Watercolour on prepared ground, 8 × 11½ (203 × 292)
Cambridge, Fitzwilliam Museum

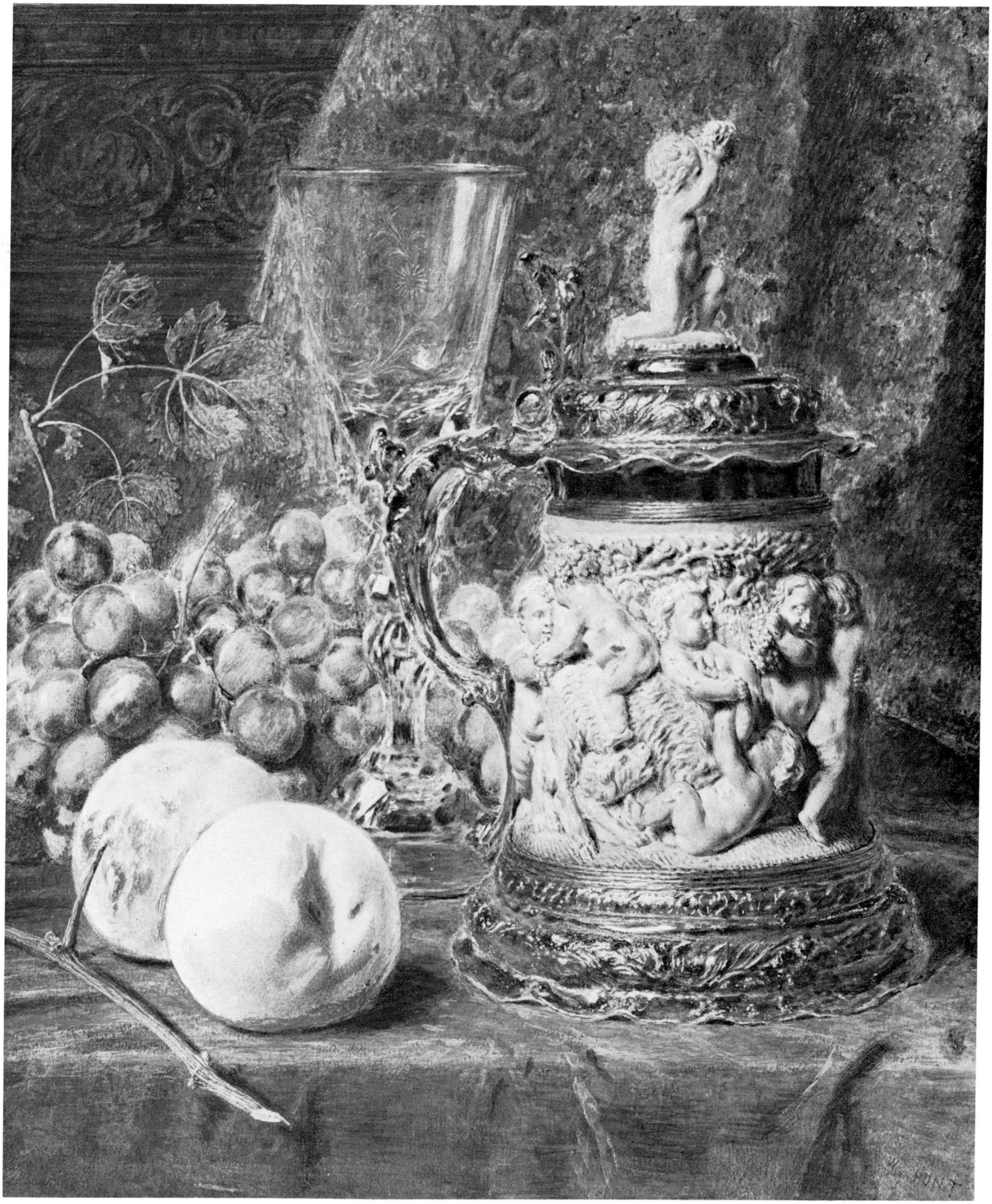

101 (668) Fruit and Tankard
Watercolour on prepared ground, $14\frac{3}{8} \times 12$ (366 × 306)
Manchester, Whitworth Art Gallery

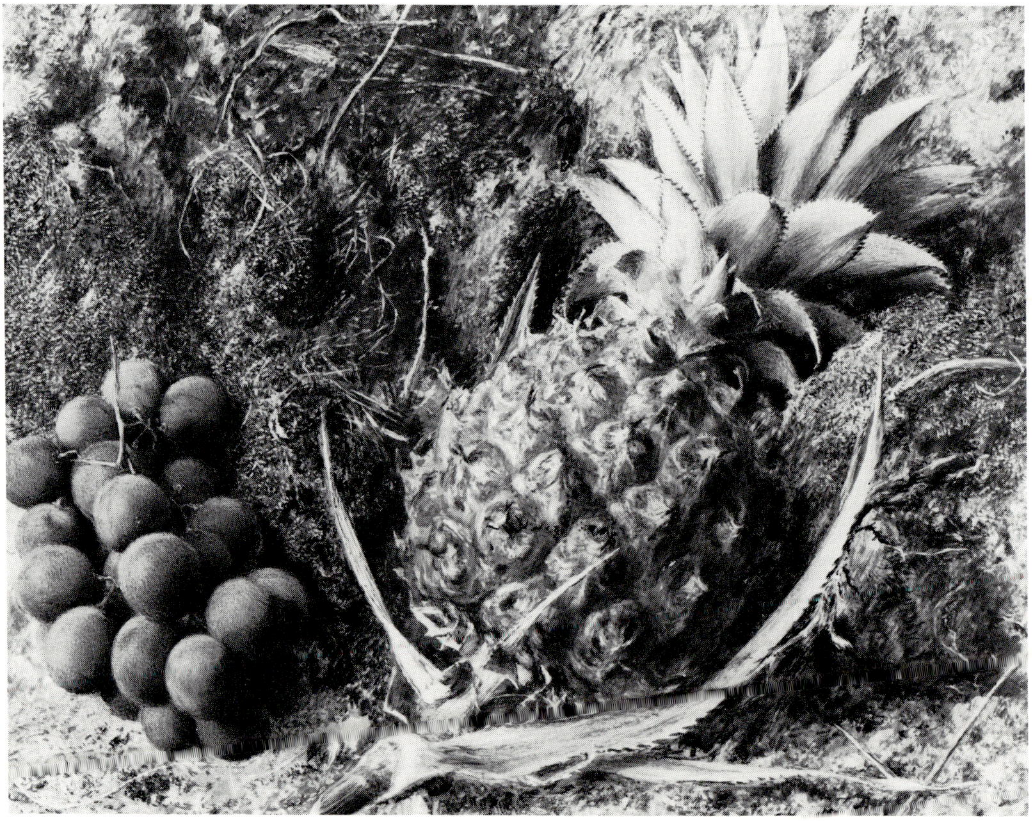

102 (726) Still Life: Grapes and Pineapple
Watercolour on prepared ground heightened with white, $8\frac{1}{8} \times 11$ (205 × 280)
Sheffield, Graves Art Gallery

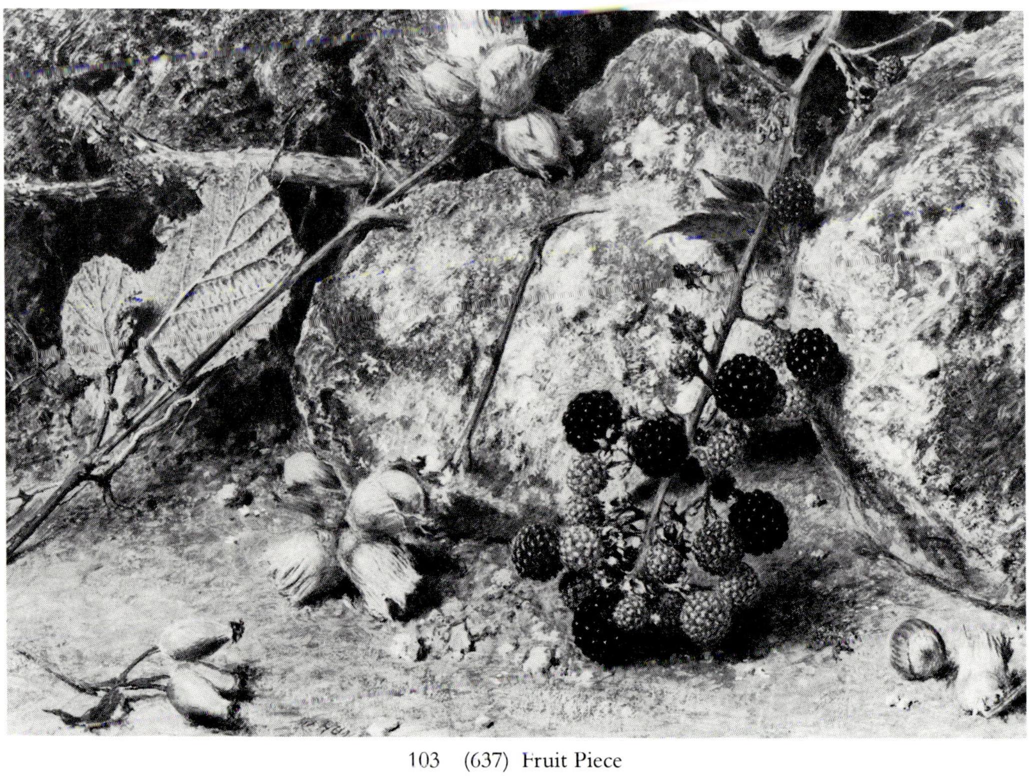

103 (637) Fruit Piece
Watercolour heightened with white, $8\frac{1}{4} \times 15\frac{1}{2}$ (209 × 395)
Gateshead, Shipley Art Gallery

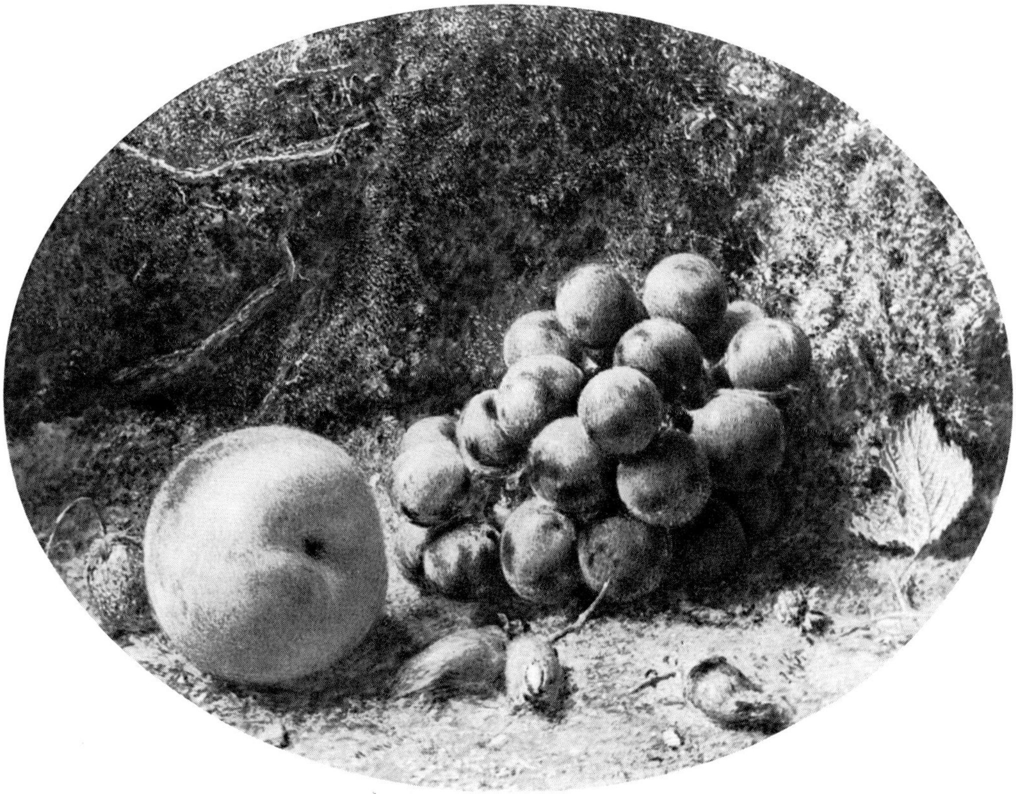

104 (599) Peach and Grapes
Watercolour on prepared ground, $8 \times 10\frac{3}{4}$ (203×273) oval
The Brantwood Trust, Brantwood, Coniston

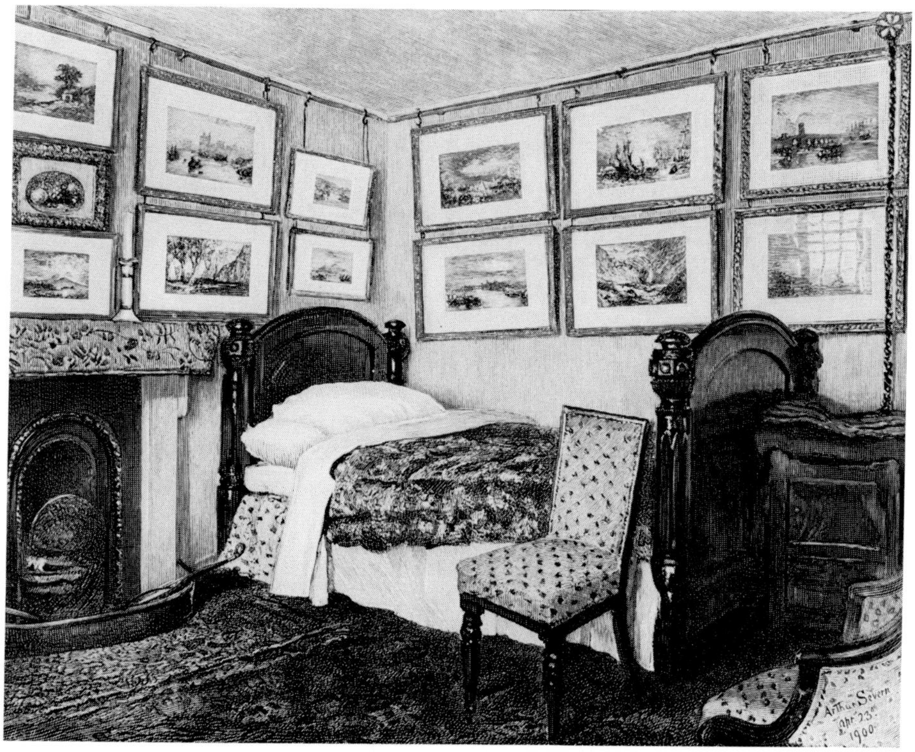

105 Ruskin's Bedroom at Brantwood – Engraving, April 1900
from a drawing by Arthur Severn. The middle watercolour above the fireplace is 'Peach and Grapes' (Plate 104)

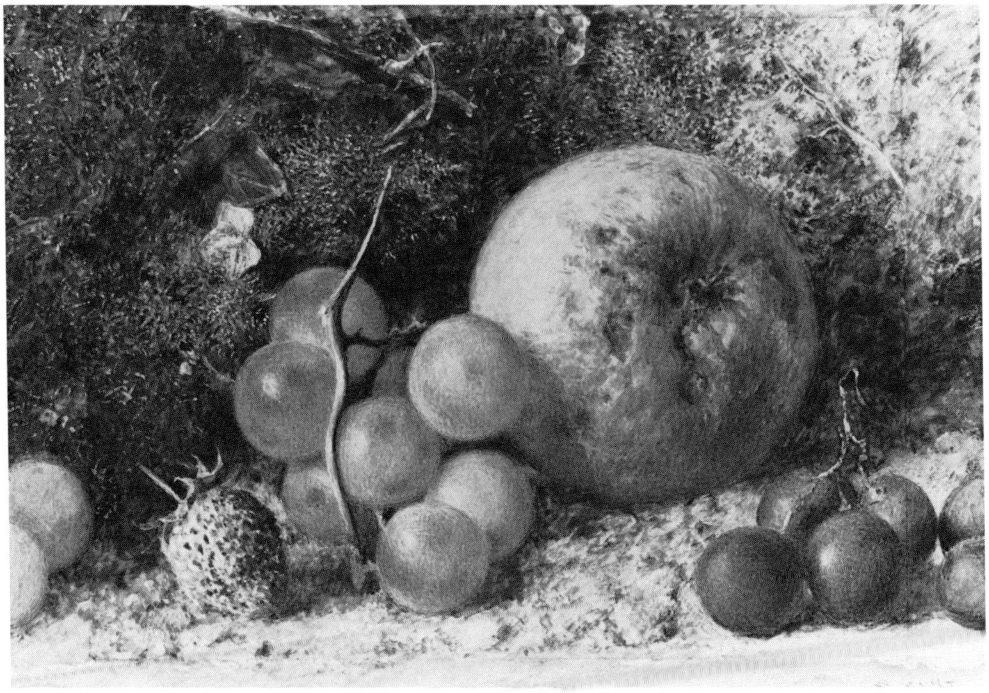

106 (673) Fruit Piece
Watercolour on prepared ground, $5\frac{1}{4} \times 7\frac{3}{4}$ (133 × 197)
National Museum of Wales, Cardiff

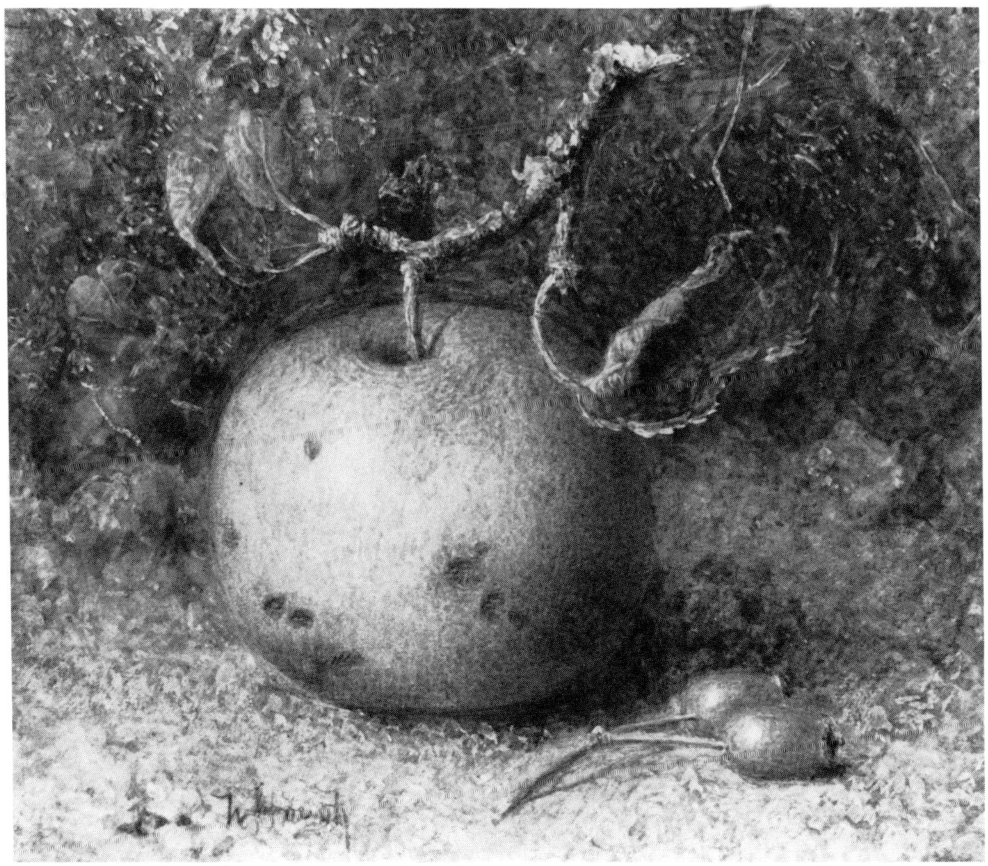

107 An Apple by William Hough
$4\frac{5}{8} \times 5\frac{1}{2}$ (117 × 140)
Witt Collection

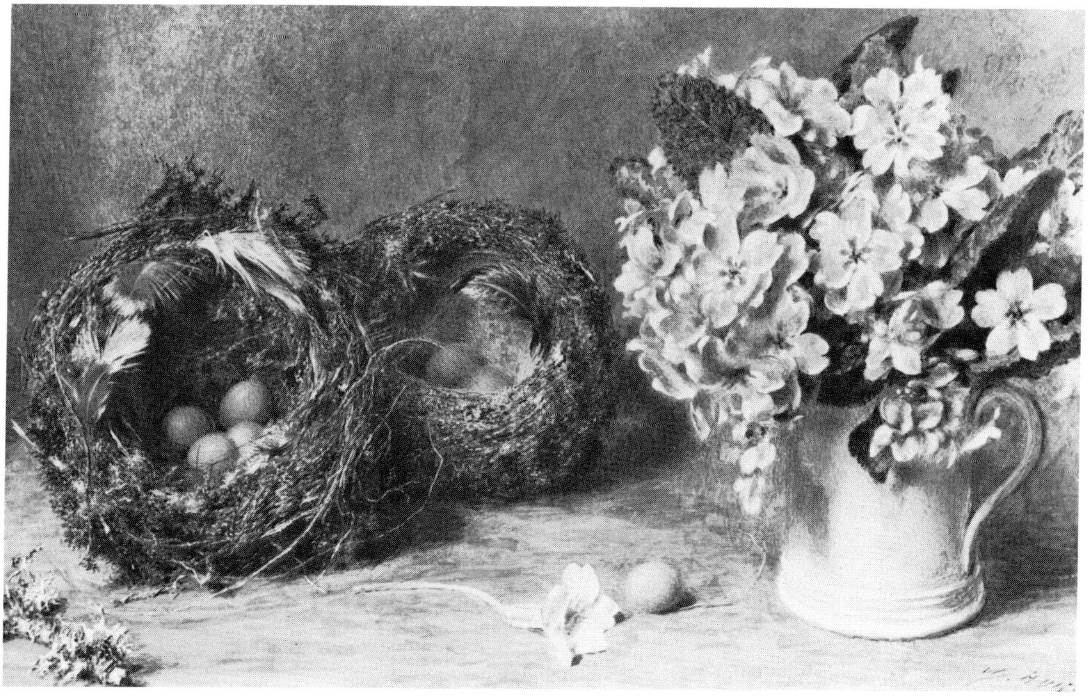

108 (658) Spring Flowers and Birds' Nests
Watercolour, $8\frac{1}{2} \times 13\frac{1}{2}$ (216 × 343)
Manchester, City Art Gallery

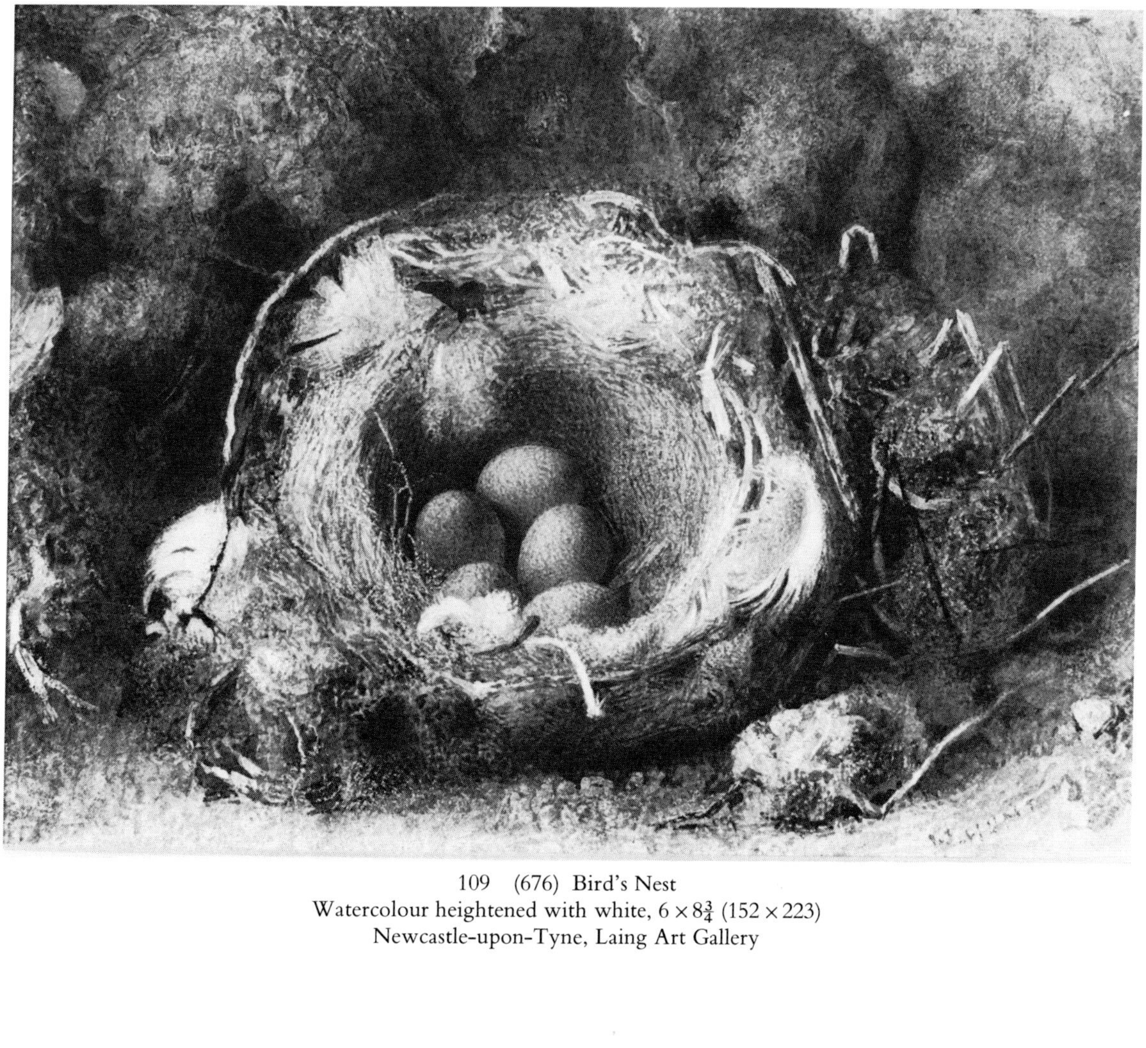

109 (676) Bird's Nest
Watercolour heightened with white, $6 \times 8\frac{3}{4}$ (152 × 223)
Newcastle-upon-Tyne, Laing Art Gallery

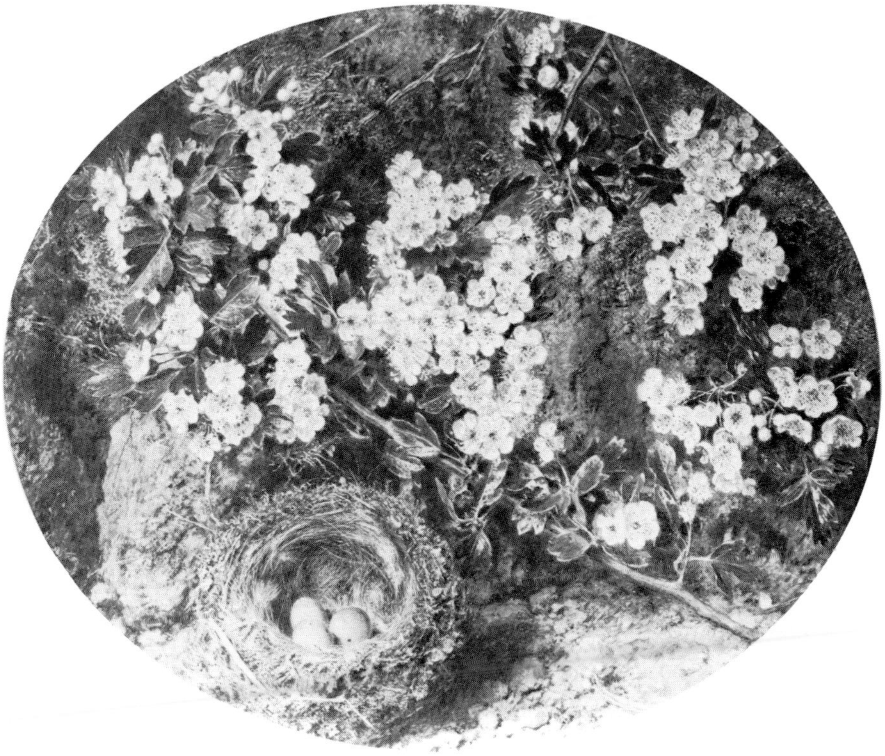

110 (659) Bird's Nest and Blossom
Watercolour heightened with white, $11\frac{1}{2} \times 13$ (293 × 330) oval
Manchester, City Art Gallery

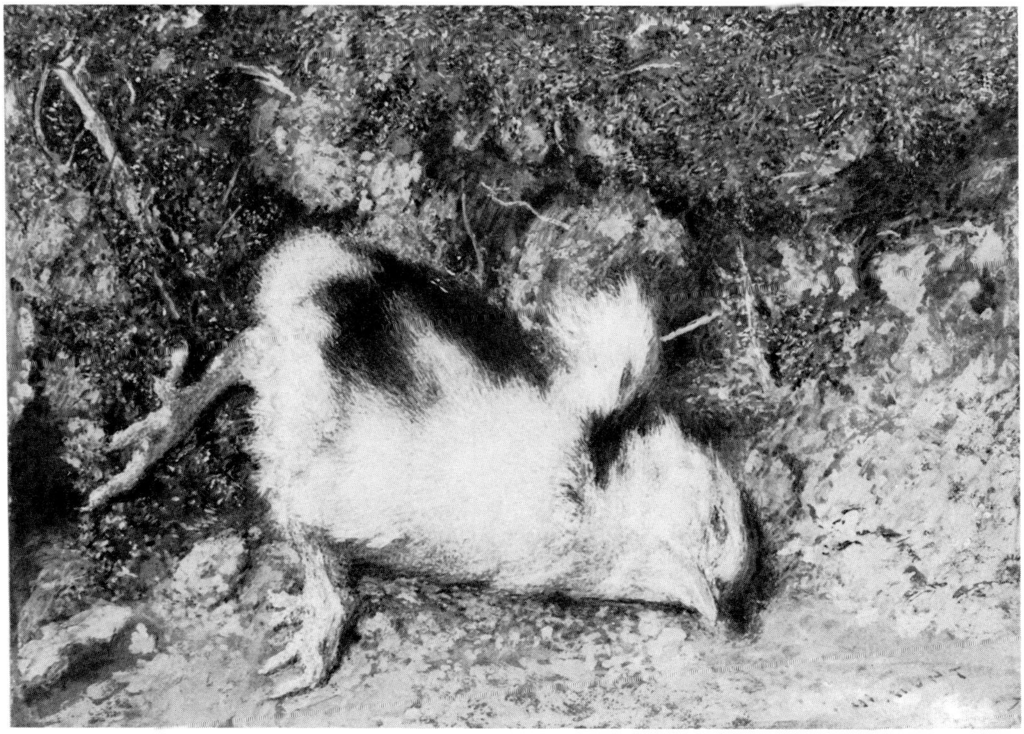

111 (653) John Ruskin's Dead Chick
Watercolour heightened with white, $4\frac{1}{4} \times 6\frac{1}{8}$ (108 × 154)
Liverpool, Walker Art Gallery

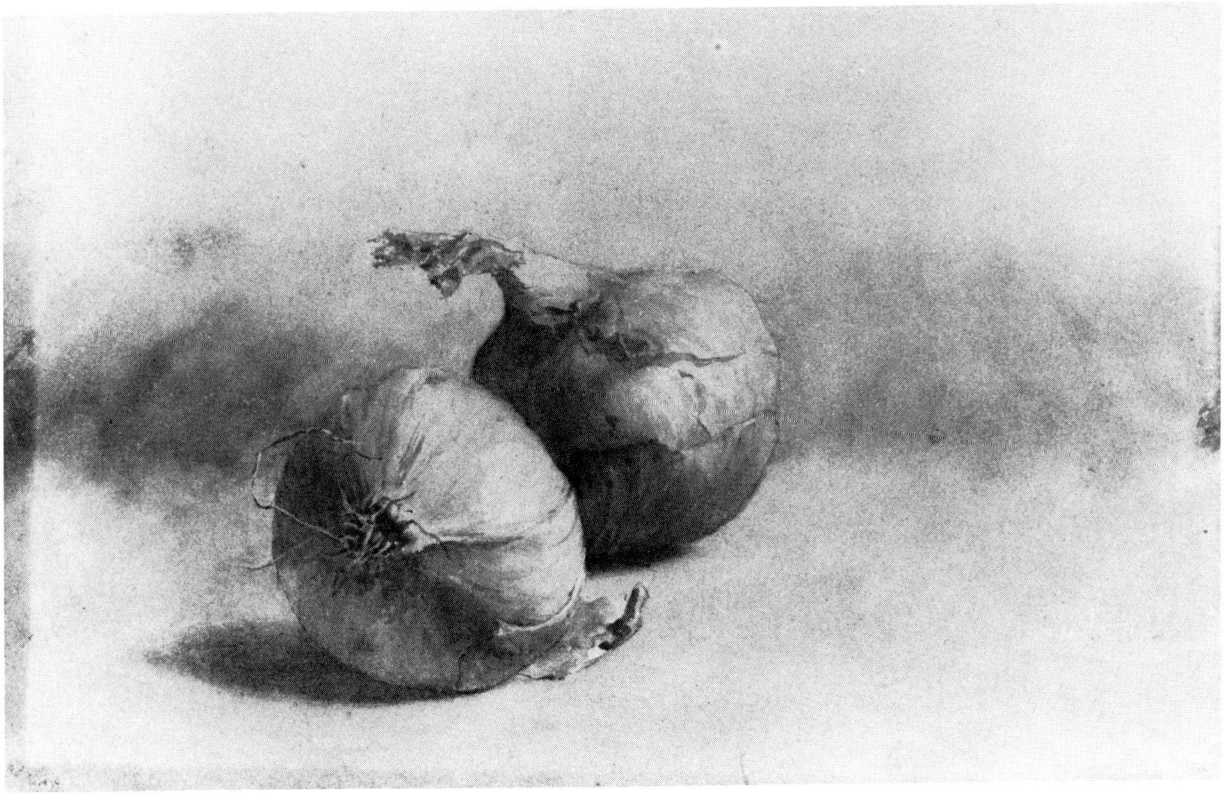

112 (630) Study of Two Onions
Watercolour, $5\frac{1}{2} \times 8\frac{1}{4}$ (145×220)
Fry Collection

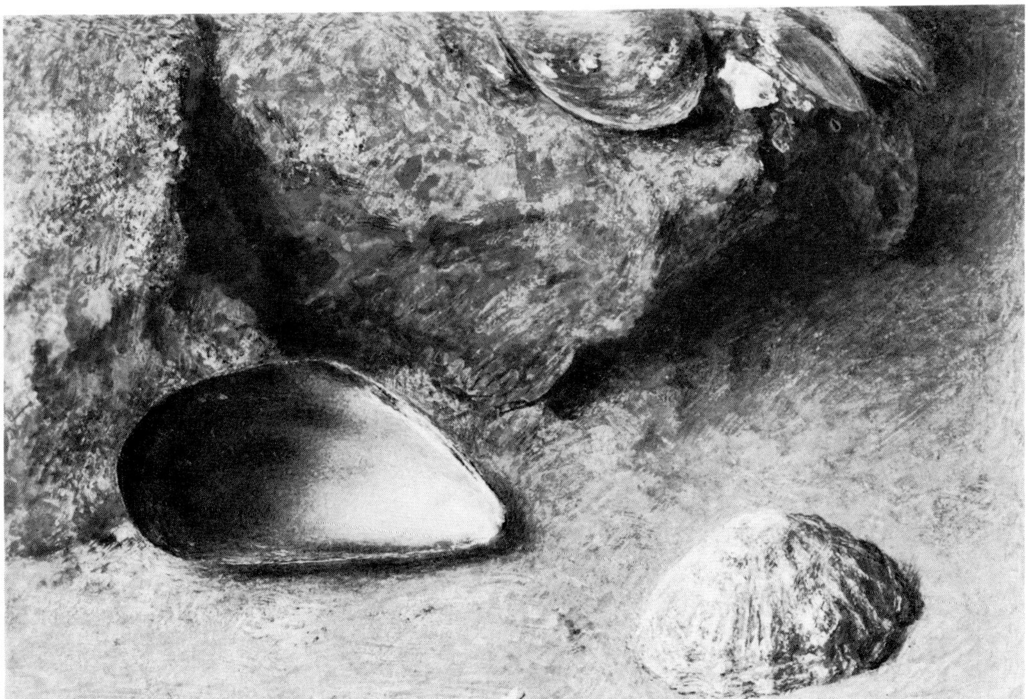

113 (620) Shells
Watercolour heightened with white, $4\frac{1}{2} \times 6\frac{1}{2}$ (114×165)
Cambridge, Mass., Fogg Art Museum, Harvard University:
Bequest — Grenville L. Winthrop

—PART II—

Catalogue

Basis of Catalogue and Abbreviations used

1. The Catalogue is arranged under the following three subject headings:

   1. LANDSCAPES (including seascapes, shore scenes and church interiors).
   2. FIGURES (including domestic interiors).
   3. STILL LIFE (including live animals and birds).

2. Entries under each subject heading are arranged, in the case of national collections and of public collections in London, alphabetically under the name of the collection; in the case of public collections elsewhere in the United Kingdom, under the place name of the town or city where the collection is situated; and in the case of public collections abroad, and all private collections, under the name of the collection or owner.

3. Where several works are owned by the same national, public or private collection the entries are arranged as far as possible in order of date.

4. Where a work is entered as dated in an individual year, e.g. 1830, it is:

   (i) if entered as 'Dated 1830', dated in that year by the artist himself, or
   (ii) if entered as 'Exh. 1830', exhibited in that year at the Society of Painters in Water-Colours (the Old Water-Colour Society) (see Part III, Section 1), or
   (iii) if entered as '*c.*1830' is regarded by the compiler either on documentary evidence or on stylistic grounds as executed circa that date.

   Where the work is not entered under (i), (ii) or (iii) above, it is entered under either five- or ten-yearly periods, e.g. '1830–35' or '1830–40'.

   Where the work is not entered under any date or period, it is to be regarded as undated and the entry is included at the end of the list of the relevant owner's works.

5. In some respects it would have been advantageous for the entries under each subject heading to have been made chronologically. However, the dating of Hunt's work presents considerable difficulty, which is increased by the fact that he dated comparatively few of his works, and also that throughout his career he repeated his particularly successful and sought-after works almost exactly and often in the same original style. Moreover, the list of 'Works Exhibited at the Society of Painters in Water-Colours' (Part III, Section 1) gives only the title of the work with no detailed

description, and with no particulars of size or date. Only seventy-six works dated by the artist have been traced for inclusion in this Catalogue, of which seventy-three are dated by him before 1840, none between 1840 and 1859, and three from 1860 to his death in 1864. Of the seventy-six dated works, fifty-five are of figures.

The dating of many of Hunt's works must inevitably be a highly subjective matter, and is not therefore suitable as the fundamental basis for this Catalogue.

6. On the other hand, there are three factors which are of help in dating. First, there are Hunt's 'boy models', who are easily recognisable, and sat for him repeatedly from about 1830 for approximately the next ten years. Secondly, there are works where he used his wife Sarah as a model. The marriage took place on 13 September 1830, and according to F. G. Stephens she was then eighteen years of age. She was shown as aged thirty-eight in the census return for 30 March 1851 which puts the date of her birth as 1812–13. Her face is recognisable, and her age can be estimated from time to time as she appears in Hunt's work. Thirdly, he often used his daughter Emma as a model. Emma was shown as aged nineteen in the census return for 30 March 1851 and thus must have been born before 30 March 1832. Her birth certificate has not been traced and for the purpose of this Catalogue her birth has been assumed to be the beginning of January 1832. She is recognisable by her somewhat round face, and again her age can be estimated as she appears from time to time in Hunt's work.

7. Detailed descriptions (in addition to the actual title) are included where it is considered that such a description will help identification.

8. Details of medium are given in the same order throughout, i.e. pencil, chalk, pen, reed pen, ink, watercolour, body-colour, heightened with white, on prepared ground. 'Body-colour' means an admixture of watercolour and Chinese white. 'Heightened with white' means Chinese white used as a means of highlighting. 'On prepared ground' means Chinese white used as a ground on which to paint in pure watercolour, a method Hunt used particularly in his later fruit pieces. See Part I, Chapter 4, 'Technique'.

9. Measurements are given first in inches, then in millimetres, height before width.

10. 'Signed' means signed by the artist 'W. Hunt'. Other forms of signature, e.g. initials, are detailed in full. Where there is no reference to signature, the work is unsigned.

11. 'Inscribed' refers to any inscription on the work other than a signature or date. If made by the artist himself it is so stated.

12. Works are included only when their present ownership in a national, public or private collection is known to the compiler. Details of present ownership are as complete as can be ascertained or as permitted by the owner. 'Provenance' includes details of such previous ownership as are known to or regarded as significant by the compiler. 'Collection' denotes ownership irrespective of the number of works owned.

13. Where accession numbers are known, they are given in square brackets immediately following the title of the work.

14. The numbers of a few late additions to the Catalogue are suffixed (a), e.g. 472(a).

15. The following abbreviations are used in the Catalogue:

GENERAL:

b/c	Body-colour	No.	Number
BIB.	Bibliography	Pl.	Plate
Bt	Bought	PROV.	Provenance
Cat.	Catalogue	Repr.	Reproduced
EXH.	Exhibited	w/c	Watercolour

BIBLIOGRAPHY and EXHIBITIONS:

Hunt Exhibition Fry Collection 1967	Hunt Exhibition from Fry Collection, Castle Museum, Norwich, and J. S. Maas Gallery, London, 1967, and Exhibition Catalogue, 1967
Hunt Exhibition 1981	Hunt Exhibition, Wolverhampton Art Gallery and Museums, Harris Museum and Art Gallery, Preston, and Hastings Museum and Art Gallery, 1981, and Exhibition Catalogue, 1981
Martin Hardie	Martin Hardie's *Water-colour Painting in Britain* edited by Dudley Snelgrove with Jonathan Mayne and Basil Taylor, 3 vols, B. T. Batsford, London, 1966–68
OWCS	Society of Painters in Water-Colours (Old Water-Colour Society)
Roget	J. L. Roget, *A History of the Old Water-Colour Society* (now the Royal Society of Painters in Water-Colours), 2 vols, Longmans Green, London, 1891
Ruskin Hunt Exhibition 1879–80	Ruskin's Exhibition of Prout and Hunt at the Fine Art Society, London, 1879–80
Ruskin *Works*	*The Works of John Ruskin*, Library Edition edited by Sir E. T. Cook and A. Wedderburn, 39 vols, George Allen, London, 1903–12
Stephens 1934–35	'William Henry Hunt' by F. G. Stephens, PRB, *Fraser's Magazine*, November 1865. Reprinted Old Water-Colour Society, Vol. XII, London, 1934–35

COLLECTIONS

Bedford, Cecil Higgins	Bedford, Cecil Higgins Art Gallery
Courtauld Institute	Courtauld Institute of Art, University of London
Fry Collection	Mr and Mrs Cyril Fry Collection, London
Huntington Library	Henry E. Huntington Library and Art Gallery, San Marino, California, USA
Oppé Collection	Mr D. L. T. Oppé, London
Whitworth Art Gallery, Manchester	Manchester, Whitworth Art Gallery, University of Manchester
Witt Collection	Sir John and Lady Witt Collection, London
Yale Center	Yale Center for British Art, Paul Mellon Collection, New Haven, Connecticut

1

Landscapes

including seascapes, shore scenes and church interiors

BARLOW, Estate of the late Miss Helen, London

1 *c.*1815

Farmyard with Implements and Figure [Probate No. 187]

Boy standing at yard entrance with grindstone and garden tools.
Reed pen, ink and w/c. 9 × 12 (228 × 304).
PROV. H. Reitlinger.
COMMENT. Bushey neighbourhood. Compare same grindstone in Huntington Library (88).

2 1815–20

Interior of Aldenham Church [Probate No. 186]

Three young children on bench under gallery.
Reed pen, ink and w/c. $12\frac{1}{2} \times 9$ (317 × 228).
COMMENT. A more finished and somewhat different version is in the Fry Collection (74).

3 1815–20

Interior of Aldenham Church [Probate No. 184]

Children sitting on staircase.
Reed pen, ink and w/c. $16\frac{3}{4} \times 12\frac{1}{4}$ (425 × 311).
COMMENT. The staircase no longer exists.

4 1815–20

Stable Yard in Hertfordshire [Probate No. 185]

Ladder up to loft and inner yard beyond.
w/c. $14\frac{1}{2} \times 10\frac{3}{4}$ (368 × 273).
COMMENT. Bushey neighbourhood.

BARNSLEY, Cooper Art Gallery

5 1817–20

Waterloo Bridge [SYCMS.CP.TR.28]

Pencil and w/c. $5\frac{3}{4} \times 8$ (146 × 203). Signed.
Gift. Sir Michael Sadler through the National Art-Collections Fund, 1932.
COMMENT. Not Waterloo Bridge but Blackfriars. Compare with Yale Center (244, Plate 10) and Huntington Library (94). Sir Michael Sadler wrote in his *Notes on a Collection of English Drawings*, Oxford University Press, 1937, p. 38: 'William Henry Hunt won fame by the naturalism of his still life, but we of a later generation like in his London sketches what is spontaneous and unlaboured.'

BEDFORD, Cecil Higgins Art Gallery

6 1815–20

Village Scene with Timbered Houses [P.77/P.76]

Stormy sky, buildings with ladders on left in deep shadows.
Reed pen, ink and w/c. $10\frac{1}{4} \times 13$ (272 × 330).
Bt 1953.
PROV. Gilbert Davis.
COMMENT. Bushey neighbourhood.

7 1815–20

Courtyard and Archway (Old Bell Yard, Bushey) [P.109/P.99]

Reed pen, ink and w/c. $15\frac{5}{8} \times 13$ (395 × 328).
Bt 1955.
PROV. Major R. C. Hans Sloane Stanley.
BIB. Repr. Pl. 4 in Grant Longman, *Bushey Then and Now*, No. 4, 1968.

8 (Plate 17) 1815–20
The Water Mill, Bushey [P.108/P.98]

Stormy sky.
Reed pen, ink and w/c. $13\frac{1}{4} \times 16\frac{7}{8}$ (335 × 427).
Bt 1955.
PROV. Major R. C. Hans Sloane Stanley.
EXH. Reading Art Gallery, 1965.
BIB. Repr. Pl. 3 in Grant Longman, *Bushey Then and Now*, No. 4, 1968.

9 1815–20
Village Scene with Cottages (View of Bushey High Street) [P.110/P.100]

Reed pen, ink and w/c. $11\frac{5}{8} \times 14\frac{1}{2}$ (294 × 367).
Bt 1955.
PROV. Major R. C. Hans Sloane Stanley.
BIB. Repr. Pl. 2 in Grant Longman, *Bushey Then and Now*, No. 4, 1968.
COMMENT. Compare back view of same cottages in Yale Center (241).

10 1815–20
Village Scene with White Hart Inn in Bushey High Street [P.111/P.101]

Reed pen, ink and w/c. $13 \times 16\frac{3}{4}$ (328 × 424).
Bt 1955.
PROV. Major R. C. Hans Sloane Stanley.
EXH. Hunt Exhibition 1981.
BIB. Repr. Pl. 1 in Grant Longman, *Bushey Then and Now*, No. 4, 1968.

BEMBRIDGE, Ruskin Galleries, Bembridge School, Isle of Wight

11 1820–30
Seashore with Boats [247]

Pencil. $3\frac{1}{2} \times 5\frac{1}{2}$ (89 × 140). Signed.

BIRMINGHAM, City Museum and Art Gallery

12 *c.*1821
St Jacques, Dieppe [259/53]

Reed pen, ink and grey wash. 17 × 12 (433 × 305).
Bequest. J. Leslie Wright, 1953.
EXH. Royal Academy, 1949 [283].
COMMENT. Same series as other views in Normandy, e.g. Rouen, in Huntington Library, which is inscribed on verso in Hunt's handwriting, with watermark of 1821 (see under 96).

BLOFIELD, T. R .C., Norfolk

13 1815–20
Farm Buildings at Bushey

Ladder and wheelbarrow in middle foreground.
Reed pen, ink and w/c. $9\frac{1}{8} \times 12\frac{5}{8}$ (231 × 332).
Signed.
PROV. Henry S. Theobald, KC.

BRADFORD, Art Galleries and Museums

14 1815–20
Yard of a Farm House [127-33]

Reed pen, sepia ink and w/c. $14\frac{1}{4} \times 10\frac{1}{4}$ (363 × 259).
Gift. Francis V. Gill, 1933.
COMMENT. Bushey neighbourhood. Compare similar buildings in Witt Collection (195) and in Victoria and Albert Museum (171).

15 1815–20
Cottages in Hertfordshire [22–21]

Reed pen, sepia ink and w/c. $9\frac{1}{8} \times 12\frac{3}{4}$ (232 × 324).
Bt 1921.
COMMENT. Bushey neighbourhood.

16 1815–20
North Porch of Bushey Church [12–34]

Looking into church with figures of two boys and spade in foreground.
Reed pen, sepia ink and w/c. $15\frac{7}{8} \times 13$ (403 × 330).
Gift. Francis V. Gill, 1934.
COMMENT. Compare same porch, but looking out on to Bushey Village at Oxford, Ashmolean Museum (138).

17 (Plate 26) 1815–20
The Nave, Bushey Church [13–32]

Reed pen, ink and w/c. $16\frac{5}{8} \times 12\frac{1}{2}$ (423 × 317).
COMMENT. Similar version in Victoria and Albert Museum (172). Compare The Nave, Aldenham Church (230).

BRANDT, Estate of the late Walter, London

18 *c.*1823
Door into the Belfry, Bushey Church

Reed pen, brown ink and w/c. $14 \times 10\frac{1}{4}$ (355 × 260).

PROV. L. G. Duke, who notes 'From the Round family of Suffolk'.
COMMENT. Almost identical versions in Mrs Cecil Keith Collection (104) and Miss F. Mills Collection (108). Compare same door looking outwards, Yale Center (251, Plate 29).

BRITISH MUSEUM, London

19 *c.*1810
Piazza S. Marco [1957.8.10.1]

Copied for Dr Monro after drawing by Canaletto.
Pen, bistre ink and sepia wash. $9 \times 13\frac{1}{4}$ (228 × 337).

20 *c.*1810
Venetian Scene with Church and Large Building [1895.9.15.862]

Copied for Dr Monro after drawing by Canaletto.
Pen, bistre ink and sepia wash. $11\frac{5}{8} \times 16\frac{7}{8}$ (294 × 428).

21 *c.*1810
Venetian Scene with Bridge over Canal [1919.7.30.1]

Copied for Dr Monro after drawing by Canaletto.
Pen, bistre ink and sepia wash. $8\frac{1}{2} \times 13\frac{3}{4}$ (217 × 350).
Bequest. Captain E. G. Spencer-Churchill, 1919.

22 *c.*1810
Ponte Rotto, Rome [1878.12.28.2]

Copied for Dr Monro after drawing by Canaletto.
Pen, bistre ink and sepia wash. 11 × 17 (278 × 430).
Bequest. John Henderson, 1878.

23 (Plate 12) *c.*1815
Dr Monro Inspecting his Burnt-out Stables at Bushey [1920.11.16.25]

Reed pen, brown ink and w/c. $13\frac{7}{8} \times 10\frac{1}{4}$ (354 × 262).
BIB. Entry in unpublished diary of E. T. Monro (eldest son of Dr Monro): '1815, 19 Aug. Hunt drawing the stables this evening'.
COMMENT. Slightly larger version, Cambridge, Fitzwilliam Museum (41).

24 (Plate 27) 1815–20
Bushey Church, South Side [1921.11.9.7]

Showing tombs of H. Monro and T. Hearne.
Reed pen, ink and w/c. $12\frac{5}{8} \times 16\frac{1}{2}$ (322 × 420).
Gift. F. R. Meatyard, 1921.
PROV. Dr T. Monro.

25 1815–20
East End of Aldenham Church [1944.10.14.111]

Five children in churchyard.
Reed pen, bistre ink and w/c. $10\frac{5}{8} \times 14\frac{1}{8}$ (270 × 360).
Gift. Miss M. H. Turner, 1944.

26 (Plate 20) *c.*1820
The Village in the Valley [1958.7.12.352]

w/c. $10\frac{1}{2} \times 14\frac{3}{4}$ (267 × 375). Signed.
Bequest. R. W. Lloyd, 1958.
EXH. Hunt Exhibition 1981.
COMMENT. Unidentified village probably in Hertfordshire.

27 *c.*1820
Bushey Churchyard [1958.7.12.354]

Looking down towards Bushey High Street.
w/c. $12\frac{1}{2} \times 16\frac{1}{2}$ (317 × 420).
Bequest. R. W. Lloyd, 1958.

28 Dated 1821
View in a Park [1920.5.6.1]

Outbuildings on left with man digging and two white cows in field on right.
Reed pen, ink and w/c. $12\frac{3}{8} \times 16\frac{1}{8}$ (314 × 409). Signed and dated 1821.
COMMENT. Probably Cassiobury Park, Watford.

29 (Colour Plate 5) 1820–25
Merry Hill, Bushey [1958.7.12.351]

Woman on balcony, probably Mrs Monro, and another in doorway, probably his daughter Sally.
Pencil and w/c, slightly heightened in white. $13\frac{1}{4} \times 10\frac{1}{2}$ (336 × 267). Signed.
Bequest. R. W. Lloyd, 1958.
COMMENT. Dr Monro's country house where he lived between 1808 and 1832 and where Hunt used to pay summer visits.

30 *c.*1822
Bushey Churchyard [1921.7.14.14]

Showing the tombs of Henry Monro, Thomas Hearne and Henry Edridge, with Dr Monro on horseback.
Reed pen, ink and w/c. $12\frac{5}{8} \times 16\frac{3}{8}$ (320 × 415).
EXH. Hunt Exhibition 1981.
COMMENT. Compare other versions at Yale Center (252, Plate 25) and Whitworth Art Gallery, Manchester (107). There is a lithograph of the above [BM.47.8.11.16], black on white paper, inscribed: 'Presented to the Print Room of the British Museum July 1847 by Henry Hunt Esq.'

31 (Plate 11) Dated 1825
London Bridge with Pool of London Beyond [1935.6.8.6]

Reed pen, brown ink and w/c. $13\frac{3}{8} \times 21\frac{3}{8}$ (342 × 544). Signed and dated 1825.
Bt 1935, through Dyson Perrins donation.
PROV. J. P. Heseltine.
EXH. Hunt Exhibition 1981.
COMMENT. Compare similar version, without watercolour, at Yale Center (253); also later version exh. 1862 in British Museum (32). Probably Lot 310 in Hunt sale at Christie's 17 May 1864. London Bridge was rebuilt 1823–31.

32 Exh. 1862
View of London Bridge [1864.6.11.1(LB11)]

With no sailing barge.
Pencil and w/c. $15\frac{3}{8} \times 21\frac{3}{8}$ (392 × 542). Signed.
Bt 1864 at Hunt sale at Christie's, 17 May 1864, Lot 305.
EXH. (1) OWCS, Winter 1862, No. 65. (2) Hunt Exhibition 1981.
COMMENT. Later copy by Hunt of British Museum (31, Plate 11) and Yale Center (253) versions, both dated 1825.

33
A Thatched Shed [1944.10.14(112)]

Pencil. $3\frac{3}{8} \times 5$ (86 × 127). Signed.
Gift. Miss M. H. Turner, 1944.
EXH. Hunt Exhibition 1981.

34
Coast Scene – Fishing [1944.10.14(113)]

Pencil. $5\frac{3}{8} \times 4\frac{1}{2}$ (137 × 114). Signed.
Gift. Miss M. H. Turner, 1944.
EXH. Hunt Exhibition 1981.

35
Landscape with Pond and Bridge [1944.10.14(114)]

Pencil. $3\frac{1}{4} \times 4\frac{1}{2}$ (83 × 114).
Gift. Miss M. H. Turner, 1944.
EXH. Hunt Exhibition 1981.

36
A Cottage [1944.10.14(115)]

Pencil. $4\frac{1}{2} \times 7$ (114 × 178). Signed.
Gift. Miss M. H. Turner, 1944.
EXH. Hunt Exhibition 1981.

37
Album A.7 [1934.9.22]

Consists of 'Drawings by William Henry Hunt and others from a scrap book once in the possession of Mrs Baxter of Compton Terrace, Highbury, a great niece of the artist'. Hunt drawings numbered 1–124 inclusive with a number of gaps. They comprise mainly portrait and figure drawings, a number of members of his family; e.g. Nos 2–7 inclusive, of his sister-in-law Maria Hunt; Nos 9–14 inclusive, of his nephew Charles Steedman (born 1826) as a baby (No. 9) and at varying ages up to 18 (No. 14); his niece Sophia Steedman (born 1830) as a baby (No. 18); and other members of the Steedman family. Nos 60 and 61 are of chess players. The album also includes (91–120 inclusive) shore scenes around Hastings and a few landscapes mainly in pencil and small in size. No. 93 is of shipping and is more elaborate than the usual landscape/seascape – $6\frac{5}{8} \times 8\frac{5}{8}$ (167 × 218) – and inscribed on verso: 'W. Hunt, 6 Marchmont Street.' As Hunt lived at that address from 1825 to 1842, No. 93 is dateable between those years. No. 121 is of Caroline Place, Hastings, in pen and sepia ink and inscribed in Hunt's handwriting 'this our prospect one way, with the sea to our right'. Also inscribed on verso: '1 Caroline House, Caroline Place, Hastings'.
The album also includes the following small pencil drawings of animals: Nos 83 and 84, cats; 85 and 86, pug dog asleep; 87, two pigs.
Bt 2 September 1934 from Mr A. Brandon through the Florence Fund.

38
Sketch Book [1877.2.10.73(LB12)]

Inscribed on fly leaf 'Sol Club'.
$6\frac{1}{4} \times 9\frac{1}{4}$ (158 × 235).
Contains: (1) 21 pages of men's portraits,

members of the Sol Club, including one inscribed 'Hunt the Slipper'. Pencil and pen. Signed. (2) A man with glasses, perhaps a singing teacher, with a mixed group of young pupils. Pencil and pen. (3) 8 landscapes and buildings, 2 with windmills. Pencil.
EXH. Hunt Exhibition 1981.
COMMENT. No record of the Sol Club has been traced but it may be connected with the Sol Arms in St Pancras.

BYAM SHAW, James, London

39 1820–30
Fishing Boats at Hastings

Black chalk. $3\frac{1}{4} \times 4\frac{1}{8}$ (83 × 104). Signed.
PROV. Gift from A. Paul Oppé.

CAMBRIDGE, Fitzwilliam Museum

40 1810–15
Shore Scene [1379]

With houses and boats. Wooden steps with hand rails and ladders from houses to the beach. Boats on left.
Pencil on grey paper. $10\frac{1}{4} \times 16$ (262 × 408).
Bequest. J. R. Holliday, 1927.
COMMENT. Perhaps at Margate.

41 *c.*1815
Dr Monro Visiting his Stables at Bushey being Rebuilt after a Fire [1380]

Reed pen, brown ink and w/c. $14\frac{5}{8} \times 10\frac{5}{8}$ (372 × 270).
Bequest. J. R. Holliday, 1927.
PROV. Sir Charles Robinson; his sale, Sotheby, 24 February 1914, Lot 57.
COMMENT. Entry in unpublished diary of E. T. Monro (Dr Monro's eldest son): '1815, 19 Aug Hunt drawing the stables this evening'. Compare similar version in British Museum (23, Plate 12).

42 1815–20
Roadside Cottage [1567]

Pencil and w/c. $13 \times 16\frac{5}{8}$ (333 × 422).
Bequest. J. R. Holliday, 1927; bt by him 1909.

43 *c.*1821
Street Scene in a Foreign Town (Bretagne) [1568]

Church tower at end of street with many figures.
Reed pen, ink and grey wash. $17\frac{3}{8} \times 12\frac{5}{8}$ (441 × 321).
Bequest. J. R. Holliday, 1927.
COMMENT. Same series as Rouen in Huntington Library (see under 96).

44 *c.*1821
In Normandy [1569]

Church and market square with fountain.
Reed pen, ink and grey wash. $14\frac{1}{2} \times 18\frac{3}{8}$ (337 × 464).
Bequest. J. R. Holliday, 1927.
COMMENT. Same series as other views in Normandy, e.g. Rouen, in Huntington Library, inscribed on verso in Hunt's handwriting and watermarked 1821. (See under 96.)

CAMBRIDGE, Massachusetts, Fogg Art Museum, Harvard University

45
A Tree Study [1934.192]

Pencil and w/c. $4\frac{7}{8} \times 3\frac{1}{2}$ (124 × 89). Signed.
Gift. Miss Eleanor B. Eaton, 1934.

CATER, Mrs Sarah, Essex

46 1820–30
Fishing Boats

With group of fishermen on beach.
Pencil. $3\frac{3}{8} \times 4\frac{1}{4}$ (87 × 108).

COURTAULD Institute of Art, University of London

47 (Plate 16) *c.*1818
Houses at Watford [14.71]

w/c. $10\frac{1}{2} \times 14\frac{13}{16}$ (267 × 376).
Gift. Mrs W. Spooner, 1971.
COMMENT. Originally laid down on newspaper and a note on the mount states that the newspaper was dated 1818 at Watford.

48 1820–30
A Sailing Vessel in Harbour [2303(a)]

With buildings behind.
Pencil. $4\frac{3}{8} \times 3\frac{1}{4}$ (109 × 84).
Bequest. Sir Robert Witt, 1952.

49 1820–30
Two Sailing Boats at Sea [2303(b)]

Two ships under sail and one rowing boat.
Pencil. $2\frac{3}{4} \times 4\frac{1}{4}$ (70 × 105).
Bequest. Sir Robert Witt, 1952.

50 1820–30
Coast Scene [2303(c)]

Boats unloading into cart pulled by horses.
Pencil. $3\frac{3}{4} \times 6\frac{1}{4}$ (95 × 116).
Bequest. Sir Robert Witt, 1952.

51 1820–30
Landscape with Trees [3738]

Black chalk and w/c. $3\frac{1}{2} \times 4\frac{3}{4}$ (89 × 122). Signed.
Bequest. Sir Robert Witt, 1952.

52 *c.*1833
Elm Tree [2921]

Pencil and w/c. $21\frac{7}{8} \times 14\frac{5}{8}$ (556 × 369). Signed.
Bequest. Sir Robert Witt, 1952.
COMMENT. Perhaps a study for Pollard Elm, dated 1833, at Preston, Harris Museum (144, Colour Plate 13). Compare also Elm Log in Farmyard (217).

DEVONSHIRE Collection Chatsworth, Derbyshire

53 *c.*1822
In the Gardens, Chiswick House

Statues under the trees.
Reed pen, ink and w/c. $6\frac{1}{8} \times 9\frac{1}{4}$ (154 × 233). Signed.
COMMENT. Two views of the gallery at Chiswick House, one dated 1822, are also at Chatsworth (333 and 334, Plate 45). Another view of the gardens at Chiswick with garden statuary is in the Rijksmuseum, Amsterdam (148).

54 Dated 1828
View of Old Hall Ruins, Hardwick

Taken from Hardwick Hall.
Pencil. $4\frac{1}{4} \times 9\frac{1}{4}$ (108 × 235). Signed and dated 1828.
COMMENT. Contained in grangerised large paper edition of the 6th Duke's *Handbook to Chatsworth*, p. 218(c). Compare identical version, same size, signed but undated, Witt Collection (214).

ENFIELD, Forty Hall Museum

55 *c.*1806
Gravel Pit Near Twickenham

w/c. $6\frac{1}{2} \times 9\frac{1}{8}$ (168 × 232). Signed.
Bt 1971.
COMMENT. Compare oil, inscribed 'Study from Nature at Twickenham' *c.*1806, Tate Gallery (158, Plate 2).

ETON COLLEGE, Brewhouse Gallery, Windsor

56 *c.*1820
Fishing Boat [Pi.109]

With furled sails.
Pencil and wash. $6\frac{3}{8} \times 12\frac{7}{8}$ (162 × 328). Signed.
Gift. Alan Pilkington, 1960.

57 1820–30
Tonbridge, Kent [Pi.108]

Pencil and w/c. $6\frac{3}{8} \times 10$ (16 × 254). Signed.
Gift. Alan Pilkington, 1960.

58 (Plate 9) *c.*1830
Rebuilding London Bridge [Pi.110]

w/c. $6\frac{3}{4} \times 9\frac{1}{8}$ (160 × 233). Signed.
Gift. Alan Pilkington, 1960.
COMMENT. London Bridge was rebuilt 1823–31.

FRY, Mr and Mrs Cyril, London

59 1806–10
Hampstead Heath

Inscribed on mount: 'during the time he was with John Varley'.
w/c. $8\frac{1}{2} \times 12\frac{1}{2}$ (224 × 322).
EXH. Hunt Exhibition Fry Collection 1967.
BIB. Fry Cat. 1967, No. 5.

60 1806–10
A Barge

Pencil and w/c. $4\frac{5}{8} \times 7\frac{5}{8}$ (119 × 195). Signed.
EXH. Hunt Exhibition Fry Collection 1967.
BIB. Fry Cat. 1967, No. 6(b).
COMMENT. Strong Varley influence.

61 1810–15
Study of a Farm with Trees Behind

Black chalk and w/c. $3\frac{1}{4} \times 4\frac{1}{8}$ (85 × 105). Signed.
EXH. Hunt Exhibition Fry Collection 1967.
BIB. Fry Cat. 1967, No. 6(a).

62 1810–15
Ruined Farm

w/c. $2\frac{5}{8} \times 4\frac{1}{8}$ (65 × 105). Signed.
EXH. Hunt Exhibition Fry Collection 1967.
BIB. Fry Cat. 1967, No. 9(a).

63 1810–15
Riverside Quay with Barge

Pencil. $7\frac{1}{4} \times 9$ (185 × 227).
EXH. Hunt Exhibition Fry Collection 1967.
BIB. Fry Cat. 1967, No. 11(b).

64 *c.*1815
Study of a Farm House

Pencil and w/c. $7\frac{1}{2} \times 11\frac{1}{8}$ (192 × 282).
EXH. Hunt Exhibition Fry Collection 1967.
BIB. Fry Cat. 1967, No. 8.

65 1815–20
Exterior of a Church in Hertfordshire

With graves and trees in churchyard.
Reed pen, ink and w/c. $9 \times 12\frac{3}{4}$ (233 × 325).
EXH. Hunt Exhibition Fry Collection 1967.
BIB. Fry Cat. 1967, No. 2.

66 1815–20
Horse and Cart

Pencil. $3\frac{3}{8} \times 5\frac{1}{4}$ (85 × 133). Signed.
EXH. Hunt Exhibition Fry Collection 1967.
BIB. Fry Cat. 1967, No. 14(1).

67 1815–20
Farm Cottage

Pencil. $3\frac{3}{4} \times 4\frac{3}{4}$ (95 × 122). Signed.
EXH. Hunt Exhibition Fry Collection 1967.
BIB. Fry Cat. 1967, No. 14(3).

68 1815–20
Distant Landscape with Trees

Pencil. $2 \times 3\frac{1}{8}$ (52 × 80). Signed.
EXH. Hunt Exhibition Fry Collection 1967.
BIB. Fry Cat. 1967, No. 14(5).

69 1815–20
Cottage and Trees

Pencil. $2\frac{1}{8} \times 3\frac{3}{4}$ (52 × 95). Signed.
EXH. Hunt Exhibition Fry Collection 1967.
BIB. Fry Cat. 1967, No. 14(4).

70 1815–20
Boats Off Shore

With two men and two donkeys.
Pencil. $2\frac{1}{2} \times 3\frac{3}{8}$ (64 × 92). Signed.
EXH. Hunt Exhibition Fry Collection 1967.
BIB. Fry Cat. 1967, No. 15(2).

71 1815–20
Fishing Boats on the Beach

Pencil. $2\frac{1}{2} \times 3\frac{3}{8}$ (64 × 85). Signed.
EXH. Hunt Exhibition Fry Collection 1967.
BIB. Fry Cat. 1967, No. 15(3).

72 1815–20
Beach Scene with Boats

Black chalk. $2\frac{1}{2} \times 4\frac{1}{2}$ (64 × 115).
EXH. Hunt Exhibition Fry Collection 1967.
BIB. Fry Cat. 1967, No. 15(4).

73 1815–20
Farm House

With tree and barn.
w/c heightened with white. $10 \times 13\frac{3}{4}$ (254 × 358). Signed.
EXH. Hunt Exhibition Fry Collection 1967.
BIB. Fry Cat. 1967, No. 28.

74 *c.*1820
Interior of Aldenham Church

Young children on bench under gallery.
Reed pen, ink and w/c. $16\frac{1}{8} \times 13$ (408 × 330).
PROV. L. G. Duke.
COMMENT. A less finished and somewhat different version belongs to the Estate of the late Miss Helen Barlow (2).

75 1820–25
Farm Yard Scene in Winter

Pencil and w/c. $8\frac{3}{8} \times 12$ (214 × 310).
EXH. Hunt Exhibition Fry Collection 1967.
BIB. Fry Cat. 1967, No. 25.

76 1820–30
Trees Outlined Against a Brilliant Sunset

w/c. $3\frac{3}{4} \times 5$ (95 × 127). Signed.
EXH. Hunt Exhibition Fry Collection 1967.
BIB. Fry Cat. 1967, No. 34(1).

77 *c.*1825
A Water Pump

w/c. $8\frac{5}{8} \times 5\frac{3}{4}$ (220 × 150).
EXH. Hunt Exhibition Fry Collection 1967.
BIB. Fry Cat. 1967, No. 32.

78 *c.*1825
Beach at Hastings

Sun shining through cloud.
w/c. $3\frac{1}{2} \times 4\frac{1}{2}$ (89 × 115). Signed.
EXH. Hunt Exhibition Fry Collection 1967.
BIB. Fry Cat. 1967, No. 34(2).

79 *c.*1825
Sunset Study from the Shore

Pencil, w/c heightened with white. $5 \times 8\frac{3}{4}$ (127 × 225).
EXH. Hunt Exhibition Fry Collection 1967.
BIB. Fry Cat. 1967, No. 33.

80 1820–30
Sky and Trees

w/c. $3\frac{1}{4} \times 4\frac{5}{8}$ (84 × 118).
EXH. Hunt Exhibition Fry Collection 1967.
BIB. Fry Cat. 1967, No. 34 (3).

81 *c.*1840
Capstan and Bench

Pencil. $2\frac{3}{8} \times 3\frac{3}{8}$ (62 × 86). Signed.
EXH. Hunt Exhibition Fry Collection 1967.
BIB. Fry Cat. 1967, No. 15(5).
COMMENT. Compare similar capstan in Huntington Library (99, Plate 90) and Witt Collection (215, Plate 88).

82 *c.*1841

A series of 12 letters, each decorated at the top with a small watercolour drawing including a peacock, flowers in a vase, a spray of lilac, a hyacinth, fruit, a bird's nest and 2 landscapes. The letters are addressed to a Miss Moore, who was evidently a pupil, living in Cheyne Walk. Hunt writes from three different addresses in Hastings and from one address in London. Some of the letters are dated with the day of the month, but none with the year. Apart from references to Miss Moore's health, Hunt's drawings, and Miss Moore's copies of them, the letters contain requests for orders from Mr Moore for theatre seats, and this may have been the form of Hunt's remuneration for helping Miss Moore with her studies.
w/c.
Gift. From L. G. Duke.
COMMENT. Note by L. G. Duke: 'The letters may all be dated *c.*1841 as "London Assurance" referred to in one of them was a comedy by Dion Boucicault, which was produced at Covent Garden in that year'. Hunt's great fondness for the theatre is referred to in Roget, Vol. II, p. 197.

HARROW School, Harrow-on-the-Hill

83 1815–20
Old Houses at Harrow

w/c. $10\frac{3}{4} \times 11\frac{3}{4}$ (273 × 298).
PROV. W. O. Hewlett.

HASTINGS, Museum and Art Gallery

84 *c.*1818
Hastings from White Rock [W.245]

View of Old Town looking east across beach at low tide. Inscribed verso: 'sketch taken on the spot by W. Hunt in July 1818'.
w/c. $10\frac{1}{4} \times 15\frac{3}{4}$ (260 × 400).
Bt 1931.
EXH. Hunt Exhibition 1981.
COMMENT. Compare views of Hastings looking west and down from the cliff in Oxford, Ashmolean Museum (137, Plate 6) and with cliffs behind looking east in Witt Collection (192).

HENRY E. HUNTINGTON Library and Art Gallery, San Marino, California

85 1810–15
Landscape with Hills [59.55.756]

w/c. $3\frac{3}{8} \times 4\frac{5}{8}$ (86 × 117).
PROV. Sir Robert Witt. Gilbert Davis.

86 1810–15
The Square [59.55.766]

w/c. $6\frac{1}{2} \times 7$ (165 × 178). Signed.
PROV. Gilbert Davis; bt by him, 1948.

87 *c.*1815
On the Sea Shore [59.55.764]

w/c. $8\frac{1}{4} \times 10\frac{1}{4}$ (208 × 262).
PROV. Gilbert Davis; bt by him, 1948.

88 *c.*1815
The Grindstone [59.55.750]

Reed pen, brown ink and w/c. $12\frac{1}{8} \times 9$ (308 × 228).
PROV. Gilbert Davis; bt by him, 1954.
COMMENT. Compare same grindstone in Estate of the late Miss Helen Barlow (1).

89 (Colour Plate 2) *c.*1815
Saw Mill, Bushey [59.55.735]

Reed pen, brown ink and w/c. $10\frac{1}{8} \times 14\frac{1}{8}$ (257×358).
PROV. Dr T. Monro. Lord Northwick. Victor Rienacker. Gilbert Davis; bt by him, 1947.

90 (Colour Plate 3) 1815–20
View over Bushey with Bushey Church in the Distance [59.55.736]

w/c. $10\frac{3}{8} \times 13$ (263×330).
PROV. Gilbert Davis; bt by him, 1953.

91 1815–20
Farmyard Scene [59.55.743]

With farm cart and three figures.
w/c. $8\frac{1}{8} \times 10\frac{1}{2}$ (206×267).
PROV. Gilbert Davis; bt by him, 1947.
COMMENT. Compare similar farm cart in Witt Collection (190).

92 *c.*1817
The Stable Yard [59.55.767]

w/c. $14\frac{1}{4} \times 10\frac{5}{8}$ (363×270).
PROV. Gilbert Davis; bt by him, 1948.
COMMENT. Verso various newspaper clippings of law cases with the date 1817 mentioned but not as the date of the hearing reported.

93 *c.*1817
Farm Yard [59.55.744]

With spire of unidentified church in background. Paper watermarked 1817.
Reed pen, brown ink and w/c. $10\frac{3}{4} \times 14\frac{7}{8}$ (274×377)
PROV. Gilbert Davis; bt by him, 1948.
COMMENT. Compare view of same yard with same church spire behind in Oxford, Ashmolean Museum (136) and in A. Stirling Collection (155).

94 1817–20
Thames Scene [59.55.769]

Boats and Blackfriars Bridge in the distance on left.
w/c. $5\frac{3}{4} \times 9\frac{3}{8}$ (147×238). Signed.
PROV. Gilbert Davis; bt by him, 1948.
COMMENT. Compare Blackfriars Bridge at Barnsley, Cooper Art Gallery (5).

95 *c.*1820
The Nave, Aldenham Church [59.55.752]

With three children.
Signed, and inscribed verso in Hunt's handwriting: 'Aldernham [sic], Herts'.
Reed pen, brown ink and w/c. $17\frac{1}{8} \times 12\frac{7}{8}$ (434×327).
PROV. Gilbert Davis; bt by him, 1952.

96 *c.*1821
Rouen [59.55.763]

Inscribed verso in Hunt's handwriting: 'The Church of St. Ouen from the Place Robes – Rouen'. Watermarked 1821.
Reed pen and wash. $18\frac{1}{2} \times 13$ (470×330).
PROV. Gilbert Davis; bt by him, 1947.
COMMENT. Other works in the same series: St Jacques, Birmingham, City Museum and Art Gallery (12); In Normandy, Cambridge, Fitzwilliam Museum (44); Street Scene in a Foreign Town, Cambridge, Fitzwilliam Museum (43). Compare also Beauvais, Yale Center, where paper watermarked Whatman Turkey, 1830 (254) and View of a Street in a French Town, Yale Center (255).

97 *c.*1822
Moor Park [59.55.757]

Unfinished trees on left.
Pencil, reed pen, brown ink and w/c. $6\frac{3}{4} \times 10\frac{1}{8}$ (173×257).
PROV. Gilbert Davis; bt by him, 1947.
COMMENT. Paper watermarked '22'.

98 1835–40
Fishing Boats Beached [59.55.734]

w/c. $2\frac{1}{2} \times 5\frac{1}{4}$ (64×134). Signed.
PROV. Gilbert Davis; bt by him, 1956.

99 (Plate 90) *c.*1840
Hastings Beach [59.55.751]

w/c. $9\frac{1}{4} \times 12\frac{3}{4}$ (235×323). Signed.
PROV. Gilbert Davis; bt by him, 1951.
COMMENT. Inscribed (according to notes of Gilbert Davis) verso in the artist's hand 'Old Hastings Beach W. Hunt, 1840'. This inscription has disappeared and must have been on an old mount, the drawing having since been remounted.

INGRAM family, Gloucestershire

100
Farmyard

With church spire behind.
Reed pen, bistre ink and w/c. 11 × 15¼ (280 × 387). Signed.
Bt 1961.
COMMENT. Bushey neighbourhood.

101
Landscape

With thatched, half-timber cottage.
Reed pen, ink and w/c. 9¼ × 12½ (235 × 317). Signed.
Bt 1961.

JEANNERAT, Pierre, London

102 *c.*1820
Look-out Hut at Hastings

w/c. 7½ × 9⅛ (190 × 232). Signed.

JEFFERISS, Dr F. J. G., Kent

103 1820–30
Ships on the Beach with Horse and Cart

Pencil. 8 × 6 (203 × 153).

KEITH, Mrs Cecil, Sussex

104 *c.*1823
The Door into the Belfry, Bushey Church

Inscribed verso as by W. Hunt and as of date 1823.
Reed pen, brown ink and w/c. 13¾ × 10¼ (349 × 261).
EXH. Worthing Art Gallery, English Watercolour Drawings from the Collection of Mrs Cecil Keith, 1963 [74].
COMMENT. Almost identical versions in Miss F. Mills Collection (108) and in the Collection of the Estate of the late Walter Brandt (18). Compare same door looking outwards at Yale Center (251, Plate 29).

LEEDS, City Art Gallery

105 (Plate 89) 1835–40
Fishing Smack

Drawn up on shore (at Hastings).
Pencil, pen, ink and w/c. 14⅝ × 10¼ (377 × 261). Signed.
Bequest. Agnes and Norman Lupton, 1952; bt by them, 1946.

McLAREN, Mr and Mrs Andrew, London

106 1820–30
Shipping at Sea

w/c. 4½ × 7¾ (114 × 197). Signed.

MANCHESTER, Whitworth Art Gallery, University of Manchester

107 *c.*1822
Bushey Churchyard [D.29.1895]

With the tombs of Henry Monro, Thomas Hearne and Henry Edridge, with Dr Monro on horseback.
Reed pen, bistre ink and w/c. 13⅜ × 17⅛ (340 × 433).
Gift. J. E. Taylor, 1895.
COMMENT. Compare other versions in British Museum (30) and Yale Center (252, Plate 25). See comment under 252.

MILLS, Miss Fiona, London

108 *c.*1823
The Door into the Belfry, Bushey Church

Reed pen, brown ink and w/c. 13½ × 10 1/16 (343 × 255).
COMMENT. Almost identical version in Mrs Cecil Keith Collection inscribed verso with date 1823 (104) and in the Collection of the Estate of the late Walter Brandt (18). Compare same door looking outwards at Yale Center (251, Plate 29).

NATIONAL TRUST, Fairhaven Collection, Anglesey Abbey, Cambridgeshire

109 (Plate 3) Exh. 1811
Windsor Castle

Oil on canvas. 20 × 26 (508 × 660).
PROV. Lord Fairhaven.
EXH. (1) British Institution, 1811. (2) OWCS, 1814, No. 41. (3) Royal Dublin Society, 1861.
COMMENT. A preliminary pencil sketch for the picture is in the Witt Collection (188).

NEWPORT, Museum and Art Gallery, Gwent

110 1815–20
Old Houses, Watford [35–50]

w/c. $10\frac{3}{4} \times 14\frac{3}{4}$ (273 × 374).
Bt 1935.
EXH. Empire Art Loan Exhibitions Society, 1947–48, in Australia, New Zealand and London.

111
Low Foreshore and Sea

w/c. $2\frac{3}{4} \times 4\frac{3}{4}$ (70 × 121).
Gift. From anonymous local donor, 1940.

OPPÉ, D. L. T., London

112 *c.*1815
A Horse in a Stable [419]

Black chalk and w/c. 14 × 13 (355 × 330).
PROV. A. Paul Oppé; bt by him, 1914; he suggested it may be contemporaneous with 113.

113 *c.*1815
Stables at the Old Priory Dover [2570]

Reed pen, ink and w/c. $12\frac{1}{8} \times 17\frac{3}{4}$ (307 × 451).
PROV. E. H. Coles. A. Paul Oppé, who suggested it may be contemporaneous with 112.

114 1815–20
Near Bushey [2571]

Looking down on Bushey Church.
w/c. $10\frac{1}{2} \times 14\frac{3}{4}$ (267 × 375).
PROV. Lord Northwick. E. H. Coles. A. Paul Oppé.

115 *c.*1820
Near Bushey [851]

Landscape with pond and horses.
w/c. $9\frac{1}{4} \times 13\frac{1}{8}$ (235 × 333).
PROV. Dr T. Monro. Captain E. G. Spencer Churchill. A. Paul Oppé; bt by him, 1919.

116 *c.*1820
Bushey [852]

Looking across valley at Bushey Church.
Reed pen, ink and w/c. $7\frac{7}{8} \times 11\frac{7}{8}$ (201 × 303).
PROV. Dr T. Monro. Captain E. G. Spencer Churchill. A. Paul Oppé; bt by him, 1919.

117 1820–30
Seascapes [1344]

Three on one mount.
w/c. $3\frac{3}{8} \times 4$ (86 × 101), $3 \times 4\frac{5}{8}$ (76 × 117), $3\frac{1}{8} \times 4$ (80 × 101). Signed.
PROV. A. Paul Oppé; bt by him, 1921.

118 1820–30
Coast Scene [2569(a)]

With figures on right.
w/c. $3\frac{1}{4} \times 4\frac{5}{8}$ (83 × 117). Signed.
PROV. E. H. Coles. A. Paul Oppé.

119 1820–30
Coast Scene [2569(b)]

With ships on left.
w/c. $3\frac{1}{2} \times 5$ (89 × 127). Signed.
PROV. E. H. Coles. A. Paul Oppé.

120
Hunt Box [1180]
Contains 30 drawings, all in pencil, consisting of 18 landscapes, 11 figures and 1 sketch of a dog.

Landscapes:
(1) A Tree
$6\frac{3}{4} \times 4\frac{1}{4}$ (177 × 108). Signed.
(2) Cliff Scene
$4\frac{1}{4} \times 3\frac{1}{2}$ (108 × 89). Signed.
(3) Barn
5 × 3 (127 × 76).
(4) Shipping Sketch
$5 \times 3\frac{1}{2}$ (127 × 89). Signed.
(5) Harbour Scene
$4 \times 2\frac{1}{2}$ (102 × 63). Signed.
(6) Haywain
$3\frac{1}{2} \times 3$ (89 × 76). Signed.
(7) Cliff
$4 \times 3\frac{1}{4}$ (102 × 83). Signed.
(8) Seascape
$3\frac{1}{2} \times 2\frac{1}{2}$ (89 × 63).
(9) Bridge
$3\frac{1}{2} \times 2\frac{1}{2}$ (89 × 63).
(10) Horse and Cart and Boats
$3\frac{3}{4} \times 2\frac{3}{4}$ (95 × 70). Signed.
(11) Boat and Figure
$4\frac{1}{4} \times 3\frac{1}{4}$ (108 × 83). Signed.
(12) Figure on a Beach
$4\frac{1}{4} \times 3\frac{1}{4}$ (108 × 83). Signed.
(13) Marine Scene
$4\frac{1}{2} \times 3\frac{1}{2}$ (114 × 89). Signed.
(14) Boats and Two Figures
$3\frac{3}{4} \times 2\frac{3}{4}$ (95 × 70). Signed.

(15) Boat on Beach
$3\frac{1}{2} \times 2\frac{3}{4}$ (89 × 70). Signed.
(16) Sailing Boats
$3\frac{1}{2} \times 2\frac{1}{2}$ (89 × 63). Signed.
(17) Sailing Boat and Roof
$4 \times 3\frac{1}{4}$ (102 × 95).
(18) Sailing Boat and Two Figures
$3\frac{1}{2} \times 2\frac{1}{2}$ (89 × 63). Signed.
PROV. A. Paul Oppé; bt by him, 1921.

121
Shipping [2568(a)]

Fishing vessels on the beach at Hastings.
Pencil. $3\frac{3}{8} \times 5\frac{3}{8}$ (86 × 136). Signed.
PROV. E. H. Coles. A. Paul Oppé.

122
Shipping [2568(b)]

Two sailing ships, beached.
Pencil. $3\frac{3}{4} \times 4\frac{7}{8}$ (95 × 123). Signed.
PROV. E. H. Coles. A. Paul Oppé.

123
Cottage in a Marsh [2572(a)]

Pen and w/c. $2\frac{5}{8} \times 4\frac{1}{4}$ (67 × 108). Signed.
PROV. E. H. Coles. A. Paul Oppé.

124
Cairn under a Stormy Sky [2572(b)]

w/c. $3\frac{1}{4} \times 4\frac{1}{8}$ (83 × 102). Signed.
PROV. E. H. Coles. A. Paul Oppé.

125
Wide Landscape near Hastings [2572(c)]

Pencil. $2\frac{1}{4} \times 7$ (57 × 178). Signed.
PROV. E. H. Coles. A. Paul Oppé.

126
Two Ships at Sea and Hulk on Shore [2572(d)]
w/c. $3\frac{1}{4} \times 4\frac{1}{8}$ (83 × 102). Signed.
PROV. E. H. Coles. A. Paul Oppé.

127
Small Ships at Sea under a Bank of Cloud [2572(e)]

w/c. $3\frac{3}{4} \times 4\frac{7}{8}$ (95 × 125). Signed.
PROV. E. H. Coles. A. Paul Oppé.

128
Ten Shipping Scenes [2574]
Pencil. All small.
PROV. E. H. Coles. A. Paul Oppé.

129
Shore Scene with Cloud [2575(a)]

w/c. $4\frac{1}{4} \times 5\frac{1}{2}$ (108 × 140). Signed.
PROV. E. H. Coles. A. Paul Oppé.

130
Cottage [2575(b)]

w/c. $3 \times 4\frac{1}{4}$ (76 × 108).
PROV. E. H. Coles. A. Paul Oppé.

131
Man in Top Hat Leaning against a Felled Tree [2575(c)]

w/c. $5\frac{1}{4} \times 8$ (134 × 203).
PROV. E. H. Coles. A. Paul Oppé.

132
A Grindstone [2575(d)]

Pencil. $9\frac{1}{8} \times 7$ (232 × 178).
PROV. E. H. Coles. A. Paul Oppé.

133
Shore Scene [2575 (e)]

Ships on the beach (unfinished).
w/c. $7\frac{5}{8} \times 11\frac{1}{4}$ (193 × 286). Signed.
PROV. E. H. Coles. A. Paul Oppé.

OXFORD, Ashmolean Museum

(None of the following works has an accession number.)

134 (Plate 4) *c.*1810
A Scene in Venice – Crowds Watching the Comedy Players.

View in the Piazza S. Marco with stage for Commedia dell' Arte performers at base of Campanile
Reed pen, brown ink and grey wash. $8\frac{1}{8} \times 12\frac{1}{2}$ (206 × 319).
Bt 1934.
BIB. W. G. Constable, *Canaletto*, revised edition, edited by J. G. Links, Vol. II, p. 534.
COMMENT. Copy after Canaletto. Similar copy at Victoria and Albert Museum (164).

135 1815–20
A Country Cottage

With barn at side.
Pencil and w/c. $13\frac{1}{8} \times 16\frac{3}{4}$ (334 × 425).
Gift. Captain E. G. Spencer Churchill.
EXH. (1) Linnell and his Circle, P. and D. Colnaghi Ltd., 1973, No. 131, Pl. XLVII. (2) Hunt Exhibition 1981.

136 *c.*1817
Backs of Old Houses, Watford

With church spire behind.
Pencil and w/c. 11 × 15 (279 × 379). Signed.
Bequest. Pierepont Barnard, 1934.
PROV. Dr. T. Monro. Sir Charles Robinson.
COMMENT. Compare same yard looking through from farm yard with same spire, paper being watermarked 1817, Huntington Library (93) and similar houses, A. Stirling Collection (155). Church spire not identified but not Watford.

137 (Plate 6) Exh. 1819
View of Hastings

Looking west and down from the cliff.
Pencil and w/c. $11\frac{1}{2} \times 15\frac{1}{4}$ (291 × 393). Signed.
Bequest. Mrs Combe, 1894.
EXH. (1) OWCS, 1819, No. 32, as A Sketch from the East Cliff, Hastings. (2) Linnell and his Circle, P. and D. Colnaghi Ltd, 1973, No. 132.
COMMENT. Sky and sea somewhat faded. Compare views of Hastings from White Rock, Hastings Museum and Art Gallery, inscribed 'July 1818' (84) and looking up the cliff from the west, Witt Collection (192).

138 *c.*1820
North Porch of Bushey Church

With seated man looking out on to Bushey village.
Reed pen, ink and w/c. $12 \times 9\frac{3}{8}$ (304 × 237).
Bt 1940.
EXH. Hunt Exhibition 1981.
BIB. Repr. Pl. 7 in Grant Longman, *Bushey Then and Now*, No. 4, 1968.
COMMENT. Compare same porch looking into church at Bradford, Art Gallery and Museums (16).

139 *c.*1820
Bridge over Stream

Pencil. $2\frac{3}{4} \times 5\frac{1}{8}$ (75 × 128). Signed.

140 *c.*1820
Richmond Hill

Pencil. $5 \times 6\frac{3}{4}$ (127 × 170). Signed.

141 (Plate 24) Dated 1822
Portico of St Martin-in-the-Fields

Reed pen, brown ink and sepia wash. $19\frac{1}{2} \times 13\frac{7}{8}$ (494 × 353). Signed and dated 1822.
PROV. Dr T. Monro; sold at his Sale at Christie's, 26 June 1833, Lot 151.
EXH. Hunt Exhibition 1981.
BIB. Stephens, 1865, p. 32, states: 'About 1822 Hunt executed a superb drawing in indian ink for Dr. Monro representing the Portico of St. Martin's Church before the alteration in that neighbourhood: this was sold at the Monro Sale and it is now in the possession of the Artist's old friend Mr. C. Tidbury, Regent Street, City Road, London. A recent copy made by Hunt from this drawing was sold after his death for £17.17s.' The copy referred to by F. G. Stephens is the version drawn from behind the churchyard railings and exhibited OWCS, Winter 1862, No. 249, now at Yale Center (256).

PRESTON, Harris Museum and Art Gallery

142 1810–15
Old Mill and Lock Gates (St Catherines) [1029]

w/c. $9\frac{3}{4} \times 12\frac{5}{8}$ (248 × 320).
Gift. S. H. Pavière, 1947.

143 1815–20
Farmyard Sketch [1034]

With wagon of hay in barn.
Pencil. $9\frac{1}{4} \times 15$ (235 × 382). Signed.
Gift. S. H. Pavière, 1947.

144 (Colour Plate 13) Dated 1833
Pollard Elm and Village Pound at Hambledon, Hampshire [315]

w/c heightened with white. 30 × 22 (762 × 558). Signed and dated 1833.
Bequest. Richard Newsham, 1883.
PROV. Hunt sale, Christie's, 16–17 May 1864, Lot 308 as A Study of a Pollard, near a Pond [Pound].
EXH. Hunt Exhibition 1981.
COMMENT. Perhaps drawing of Elm at Courtauld Institute (52) is a preliminary study. Compare Elm Log in Farmyard, Witt Collection (217).

145 (Plate 86) 1830–35
Rock on the Downs near Hastings [317]
w/c. $24\frac{1}{2} \times 20$ (622 × 508).
Bequest. Richard Newsham, 1883.

146 Dated 1836
Old Oak at Faversham, Kent [314]

w/c. $25\frac{1}{2} \times 18\frac{1}{4}$ (648 × 464). Signed and dated 1836.
Bequest. Richard Newsham, 1883.
EXH. Hunt Exhibition 1981.
COMMENT. Perhaps exhibited OWCS, 1837, No. 1, as An Oak Tree near Guildford.

PRYOR, R. M. M., Hertfordshire

147 *c.*1815
Tree Study

Pencil. $3\frac{7}{8} \times 3$ (98 × 76). Signed with initials 'W.H.'
PROV. Gilbert Davis.

RIJKSMUSEUM, Amsterdam, Holland

148 *c.*1822
The Garden with Statues at Chiswick House

Reed pen, ink and w/c. $12\frac{1}{8} \times 15$ (307 × 382). Signed.
Bt 1979.
COMMENT. Another view of the gardens with garden statuary is in the Devonshire Collection, Chatsworth (53). The Gallery, Chiswick House, dated 1822, is in the same Collection (333, Plate 45).

ROSSETTI, Charles, London

149 1820–30
Boats on the Shore

Pencil. $3 \times 3\frac{5}{8}$ (76 × 92).

ROSSETTI, Mr and Mrs Harold, Suffolk

150 *c.*1815
Farm House and Yard

w/c. $9 \times 12\frac{3}{4}$ (228 × 324). Signed.
COMMENT. Bushey neighbourhood.

151 *c.*1820
Fishing Boats on the Beach at Hastings

Pencil. $6 \times 3\frac{5}{8}$ (152 × 94). Signed.

152 *c.*1820
Barn

In lane with gate.
w/c. $3\frac{1}{4} \times 5\frac{1}{8}$ (83 × 130). Signed.
Gift. Sir John and Lady Witt.

ROYAL ACADEMY OF ARTS, London

153
Jupp Catalogue [JU.9.5]

This consisted of 16 volumes compiled by E. J. Jupp (1812–77) and presented by him to the Royal Academy. Vol. IX comprised 12 drawings, all in pencil, and with one exception, Boat and Wagon – $6\frac{1}{8} \times 8\frac{5}{8}$ (155 × 220) – all small as follows: Beach and Rocks; Storm; Dark Trees in a Landscape; three of Babies; three of Dogs; two of Cats.
COMMENT. The volume contains a letter by Hunt dated 21 July 1847 from 62 Stanhope Street, Hampstead Road, to a Mr Mackinley: 'The frame is after my own fancy – hope that it would harmonise with the furniture in your drawing room. I trust you will accept of the same with best respects to Mrs Mackinley and my young moth.'

RYSKAMP, Charles, New York City

154 *c.*1820
Doorway on North Side of Aldenham Church

Looking across the churchyard.
Reed pen, ink and w/c. $13 \times 8\frac{1}{2}$ (330 × 216).

STIRLING, Angus, London

155 *c.*1818
Houses in a Hertfordshire Village

w/c. $14\frac{3}{8} \times 10\frac{1}{2}$ (365 × 265).
Bt 1968.
COMMENT. One of a pair, both of which were backed with newspaper (removed before purchase) dated 1818. Compare similar houses with same church spire (unidentified) behind, Huntington Library (93) and in Oxford, Ashmolean Museum (136).

STOKE-ON-TRENT, City Museums and Art Gallery

156 1815–20
Aldenham Churchyard [861.48]

w/c. $9\frac{3}{4} \times 13$ (247 × 330). Signed.
Bt 1948, from sale at Yildersley Hall, Ashbourne.
PROV. William Quilter; his sale, Christie's, 8 April 1875, Lot 199.

STRANGE, Mrs Mavis, London

157 1815–20
Cottage with Distant Landscape

w/c. $9\frac{1}{8} \times 11\frac{7}{8}$ (233 × 302).
COMMENT. Bushey neighbourhood.

TATE GALLERY, London

158 (Plate 2) *c.*1806
Twickenham [T.1154]

An inscription verso, presumably by Linnell, reads: 'Study from Nature at Twickenham by Hunt about 1806.'
Oil on millboard. $12\frac{3}{4} \times 6\frac{1}{2}$ (329 × 168).
Bt 1969.
PROV. Mrs John Lucas (great-granddaughter of John Linnell).
EXH. (1) Linnell and his Circle, P. and D. Colnaghi Ltd, 1973, No. 130, Pl. XLVI. (2) Hunt Exhibition 1981.
COMMENT. An almost identical view by John Linnell, dated 1806, was No. 4, repr. Pl. III in the Colnaghi exhibition, and is also in the Tate Gallery [T.934].

159 1820–30
Landscape with Barn [4315A]

Pencil. $3\frac{1}{8} \times 5$ (80 × 127). Signed.
Bequest. J. R. Holliday, 1927.

160 1820–30
Barn with Trees [4315B]

Pencil. $3\frac{1}{8} \times 5$ (80 × 127).
Bequest. J. R. Holliday, 1927.

TORBOCK, H. C., Cumbria

161 1820–30
Beach Scene with Fishing Boats [201]

Boats beached at Hastings with laundry line between.
w/c. $4\frac{1}{2} \times 7\frac{1}{2}$ (114 × 191).

VICTORIA AND ALBERT MUSEUM, London

162 1806–10
Landscape with Elm Trees and a Farm [440.1887]

Described on frame as view said to be near Bayswater.
Oil on millboard. $5\frac{1}{4} \times 7\frac{7}{8}$ (133 × 200).
EXH. Hunt Exhibition 1981.
BIB. Referred to in M. H. Grant, Vol. II, p. 311.

163 *c.*1810
Arcade, Doge's Palace, Venice [1146.1886 (BGM)]

w/c. $19\frac{5}{8} \times 14\frac{5}{8}$ (498 × 372).
Bequest. Joshua Dixon, 1886.
PROV. Hunt sale, Christie's 16–17 May 1864, Lot 306.
COMMENT. At Bethnal Green Museum. Related to a painting by Francesco Guardi in the Wallace Collection, London.

164 *c.*1810
Concert in the Piazza, Venice [E.3792.1934]

Reed pen, brown ink and sepia wash. $8\frac{1}{8} \times 13\frac{3}{8}$ (206 × 340).
EXH. Hunt Exhibition 1981.
COMMENT. Copied for Dr Monro after drawing by Canaletto. Similar version at Oxford, Ashmolean Museum (134, Plate 4).

165 1810–15
Mill at Mapledurham (?) on the Thames [A.L.5965]

Buildings and pollarded willow by water.
Pencil and w/c. $10\frac{1}{4} \times 14\frac{3}{8}$ (260 × 365).
COMMENT. Colour much faded.

166 *c.*1815
Landscape with Cottages [845a.1888]

Cottages framed in trees with stormy sky.
w/c. $6\frac{7}{8} \times 10$ (175 × 254).

167 *c*.1815
Landscape with Cottages [845.1888]

Row of trees on right.
w/c. 6⅞ × 10 (175 × 254).

168 *c*.1815
St Albans Cathedral, Hertfordshire [57.1896]

w/c. 13 × 16½ (330 × 419).
COMMENT. An early example of his work in the Bushey neighbourhood. Compare almost identical, though smaller version in Witt Collection (191).

169 (Colour Plate 4) 1815–20
Farmyard with a Pool [P3.1943]

Barn and outbuilding with trees.
Pencil and w/c. 13 × 16⅝ (330 × 423).

170 1815–20
Edgware [P.26.1968]

Distant view through trees of church and village.
w/c. 9 × 13 (230 × 330).
Gift. National Art-Collections Fund 1968 from the Herbert Powell Bequest.

171 *c*.1820
Cottage Door [FA.350]

Back door with woman leaning over gate reading, with big water butt and chickens.
Reed pen, brown ink and w/c. 13¾ × 10¼ (350 × 260).
Bt probably in the late 1850s.
COMMENT. Almost identical version in Witt Collection (195).

172 *c*.1820
Interior of an Old Church [318.1891]

Nave of Bushey Church.
Reed pen, sepia ink and w/c. 15½ × 12½ (394 × 318).
COMMENT. Compare similar version, with only minor differences, at Bradford, Art Galleries and Museums (17, Plate 26).

173 *c*.1820
Side Chapel in an Old Church, with Altar Tomb [317.1891]

Tomb is Coghill Monument in Aldenham Church before it was moved from side chapel to another part of church.
Reed pen, ink and w/c. 16⅝ × 13 (423 × 330).
BIB. Repr. Pl. 6 in Grant Longman, *Bushey Then and Now*, No. 4, 1968.

174 (Colour Plate 7) 1820–25
New Court, The Temple, London [3022.1876]

Reed pen, brown ink and w/c. 16⅜ × 19¾ (416 × 502).
Bequest. William Smith, 1876.
BIB. Repr. Pl. 39, Graham Reynolds, *An Introduction to English Water-Colour Painting*, 1950.

175 1820–25
The Old Fish Market, Hastings [1797.1888]

Numerous figures with buildings, narrow street, cliffs behind, and beach on right.
w/c heightened with white. 10¾ × 17¾ (273 × 451).
Signed.
Bequest. Arthur Ditchfield, 1888.
EXH. Hunt Exhibition 1981.

176 1820–25
Royal Horticultural Society's Gardens, Chiswick [134.1892]

Garden statuary among trees.
Reed pen, brown ink and w/c. 5¼ × 8¼ (133 × 210).

177 *c*.1830
Shore Scene [E.857.1948]

Waves rolling in on beach.
w/c heightened with white. 5 × 6¾ (126 × 172).
Signed.

WITT, C. W., Bucks.

178 *c*.1830
Ships at Sea [176]

w/c. 4 × 7 (102 × 178). Signed.

WITT, Sir John and Lady, London

179 (Plate 5) 1806–10
Saltwood Castle, Kent [1748]

Pencil and w/c. 5⅞ × 8 (148 × 206).
Bt 1970.
COMMENT. Strong Varley influence.

180 1806–10
Farm Outbuildings [1999]

Pencil and w/c. $8\frac{3}{4} \times 13\frac{1}{8}$ (224 × 334).

181 1810–15
Ships in Harbour [299]

Inscribed: 'at Margate'.
Reed pen, ink and w/c. $7 \times 13\frac{1}{4}$ (177 × 334).
Signed.
Bt 1934.

182 1810–15
Church, Farm Buildings and Cart [1011]

Pencil. $5\frac{5}{8} \times 5\frac{1}{4}$ (143 × 134). Signed.
Bt 1963.

183 1810–15
Oxsprings Farm [1663]

Farmyard with water barrel and chickens.
w/c. $8\frac{7}{8} \times 13\frac{5}{8}$ (224 × 346). Signed.
Bt 1970.

184 1810–15
Gate and Split Rail Fence [1844]

Reed pen, ink and w/c. $3\frac{7}{8} \times 6\frac{1}{8}$ (96 × 154).

185 1810–15
Study of a Gateway [1882]

w/c. $3\frac{3}{4} \times 4\frac{7}{8}$ (95 × 122). Signed.
Bt 1973.

186 1810–15
House in Trees [2105]

With distant landscape.
w/c. $3\frac{1}{4} \times 6$ (83 × 152). Signed.
Bt 1980.

187 *c.*1810
Thames Barges [2114]

Inscribed in Hunt's handwriting: 'Thames Barges seldom seen above Putney Bridge'. Verso ships and buildings.
Pencil and w/c. $6\frac{5}{8} \times 9\frac{3}{4}$ (167 × 248). Signed.
Bt 1980.

188 *c.*1811
Windsor Castle [2103]

Pencil heightened with white on grey green paper. $6\frac{1}{2} \times 11\frac{1}{2}$ (165 × 293). Signed.
Bt 1980.
COMMENT. Preliminary drawing for oil painting of Windsor Castle, National Trust (Fairhaven Collection), Anglesey Abbey (109, Plate 3). Oil painting was exhibited at British Institution, 1811, and OWCS, 1814, No. 41.

189 *c.*1811
Windsor Castle [2104]

Pencil on Whatman paper watermarked 1794.
$5\frac{7}{8} \times 12$ (148 × 205).
Bt 1980.
COMMENT. Different view of Castle to Witt Collection (188).

190 1815–20
Farm Cart [1003]

Pencil and w/c. 10×14 (254 × 355).
Bt 1963.
COMMENT. Compare farm cart in Huntington Library (91).

191 *c.*1815
St Albans Abbey, Hertfordshire [2124]

w/c. $11\frac{1}{2} \times 14\frac{3}{4}$ (292 × 375). Signed.
Bt 1981.
PROV. Michael John Holroyd of Halifax, *c.*1860. By descent to the immediate past owner, his granddaughter Miss Sybil Holroyd.
COMMENT. An early example of his work in the Bushey neighbourhood. Compare almost identical, though larger version in Victoria and Albert Museum (168).

192 *c.*1818
View of Old Hastings [2113]

Cliffs behind looking east.
Pencil and w/c. $7\frac{1}{2} \times 10$ (190 × 254). Signed.
Bt 1980.
COMMENT. Compare views of Hastings from White Rock, Hastings Museum and Art Gallery, inscribed 'July, 1818' (84) and looking west and down from the cliff in Oxford, Ashmolean Museum (137, Plate 6).

193 *c.*1820
The River Bank [1662]

w/c. $9\frac{5}{8} \times 13\frac{3}{4}$ (244 × 348). Signed.
Bt 1970.
EXH. Hunt Exhibition 1981.

194 *c*.1820
Beach Scene Hastings [1791]

Two figures looking out to sea.
w/c. 3 × 3¾ (77 × 95). Signed.
Bt 1971.
EXH. Hunt Exhibition 1981.

195 *c*.1820
Cottages near Bushey [2095]

Reed pen, brown ink and w/c. 14½ × 10¾ (370 × 275).
Bt 1980.
PROV. J. M. W. Turner. Charles Mallord Turner.
COMMENT. Almost identical version at Victoria and Albert Museum (171).

196 *c*.1820
Three Goats on the Beach under a Cliff [2117]

Black, yellow, and brown chalk. 4¼ × 6⅝ (108 × 168). Signed.

197 (Plate 28) *c*.1823
Interior of the Belfry, Bushey Church [2120]

Numbered 1 to 24 on right hand side in pencil, and squared for enlargement in pencil.
Reed pen and brown ink. 10⅞ × 8 (277 × 203).
COMMENT. Preliminary drawing for same subject at Yale Center (251, Plate 29).
Bt 1980.

198 1820–30
Path Through a Wood [52]

Pencil. 2¾ × 3⅛ (70 × 80).
Bt 1920.

199 1820–30
Horse and Cart and Boats on Beach [53]

Pencil. 3¾ × 5⅛ (95 × 130). Signed.
Bt 1920.

200 1820–30
Pull-cart, Boats and Figures on Beach [54]

Pencil. 3¼ × 4⅜ (83 × 112). Signed.
Bt 1920.

201 1820–30
River Estuary with Boats and Buildings [1239]

Pencil. 4½ × 7⅛ (114 × 182). Signed.
Bt 1965.

202 1820–30
A Country House with Cemetery in Foreground [2063]

Pencil. 4⅛ × 2⅝ (104 × 67).
Bt 1979.

203 1820–30
A Country House with Church in Foreground [2064]

Pencil. 3½ × 4¼ (90 × 122). Signed.
Bt 1979.

204 1820–30
Courtyard of a Large House in French Architectural Style [2065]

Pencil. 4⅝ × 3½ (117 × 90). Signed.
Bt 1979.

205 1820–30
Cart [2066]

Drawn by three horses on beach.
Pencil. 3⅜ × 4¼ (87 × 108).
Bt 1979.

206 1820–30
Three Fishing Boats on the Beach [2067]

Pencil. 3⅛ × 4⅛ (80 × 105).
Bt 1979.

207 1820–30
Fishing Boats [2068]

With group of fishermen on beach.
Pencil. 3⅜ × 4¼ (87 × 108).
Bt 1979.

208 1820–30
Group of Fishing Boats [2069]

Beached close together.
Pencil. 4 × 6⅜ (102 × 163). Signed.
Bt 1979.

209 1820–30
Study of Trees in Winter [2089]

Pencil. $5\frac{1}{2} \times 3\frac{3}{4}$ (140 × 94). Signed.
Bt 1979.

210 (Plate 21) 1820–30
Snow Scene [376]

w/c. $4 \times 6\frac{1}{2}$ (102 × 166). Signed.
Bt 1935.
PROV. J. P. Heseltine.
EXH. Hunt Exhibition 1981.

211 1820–30
Castle of Arques [2110]

So inscribed in Hunt's handwriting.
Pencil. $3\frac{1}{2} \times 4\frac{1}{4}$ (90 × 107). Signed.
Bt 1980.
COMMENT. This gives the impression of a sketch done on the spot. Arques is just south of St Omer in the Pas-de-Calais, and within 25 miles of Calais, Boulogne or Dunkerque. It has always been assumed that Hunt never went abroad, but spending so many winters at Hastings it would have been a comparatively easy matter for him to have crossed the Channel for a brief trip to France.

212 1820–30
Castle of Arques [2119]

So inscribed in Hunt's handwriting.
Black chalk slightly heightened with white. $6\frac{1}{2} \times 9\frac{3}{4}$ (165 × 247). Signed.
Bt 1980.
COMMENT. See under 211.

213 1825–30
Water Butt in the Snow [1291]

w/c. $3\frac{1}{4} \times 5$ (83 × 127).
Bt 1966.

214 *c.*1828
View of Old Hall Ruins, Hardwick [2081]

Taken from Hardwick Hall.
Pencil. $4\frac{1}{4} \times 9\frac{1}{4}$ (108 × 235). Signed.
Bt 1979.
COMMENT. The decorations on top of the wall are typical of Hardwick. Compare identical version, same size, signed and dated 1828 in Devonshire Collection Chatsworth (54).

215 (Plate 88) *c.*1830
Sunset Off Hastings Beach [1892]

w/c. $4\frac{3}{4} \times 6\frac{5}{8}$ (121 × 167). Signed.
Bt 1973.

216 *c.*1830
Late Sunset off Hastings Beach [1893]

w/c. $5 \times 6\frac{1}{2}$ (127 × 165). Signed.
Bt 1973.

216(a) *c.*1830
Chained Ship's Fender and Starfish on the Beach [2124]

w/c. $9 \times 13\frac{1}{2}$ (228 × 343). Signed.
Bt 1981.

217 *c.*1833
Elm Log in Farmyard [816]

w/c slightly heightened with white. $12\frac{1}{2} \times 16\frac{1}{2}$ (317 × 418). Signed.
Bt 1958.
COMMENT. Compare Pollard Elm, dated 1833, at Preston, Harris Museum (144, Colour Plate 13), and Elm Tree, Courtauld Institute (52).

218 1830–40
Fishing Boats on the Beach at Hastings [1635]

Pencil. $3\frac{1}{8} \times 5\frac{1}{8}$ (80 × 130).
Bt 1969.

219 (Plate 87) 1830–40
Fishing Boats on the Beach at Hastings [2049]

Pencil. $8\frac{1}{8} \times 10$ (206 × 254).
Bt 1978.
EXH. Hunt Exhibition 1981.

220 1830–40
Large Fishing Boat on the Beach at Hastings [2070]

Pencil. $6 \times 3\frac{3}{4}$ (153 × 95). Signed.
Bt 1979.

221 1830–40
Large Fishing Boat with Sails [2071]

Beached at Hastings with horse and carts alongside.
Pencil. $5\frac{7}{8} \times 4\frac{3}{8}$ (148 × 113).
Bt 1979.

222 1830–40
Group of Fishing Boats on the Beach [2091]

Pencil and faint w/c. $2\frac{3}{4} \times 3\frac{3}{4}$ (70 × 95).
Bt 1979.

223 *c*.1843
Race Meeting with Grandstand [2109]

Pencil. $3\frac{1}{2} \times 5\frac{1}{4}$ (90 × 133). Signed.
Bt 1980.
COMMENT. Sketch for more finished work of same subject, Witt Collection (224).

224 *c*.1843
Race Meeting with Grandstand [2108]

Pencil, pen and bistre ink on Whatman paper watermarked 1843. $7\frac{3}{8} \times 12\frac{1}{4}$ (187 × 312).
Bt 1980.
COMMENT. Compare pencil sketch of same subject, Witt Collection (223).

225
Wooded Landscape [140(a)]

Pencil. $2\frac{3}{8} \times 4\frac{1}{2}$ (60 × 114). Signed.
Bt 1927.

226
Cliff and Foreshore [140(b)]

Pencil. $3\frac{1}{4} \times 4\frac{1}{2}$ (83 × 114).
Bt 1927.

227
Ruined Church and House Behind [140(c)]

Pencil. $2\frac{1}{8} \times 3\frac{1}{2}$ (53 × 90). Signed.
Bt 1927.

228
Boats at Sea [140(d)]

Pencil. 2 × 4 (51 × 102). Signed.
Bt 1927.

229
Pulling in Boats [140(e)]

Pencil. $2\frac{3}{4} \times 4\frac{1}{8}$ (70 × 105). Signed.
Bt 1927.

WRIGHT, Mrs P. L. M., Somerset

230 *c*.1820
The Nave, Aldenham Church

Reed pen, ink and w/c. 16 × 13 (406 × 330).
COMMENT. Compare The Nave, Bushey Church (17, Plate 26).

231 *c*.1820
Side Chapel and Pulpit, Aldenham Church

Reed pen, ink and w/c. 16 × 13 (406 × 330).

YALE CENTER FOR BRITISH ART (Paul Mellon Collection), New Haven, Connecticut

232 *c*.1810
Buildings in Venice [B.1975.3.1070]

Reed pen, bistre ink and sepia wash. $9\frac{1}{8} \times 13\frac{3}{8}$ (232 × 340).
PROV. T. Girtin, 1909. Tom Girtin.
EXH. Royal Academy, London, Girtin Collection, 1962, No. 45.
COMMENT. Copy after drawing by Canaletto. Similar copies after drawings by Canaletto at British Museum (19), Oxford, Ashmolean Museum (134, Plate 4), Victoria and Albert Museum (164).

233 1811–15
Singer's Farm, Bushey [B.1975.3.964]

Pencil and w/c. $12\frac{13}{16} \times 17\frac{3}{4}$ (325 × 450).
PROV. Dr T. C. Girtin. G. W. Girtin. T. Girtin. Tom Girtin.
EXH. (1) Grosvenor Gallery, London, Water-Colour Drawings by Deceased Masters of the British School, 1877–78, No. 289 (as by Edridge). (2) Fitzwilliam Museum, Cambridge, Drawings by the Early English Watercolourists, 1920, No. 100.
COMMENT. T. Girtin notes in his Cat. card that 'this drawing was formerly attributed to Edridge, but is in fact a copy by Hunt of a drawing by Edridge in the Print Room, British Museum, dated on the old mount Oct. 17, 1811.' Size $12\frac{3}{8} \times 18\frac{3}{8}$ (315 × 467) [1845.8.18.7].

234 *c*.1815
Dr Monro's Carpenter at Work [B.1975.3.864]

Pencil and w/c. $11\frac{7}{8} \times 9$ (302 × 228).
PROV. T. Girtin, 1927. Tom Girtin.

EXH. Royal Academy, London, The Girtin Collection, 1962, No. 46.
BIB. Royal Academy 1962 Exhibition Cat. states that it has been suggested that the distant figure might be Dr Monro's son Alexander. Repr. Martin Hardie, Vol. III, Pl. 125.

235 *c.*1815
A Farmyard [B.1977.14.5921]

Water butts and poultry.
Pencil, reed pen, brown ink and w/c. $9\frac{7}{16} \times 11\frac{13}{16}$ (240 × 300).
PROV. Martin Hardie.
COMMENT. Martin Hardie's note on mount: 'early work c.1810–15'.

236 *c.*1815
Street in a Country Village [B.1975.3.1045]

With farm cart.
Pencil and w/c. $11 \times 14\frac{3}{16}$ (280 × 360).
PROV. T. Girtin, 1917. Tom Girtin.
COMMENT. More finished version at Yale Center (237).

237 *c.*1815
Street in Country Village [B.1975.4.1698]

With farm cart.
Reed pen and brown ink with faded green w/c. $10\frac{5}{8} \times 14\frac{1}{2}$ (271 × 371). Signed.
COMMENT. Preliminary drawing for same scene at Yale Center (236).

238 *c.*1815
A Fallen Oak [B.1977.14.5477]

w/c. $14\frac{5}{8} \times 21\frac{1}{4}$ (371 × 536).
PROV. Randall Davis. L. G. Duke.
COMMENT. Unusual Rowlandson/Howitt-type landscape, but main figure typical Hunt.

239 (Plate 8) *c.*1816
Building Waterloo Bridge [B.1975.3.1041]

With Somerset House in distance across river.
Reed pen and brown ink with brown and grey wash. $9\frac{7}{16} \times 15\frac{5}{8}$ (252 × 396). Signed.
PROV. Sir J. C. Robinson. T. Girtin, 1919. Tom Girtin.
EXH. Ruskin Hunt Exhibition 1879–80, No. 124, as 'Somerset House'.
BIB. Ruskin's note on No. 124 in Ruskin, *Works*, Vol. XIV, p. 446: 'Compare the entirely magnificent sketch of the riverside No. 124 which is as powerful in lines as Rembrandt'.

240 (Plate 15) 1815–20
Bushey Church from the South-West [B.1975.3.865]

Two young children sitting on stile outside churchyard.
Pencil and w/c. $7\frac{1}{4} \times 10\frac{1}{8}$ (183 × 251).
PROV. T. Girtin, 1902. Tom Girtin.
COMMENT. Aldenham Church, not Bushey.

241 1815–20
Old Farm Buildings and Farm Yard [B.1975.3.1046]

Pencil and w/c. $13\frac{1}{8} \times 16\frac{3}{4}$ (331 × 423).
PROV. T. Girtin, 1927. Tom Girtin.
COMMENT. Back view of Cottages in Bedford, Cecil Higgins (9).

242 1815–20
Back Yard of a Cottage [B.1975.3.1047]

Tree, water butts and figure of young woman.
Pencil and w/c. $9\frac{3}{8} \times 12\frac{1}{2}$ (238 × 318).
PROV. T. Girtin, 1909. Tom Girtin.

243 (Plate 14) 1815–20
A Farm House [B.1975.3.1044]

With man in doorway.
Pencil and w/c. $11\frac{13}{16} \times 15\frac{3}{4}$ (300 × 400).
PROV. T. Girtin, 1911. Tom Girtin.

244 (Plate 10) 1815–20
St Paul's Cathedral and Blackfriars Bridge [B.1977.14.5922]

Reed pen, brown ink and w/c. $9 \times 13\frac{3}{8}$ (228 × 340).
PROV. Martin Hardie.
COMMENT. Martin Hardie noted on mount: 'c.1815–20'.

245 (Plate 19) *c.*1820
A Lodge at Cassiobury [B.1975.4.1815]

Reed pen, ink and w/c. $10\frac{5}{8} \times 15$ (271 × 381). Signed.
Bt 1972.

246 (Plate 13) *c.*1820
The Lecture House, Watford [B.1977.14.4908]

w/c. $12\frac{7}{8} \times 16\frac{13}{16}$ (327 × 427).
PROV. Dr T. Monro. Lord Northwick. T. Girtin, 1920. Tom Girtin.

247 (Plate 18) *c.*1820
Village Street in St Albans [B.1975.3.1042]

Distant view over countryside.
Pencil and w/c. $9\frac{3}{8} \times 11\frac{3}{4}$ (237 × 297).
PROV. Dr T. Monro. Lord Northwick. T. Girtin; bt Northwick sale, 1921. Tom Girtin.

248 *c.*1820
The Essex Chantry, Watford Church [B.1975.3.963]

With tombs and banners of Essex family.
Reed pen, brown ink and w/c. $18\frac{1}{8} \times 14\frac{3}{8}$ (460 × 364).
PROV. Sir J. C. Robinson. T. Girtin, 1919. Tom Girtin.
EXH. Royal Academy, London, The Girtin Collection, 1962, No. 51.

249 *c.*1820
Bushey Church from the South West [B.1975.3.1040]

w/c. $7\frac{15}{16} \times 13$ (198 × 330).
PROV. Dr T. Monro. Lord Northwick. A. P. Oppé. T. Girtin, 1921. Tom Girtin.
EXH. Royal Academy, London, The Girtin Collection, 1962, No. 47.

250 (Plate 7) *c.*1820
The Flagstaff, Margate [B.1975.3.1217]

Pencil and w/c. $7\frac{15}{16} \times 11\frac{5}{8}$ (201 × 295).
PROV. Finberg. T. Girtin, 1924. Tom Girtin.
EXH. Royal Academy, London, The Girtin Collection, 1962, No. 56.

251 (Plate 29) *c.*1822
Interior of the Belfry, Bushey Church [B.1975.3.1039]

Pencil, reed pen, brown ink and w/c. $14\frac{7}{16} \times 10\frac{5}{16}$ (366 × 266).
PROV. Dr T. Monro. Lord Northwick. T. Girtin; bt Northwick sale, 1921. Tom Girtin.
COMMENT. Preliminary drawing, without w/c, numbered and squared for enlargement, Witt Collection (197, Plate 28).

252 (Plate 25) *c.*1822
Bushey Churchyard [76.1.8.10]

With the tombs of Henry Monro, Thomas Hearne and Henry Edridge, with Dr Monro on horseback.
Reed pen, brown ink and w/c. $12\frac{1}{4} \times 16\frac{1}{4}$ (312 × 413).
PROV. Dr T. Monro. Lord Northwick. George Guillemard. Mr and Mrs Paul Mellon.
COMMENT. The first tomb on the right is of Henry Monro, Dr Monro's second son who died in 1814 at the early age of 23. The next tomb to the left is of Henry Edridge who died in 1821, and the next small upright tomb to the left is of Thomas Hearne who died in 1817. Both Hearne and Edridge were intimate friends of Dr Monro, and his son Henry was a promising artist. Henry Monro's tomb was removed after Dr Monro's death to make way for flat tombstones under which many members of the Monro family were buried. This must be the original version. Other similar versions are in the British Museum (30) and at Whitworth Art Gallery, Manchester (107).

253 Dated 1825
View of Old London Bridge [B.1975.3.1236]

Reed pen and brown ink. $13\frac{3}{16} \times 21\frac{3}{16}$ (336 × 533). Signed and dated 1825.
Bt 1975.
COMMENT. Compare similar version, but with reed pen, brown ink and w/c, also dated 1825, in British Museum (31, Plate 11). Also later version exhibited in 1862, also in British Museum (32). London Bridge was rebuilt 1823–31 to Rennie's design by his son.

254 *c.*1831
Beauvais [B.1975.3.1043]

Street scene with the Cathedral in the distance on the right.
Reed pen, brown ink and w/c. $17 \times 13\frac{5}{8}$ (431 × 347).
PROV. Randall Davies. T. Girtin. Tom Girtin.
BIB. T. Girtin Cat. entry notes that an old mount, now missing, was inscribed and dated 1831. Yale Center Cat. entry states: 'probably after a drawing by Edridge'.
COMMENT. Woman's figure in doorway looks typically Hunt. Paper watermarked 'Whatman Turkey Mills 1830'.

255 *c.*1831
View of a Street in a French town [B.1975.3.1048]

So inscribed verso but now laid down.
Reed pen and brown ink. $18\frac{1}{8} \times 13\frac{3}{8}$ (461 × 340).
PROV. Dr Monro. Madelaine Le Geyt; given by her, 1929, to T. Girtin. Tom Girtin.

BIB. Yale Cat. entry states: 'believed to be after a drawing by Edridge'.
COMMENT. Unfinished. Compare Beauvais, Yale Center (254).

256 Exh. 1862
The Portico of St Martin-in-the-Fields
[B.1977.14.4909]

Reed pen, ink and w/c. $19\frac{1}{2} \times 13\frac{1}{2}$ (495×353). Signed.
PROV. C. J. Pooley. C. A. Coutts. William Quilter; his sale, Christie's, 8 April 1875, Lot 219. Wynne Ellis. T. Girtin, 1919. Tom Girtin.
EXH. (1) OWCS, Winter 1862, No. 249. (2) Ruskin Hunt Exhibition 1879–80, No. 123, lent by Mr Ellis. (3) Burlington Fine Arts Club, 1919, No. 34, repr. Pl. XV. (4) British Empire Exhibition, Wembley, 1924. (5) Royal Academy, London, The Girtin Collection, 1962, No. 50.
BIB. (1) Ruskin's note on No. 123 in Ruskin Hunt Exhibition 1879–80, Ruskin, *Works*, Vol. XIV, p. 446: 'Compare the St Martins Church No. 123 which is like a bit of Hogarth'. (2) Stephens, 1865, p. 32, refers to this work as 'A recent copy made by Hunt from this drawing [the Ashmolean drawing (141, Plate 24)] sold after his death for £17.17s.' (3) Repr. Pl. 132, John Baskett and Dudley Snelgrove, 1972; (4) Pl. 135, Andrew Wilton, 1977.
COMMENT. Compare earlier version of The Portico, dated 1822, commissioned by Dr Monro, at Oxford, Ashmolean Museum (141, Plate 24).

—2—
Figures
including domestic interiors

ABERDEEN, Art Gallery and Museums

257 Exh. 1841
The Ballad Singer

Boy holding sheaf of ballads.
w/c. $15\frac{1}{4} \times 10\frac{1}{8}$ (387 × 257).
Bt 1938.
EXH. (1) OWCS, 1841, No. 153, as Boy with Ballads. (2) Art Treasures, Manchester, 1857, No. 522 as owned by James Fallows.
COMMENT. Boy model.

ASPREY, Mrs Bridget, London

258 (Plate 34) Dated 1822
An Old Man Fishing by a Lock Gate

Reed pen, brown ink and w/c. 11 × 15 (280 × 382). Signed and dated 1822.
PROV. L. G. Duke.

BARKER, J., Newark, Notts

259 Dated 1831
The Art Critic

Young boy inspecting picture on easel, with two young girls sitting watching.
w/c heightened with white. $20\frac{3}{4} \times 25$ (526 × 635). Signed and dated 1831.
PROV. W. Barfoot.
EXH. Ruskin Hunt Exhibition 1879–80, No. 184.

BARLOW, Estate of the late Miss Helen, London

260 *c.*1835
Old Man Asleep [Probate No. 88]

Inscribed: 'Asleep May 4th 1835 aged 81 at near midsummer'.
Pencil and w/c. $9\frac{3}{4} \times 6\frac{1}{8}$ (247 × 155). Signed.

BASKETT, John, London

261 *c.*1835
Girl Standing in a Window

She stands against white curtain with one hand on her head, the other holding red-coloured book.
w/c heightened with white. $9\frac{1}{4} \times 6\frac{1}{4}$ (235 × 159).

262 *c.*1835
For the Squire

Young boy in profile with anxious expression, holding his hat, and probably expecting a dressing down.
w/c. $7\frac{5}{8} \times 5\frac{1}{4}$ (193 × 133). Signed.
PROV. Barnet Lewis, 1930.

263
Man Sitting at Table with Food and Tankard

Pencil. $4\frac{1}{8} \times 3\frac{1}{2}$ (103 × 89).
PROV. J. P. Heseltine. Sir Robert Witt.

BATH, Victoria Art Gallery

264 Exh. 1830
Fisherboy [P.1917.18]

Standing on beach with fishing basket.
w/c. $11\frac{3}{4} \times 8$ (297 × 203).

Bequest. Hon. Caroline Jervis, 1917.
EXH. OWCS, 1830, No. 273 as A Fishing Boy.

BEDFORD, Cecil Higgins Art Gallery

265 1825–30
Mrs Gurney Hoare [P.320/P.165]

Inscribed: 'Mrs. Gurney Hoare' not in Hunt's hand.
Pencil and w/c slightly heightened with white. $12\frac{3}{8} \times 9\frac{1}{8}$ (313 × 231). Signed.
Bt 1960.
EXH. Reading Art Gallery, 1965.
COMMENT. Mrs Gurney Hoare was Caroline Bradley of a Quaker family and married to John Gurney Hoare (1810–76).

266 (Plate 41) *c.*1830
Young Girl Reclining on a Couch
[P.194/P.212]

w/c. $14 \times 10\frac{1}{4}$ (354 × 260).
Bt 1958.
EXH. Reading Art Gallery, 1965.
BIB. Repr. OWCS Club, Vol. 1961, Pl. V.

267 (Plate 75) Exh. 1834
The Maid and the Magpie, a Cottage Interior at Shillington, Bedfordshire [P.609/PE234]

w/c slightly heightened with white. $17\frac{3}{8} \times 22\frac{3}{8}$ (441 × 569).
Bt 1970.
PROV. George A. Musgrave. Horace Musgrave. C. Fairfax Murray.
EXH. (1) OWCS, 1834, No. 20 as The Maid and the Magpie. (2) Royal Academy, London, 1908, No. 214.
COMMENT. On label verso: 'William Hunt date 1838 exposed to the light for 48 years. Interior of Cottage at Shillington now the property of Horace Musgrave Esq. Painted for George Musgrave Esq. deceased of Shillington Manor, Beds'.
Another label (in different handwriting): 'Shillington, Beds. Cottage David Coopers daughter paring apples. Drawn by Wm. Hunt for my father in 1838.'
The date of OWCS exh., 1834, must be preferred to 1838.

BIRKENHEAD, Williamson Art Gallery and Museum

268 Exh. 1825
The Poacher [BIKGM.1681]

w/c. $12\frac{1}{2} \times 9\frac{1}{2}$ (317 × 242).
Gift. John McKay, 1930.
EXH. OWCS, 1825, No. 139 as A Poacher.

269 *c.*1831
Interior of Cockshot Farm. June 17, 1831.
[BIKGM.2255]

So inscribed. Man sitting by fire.
w/c. $6\frac{1}{2} \times 10$ (166 × 254).
Bequest. Dr H. Nazeby Harrington, 1936.

270 Exh. 1841
The Young Shaver [BIKGM.1782]

w/c. $15 \times 10\frac{3}{4}$ (381 × 273). Signed.
Bt 1930.
EXH. (1) OWCS, 1841, No. 105 as Giving himself (H)Airs. (2) Hunt Exhibition 1981.
BIB. Roget, Vol. II, p. 192.

BIRMINGHAM, City Museum and Art Gallery

271 (Plate 32) *c.*1820
Farmer in a Barn [258/53]

w/c heightened with white. $10\frac{3}{4} \times 7\frac{1}{8}$ (274 × 182).
Bequest. J. Leslie Wright, 1953.
EXH. (1) Royal Academy, London, 1949, No. 269. (2) Tokyo, 1967, No. 122. (3) Detroit Institute of Arts, 1968, No. 155. (4) Philadelphia Museum of Art, 1968, No. 155.

272 (Plate 36) Exh. 1824
A Miller in his Mill [57/31]

Reed pen, ink and w/c. $15\frac{1}{4} \times 11\frac{7}{8}$ (387 × 303). Signed with initials 'W.H.'
Bequest. J. R. Holliday, 1927.
EXH. OWCS, 1824, No. 286 as The Miller.
COMMENT. Probably Hunt's future father-in-law. Compare Self Portrait (wrongly so-titled) at Port Sunlight, The Lady Lever Art Gallery, of what is suggested to be the same sitter (473, Plate 37). See under 473.

273 *c.*1829
David Cox Senior and Junior Playing a Game [895/27]

Black chalk. $3\frac{5}{8} \times 4\frac{1}{2}$ (93 × 114).
Bequest. J. R. Holliday, 1927.
EXH. Hunt Exhibition 1981.
COMMENT. David Cox Senior (1783–1859) looks about 45, David Cox Junior (1809–85) about 20, therefore date *c.*1829.

274 (Plate 77) 1835–40
Slumber [168/28]

w/c. $13\frac{5}{8} \times 16\frac{7}{8}$ (342 × 428). Signed.
Bequest. John Feeney, 1928.
EXH. (1) Royal Academy, London, Primitives to Picasso, 1962, No. 400. (2) Arts Council Touring Exhibition of British Watercolours 1760–1930, from the Birmingham Museums and Art Gallery, 1980, No. 61, repr. p. 19.
BIB. Repr. Pl. 44, Graham Reynolds, *An Introduction to English Water-Colour Painting*, 1950.

BLACKBURN, Museum and Art Gallery

275 1820–25
Figure of Man with Sword and Shield [453]

w/c. $13\frac{1}{8} \times 9\frac{7}{8}$ (334 × 250). Signed.
Bequest. Mrs E. A. Yerburgh, 1948.

276 *c.*1830
Self Portrait [449]

w/c. $7\frac{3}{8} \times 5\frac{5}{8}$ (180 × 145).
Bequest. Mrs E. A. Yerburgh, 1948.
EXH. Hunt Exhibition 1981.
COMMENT. Aged about 40.

277 *c.*1833
Girl at Prayer [23]

w/c. $11 \times 18\frac{1}{8}$ (280 × 460). Signed.
Bequest. Mrs R. B. Dodgson, 1884.
COMMENT. This is one of a notable group of bedroom interiors of the early 1830s. Compare same patchwork quilt, chest of drawers and chair in Sunday Morning, dated 1833, in Huntington Library (407, Plate 74). Also same patchwork quilt and similar furniture in Witt Collection (553, Colour Plate 16); also similar furniture in Girl Reading at a Window, dated 1832, Duke of Norfolk Collection (458, Plate 78), and in *Preparing for Sunday*, Preston, Harris Museum and Art Gallery (482).

278 *c.*1835
The Rustic Artist [537]

Boy holding palette and brush seated at easel.
w/c. $17\frac{3}{8} \times 11\frac{3}{4}$ (440 × 330). Signed.
Bequest. E. L. Hartley, 1954.
PROV. Edwin Heritage. Sold Christie's, 18 March 1871, Lot 18; bt by Gurney. George Gurney. Sold Christie's, 11 July 1903, Lot 19.
EXH. (1) Ruskin Hunt Exhibition 1879–80, No. 164, as A Young Artist, lent by Mr George Gurney. (2) Hunt Exhibition 1981.
BIB. Ruskin, *Works*, 'Notes on the Exhibition', p. 446, refers to this work as 'Full of Humour; but there is no place for humour in true painting.'

BOURNEMOUTH, Russell-Cotes Art Gallery and Museum and The Rothesay Museum

279 *c.*1825
Head of a Boy Wearing a Hat [258]

w/c. $4\frac{1}{2} \times 3\frac{1}{2}$ (115 × 90). Signed.
Gift. Sir Merton Russell-Cotes, 1922.

BRANDT, Estate of the late Walter, London

280 1815–20
Portrait of a Youth

w/c. $6\frac{1}{2} \times 4\frac{5}{8}$ (160 × 117) oval.

281 *c.*1820
Farm Boy

Sitting in barn.
w/c slightly heightened with white. $11 \times 8\frac{1}{2}$ (280 × 216).

282 Dated 1827
Fisher Boy and Young Girl

w/c. $10\frac{1}{4} \times 7\frac{1}{2}$ (260 × 190). Signed and dated 1827.

283 1820–30
Portrait of a Man

With long side-burns.
Pencil. $4 \times 3\frac{1}{2}$ (101 × 89).

284 *c.*1830
An Old Gentleman

Inscribed: 'from W. Hunt'.
Pencil and w/c. $9 \times 3\frac{1}{2}$ (229 × 89).

285 Dated 1831
School Boy

w/c heightened with white. $12 \times 8\frac{1}{2}$ (305×216).
Signed and dated 1831.

THE BRANTWOOD TRUST, Brantwood, Coniston, Cumbria

286 *c.*1835
An Interior of a Farm Shed [734]

w/c heightened with white. $17\frac{1}{4} \times 13\frac{1}{2}$ (438×343).
Bt from Sharp Estate, 1960.
PROV. John Ruskin. Severn Family. F. J. Sharp.
EXH. Ruskin Hunt Exhibition 1879–80, No. 174.
BIB. Ruskin, *Works*, Vol. XIV, pp. 378, 383 and 442. p. 378: 'For an especial instance, the drawing of the interior No. 174, may be taken as a final example of the confidence which the painter felt in his power of giving some kind of interest to the most homely objects, and rendering the transitions of ordinary light and shade impressive, though he had nothing more sacred to illuminate than a lettuce and nothing more terrible to hide than a reaping hook'.

BRIGHTON, The Royal Pavilion, Art Gallery and Museums

287 *c.*1830
The Pursuit of Knowledge under Difficulties [101273]

Two boys, one reading by lantern light.
w/c. $10\frac{7}{8} \times 12\frac{7}{8}$ (276×328). Signed.
Bt 1961.

BRISTOL, Museum and Art Gallery

288 *c.*1825
Sporting Gentleman in a High Straw Hat Cleaning his Gun

Squared for enlargement, but lines have been carefully rubbed out of the background.
Pencil and w/c. $11\frac{1}{2} \times 8$ (292×202).
Bt 1947.
COMMENT. Compare stylistically with Man Playing Flute, Witt Collection (547).

BRITISH MUSEUM, London

289 *c.*1815
Portrait of Robert Clutterbuck
[1888.1.16(12) & (13) LB10 (a) (b)]

Indian ink (pale). $5 \times 3\frac{7}{8}$ (127×97).
EXH. Hunt Exhibition 1981.
COMMENT. Mounted with engraving by W. Bond.

290 1815–20
Boy Holding a Puppy [1889.7.24.362 (LB4)]

Reed pen, brown ink and w/c. $6\frac{3}{4} \times 4\frac{7}{8}$ (170×123).
COMMENT. Compare same boy holding puppy, in same medium, in Witt Collection (542).

291 1815–20
Portrait of a Young Man [1877.8.11.18 (LB8)]

Pencil. $7\frac{1}{2} \times 5\frac{1}{2}$ (190×140).
Bt 1877.

292 1815–20
Portrait of an Elderly Man Wearing Spectacles and Reading [1877.8.11.19 (LB9)]

Pencil. $6\frac{1}{8} \times 4$ (155×103).
Bt 1877.

293 (Plate 39) *c.*1820
Group of Three Women [1884.3.8.82 (LB6)]

Pencil and w/c. $7\frac{1}{8} \times 5\frac{5}{8}$ (180×142). Signed.

294 *c.*1820
Girl Threading a Needle [1884.3.8.33 (LB7)]

Pencil. $5\frac{3}{4} \times 4\frac{1}{8}$ (145×104). Signed (in ink).

295 *c.*1825
Three Figures on the River Bank
[1889.7.24.363 (LB3)]

Two girls with bonnets and man in bluish tail-coat and top hat.
Black chalk and w/c. $10\frac{1}{4} \times 6\frac{7}{8}$ (260×175).

296 1825–30
Girl Seated [1889.7.24.364 (LB2)]

With reddish hair at table with lamp.
Pencil and w/c. $6\frac{1}{4} \times 4\frac{1}{2}$ (158×114) oval.

297 *c.*1830
Portrait of a Woman in Purple Dress
[1934.9.22 No. 42]

w/c. Diameter $5\frac{7}{8}$ (150) circular. Signed.
EXH. Hunt Exhibition 1981.
COMMENT. Separately mounted from Album A.7 (see under 306).

298 (Colour Plate 14) Dated 1832
Plucking the Fowl [1958.7.12.353]

Girl in blue blouse plucking pink-breasted chicken.
w/c with much scratching. $13\frac{5}{8} \times 14\frac{1}{4}$ (346 × 362). Signed and dated 1832 (on brick wall).
Bequest. R. W. Lloyd, 1958.
EXH. OWCS, 1833, No. 309, as Picking a Fowl.

299 1830–35
The Poacher [1935.6.8.7]

Head and shoulders, face stippled.
w/c slightly heightened with white. $7 \times 6\frac{1}{2}$ (178 × 165). Signed.

300 Dated 1836
Sleeping Man [1934.9.22 No. 40]

Pencil. $5\frac{3}{8} \times 3\frac{3}{4}$ (136 × 96). Signed W.H. and dated 5 Nov. 1836.
COMMENT. Separately mounted from Album A.7 (see under 306).

301 *c.*1837
Little Emma Reclining [1934.9.22 No. 18]

Two separate studies of Emma on sofa. Inscribed with above title and: 'at Mr Hunt's 7 January, 1832'.
Pencil. $5 \times 6\frac{1}{8}$ (112 × 157).
COMMENT. Emma, born in 1832, looks about 5, so the date 1832 must be mistaken. Separately mounted from Album A.7 (see under 306).

302 *c.*1840
Self Portrait [1889.9.8.1 (LB1)]

w/c slightly heightened with white on hair and collar. $13\frac{3}{4} \times 10\frac{7}{8}$ (351 × 277).
EXH. Hunt Exhibition 1981.
COMMENT. Aged about 50.

303 *c.*1840
Girl Standing Full Length Reading a Letter
[1923.3.2.4]

Black chalk heightened with white. $12\frac{1}{8} \times 8\frac{1}{2}$ (318 × 216).
Gift. Miss C. Nowlan, 1923.
COMMENT. Unusually broad and free drawing.

304 *c.* 1843
Portrait of his Daughter [1934.9.22 No. 58]

Looking out of lattice window. Inscribed with above title.
w/c. $4\frac{1}{8} \times 5\frac{1}{8}$ (103 × 132).
COMMENT. His daughter Emma aged about 11. Separately mounted from Album A.7 (see under 306).

305 *c.*1844
Young Girl Full Length in Blue Dress
[1934.9.22 No. 53]

w/c. $7\frac{1}{2} \times 4\frac{1}{4}$ (190 × 108). Signed with initials 'W. H.'
COMMENT. His daughter Emma aged about 12. Mounted separately from Album A.7 (see under 306).

306
Album A.7 [1934.9.22]

Consists of 'Drawings by William Henry Hunt and others from a scrap book once in the possession of Mrs Baxter of Compton Terrace, Highbury, a great niece of the artist'. Hunt drawings numbered 1–124 inclusive with a number of gaps. They comprise mainly portrait and figure drawings, a number of members of his family; e.g. Nos. 2–7 inclusive, of his sister-in-law Maria Hunt; Nos. 9–14 inclusive, of his nephew Charles Steedman (born 1826) as a baby (No. 9) and at varying ages up to 18 (No. 14); his niece Sophia Steedman (born 1830) as a baby (No. 18); and other members of the Steedman family. Nos. 60 and 61 are of chess players. The album also includes (91–120 inclusive) shore scenes around Hastings and a few landscapes mainly in pencil and small in size. No. 93 is of shipping and is more elaborate than the usual landscape/seascape – $6\frac{5}{8} \times 8\frac{5}{8}$ (167 × 218) – and inscribed on verso: 'W. Hunt, 6 Marchmont Street.' As Hunt lived at that address from 1825 to 1842, No. 93 is dateable between those years. No. 121 is of Caroline Place, Hastings, in pen and sepia ink and inscribed in Hunt's handwriting: 'this our prospect one way, with the sea to our right'. Also inscribed on verso: '1 Caroline House, Caroline Place, Hastings'. The album also includes the following small pencil drawings of animals: Nos 83 and 84 Cats; 85 and 86 Pug Dog Asleep; 87 Two Pigs.
Bt 2 September 1934 from Mr A. Brandon through the Florence Fund.

307
Sketch Book [1877.2.10.73 (LB12)]

Inscribed on fly leaf 'Sol Club'.
$6\frac{1}{4} \times 9\frac{1}{4}$ (158 × 235).
Contains: (1) 21 pages of men's portraits,

members of the Sol Club, including one inscribed 'Hunt the Slipper'. Pencil and pen. Signed. (2) A man with glasses, perhaps a singing teacher, with a mixed group of young pupils. Pencil and pen. (3) 8 landscapes and buildings, 2 with windmills. Pencil.
EXH. Hunt Exhibition 1981.
COMMENT. No record of the Sol Club has been traced, but it may be connected with the Sol Arms in St Pancras.

BURNLEY, Towneley Hall Art Gallery and Museums

308 1830–35
The Frugal Meal [WA/CO.72]

Boy sitting on chest in outhouse feeding a dog.
w/c. $14\frac{1}{4} \times 10\frac{1}{4}$ (362 × 261). Signed.
Bt 1933.
COMMENT. Boy model.

309 1830–35
Study: A Boy on a Chair [WA/CO.74]

w/c. $12\frac{1}{4} \times 9$ (312 × 228).
Gift. Wilfrid Dean of Burnley, 1933.

310 1835–40
A Warrior Bold [WA/CO.78]

Boy wearing hat with feather holding large sword, with suit of armour on the ground.
w/c heightened with white. $18\frac{1}{2} \times 13$ (470 × 330). Signed.
Gift. Wilfrid Dean of Burnley, 1933.
PROV. Barnet Lewis.
EXH. Hunt Exhibition 1981.
COMMENT. Boy model.

311 Dated 1837
Cimon and Iphigenia [WA/CO.32]

w/c heightened with white. $22\frac{1}{4} \times 18$ (540 × 457). Signed and dated 1837.
Bt 1924.
PROV. Sam Mendel. William Quilter; his sale, Christie's, 9 April 1875, Lot 228.
EXH. (1) OWCS, 1837, No. 9 as Girl in a Woodhouse. (2) Hunt Exhibition 1981.
COMMENT. Boy model. Compare larger version of same subject in Captain R. Sheepshanks's Collection (501). The legend of Cimon and Iphigenia is derived from the *Decameron* of Boccaccio. Cimon, the son of a nobleman of Cyprus, was a handsome youth though coarse and unlettered. He fell in love with Iphigenia and after certain vicissitudes married her. The effects of love were wholly beneficial, changing him into an accomplished and polished gallant. This moral allegory was popular with seventeenth-century artists who depicted the moment that Cimon first set eyes on Iphigenia.

312 Exh.1847
Christmas Pie [WA/CO.71]

Smiling boy sitting at table with pie in front of him and holding knife and fork.
w/c. $15\frac{1}{2} \times 11\frac{1}{2}$ (394 × 293). Signed.
Bt 1933.
EXH. (1) OWCS, 1847, No. 232. (2) Hunt Exhibition 1981.

BURY, Art Gallery

313 *c.*1836
Pickaback [78]

Mother and daughter, probably Mrs Hunt and Emma aged about 4.
w/c. 13 × 12 (330 × 306) oval. Signed.
Gift. Wrigley Family, 1901.
PROV. Thomas Wrigley, a local paper manufacturer who died 1880.
COMMENT. Compare preliminary version, Derby, Museum and Art Gallery (330).

314 *c.*1844
Peasant Woman [75]

Seated, three-quarter length, with hands folded in her lap.
w/c. $14 \times 9\frac{1}{2}$ (355 × 242).
Gift. Wrigley Family, 1901.
PROV. Thomas Wrigley, a local paper manufacturer who died 1880.
COMMENT. His daughter Emma aged about 12.

BUXTON, John, Wiltshire

315
Man Seated at a Table

Pencil. $4\frac{1}{8} \times 3\frac{1}{2}$ (105 × 89).

BYAM SHAW, James, London

316 1825–30
Young Girl Reading by Lamplight

w/c on blue paper. $5\frac{7}{8} \times 5\frac{3}{8}$ (149 × 137).

317 *c*.1830
Young Boy Standing and Leaning on a Table Wearing Cap.

Black and red chalk and sepia wash. $14\frac{1}{8} \times 10$ (358 × 254). Signed.

CAMBRIDGE, Fitzwilliam Museum

318 Exh. 1832
The Gleaner [1796]

Young girl with a sheaf of corn.
w/c heightened with white with surface scratching. $11 \times 7\frac{5}{8}$ (280 × 194).
Bequest. Arthur W. Young, Trinity College, 1936.
EXH. OWCS, 1832, No. 34.
BIB. Repr. Pl. 19 (lithograph), Thomas Fairland, *Hunt's Comic Sketches*, 1844.
COMMENT. Almost identical version in Fry Collection (383).

319 *c*.1833
Portrait of Samuel Prout [742]

Black chalk heightened with white on buff paper. $6\frac{5}{8} \times 5$ (170 × 126).
Gift. C. Fairfax Murray, 1912.
EXH. Ruskin Hunt Exhibition 1879–80, No. 177.
COMMENT. Samuel Prout (1783–1852) was a landscape and architectural artist greatly admired by Ruskin. He shared with Hunt Ruskin's Exhibition of Prout and Hunt in 1879–80. Aged about 50.

320 *c*.1833
Mr W. Scott, Member of the Water Colour Society [743]

Inscribed with above title.
Pencil. $4\frac{3}{8} \times 3\frac{1}{2}$ (111 × 89). Signed.
Gift. C. Fairfax Murray, 1912.
COMMENT. William Scott (1783–1855) exhibited works mainly of rustic architecture. Cat. of the Hunt sale at Christie's, 17 May 1864, Lot 229 comprised: 'Five portraits of members of the Old Society of Water-Colours: Mr Fielding, Mr Nash, Mr Scott, and two others'. Scott aged about 50. See also Halifax, Bankfield Museum for portrait of Copley Fielding (393).

321 (Colour Plate 15) Dated 1838
The Outhouse [739]

Young woman (Mrs Hunt) standing in doorway.
w/c heightened with white and much scratching. $21\frac{1}{4} \times 29\frac{1}{2}$ (540 × 749). Signed and dated 1838.
Gift. C. Fairfax Murray, 1912.
EXH. Linnell and his Circle, P. and D. Colnaghi Ltd, 1973, No. 135.
BIB. Repr. Pl. 139, Wilton, 1977.

CLARK, Colin, London

322 *c*.1820
Portrait of a Bearded Man

w/c. $7\frac{1}{2} \times 8\frac{7}{8}$ (191 × 226). Signed with initials 'W. H.'

COLMAN, the late Sir Jeremiah Colman, Bt

323 (Plate 62) Exh. 1840
A Young Cricketer

w/c. $18\frac{1}{8} \times 14\frac{1}{8}$ (462 × 360). Signed.
EXH. OWCS, 1840, No. 236.
COMMENT. Compare Boy Cricketer at Marylebone Cricket Club, Lords (442). Boy model.

COURTAULD Institute of Art, University of London

324 (Plate 35) *c*.1825
The Vegetable Seller [86]

Man wearing top hat, with yoke on his back with two baskets of vegetables attached.
Reed pen, ink and w/c. $15 \times 10\frac{3}{8}$ (381 × 264). Signed.
Bequest. W. W. Spooner, 1967.
PROV. G. Reitlinger.
EXH. (perhaps) OWCS, 1825, No. 194 as The Gardener.
COMMENT. Preliminary drawing at Victoria and Albert Museum (521).

325 1820–30
Head of a Young Girl [3546(a)]

Pencil, black and red. $2\frac{7}{8} \times 2$ (73 × 52).
Bequest. Sir Robert Witt, 1952.

326
Man's Portrait [3546(b)]

Pencil. $4\frac{1}{4} \times 3\frac{1}{8}$ (105 × 79).
Bequest. Sir Robert Witt, 1952.

327
Portrait of a Young Boy [3546(c)]

Pencil. $3\frac{7}{8} \times 3\frac{1}{8}$ (99 × 81).
Bequest. Sir Robert Witt, 1952.

CUTHBERTSON, Allan, London

328 (Plate 73) *c*.1835
The Young Apple Seller

w/c. $13\frac{5}{8} \times 9\frac{1}{2}$ (346 × 242).

DANIELS, David, New York City

329 (Colour Plate 10) *c*.1830
Negro Boxer

w/c heightened with white. $14 \times 9\frac{1}{2}$ (355 × 242).
Signed.

DERBY, Museum and Art Gallery

330 *c*.1835
Pickaback

Mother and daughter, probably Mrs Hunt and Emma aged about 4.
w/c. $12 \times 9\frac{3}{4}$ (306 × 247).
Bequest. Col. Richard Sale, 1904. Col. Sale, of the Royal Bengal Engineers, was a member of an old Derby family, and died in 1903.
COMMENT. Compare more finished version, Bury Art Gallery (313).

331 Exh. 1839
All Fours – A Critical Moment

Two boys playing cards in kitchen.
w/c. $19\frac{1}{2} \times 15\frac{1}{4}$ (496 × 387).
Bequest. Col. Richard Sale, 1904. Col. Sale, of the Royal Bengal Engineers, was a member of an old Derby family, and died in 1903.
EXH. (1) OWCS, 1839, No. 127 as All Fours.
(2) Hunt Exhibition 1981.
COMMENT. Boy model.

DEVONSHIRE Collection Chatsworth, Derbyshire

332 (Plate 47) Dated 1822
The Saloon, Devonshire House [WC45]

w/c. $10\frac{3}{8} \times 12\frac{1}{4}$ (265 × 310). Signed and dated 1822.
EXH. Treasures from Chatsworth, Royal Academy, London, 1980, No. 126.

333 Dated 1822
The Gallery, Chiswick House [WC46]

w/c. $11\frac{7}{8} \times 9\frac{1}{8}$ (290 × 232). Signed and dated 1822.

334 (Plate 45) Dated 1822
The Gallery, Chiswick House [WC44]

w/c. $12\frac{3}{4} \times 10$ (325 × 255). Signed and dated 1822.
EXH. Treasures from Chatsworth, Royal Academy, London, 1980, No. 125.

335 Dated 1822
The Morning Room, Chatsworth [WC47]

w/c. $9\frac{7}{8} \times 11\frac{1}{4}$ (253 × 285). Signed and dated 1822.
BIB. Repr. Pl. 79, Francis Thompson, *History of Chatsworth*, Country Life, 1949.
COMMENT. Later altered to the library.

336 *c*.1822
North Entrance Hall, Chatsworth

w/c. $7\frac{3}{4} \times 13$ (197 × 330). Signed.
BIB. Contained in a grangerised large paper edition of the 6th Duke's *Handbook to Chatsworth and Hardwick*.

337 Dated 1822
Canova's Bust of Laura

w/c. $7\frac{1}{4} \times 4\frac{3}{8}$ (184 × 111). Signed and dated 1822.
BIB. Contained in a grangerised large paper edition of the 6th Duke's *Handbook to Chatsworth and Hardwick*.

338 Dated 1823
The Butler's Room, Chatsworth

w/c. $9 \times 10\frac{3}{4}$ (229 × 273). Signed and dated 1823.
BIB. Contained in a grangerised large paper edition of the 6th Duke's *Handbook to Chatsworth and Hardwick*.

339 *c*.1823
The Kitchen, Chatsworth

w/c. $11\frac{3}{4} \times 9\frac{1}{2}$ (298 × 241). Signed.
BIB. Removed from grangerised large paper edition of the 6th Duke's *Handbook to Chatsworth and Hardwick*. Contemporaneous with The Butler's Room, Chatsworth which is dated 1823 (338).

340 Dated 1827
The First Duke's Staircase in the Painted Hall

w/c heightened with white. $11 \times 8\frac{1}{2}$ (280 × 215). Signed and dated 1827.

BIB. Repr. Pl. 11, Francis Thompson, *History of Chatsworth*, Country Life, 1949.

341 (Colour Plate 6) *c.*1827
The Library, Chatsworth [WC52]

w/c. $10 \times 11\frac{1}{4}$ (255 × 285).
EXH. Treasures from Chatsworth, Royal Academy, London, 1980, No. 127.
BIB. Repr. Pl. 77, Francis Thompson, *History of Chatsworth*, Country Life, 1949.

342 *c.*1827
The Old Library, Chatsworth [WC48]

w/c heightened with white. $9\frac{3}{8} \times 9\frac{5}{8}$ (238 × 244).
BIB. Repr. Pl. 81, Francis Thompson, *History of Chatsworth*, Country Life, 1949.

343 *c.*1827
Member of the 6th Duke's Orchestra, Chatsworth

Standing playing violin with book of music on chair behind.
w/c. $9\frac{3}{4} \times 6$ (248 × 152).

344 *c.*1827
Groom of Chambers, Chatsworth

Standing holding billiard cue with billiard table behind.
w/c. $9\frac{3}{4} \times 6$ (248 × 152).

345 *c.*1827
Butler, Chatsworth

Standing holding gold jug and goblet.
w/c. $10\frac{1}{4} \times 6\frac{1}{8}$ (260 × 155).

346 *c.*1827
Footman, Chatsworth

Standing doing slight dance.
w/c. $10\frac{1}{4} \times 6\frac{1}{8}$ (260 × 155).

347 *c.*1827
Portrait of a Woman

She is sitting, wearing tall white hat, her feet on footstool, with her work basket, and small dog jumping up.
w/c. $18\frac{3}{4} \times 13\frac{7}{8}$ (476 × 352).
COMMENT. Perhaps the housekeeper.

348 *c.*1827
Portrait of Mrs Gregory

Pencil and red chalk. $6\frac{1}{4} \times 4\frac{1}{8}$ (159 × 105).
COMMENT. Mrs Gregory was housekeeper at Chatsworth during part of the 1820s.

349 *c.*1827
Portrait of Miss Sarah Bown

Pencil. $7 \times 4\frac{1}{2}$ (178 × 114).
COMMENT. Sarah Bown was the niece of the then housekeeper Mrs Gregory, and subsequently married Joseph Paxton who came to Chatsworth in 1826, and later built the great conservatory. He was later knighted and his wife Sarah became Lady Paxton.

350 Dated 1828
The Library, Hardwick [WC49]

w/c. $10\frac{1}{2} \times 17\frac{3}{8}$ (266 × 440). Signed and dated 1828.
EXH. OWCS, 1828, No. 346, under title Library of His Grace the Duke of Devonshire at Hardwick, as belonging to the Duke of Devonshire.

351 (Plate 46) Dated 1828
The Long Gallery, Hardwick [WC50]

w/c. $11\frac{1}{4} \times 16\frac{3}{4}$ (286 × 427). Signed and dated 1828.
EXH. OWCS, 1828, No. 365, as belonging to the Duke of Devonshire.

352 Dated 1828
Mary Queen of Scots' Room, Hardwick [WC51]

w/c. 9 × 13 (230 × 329). Signed and dated 1828.
EXH. OWCS, 1828, No. 330, as belonging to the Duke of Devonshire.

DURLACHER, Sir Esmond, Dorset

353 1830–40
Boy Asleep, Sitting in a Wooden Backed Chair

w/c. $10\frac{1}{2} \times 8$ (267 × 203).
PROV. Bt by the owner's maternal grandfather Sir Reginald Hanson, *c.*1880.

DURLACHER, Mrs R., London

354
Contented with Little

Boy seated on tub at table, holding dumpling on fork.
11 × 7¾ (280 × 197).
PROV. R. Bernal. E. H. Lawrence.
EXH. Royal Academy, London, Works by Old Masters, 1892.

EDWARDS, Miss Olivia, London

355 *c.*1830
Portrait of a Gipsy

Wearing hat, and with long hair.
w/c. 10⅛ × 9 (257 × 228). Signed.
PROV. Ralph Edwards.

EGERTON, Mrs Judy, London

356
Group of Figures Sitting on a Bench Seen from Behind

Pencil. 3¼ × 3¼ (83 × 83).

FORD, Brinsley, London

357 1825–30
Head of a Boy

Pencil. 3½ × 3 (90 × 77). Signed.

358 1825–30
Head of a Laughing Boy

Pencil. 3¼ × 3½ (83 × 90). Signed.

FREE, Mrs R., Sydney, Australia

359 *c.*1848
Resting by the Wayside

Young girl leaning against bank with right hand on cheek.
w/c. 14 × 10 (356 × 254). Signed.
COMMENT. His daughter Emma aged about 16.

FRY, Mr and Mrs Cyril, London

360 Dated 1814
Young Girl Seated

Pencil. 6 × 5 (155 × 128) oval. Signed and dated 1814.
EXH. Hunt Exhibition Fry Collection 1967.
BIB. Fry Cat., 1967, No. 16(a).

361 (Colour Plate 1) 1810–15
The Reaper

Oil on canvas. 11½ × 9½ (292 × 241). Signed.

362 (Plate 30) *c.*1815
Self Portrait Aged 25 Years

Pencil and w/c. 3¾ × 3⅛ (95 × 80). Signed.
PROV. L. G. Duke.
EXH. Hunt Exhibition Fry Collection 1967.
BIB. Fry Cat., 1967, No. 12(c). Repr. M. H. Grant, Vol. II, p. 311.

363 *c.*1815
Portrait of a Man

Inscribed on old mount as 'William Hunt's Father'.
Pencil and w/c. 3⅝ × 4½ (92 × 117). Signed.
EXH. Hunt Exhibition Fry Collection 1967.
BIB. Fry Cat., 1967, No. 12(b).
COMMENT. Compare corresponding drawing inscribed 'William Hunt's Mother' in Fry Collection (364).

364 *c.*1815
Portrait of a Woman

Inscribed on old mount as 'William Hunt's Mother'.
Pencil and w/c. 3⅝ × 4½ (92 × 117). Signed.
EXH. Hunt Exhibition Fry Collection 1967.
BIB. Fry Cat., 1967, No. 12(a).
COMMENT. Compare corresponding drawing of his father in Fry Collection (363).

365 1815–20
Young Girl Sleeping in a Chair

Pencil. 4½ × 3¼ (116 × 84). Signed.
EXH. Hunt Exhibition Fry Collection 1967.
BIB. Fry Cat., 1967, No. 17(1).
COMMENT. Compare same girl in similar pose in Mr and Mrs H. Rossetti Collection (492).

366 1815–20
Portrait of J. M. W. Turner

Inscribed verso: 'Sketch on a steam boat J. M. W. Turner RA'.
Pencil. 10 × 7 (254 × 178).
EXH. Hunt Exhibition Fry Collection 1967.
BIB. Fry Cat., 1967, No. 18.

367 1815–20
Seated Man in Top Hat Smoking a Pipe

Black chalk. 5 × 3⅝ (127 × 91).
EXH. Hunt Exhibition Fry Collection 1967.
BIB. Fry Cat., 1967, No. 16(3).

368 *c.*1820
Two Young Girls Standing

Pencil and w/c. 7½ × 3½ (192 × 105). Cut edges.
EXH. Hunt Exhibition Fry Collection 1967.
BIB. Fry Cat., 1967, No. 19.

369 *c.*1820
Young Woman Seated

Pencil. 5¾ × 4¼ (145 × 109).
EXH. Hunt Exhibition Fry Collection 1967.
BIB. Fry Cat., 1967, No. 17(2).

370 *c.*1820
Young Woman Sleeping

Pencil. 3⅛ × 2¼ (80 × 57). Signed.
EXH. Hunt Exhibition Fry Collection 1967.
BIB. Fry Cat., 1967, No. 16(2).

371 1820–25
Girl with a Basket

Pencil and w/c. 6¼ × 3½ (159 × 90).
EXH. Hunt Exhibition Fry Collection 1967.
BIB. Fry Cat., 1967, No. 20.

372 1820–25
Kitchen Interior with Young Man Sitting by the Fire

Inscribed verso: 'Paddy at Home'.
w/c heightened with white. 7⅝ × 10¾ (195 × 273).
EXH. Hunt Exhibition Fry Collection 1967.
BIB. Fry Cat., 1967, No. 26.

373 1820–25
Interior of a Barn

With young man holding beer mug.
Pencil and w/c heightened with white. 15¼ × 13¼ (395 × 340).
EXH. (1) Hunt Exhibition Fry Collection 1967. (2) Hunt Exhibition 1981.
BIB. Fry Cat., 1967, No. 30.

374 1820–25
Portrait of a Negro Boy

Pencil and w/c. 4¼ × 3½ (118 × 89). Signed.

375 (Plate 22) Dated 1821
The Dining Room at Cassiobury Park, the Seat of the Earl of Essex

w/c. 9⅝ × 13¼ (245 × 336). Signed and dated 1821.
EXH. (1) Royal Academy, London, 1822, No. 918 as The Winter Dining Room. (2) Hunt Exhibition Fry Collection 1967.
BIB. Fry Cat., 1967, No. 22.

376 (Plate 23) Dated 1823
The Drawing Room at Cassiobury Park, the Seat of the Earl of Essex

w/c. 8⅜ × 10¾ (211 × 270). Signed and dated 1823.
EXH. Hunt Exhibition Fry Collection 1967.
BIB. Fry Cat., 1967, No. 23.

377 Exh. 1824 or 1825
The Gamekeeper

Reed pen, ink and w/c. 13⅝ × 9 (345 × 228).
EXH. (1) OWCS, 1824, No. 62 or 1825, No. 133 or No. 341. (2) Hunt Exhibition Fry Collection 1967.
BIB. Fry Cat., 1967, No. 36.
COMMENT. Compare other gamekeepers in Mr and Mrs D. J. Methven's Collection (444) and Yale Center (573).

378 *c.*1825
Portrait of a Negro

Reed pen, ink and w/c. 4 × 3¼ (102 × 83). Signed.
EXH. Hunt Exhibition Fry Collection 1967.
BIB. Fry Cat., 1967, No. 38(a).

379 (Plate 43) *c.*1827
Girl Reading by Lamplight

w/c. 12¼ × 8½ (312 × 220). Signed.
EXH. (1) (perhaps) OWCS, 1829, No. 13 or No. 214, both entitled A Lady Reading by Lamplight. (2) Hunt Exhibition Fry Collection 1967.
BIB. Fry Cat., 1967, No. 44.
COMMENT. Same girl as in Witt Collection, dated 1827 (548), and in Huntington Library (403).

380 Dated 1828
Interior of a Barn

Inscribed verso: 'Drawn from life by me, 1828, two Shillington boys, Joe Watts and Bill Furse'.
w/c. 13⅝ × 10⅛ (346 × 263).
EXH. Hunt Exhibition Fry Collection 1967.
BIB. Fry Cat., 1967, No. 43.

381 *c.*1830
The Turnip Boy

w/c heightened with white. $11\frac{1}{4} \times 7\frac{3}{4}$ (286 × 197).
EXH. Hunt Exhibition Fry Collection 1967.
BIB. Fry Cat., 1967, No. 37.

382 *c.*1830
Boy Sleeping in a Chair

w/c. $4\frac{3}{8} \times 5\frac{7}{8}$ (110 × 150). Signed.
EXH. Hunt Exhibition Fry Collection 1967.
BIB. Fry Cat., 1967, No. 38(b).

383 *c.*1832
Girl with a Sheaf of Corn

w/c heightened with white with surface scratching. $11 \times 7\frac{3}{4}$ (280 × 197).
EXH. Hunt Exhibition Fry Collection 1967.
BIB. Fry Cat., 1967, No. 50.
COMMENT. Almost identical version in Cambridge, Fitzwilliam Museum (318).

384 *c.*1835
Boy with a Cabbage

w/c heightened with white. $15 \times 11\frac{3}{8}$ (380 × 295).
EXH. Hunt Exhibition Fry Collection 1967.
BIB. Fry Cat., 1967, No. 45.

385 *c.*1835
Old Man with Pipe Seated at a Table

w/c heightened with white. 19 × 12 (487 × 310). Signed.
EXH. Hunt Exhibition Fry Collection 1967.
BIB. Fry Cat., 1967, No. 46.

386 *c.*1839
Miss Moore Sewing

Inscribed on old mount: 'Miss Moore's Room Aldersgate 1824'.
w/c. $9\frac{1}{4} \times 10\frac{3}{4}$ (235 × 275).
EXH. (1) Hunt Exhibition Fry Collection 1967. (2) Hunt Exhibition 1981.
BIB. Fry Cat., 1967, No. 21.
COMMENT. Miss Moore was one of Hunt's pupils. The reference in the inscription to 'Aldersgate 1824' is a confusion with a Miss Maw whose father was a surgical instrument maker at Aldersgate and friend of Hunt. Compare larger and more finished drawing in the Whitworth Art Gallery, Manchester, dated 1839, for which the Fry drawing is clearly a preliminary sketch (439, Plate 79). The date '1824' in the inscription must also be wrong and the drawing should be dated *c.*1839 on the basis of the Whitworth drawing. This ties in with the series of illustrated letters from Hunt to Miss Moore in the Fry Collection which can be dated *c.*1841 (82). Miss Moore is also the sitter in Oldham, Art Galleries and Museums (462) and Whitworth Art Gallery, Manchester (439, Plate 79).

387 (Plate 65) *c.*1840
Musical Party with Three Young Girls Dancing

Pen and ink. $5\frac{1}{8} \times 7\frac{1}{4}$ (130 × 184). Signed with initials 'W.H.'
PROV. Mrs Baxter, great-niece of the artist. L. G. Duke, who acquired it from a scrapbook before its sale in 1934 to the British Museum, now Album A. 7 (see under 306).

388 (Plate 69) Exh. 1848
The Orphan

Woman (Mrs Hunt) feeding pig from bottle.
w/c heightened with white. $11\frac{1}{2} \times 13\frac{1}{4}$ (297 × 355). Signed.
EXH. (1) OWCS, 1848, No. 112. (2) Hunt Exhibition Fry Collection 1967. (3) Hunt Exhibition 1981.
BIB. Fry Cat., 1967, No. 42.
COMMENT. Mrs Hunt aged about 36.

GATELEY, Alan B., West Midlands

389 *c.*1840
A Monk Sitting in his Cell

With hand resting on Bible.
w/c. 21 × 15 (533 × 381). Signed.

GLASGOW, Art Gallery and Museum, Kelvingrove

390 (Plate 92) *c.*1840
Interior [706]

Woman standing with lute by chair upholstered in brocade.
w/c heightened with white. $17\frac{1}{8} \times 12\frac{3}{4}$ (434 × 323). Signed.
Gift. James Orrock, 1892.

HALIFAX, Bankfield Museum

391 (Plate 40) *c*.1825
Portrait of a Girl [974.583]

Portrait of young woman wearing wide-brimmed black hat.
w/c. 7 × 4 (177 × 100).
Gift. Alderman W. Smith, 1907.
COMMENT. Incorrectly titled The Artist's Daughter.

392 1825–30
On the Cliff [1975.585]

Young girl standing at cliff edge peeling apple.
w/c slightly heightened with white. $12\frac{1}{4} \times 8\frac{1}{2}$ (310 × 215). Signed.
Gift. Alderman W. Smith, 1907.

393 *c*.1833
Portrait of Copley Fielding [132.104]

Pencil. $4\frac{1}{2} \times 3\frac{1}{4}$ (115 × 83). Signed.
Bt 1932.
COMMENT. Inscribed in Hunt's handwriting: 'Mr Fielding President of the Society of Painters in Water-Colours'. Christie's sale of Hunt's works, 17 May 1864, Lot 229, comprised: 'Five portraits of members of the Old Society of Water-Colours: Mr Fielding [Anthony Vandyke Copley Fielding, 1787–1885], Mr Nash, Mr Scott and two others'. The portrait of Mr Scott is in Cambridge, Fitzwilliam Museum (320).

SMITH, Hammond, Leicester

394 Exh. 1838
A Marine Effect

Seasick-looking boy wearing top hat sitting with his mother on boat. Inscribed verso: 'W. Hunt, 6 Marchmont Street, Russell Square'.
w/c heightened with white. $16\frac{1}{2} \times 12\frac{3}{4}$ (420 × 324).
EXH. (1) OWCS, 1838, No. 49. (2) Hunt Exhibition 1981.

HARRISON, Mr and Mrs D. C., Bucks

395 Dated 1837
The Barber

Old bespectacled barber stands cutting young boy's hair. Inscribed verso in Hunt's handwriting: 'Lady Rolle, the Barber 1837 Watercolour Exhibition'.
w/c heightened with white. $18 \times 12\frac{1}{4}$ (457 × 311). Signed and dated 1837.
PROV. Lady Rolle, by whom bt at OWCS, 1837. Sale Sotheby Bearne, Torquay, 23 July 1980, Lot 257.
EXH. (1) OWCS, 1837, No. 251. (2) Hunt Exhibition 1981.
BIB. Engraved C. Turner, and published by Mrs C. Turner, 19 June 1841, with the dedication to Lady Rolle.

HASTINGS, Museum and Art Gallery

396 1825–30
Portrait of a Young Negro Boy

Head and shoulders, looking left.
w/c. $7\frac{7}{8} \times 5\frac{7}{8}$ (200 × 150). Signed.

397 *c*.1840
Portrait of Lullam [911.36.3]

Lithograph. $12\frac{5}{8} \times 8\frac{5}{8}$ (320 × 220).
Gift. Miss Clara Allen, 1911.
COMMENT. Note (verso) states: 'Lithographic Portrait of Lullam organ blower at St Clement's Church, Hastings by W. Hunt. To be sent at my death to the Hastings Museum. S. G. Prout'.

398 *c*.1842
Portrait of the Artist's Daughter [973.13.1]

Emma aged about 10. Head in profile.
w/c. $8\frac{1}{4} \times 6\frac{1}{4}$ (210 × 160).
Gift. Miss D. Perratt of St Leonards, 1973.
PROV. William Quilter; his sale, Christie's, 8 April 1875, Lot 216, as Portrait of the Artist's daughter.
EXH. Hunt Exhibition 1981.
COMMENT. The museum's records state that the donor's family were in some way connected with Hunt, and the drawing has always been traditionally regarded in the Perratt family as being of his daughter. Miss Perratt has left the neighbourhood and no further details of her family's connection are available. Emma was born in 1832.

HUDDERSFIELD, Libraries and Museum, West Yorkshire

399 (Plate 91) *c*.1840
Light and Shade

Portrait of young girl.
w/c heightened with white. $13 \times 9\frac{1}{2}$ (330 × 242).
Bt 1930.

HENRY E. HUNTINGTON Library and Art Gallery, San Marino, California

400 (Plate 70) *c.*1825
Portrait of a Young Lady [59.55.755]

w/c. $10\frac{3}{8} \times 5$ (263 × 127). Signed.
PROV. Gilbert Davis; bt by him, 1948.

401 (Colour Plate 8) Dated 1827
Westminster Schoolboy in Rowing Attire [59.55.770]

View of Westminster Abbey on opposite bank.
w/c. $13 \times 7\frac{3}{4}$ (330 × 197). Signed and dated 1827.
PROV. Gilbert Davis; bt by him, 1947.
EXH. OWCS, 1828, No. 18 as Westminster Scholar.

402 Dated 1827
An Irish Labourer [59.55.754]

Holding hod with two bricks.
w/c. $14\frac{1}{2} \times 8\frac{3}{4}$ (368 × 223). Signed and dated 1827.
PROV. Gilbert Davis; bt by him, 1950.

403 *c.*1827
Reading by Lamplight [59.55.761]

w/c. $8\frac{1}{2} \times 12\frac{1}{2}$ (216 × 317). Signed.
PROV. Gilbert Davis; bt by him, 1950.
EXH. (perhaps) OWCS, 1829, No. 13 or No. 214, both entitled Girl Reading by Lamplight.
COMMENT. Same girl as in Witt Collection, dated 1827 (548), and in Fry Collection (379, Plate 43).

404 *c.*1830
The Fireplace, Cottage Interior [59.55.745]

w/c. $10\frac{1}{2} \times 15$ (268 × 382). Signed.
PROV. Gilbert Davis; bt by him, 1952.

405 Dated 1830
A Greenwich Pensioner [59.55.749]

Seated, holding pipe and stick.
w/c slightly heightened with white. $21\frac{3}{4} \times 17\frac{3}{4}$ (554 × 452). Signed and dated 1830.
PROV. Gilbert Davis; bt by him, 1948.

406 *c.*1832
Sleeping Woman [59.55.771]

Mrs Hunt aged about 20.
Pencil. $4\frac{7}{8} \times 3$ (123 × 78). Signed.
PROV. J. P. Heseltine. Gilbert Davis; bt by him, 1947.

407 (Plate 74) Dated 1833
Sunday Morning [59.55.768]

Girl sitting reading in bedroom.
w/c. $15\frac{3}{8} \times 21\frac{7}{8}$ (391 × 556). Signed and dated 1833.
PROV. Gilbert Davis; bt by him, 1947.
EXH. (1) (probably) OWCS, 1833, No. 236 as An Interior. (2) Ruskin Hunt Exhibition 1879–80, No. 158.
COMMENT. Ruskin, in his Preface to the Exhibition, refers to this drawing as Hunt enlivening 'a study of his parlourmaid at her glass with the elegance of a red and green pincushion'. One of a notable group of bedroom interiors of the early 1830s, e.g., with the same patchwork quilt, in Blackburn, Museum and Art Gallery (277) and in Witt Collection (553, Colour Plate 16).

408 (Plate 67) Dated 1835
At the Cottage Door [59.55.711]

Mrs Hunt (aged about 23) wearing pink spotted dress and holding flower.
w/c. $12\frac{1}{2} \times 7\frac{1}{4}$ (324 × 184). Signed and dated 1835.
PROV. Gilbert Davis; bt by him, 1948.

409 (Colour Plate 17) *c.*1835
The Jewels [59.55.753]

Young woman sitting at dressing table with jewels.
w/c heightened with white. $10\frac{1}{2} \times 12\frac{1}{2}$ (267 × 317).
PROV. Gilbert Davis; bt by him, 1948.

410 (Plate 61) *c.*1835
The Young Artist [59.55.733]

Boy sitting on chair drawing small white dog.
w/c heightened with white. $17\frac{7}{8} \times 12\frac{3}{4}$ (456 × 324).
PROV. Gilbert Davis; bt by him, 1948.
COMMENT. Boy model.

411 (Plate 72) *c.*1840
The Sisters [59.55.765]

w/c. $12\frac{1}{8} \times 9\frac{1}{4}$ (308 × 235).
PROV. Gilbert Davis; bt by him, 1948.
COMMENT. Right hand sister is Hunt's daughter Emma aged about 8. Same girl models as in National Museum of Wales (450).

412 *c.*1840
The Outhouse [59.55.758]

Boy leaning on barrel, with large chest and baskets.

w/c. $15\frac{3}{4} \times 22$ (400 × 558).
PROV. Gilbert Davis; bt by him, 1948.

413 *c.*1842
At Prayer [59.55.760]

His daughter Emma aged about 10.
w/c. Diameter 7 (178) circular. Signed (signature partly cut off).
PROV. Gilbert Davis; bt by him, 1947.

414 *c.*1842
Gypsy Girl [59.55.747]

His daughter Emma aged about 10.
w/c. $12\frac{1}{2} \times 9\frac{3}{4}$ (317 × 246).
PROV. Gilbert Davis; bt by him, 1948.

415 Exh. 1843 or 1848
Mrs John Curteis in her Boudoir in Devonshire Place [59.55.738]

w/c heightened with white. $15\frac{1}{4} \times 11$ (385 × 286). Signed.
PROV. Gilbert Davis; bt by him, 1947.
EXH. Either OWCS, 1843, No. 200 as An Interior in Devonshire Place, or OWCS, 1848, No. 276 as An Interior, at the Residence of John Curteis, Esq., Devonshire Place. Companion w/c of Mr John Curteis, Huntington Library (416).
COMMENT. Both these works appear stylistically earlier but are examples of how Hunt reverted to an earlier style, as in Whitworth Art Gallery, Manchester (see under 441).

416 Exh. 1843 or 1848
Mr John Curteis in his Drawing Room in Devonshire Place [59.55.737]

w/c. $15\frac{3}{8} \times 11\frac{1}{4}$ (390 × 286). Signed.
PROV. Gilbert Davis; bt by him, 1947.
EXH. Either OWCS, 1843, No. 200 as An Interior in Devonshire Place, or OWCS, 1848, No. 276 as An Interior, at the Residence of John Curteis, Esq., Devonshire Place. Companion w/c of Mrs John Curteis, Huntington Library (415).

JEANNERAT, Pierre, London

417 *c.*1835
New Red Shoes

Mrs Hunt, wife of the artist, wearing red dress; candle on left.
w/c. $13 \times 8\frac{3}{8}$ (325 × 210).

LEEDS, City Art Gallery

418 *c.*1825
Interior

With two men at table, smoking.
Pencil and w/c. $10\frac{5}{8} \times 7\frac{1}{2}$ (270 × 189). Signed.
Bequest. Agnes and Norman Lupton, 1952.

LEICESTER, Museums and Art Galleries

419 (Plate 58) Dated 1838
The Turnip Lantern [I.A.1895]

w/c heightened with white. $13\frac{1}{8} \times 8\frac{7}{8}$ (336 × 225). Signed and dated 1838.
Bt 1895.
PROV. C. F. Huth. Sold Christie's, 6 July 1895, Lot 34.
EXH. (1) OWCS, 1838, No. 301 A Turnip Bogle. (2) Hunt Exhibition 1981.
COMMENT. 'Bogle' is defined in the Oxford English Dictionary as 'a phantom causing fright'. Boy model.

420 (Plate 60) Dated 1839
Puzzled [5A.1886]

Pencil and w/c slightly heightened with white. $13\frac{1}{8} \times 8\frac{3}{4}$ (333 × 223). Signed and dated 1839.
Bt 1886.
COMMENT. Boy model.

LIVERPOOL, Walker Art Gallery

421 *c.*1835
Contemplation [14]

Boy sitting by river with fishing rod.
w/c. $13\frac{1}{4} \times 9\frac{3}{8}$ (334 × 240). Signed.
Bequest. Mrs Margaret Harvey, 1878.
COMMENT. Boy model.

MAAS, J. S., London

422 *c.*1820
Girl Asleep in an Armchair

w/c heightened with white. $12 \times 9\frac{3}{4}$ (305 × 247).
BIB. Repr. Maas, *Victorian Painters*, 1969, p. 109.

423 *c.*1830
Young Girl with a Book in her Lap

w/c. $5\frac{3}{4} \times 4$ (146 × 102).

424 *c*.1830
Thought before the Looking Glass

w/c heightened with white. $14\frac{1}{4} \times 10$ (362×254). Signed.
PROV. Thomas Brown. Sold Christie's, 4 June 1869, Lot 344. Mrs Henri Rivière, sold Christie's, 5 June 1930, Lot 42.

425 *c*.1835
Girl Writing by Candlelight

Pencil, pen, ink and faint w/c in girl's cheeks. $4 \times 5\frac{3}{8}$ (101×137).
COMMENT. Preliminary sketch for finished version of same subject in J. S. Maas Collection (426).

426 *c*.1835
Girl Writing by Candlelight

w/c heightened with white with surface scratching. 11×15 (279×381).
PROV. E. Gambart. Joseph Gillott, sale Christie's, 4 May 1872, Lot 450.
EXH. Hunt Exhibition 1981.
BIB. Repr. Maas, *Victorian Painters*, 1969, p. 110.
COMMENT. Finished version. (See 425).

McLAREN, Mr and Mrs Andrew, London

427
Seated Girl

Black and red chalk. $5\frac{5}{8} \times 4\frac{1}{8}$ (143×105).

MANCHESTER, City Art Gallery

428 1825–30
Cottage Interior with Girl Sewing [1890/50]

w/c. $7\frac{1}{2} \times 10\frac{7}{8}$ (191×277). Signed.
Gift. Roger R. Ross, 1890.

429 (Plate 44) Dated 1829
Boy Blowing a Horn [1920.589]

w/c. $14 \times 10\frac{1}{4}$ (356×262). Signed and dated 1829.
Bequest. Dr D. Lloyd Roberts, 1920.
EXH. (1) OWCS, 1829, No. 18 as Cow Boy. (2) Hunt Exhibition 1981.

430 (Plate 42) Dated 1829
A Radish Stall [1918.1069]

w/c heightened with white. $8\frac{3}{4} \times 10\frac{7}{8}$ (223×277). Signed and dated 1829.
Bequest. Mothersill, 1880.
EXH. OWCS, 1829, No. 280.
COMMENT. Entitled, in Manchester Cat., The Market Woman.

431 *c*.1830
Lady Sewing [1918.441]

w/c heightened with white. 15×11 (382×279).
Bequest. Mothersill, 1880.
PROV. T. C. Horsfall.
EXH. Thos Agnew & Sons Ltd, English Watercolours and Drawings from Manchester City Art Gallery, 1977, No. 43.

432 Dated 1833
Saying her Lesson (Candlelight) [1890.51]

Young girl in bonnet reading to seated man, with young boy with stick looking on.
w/c. $11\frac{3}{4} \times 13\frac{1}{4}$ (297×337). Signed and dated 1833.
Gift. Roger R. Ross, 1890.

433 Dated 1833
The Flower Girl [1920.596]

w/c. $10\frac{3}{4} \times 7\frac{3}{4}$ (273×197). Signed and dated 1833.
Bequest. Dr Lloyd Roberts, 1920.
EXH. OWCS, 1833, No. 297.

434 1835–40
The Scrub [1920.633]

Boy standing by stone sink vigorously rubbing face with towel.
w/c heightened with white. $13\frac{1}{2} \times 9\frac{1}{2}$ (343×242). Signed and dated 18 . . . (illegible).
Bequest. Dr Lloyd Roberts, 1920; bt by him 1895.
PROV. F. Craven. Sold Christie's, 18 May 1895, Lot 22.
EXH. (1) Royal Jubilee Exhibition, Manchester, 1887, No. 1728. (2) Glasgow International Exhibition, 1901, No. 882. (3) Hunt Exhibition 1981.
COMMENT. Boy model.

435 1836–42
Devotion [1920.639]

Kneeling boy with rosary on the ground.
w/c heightened with white. $18\frac{1}{4} \times 11\frac{3}{4}$ (463×297). Signed.
Bequest. Dr Lloyd Roberts, 1920; bt by him, 1895.
COMMENT. Compare with Devotion at Whitworth Art Gallery, Manchester (436). See under 436 for other works entitled Devotion.

MANCHESTER, Whitworth Art Gallery, University of Manchester

436 1833–36
Devotion [D.25.1887]

Kneeling boy in yellow smock with hat and rosary on ground.
w/c. $14\frac{1}{4} \times 10\frac{3}{8}$ (363 × 264). Signed.
Gift. Guarantors of the Royal Jubilee Exhibition, Manchester, 1887.
EXH. Hunt exhibited nine works entitled Devotion at the OWCS: in 1833, No. 392; in 1836, No. 154; in 1841, No. 284; in 1842, No. 289; in 1850, No. 351; in 1853, No. 254; in 1856, No. 271; in 1860, No. 220; and in 1862, No. 404. Two works entitled Devotion were exhibited at the Art Treasures Exhibition, Manchester, 1857, Nos 531 and 538, lent respectively by J. J. Jenkins and J. Dillon. Hunt Exhibition 1981.
COMMENT. Stylistically this work belongs to the early 1830s and is therefore dated 1833–36.

437 (Plate 57) Dated 1835
A Shrimper [D.33.1887]

w/c. $15\frac{1}{8} \times 12\frac{1}{8}$ (384 × 307). Signed and dated 1835.
Gift. The Guarantors of the Royal Jubilee Exhibition, Manchester, 1887.

438 Dated 1836
The Valentine

Young, smiling boy reading letter by candlelight.
w/c heightened with white. $9\frac{1}{8} \times 6\frac{7}{8}$ (231 × 174). Signed and dated 1836.
Bequest. Sir E. Tootal Broadhurst, 1922.
EXH. (1) Royal Jubilee Exhibition, Manchester, 1887, No. 1726. (2) Hunt Exhibition 1981.
COMMENT. Boy model.

439 (Plate 79) Dated 1839
A Bedchamber [D.32.1887]

Miss Moore sitting on four-poster bed sewing.
w/c. $11\frac{3}{8} \times 17\frac{3}{8}$ (288 × 443). Signed and dated 1839.
Gift. Guarantors of the Royal Jubilee Exhibition, Manchester, 1887, who bt Christie's sale, 22 June 1891.
EXH. (1) (probably) OWCS, 1840, No. 321 as An Interior. (2) Hunt Exhibition 1981.
COMMENT. Compare with preliminary, unfinished version (with only one window) of Miss Moore Sewing in Fry Collection (386). The illustrated letters from Hunt to Miss Moore in the Fry Collection (82) are dateable *c*.1841. Miss Moore is also the sitter in Fry Collection (386) and Oldham, Art Galleries and Museums (462).

440 *c*.1842
Peasant Girl Seated on a Rock [D.10.1977]

His daughter Emma (aged about 10) wearing pinkish dress.
w/c. $16\frac{5}{8} \times 12\frac{5}{8}$ (424 × 320). Signed.
Bequest. J. E. Whitehead, 1977.

441 Exh. 1848
What Shall I Sing? [D.12.1944]

Girl seated at piano with music in front of her and holding sheet of music, with picture of white grapes on wall behind. Inscribed on mount: 'No. 20, what shall I sing. W. Hunt. A Portrait of his daughter.'
w/c heightened with white. $11\frac{1}{4} \times 6\frac{7}{8}$ (285 × 174). Signed.
Gift. Joseph Knight, 1944.
PROV. J. P. Heseltine.
EXH. (1) OWCS, 1848, No. 337 as What Shall I Play. (2) Hunt Exhibition 1981.
COMMENT. His daughter Emma (born 1832) and this girl aged about 16. Stylistically the work looks earlier but Hunt often reverted to an earlier style, as is shown by the drawings of Mr John Curteis in his Drawing Room in Devonshire Place and the companion work of Mrs John Curteis in her boudoir at the same address, Huntington Library (416 and 415 respectively), one of which was exhibited at OWCS, 1848, No. 276.

MARYLEBONE CRICKET CLUB, Lord's, London

442 1836–39
Boy Cricketer

w/c. 15 × 11 (381 × 280). Signed.
EXH. (perhaps) OWCS, 1836, No. 338 or 1839, No. 270.
COMMENT. Compare A Young Cricketer in the late Sir Jeremiah Colman's Collection (323, Plate 62).

MAYS, S. G., Tunbridge Wells, Kent

443 *c.*1820

Portrait of a Man
Pencil and w/c. $4\frac{3}{4} \times 4\frac{1}{8}$ (121 × 105). Signed.

METHVEN, Mr and Mrs D. J., Oxfordshire

444 Dated 1828
A Gamekeeper from Nature

With pink waistcoat and whistle.
Reed pen, ink and w/c. $14\frac{1}{4} \times 8\frac{3}{8}$ (362 × 212).
Signed and dated 'Wm. Hunt 1828' in reed pen.
EXH. OWCS, 1828, No. 359.
COMMENT. Compare with other gamekeepers in Fry Collection (377) and Yale Center (573).

445 *c.*1830
Fisherman on the Shore at Hastings

Wearing blue hat, blue breeches and stockings.
w/c. $15\frac{1}{8} \times 8\frac{3}{4}$ (384 × 222).

446 *c.*1831
Girl with a Pitcher

Three-quarter length, wearing blue skirt, and tam-o'-shanter hat.
w/c. $11\frac{1}{4} \times 8\frac{1}{8}$ (281 × 210).
PROV. Francis Llewellyn Jenks.
EXH. (perhaps) OWCS, 1831, No. 68 as A Child with Pitcher.

447 Dated 1838
The Forlorn Sailor-Boy

w/c heightened with white. $13\frac{3}{4} \times 10$ (349 × 254).
Signed and dated 1838.
EXH. OWCS, 1838, No. 192.

NATIONAL GALLERY OF SCOTLAND, Edinburgh

448 *c.*1815
Boy Lying on the Grass [D.3651]

Pencil and w/c. $4\frac{7}{8} \times 6\frac{5}{8}$ (126 × 168). Signed.
Bequest. Cowan Smith, 1919.
COMMENT. Compare same boy in Stable Boy, dated 1815, in Witt Collection (540, Plate 31).

NATIONAL GALLERY OF VICTORIA, Melbourne, Australia

449
The Industrious Pupil

w/c. $10 \times 15\frac{3}{8}$ (254 × 390).
Bt Felton Bequest, 1910, on the advice of Charles Ricketts and Frank Gibson.

NATIONAL MUSEUM OF WALES, Cardiff

450 *c.*1840
Gipsies [98.158]

Two young girls sitting with straw basket.
w/c. $21\frac{1}{2} \times 14\frac{3}{4}$ (540 × 375)
Gift. Pyke Thompson Family, 1898.
PROV. James Pyke Thompson; bt by him, 1889.
COMMENT. Same girl models as in Huntington Library (411, Plate 72).

NATIONAL PORTRAIT GALLERY, London

451 (Plate 80) *c.*1835
Self Portrait [2636]

w/c. $14\frac{3}{4} \times 11$ (374 × 279).
Bequest. H. S. Palmer, 1933.
PROV. Sutton Palmer. H. S. Palmer.
EXH. (1) Ruskin Hunt Exhibition 1879–80, No. 176 as lent by Mr Sutton Palmer. (2) Linnell and his Circle, P. and D. Colnaghi Ltd, 1973, No. 136. (3) Hunt Exhibition 1981.
BIB. Repr. Pl. 458, Richard Ormond, *Early Victorian Portraits*, 1973, Vol. II. Description p. 237: 'Healthy complexion, brown hair with grey streaks. Dressed in dark stock, white shirt and grey coat. Background colour brown.' Repr. p. 503, *Magazine of Art*, Vol. 22, 1898. *Dictionary of National Biography*, Vol. X, 1908, p. 283.
COMMENT. Aged about 45. Compare self-portrait of about same age, Rochdale Art Gallery (491).

452 (Plate 93) *c.*1850
Self Portrait [768]

Oil on paper stuck on card. $5\frac{1}{4} \times 4\frac{1}{4}$ (135 × 110). Signed.
Gift. The Earl of Leven and Melville, 1887.
BIB. Repr. Pl. 457, Richard Ormond, *Early Victorian Portraits*, 1973, Vol. II. Description p. 236: 'Healthy complexion, brown eyes, grey hair and whiskers. Dressed in a white shirt, dark

stock and loose brown coat. Background colour dark brown'.
COMMENT. Aged about 60.

NEWCASTLE-UPON-TYNE, Laing Art Gallery

453 *c.*1830
The Fisherboy [JWR 23 W/C]

w/c. $10\frac{1}{4} \times 7\frac{1}{4}$ (261 × 185). Signed.
Bequest. John Wigham Richardson, 1925.
COMMENT. Boy model.

454 Dated 1838
Woman Peeling Apples [37/133 W/C]

w/c. $11\frac{1}{4} \times 8\frac{3}{4}$ (281 × 224). Signed and dated 1838.
Bequest. G. E. Henderson, 1937.

NORFOLK, His Grace the Duke of, Arundel Castle, Sussex

455 *c.*1825
Boy and Girl in a Stable

w/c slightly heightened with white. $10\frac{3}{4} \times 7\frac{1}{2}$ (273 × 191). Signed.

456 Dated 1827
Fisherman seated on a Barrel holding a Pipe

w/c. $15\frac{1}{4} \times 11$ (388 × 279). Signed and dated 1827.

457 Dated 1830
Young Fishermen

Three young boys sitting on rocks.
w/c. $24\frac{1}{2} \times 20\frac{1}{2}$ (624 × 522). Signed and dated 1830.
EXH. OWCS, 1830, No. 79.

458 (Plate 78) Dated 1832
Girl Reading at a Window

w/c. $8 \times 10\frac{1}{2}$ (203 × 267). Signed and dated 1832.
EXH. OWCS, 1832, No. 242 under title Reading or No. 128 An Interior.
COMMENT. Compare other interiors with similar furniture, e.g. Girl at Prayer, Blackburn, Museum and Art Gallery (see under 277). An almost identical version entitled Sunday Morning, signed and dated 1831, $8\frac{1}{4} \times 10\frac{3}{4}$ (210 × 273), was sold at Christie's, 21 October 1980, Lot 102. Present owner unknown. Main difference is in the girl's white pantaloons showing in this latter version below her skirt.

NOTTINGHAM, Castle Museum

459 *c.*1830
Head of a Boy [20.42]

Black chalk. $3\frac{5}{8} \times 3\frac{1}{8}$ (93 × 79).
Bt 1920.
PROV. Charles Fairfax Murray.

460 *c.*1833
The Kitchen Maid [57.38]

Mrs Hunt seated on bench preparing vegetables.
w/c. $18\frac{1}{8} \times 22\frac{5}{8}$ (460 × 575). Signed.
Bt 1957.
COMMENT. Mrs Hunt aged about 21.

461 *c.*1835
Head of a Woman Crocheting [20.41]

Portrait of Mrs Hunt aged about 23.
Pencil. $3\frac{1}{2} \times 3\frac{3}{4}$ (89 × 95). Signed.
Bt 1920.
PROV. Charles Fairfax Murray.

OLDHAM, Art Galleries and Museums

462 *c.*1839
An Interior

Young girl seated in wooden chair reading by window.
w/c. $10 \times 7\frac{1}{2}$ (255 × 190).
Gift. C. E. Lees, 1888.
COMMENT. The sitter is Miss Moore, one of Hunt's pupils, to whom the series of 12 letters, *c.*1841, in the Fry Collection (82) are addressed. She is also the sitter in Whitworth Art Gallery, Manchester (439, Plate 79) and in Fry Collection (386).

OPPÉ, D. L. T., London

463 *c.*1820
Girl's Head [2133(a)]

Full face wearing hat.
Black and red chalks. $4\frac{1}{8} \times 8\frac{1}{8}$ (105 × 207).
PROV. J. P. Heseltine. A. Paul Oppé; bt by him, 1936.

464 *c.*1820
Girl's Head [2133(b)]

In profile to right.
Pencil and coloured chalks on brown paper.
$3\frac{3}{8} \times 2\frac{5}{8}$ (86 × 67). Signed.
PROV. J. P. Heseltine. A. Paul Oppé; bt by him, 1936.

465 *c.*1822
Portrait of Frederick Nash [2296]

In profile to the left, aged about 40.
Pencil. $5\frac{3}{4} \times 4\frac{1}{2}$ (146 × 114). Signed.
PROV. A. Paul Oppé; bt by him, 1945.
COMMENT. Frederick Nash was born in 1782.

466
Hunt Box [1180]

Containing 30 drawings, all in pencil, consisting of 18 landscapes, 11 figures and 1 sketch of a dog.
Figures:
(1) Head of a Man in High Collar
$4 \times 2\frac{3}{4}$ (102 × 70). Signed.
(2) Sketch of a Man
$4\frac{3}{4} \times 3\frac{1}{2}$ (121 × 89). Signed.
(3) Group of Figures
$4\frac{1}{4} \times 2\frac{1}{2}$ (108 × 63). Signed.
(4) Three Figures
$3\frac{3}{4} \times 2\frac{1}{4}$ (95 × 57). Signed.
(5) Group of Figures
$2\frac{1}{2} \times 2\frac{1}{2}$ (63 × 63). Signed.
(6) Sketch of Seated Woman
$3\frac{1}{4} \times 4\frac{1}{4}$ (83 × 108). Signed.
(7) Man Kneeling
$3\frac{3}{4} \times 4\frac{1}{4}$ (95 × 108). Signed.
(8) Lady Seated in Profile
$3\frac{3}{4} \times 4\frac{1}{4}$ (95 × 108). Signed.
(9) Young Woman Kneeling
$2\frac{1}{2} \times 3\frac{3}{4}$ (63 × 95). Signed.
(10) Portrait of John Linnell (?)
$3\frac{1}{4} \times 4$ (83 × 102).
(11) Man in a Top Hat
$3\frac{1}{4} \times 4\frac{1}{2}$ (83 × 114). Signed.
PROV. A. Paul Oppé; bt by him, 1921.

467
Young Man Looking Down [2573(a)]

Pencil. $3\frac{1}{4} \times 3\frac{5}{8}$ (83 × 92).
PROV. E. H. Coles. A. Paul Oppé.

468
A Boy [2573(b)]

Pencil and coloured chalks. $4\frac{7}{8} \times 3\frac{5}{8}$ (124 × 89).
PROV. E. H. Coles. A. Paul Oppé.

469
An Old Man [2573(c)]

Pencil and coloured chalks. $4\frac{7}{8} \times 3\frac{5}{8}$ (124 × 89). Signed.
PROV. E. H. Coles. A. Paul Oppé.

OXFORD, Ashmolean Museum

(None of the following works has an accession number.)

470 (Plate 38) *c.*1820
Young Woman Standing

w/c. $10\frac{7}{8} \times 7\frac{1}{8}$ (276 × 180).
Bt 1954.
PROV. Oliver Hill.

471 Dated 1833
Farm Boys

Two young boys, one holding brown pitcher.
w/c. $11\frac{1}{4} \times 8\frac{1}{8}$ (285 × 205). Signed and dated 1833.
PROV. Ruskin Art Collection (R 143).
COMMENT. Rudimentary Series. See entry under Oxford, Ashmolean Museum, in Section 3 of this Catalogue.

472 (Plate 76) Dated 1836
In Val Crucis Abbey: The Interior used as a Barn

Pencil and w/c heightened with white with surface scratching. $23\frac{3}{8} \times 15\frac{3}{4}$ (593 × 402). Signed and dated 1836.
Bt 1962.
EXH. (1) OWCS, 1836, No. 12 as Interior of an Old Priory. (2) Hunt Exhibition 1981.
PROV. F. J. Nettlefold; his sale, Christie's, 6 June 1913, Lot 287. M. E. Martineau.
COMMENT. Boy model.

PAVITT, Burnet, London

472(a) *c.*1837
Portrait of the Artist's Wife

Black and white chalk. $3\frac{1}{2} \times 3$ (89 × 76).
Gift. Lady (Jane) Clark.
COMMENT. Mrs Hunt aged about 25.

PORT SUNLIGHT, The Lady Lever Art Gallery, Cheshire

473 (Plate 37) *c.*1825
Self Portrait [WHL 741]

Balding man (about 50) sitting on wooden seat, holding walking stick and top hat, and wearing cravat and gaiters.
Pencil, reed pen, brown ink and w/c. $15\frac{1}{2} \times 11\frac{1}{2}$ (394 × 293).
Bt 1911.

PROV. C. F. Huth.
EXH. Hunt Exhibition 1981.
BIB. Repr. *Connoisseur*, August 1931, p. 81.
COMMENT. Most unlikely to be a self portrait. If the sitter is aged about 50, the work would be dateable *c*.1840. Stylistically it seems much earlier, *c*.1825. The face strongly resembles A Miller in his Mill, exh. OWCS, 1824, No. 286, at Birmingham, City Museum and Art Gallery (272, Plate 36) who was probably Hunt's future father-in-law.

474 1825–30
Woman Seated by Fireside [WHL 262]

w/c. $10\frac{3}{4} \times 7\frac{1}{2}$ (273 × 190). Signed.

475 1830–35
Young Salts [WHL 266]

Two young boys, one with the other on his back, leaning against rock with sea on right.
w/c. $10\frac{1}{2} \times 7\frac{1}{4}$ (267 × 184).
PROV. Ralph Bernal. E. H. Lawrence. James Orrock; sale, Christie's, 4 June 1904, Lot 27.

476 *c*.1835
A Hastings Fisherman [WHL 3063]

w/c. $15\frac{1}{4} \times 10\frac{1}{2}$ (394 × 267). Signed.
Bt 1916.
EXH. Hunt Exhibition 1981.

477 Exh. 1837
Jim Crow [WHL 320]

Young negro seated by brazier.
w/c. $13\frac{1}{4} \times 9\frac{1}{4}$ (334 × 235). Signed and dated. Date obscured by stuck-down mount.
PROV. James Orrock; sale, Christie's, 4 June 1904, Lot 24.
EXH. (1) OWCS, 1837, No. 62. (2) Royal Jubilee Exhibition, Manchester, 1887, No. 1724. (3) Hunt Exhibition 1981.

478 *c*.1840
The Blessing [WHL 265]

Old man sitting with clasped hands at table, with loaf of bread and mug.
w/c. $11 \times 7\frac{1}{2}$ (280 × 190). Signed.
Bt 1907.
PROV. James Orrock.
EXH. Royal Jubilee Exhibition, Manchester, 1887, No. 1730.

479 *c*.1840
The Ballad Seller [WHL 313]

Young woman sitting, wearing yellow dress and red and black shawl, with basket containing ballads.
w/c. $16\frac{3}{4} \times 11\frac{1}{4}$ (426 × 286). Signed.
PROV. L. B. Mozeley, sold Christie's, 27 May 1865, Lot 126. Sir John Fowler, sold Christie's, 6 May 1899, Lot 17.
EXH. Hunt Exhibition 1981.
COMMENT. Compare The Ballad Singer, Aberdeen, Art Gallery and Museums (257).

480 *c*.1844
Cottage Girl Seated with a Pitcher [WHL 728]

Hunt's daughter Emma, full face, with red headscarf, aged about 13.
w/c. $10\frac{1}{2} \times 7\frac{1}{4}$ (267 × 184). Signed.
PROV. James Orrock, from whom bt, 1910.
EXH. Royal Jubilee Exhibition, Manchester, 1887, No. 1695.

481 *c*.1845
An Old Man Reading the Bible [WHL 724]

w/c. $11 \times 7\frac{1}{2}$ (280 × 190).
Bt 1910.
PROV. James Orrock.

PRESTON, Harris Museum and Art Gallery

482 *c*.1832
Preparing for Sunday [1273]

w/c. 13 × 17 (330 × 432). Signed.
Bequest. Rev. J. P. Haslam, 1924, subject to his wife's life interest; received 1949.
EXH. Hunt Exhibition 1981.
COMMENT. One of a notable group of bedroom interiors, e.g. Girl at Prayer, Blackburn, Museum and Art Gallery (see under 277).

483 *c*.1835
The Broom Gatherer [312]

Wearing corduroys and high boots.
w/c. $11\frac{1}{2} \times 7\frac{1}{2}$ (293 × 189). Signed.
Bequest. Richard Newsham, 1883.

484 *c*.1835
Rustic Devotion: The Church Porch [313]

Unshaven man seated holding stick.
w/c. 14¼ × 9½ (363 × 242).
Bequest. Richard Newsham, 1883.

485 *c*.1840
The Shy Sitter

Young girl sitting with hands clasped, in profile, on a ladder-back chair.
w/c. 9 × 7¼ (228 × 184). Signed.
Bequest. Rev. J. P. Haslam, 1924, subject to his wife's life interest; received 1949.
PROV. John Ruskin. James Orrock.
EXH. (1) Ruskin Hunt Exhibition 1879–80, No. 172, as lent by James Orrock. Ruskin (*Works*, Vol. XIV, p. 447) refers to this work: 'He is here again in his utmost strength – and in qualities of essential painting – unconquerable'. No. 172 repr. as frontispiece in the illustrated (1880) edition of the *Notes*. (2) London, Grosvenor Gallery Winter Exhibition, 1877–78. (3) Manchester, Royal Jubilee Exhibition, 1887. (4) Burlington House, 1891 (No. 106) as The Diffident Sitter, lent by James Orrock. (5) Hunt Exhibition 1981.

PRIVATE COLLECTION, London

486 *c*.1825
A Little Girl Reading

Pencil and w/c. 12 × 8⅝ (304 × 219).
BIB. Repr. Pl. 136, Andrew Wilton, 1977.

PRYOR, R. M. M., Hertfordshire

487 1820–30
Head of a Man

Pencil and red chalk on grey paper. 4¾ × 3½ (122 × 89). Signed.

488 1820–30
Head of a Man Looking to the Right

Pencil. 4 × 3⅛ (102 × 79). Signed.
PROV. Gilbert Davis.

READING, Museum and Art Gallery

489 *c*.1825
Two Young Children [264.31]

Pencil and sepia wash. 7 × 10⅜ (177 × 264).
Gift. Dr G. H. R. Holden, 1923.

REED, Mrs A., London

490 (Plate 68) *c*.1835
Woman Reading by Candlelight

Pencil and w/c. 13⅜ × 9½ (340 × 242). Signed.
EXH. (probably) OWCS, 1835, No. 192 as A Lady Reading.
COMMENT. Mrs Hunt aged about 23.

ROCHDALE, Art Gallery

491 *c*.1835
Self Portrait [ROCDG.419]

w/c slightly heightened with white. 15⅜ × 11⅜ (390 × 290).
Gift. R. Heape, 1917.
COMMENT. Aged about 45. Compare Self Portrait of about the same age, National Portrait Gallery (451, Plate 80).

ROSSETTI, Mr and Mrs Harold, Suffolk

492 1815–20
Girl Asleep in an Arm Chair

Pencil and w/c. 9⅛ × 6½ (232 × 165). Signed.
COMMENT. Compare same girl in similar pose in Fry Collection (365).

493 1832–35
Woman Sewing

w/c. 13¼ × 8½ (337 × 217).
EXH. OWCS, either as The Seamstress in 1832 No. 360, or A Sempstress in 1833 No. 237, or A Lady Sewing in 1835 No. 200.

ROYAL ACADEMY OF ARTS, London

494
Jupp Catalogue [JU.9.5]

This consisted of 16 volumes compiled by E. J. Jupp (1812–77) and presented by him to the Royal Academy. Vol. IX comprised 12 drawings by Hunt all in pencil, and with one exception, Boat and Wagon – 6⅛ × 8⅝ (155 × 220), all small as follows: Beach and Rocks, Storm, Dark Trees in a Landscape, three of Babies, three of Dogs, two of Cats.
COMMENT. The volume contains a letter by Hunt dated 21 July 1847 from 62 Stanhope Street, Hampstead Road, to a Mr Mackinley: 'The frame is after my own fancy – hope that it would har-

monise with the furniture in your drawing room. I trust you will accept of the same with best respects to Mrs Mackinley and my young moth.'

ROYAL COLLEGE OF SURGEONS, Lincoln's Inn Fields, London

495 *c*.1826
Portrait of John Abernethy [PRCS 1826].

w/c on card. 70 × 55 ($2\frac{3}{4} \times 2\frac{1}{8}$).
COMMENT. Derived from the portrait by Sir Thomas Lawrence at St Bartholomew's Hospital.

ROYAL SOCIETY OF PAINTERS IN WATER-COLOURS, London

496 *c*.1826
The Broken Pitcher [RWS.H.144]

Young girl, holding brown pitcher with crack down the front, standing near gate with cottage and trees behind.
w/c. 9 × $13\frac{1}{2}$ (228 × 343). Signed.
EXH. Hunt Exhibition 1981.
COMMENT. Diploma work presented to the Society by Hunt on becoming a member in 1826.

497 Dated 1833
The Stonebreaker [RWS.PB.33]

Old man in gaiters with long-handled stone breaker standing beside a pile of stones.
w/c. $14\frac{1}{8} \times 9\frac{7}{8}$ (358 × 252). Signed and dated 1833. Bequest. R. W. S. Parsons, 1979.
PROV. Ralph Bernal; sold Christie's, 23 April 1853, Lot 342.
EXH. Hunt Exhibition 1981.

RYSKAMP, Charles, New York City

498 *c*.1831
Boy Standing in a Pantry

Boy's figure is unfinished: he is standing by a table on which sits a large orange crock.
Pencil and w/c. 11 × $7\frac{1}{2}$ (280 × 190).
COMMENT. Boy model.

SHEEPSHANKS, Captain R., Suffolk

499 (Colour Plate 11) *c*.1834
The Attack (originally entitled The Commencement)

Young boy seated at table begins to eat large pie.
w/c. $16\frac{1}{2}$ × 11 (419 × 280).
PROV. John Sheepshanks: by descent through members of the Sheepshanks family to the present owner.
EXH. (1) OWCS, 1834, No. 382 as The Commencement. (2) Exposition Universelle in the Palais des Beaux Arts, Paris, 1855, No. 1032 as L'Attaque du pâté.
BIB. Referred to Roget, Vol. II, pp. 191, 192.
COMMENT. Pendant to The Defeat (originally entitled The Conclusion) in the same Collection (500, Colour Plate 12). An almost identical version, $16\frac{1}{8} \times 11\frac{5}{8}$ (410 × 295) signed and dated 1834, was exhibited at the Exhibition of Art Treasures of the United Kingdom, Manchester, 1857, No. 526, as belonging to G. W. Moss. It subsequently formed part of the F. J. Nettlefold Collection. Present ownership unknown. Boy model.

500 (Colour Plate 12) *c*.1834
The Defeat (originally entitled The Conclusion)

Young boy seated at table, totally exhausted having just finished eating large pie.
w/c. $16\frac{3}{4}$ × 11 (426 × 280).
PROV. John Sheepshanks: by descent through members of the Sheepshanks family to the present owner.
EXH. (1) OWCS, 1834, No. 367 as The Conclusion. (2) Exposition Universelle in the Palais des Beaux Arts, Paris, 1855, No. 1033 as Le pendant de l'attaque.
BIB. Referred to Roget, Vol. II, pp. 191, 192.
COMMENT. Pendant to The Attack (originally entitled The Commencement) (499, Colour Plate 11). An almost identical version, $16\frac{1}{8} \times 11\frac{1}{4}$ (410 × 286), was exhibited at the Exhibition of Art Treasures of the United Kingdom, Manchester, 1857, No. 527, as belonging to G. W. Moss. It subsequently formed part of the F. J. Nettlefold Collection. Present ownership unknown. Boy model.

501 Exh.1838
Cimon and Iphigenia

Boy with pitchfork looking at sleeping girl.
w/c. $21\frac{3}{4} \times 30\frac{1}{2}$ (553 × 776).
PROV. John Sheepshanks: by descent through members of the Sheepshanks family to present owner.
EXH. OWCS, 1838, No. 182.
COMMENT. Compare version of same subject, dated 1837, in Burnley, Towneley Hall Art

Gallery and Museums (311) (see entry for legend of Cimon and Iphigenia). Boy model.

502 Dated 1839
Two Beggar Boys

One standing, wearing yellow smock, the other sitting wearing buff smock holding razor shells.
w/c heightened with white. $17\frac{1}{4} \times 11\frac{3}{4}$ (437×297).
Signed and dated 1839.
PROV. John Sheepshanks: by descent through members of the Sheepshanks family to present owner.
COMMENT. Pendant to Two Young Girls in same collection (503).

503 *c.*1839
Two Young Girls

One standing, wearing blue and white smock, the other sitting, wearing a red cloak, and reading a broad-sheet.
w/c heightened with white. $16\frac{5}{8} \times 13$ (423×330).
PROV. John Sheepshanks: by descent through members of the Sheepshanks family to present owner.
COMMENT. Pendant to Two Beggar Boys in same collection (502).

504 Dated 1839
The Halloween Boy

w/c heightened with white. $15\frac{3}{4} \times 12$ (402×305).
Signed and dated 1839.
PROV. John Sheepshanks: by descent through members of the Sheepshanks family to present owner.
COMMENT. Boy model.

505 1835–40
Boy Blowing a Large Bubble

w/c. $14\frac{3}{4} \times 9\frac{1}{2}$ (375×242).
PROV. John Sheepshanks: by descent through members of the Sheepshanks family to present owner.
COMMENT. Boy model.

506 1835–40
Boy Drawing on a Slate

Seated on barrel, wearing blue hat with red band.
w/c. $14\frac{1}{4} \times 9\frac{3}{8}$ (362×237). Signed.
PROV. John Sheepshanks: by descent through members of the Sheepshanks family to present owner.
COMMENT. Boy model.

507 (Colour Plate 19) Dated 1839
The Flower Girl

Sitting, wearing red bandana on her head, with a basket of flowers.
w/c slightly heightened with white. $19\frac{1}{4} \times 12\frac{1}{2}$ (488×317). Signed and dated 1839.
PROV. John Sheepshanks: by descent through members of the Sheepshanks family to present owner.

508 *c.*1840
Seated Boy Reading a Red Book

w/c. $11\frac{3}{8} \times 8\frac{3}{8}$ (289×213).
PROV. John Sheepshanks: by descent through members of the Sheepshanks family to present owner.
COMMENT. Pendant to (509).

509 *c.*1840
Seated Boy Reading a Large Book

Book propped up on barrel.
w/c. $11\frac{3}{8} \times 8\frac{3}{4}$ (289×213).
PROV. John Sheepshanks: by descent through members of the Sheepshanks family to present owner.
COMMENT. Pendant to (508).

SHEFFIELD, Graves Art Gallery

510 (Plate 63) *c.*1833
The Artist's Wife [1695]

Pencil. $3\frac{7}{8} \times 3\frac{1}{2}$ (98×90). Signed.
Bt 1949.
COMMENT. Mrs Hunt aged about 23.

SMITH, Hammond. *See* **394**

SOUTHPORT, Atkinson Art Gallery

511 *c.*1845
The Art Student [1451]

Girl wearing white smock, carrying book or portfolio.
w/c heightened with white. $8\frac{3}{4} \times 6\frac{1}{4}$ (223×159).
Bequest. Miss P. Lithgow, 1978.
COMMENT. His daughter Emma aged about 13.

STRANGE, Mrs Mavis, London

512 1820–25
Young Boy

Sitting on wall, wearing pink and blue hat, and shading his eyes.
w/c. $8\frac{7}{8} \times 5\frac{1}{2}$ (226 × 140).

TATE GALLERY, London

513 *c.*1835
A Water Carrier [1973]

Boy with yoke on his shoulders and two water barrels on the ground.
w/c. $14\frac{3}{4} \times 10\frac{1}{4}$ (375 × 260).
Bequest. C. Fraser, 1905.
COMMENT. Boy model.

514 (Plate 64) 1835–40
An Old Man's Head [1970]

w/c. $9\frac{1}{4} \times 8$ (235 × 203). Signed.
Bequest. C. Fraser, 1905.
COMMENT. Considerable knife scratching.

515 Dated 1838
Peasant Girl [1971]

w/c. $15\frac{1}{2} \times 11$ (394 × 280). Signed and dated 1838.
Bequest. C. Fraser, 1905.
EXH. OWCS, 1838, No. 74.
COMMENT. His daughter Emma aged about six.

TOLEDO, Museum of Art, Ohio

516 *c.*1832
Interior with a Young Girl [50.226]

Pencil and w/c heightened with white. $17\frac{1}{4} \times 12\frac{7}{8}$ (438 × 327).
COMMENT. Probably same girl as in Girl Reading at a Window, dated 1832, in Duke of Norfolk's Collection (458, Plate 78). See entry.

TORBOCK, H. C., Cumbria

517
Study of a Boy

Stooping and holding pencil and paper.
w/c. $8 \times 8\frac{1}{2}$ (202 × 216).

TUFF, Mrs G. M., London

518 (Plate 95) *c.*1845
The Artist's Daughter Holding a Jug

w/c. $10\frac{1}{2} \times 7\frac{1}{8}$ (267 × 182). Signed.
COMMENT. His daughter Emma aged about 13.

VICTORIA AND ALBERT MUSEUM, London

519 *c.*1820
Head of a Young Girl [E.856.1948]

w/c, sepia and pink wash. $9\frac{1}{2} \times 7\frac{1}{4}$ (242 × 185). Signed.

520 1820–25
The Faithful Old Servant [P.6.1931]

Old man sitting in barn by candlelight.
w/c. $24\frac{3}{8} \times 19\frac{3}{8}$ (620 × 493). Signed.
Bequest. F. L. Lucas, 1931.

521 *c.*1825
The Vegetable Man [P.10.1961]

Reed pen, ink and w/c. $12\frac{1}{4} \times 8\frac{5}{8}$ (312 × 220).
Gift. Captain C. B. Lyon, 1961.
COMMENT. Preliminary drawing for The Vegetable Seller, Courtauld Institute, Spooner Bequest (324, Plate 35).

522 *c.*1825
Mulatto Boy [FA.339]

Standing holding cap and basket.
w/c. $15 \times 8\frac{3}{4}$ (381 × 222).
COMMENT. Probably acquired in the late 1850s.

523 *c.*1825
Self Portrait [P.16.1921]

Oil on canvas. $4\frac{3}{8} \times 3\frac{7}{8}$ (111 × 98).
Gift. Alfred Jones, 1920.
COMMENT. Aged about 35.

524 1825–30
Lady Playing a Guitar [1760.1900]

Sitting on sofa wearing mauve dress.
w/c. $10\frac{3}{8} \times 7$ (263 × 178).
Bequest. H. S. Ashbee, 1900.

525 1825–30
Interior of a Bedroom [588.1870]

Green bed hangings, white bedspread, and red dress on chair.
Reed pen, ink and w/c. $12\frac{1}{4} \times 9\frac{1}{4}$ (311 × 235).
Bequest. J. M. Parsons, 1870.

526 (Colour Plate 9) Dated 1828
James Holland (1799–1870) Painter
[451.1887]

Inscribed in Hunt's handwriting: 'Portrait of Jas. Holland'.
w/c. $12\frac{1}{4} \times 8\frac{3}{4}$ (311 × 223). Signed and dated 'Wm. Hunt 1828'.
EXH. Hunt Exhibition 1981.
BIB. *The Portfolio*, 1891, Vol. 22, p. 12.
Connoisseur, June 1926, repr. facing p. 116.

527 *c.*1830
Coast Guardsman [FA.340]

With sword and pistol in his belt and carrying gun.
w/c. $14 \times 9\frac{1}{8}$ (356 × 232).
COMMENT. Probably acquired in the late 1850s.

528 1830–35
The Doubtful Coin [1472.1869]

Young boy closely inspecting coin, with basket of apples.
w/c. $11\frac{7}{8} \times 8\frac{1}{4}$ (302 × 210). Signed.
Bequest. Rev. C. H. Townshend, 1869.
COMMENT. Boy model.

529 *c.*1833
Love's Missive [1761.1900]

Mrs Hunt, aged about 21, looking out of the window.
w/c. $10\frac{5}{8} \times 7\frac{1}{4}$ (270 × 184). Signed.
Bequest. H. S. Ashbee, 1900.
PROV. Ralph Bernal. Henry Wallis; sold Christie's, 20 March 1861, Lot 50.
EXH. Hunt Exhibition 1981.
COMMENT. Compare same chest and chair in C. W. Witt Collection (539, Plate 66).

530 (Plate 59) Dated 1836
Boy and Goat [FA.341]

w/c heightened with white with surface scratching. $12\frac{1}{4} \times 16$ (312 × 407). Signed and dated 1836.
EXH. (1) OWCS, 1836, No. 192. (2) Hunt Exhibition 1981.
BIB. Repr. Pl. 130, Martin Hardie, Vol. III.
COMMENT. Probably acquired in the late 1850s.

531 1830–40
Head of a Negro [1205.1886BGM]

w/c. $7 \times 4\frac{7}{8}$ (178 × 125) oval.
Bequest. Joshua Dixon, 1886.
COMMENT. At Bethnal Green Museum, London.

532 1835–40
The Valentine [1031.1873]

Boy writing at table.
w/c. $9\frac{7}{8} \times 7\frac{1}{8}$ (250 × 182).
Gift. Mrs R. Ellison, 1860.
COMMENT. Boy model.

533 Exh. 1840
A Brown Study [FA.526]

Young coloured boy sitting doing sums on slate.
w/c. $14 \times 9\frac{1}{2}$ (356 × 241). Signed.
Gift. Mrs R. Ellison, 1860.
EXH. (1) OWCS, 1840, No. 116. (2) Hunt Exhibition 1981.
COMMENT. Compare Negro Boy, Yale Center (574).

534 *c.*1840
Indigence: A Girl's Head [558.1882]

In profile, with long hair.
w/c. $8\frac{1}{2} \times 6\frac{3}{4}$ (216 × 172). Signed.
Bequest. John Jones, 1882.

535 (Plate 96) *c.*1842
Portrait of the Artist, his Daughter and Niece [D.271.1905]

Inscribed on back of mount: 'whom he was in the habit of dressing up on occasion'.
Pen, ink and w/c. $4 \times 5\frac{5}{8}$ (102 × 143).
COMMENT. His daughter Emma aged about 10.

536 (Colour Plate 18) *c.*1842
Hearing Lessons [1138.1886BGM]

Mrs Hunt and her daughter Emma aged about 10.
w/c. $14\frac{1}{2} \times 13\frac{1}{2}$ (368 × 344). Signed.
Bequest. Joshua Dixon, 1886.
COMMENT. At Bethnal Green Museum, London.

537 1840–50
The Monk [FA.524]

Wearing cassock and holding book.
w/c heightened with white. $14\frac{7}{8} \times 10\frac{1}{4}$ (378 × 262). Signed.
Gift. Mrs R. Ellison, 1860.
EXH. Hunt Exhibition 1981.
BIB. Repr. *The Portfolio*, Vol. XIX, 1888, p. 197.

WHITE, Clifford G., Hertfordshire

538 *c*.1840
Young Boy and Girl in a Barn

With large wicker basket and farming tools.
w/c heightened with white. $15 \times 13\frac{7}{8}$ (380 × 327). Signed.
EXH. Royal Jubilee Exhibition, Manchester, 1887.

WITT, C. W., Bucks.

539 (Plate 66) *c*.1833
An Interesting Letter [131]

Mrs Hunt aged about 21 reading a letter.
w/c. $13\frac{1}{4} \times 9\frac{3}{4}$ (337 × 246). Signed.
PROV. J. P. Heseltine.
BIB. Repr. Plate 13, J. P. Heseltine, *John Varley and His Pupils, W. Mulready, J. Linnell, and W. Hunt. Original Drawings in the Collection of J.P.H.*, 1918.
COMMENT. Compare same chest and chair at Victoria and Albert Museum (529).

WITT, Sir John and Lady, London

540 (Plate 31) Dated 1815
Stable Boy [1795]

w/c. $10\frac{7}{8} \times 7\frac{1}{4}$ (276 × 184). Signed and dated 1815.
Bt 1971.
COMMENT. Compare same figure in National Gallery of Scotland (448).

541 *c*.1820
Man in Top Hat Cleaning Fish [1899]

Pencil. $8 \times 4\frac{3}{4}$ (203 × 122). Signed 'W.H.'
Bt 1973.

542 *c*.1820
Young Girl and Young Boy Holding Dog [2042]

Pencil, reed pen, ink and w/c. $10\frac{1}{2} \times 5\frac{1}{2}$ (267 × 140). Signed.
Bt 1978.
COMMENT. Compare same boy holding puppy, in same medium, in British Museum (290).

543 *c*.1820
Seated Man Reading a Book [2118]

Wearing smoking cap.
Pencil and w/c. $9\frac{3}{4} \times 6\frac{3}{4}$ (248 × 171).
Bt 1981.

544 (Plate 33) *c*.1820
Young Girl Standing Barefoot [2048]

Reed pen, ink and w/c. $7\frac{1}{2} \times 3\frac{7}{8}$ (190 × 97). Signed.
Bt 1978.
COMMENT. Compare same girl from slightly different angle at Yale Center (565).

545 *c*.1830
Two Young Women Seated Talking [2093]

Pencil and w/c. $7\frac{1}{4} \times 5\frac{1}{2}$ (184 × 140).
Bt 1980.

546 *c*.1820
Study of a Girl [847]

Unfinished.
Pencil and w/c. $9\frac{1}{2} \times 8\frac{1}{8}$ (242 × 207). Signed.
Bt 1958.

546(a) *c*.1820
Study of a Girl Wearing a Pink-striped Head Scarf [2133]

Pencil and w/c. $7\frac{7}{8} \times 6\frac{3}{4}$ (200 × 173). Signed.
Bt 1981.

547 *c*.1825
Man Playing Flute [1484]

w/c. $13\frac{1}{4} \times 9\frac{1}{8}$ (336 × 232).
Bt 1968.
COMMENT. Compare stylistically with Sporting Gentleman in a High Straw Hat Cleaning his Gun in Bristol, Museum and Art Gallery (288).

548 Dated 1827
Girl Reading a Letter by Lamplight [1712]

w/c heightened with white. $14\frac{5}{8} \times 10\frac{1}{2}$ (373 × 267). Signed and dated 1827.
Bt 1970.
EXH. (1) (perhaps) OWCS, 1829, No. 13 or No. 214, both entitled A Lady Reading by Lamplight. (2) Hunt Exhibition 1981.
COMMENT. Same girl as in Fry Collection (379, Plate 43) and in Huntington Library (403).

549 *c*.1827
Young Girl Looking in a Mirror by Lamplight [1894]

w/c. $10\frac{3}{4} \times 7\frac{1}{4}$ (273×184). Signed.
Bt 1973.
EXH. Hunt Exhibition 1981.
COMMENT. Compare Girl Reading a Letter by Candlelight, dated 1827, Witt Collection (548).

550 Dated 1830
A Fishing Boy [1541]

w/c. $15\frac{1}{4} \times 9\frac{3}{4}$ (387×247). Signed and dated 1830.
Bt 1969.
EXH. OWCS, 1830, No. 273 or 302.

551 1830–35
Portrait of a Young Black Girl [2132]

Pencil. $8\frac{5}{8} \times 6\frac{1}{2}$ (220×165). Signed.
Bt 1981.

552 1830–35
Woman Sitting at a Window with Landscape Outside [813]

w/c heightened with white. 14×11 (356×279). Signed.
Bt 1958.

553 (Colour Plate 16) *c*.1833
Girl at her Toilet [1920]

w/c. $12\frac{1}{4} \times 16\frac{1}{2}$ (312×420).
Bt 1974.
PROV. Muir Hetherington.
EXH. Hunt Exhibition 1981.
COMMENT. Same patchwork quilt as in Sunday Morning, dated 1833, in Huntington Library (407, Plate 74) and in Blackburn, Museum and Art Gallery (see under 277).

554 *c*.1835
Young Child Seated at a Table [2087]

Pencil and w/c. $12\frac{1}{4} \times 8\frac{1}{8}$ (312×206). Signed.
Bt 1979.
COMMENT. Same child as in Wolverhampton, Art Gallery and Museums (560).

555 1835–40
Portrait of an Elderly Woman [1514]

w/c heightened with white. $10\frac{3}{4} \times 9\frac{1}{8}$ (273×234).
Bt 1968.

556 *c*.1847
Woman Seated Reading a Book by Candlelight [1830]
Inscribed on old mount: 'The Artist's wife'.
Black and coloured crayons. $4\frac{5}{8} \times 3\frac{3}{4}$ (118×95).
Bt 1972.
COMMENT. Mrs Hunt aged about 35. She died in 1857 at the age of 45.

557 (Plate 94) *c*.1847
Portrait of his Daughter [1973]

So inscribed on old label.
w/c heightened with white. $5\frac{1}{8} \times 3\frac{3}{8}$ (130×86). Signed.
Bt 1975.
COMMENT. Emma aged about 15.

558
Portrait of a Young Man [140(g)]

Pencil. $3\frac{1}{2} \times 3$ (90×77). Signed.
Bt 1927.

559
Album [2106]

Containing 22 pen and 27 pencil studies of single figures and groups of figures, 11 pencil studies of cats and dogs, 1 study of a goat (in coloured chalks) and 1 pencil study of a fountain – all small.
Bt 1980.

WOLVERHAMPTON, Art Gallery and Museums

560 *c*.1835
Curiosity – a Sketch [W.88]

Young child crawling.
w/c. $3\frac{3}{4} \times 5\frac{1}{4}$ (95×133).
Bequest. Cartwright, 1887.
COMMENT. Same child as in Witt Collection (554).

WORTHING, Museum and Art Gallery, Sussex

561 *c*.1830
Shepherd Boy [1955.31]

w/c. $9\frac{3}{8} \times 12\frac{3}{8}$ (237×314). Signed.
Gift. Rev. Canon F. H. D. Smythe, 1955.

YALE CENTER FOR BRITISH ART (Paul Mellon Collection), New Haven, Connecticut

562 1815–20
A Postillion [B.1977.14.6206]

Pencil and w/c. $8\frac{1}{8} \times 6\frac{15}{16}$ (205 × 175). Signed.
Bt 1969.

563 *c.*1820
A Young Scholar goes Fishing
[B.1975.4.580]

Pencil and w/c. $8\frac{3}{4} \times 7\frac{7}{8}$ (222 × 201). Signed 'W.H.'
Bt 1963.

564 *c.*1820
A Countryman [B.1975.4.582]

w/c. $3\frac{3}{4} \times 3\frac{1}{8}$ (96 × 80). Signed.
Bt 1969.
PROV. A. J. Rowe.

565 *c.*1820
Young Girl Standing Barefoot
[B.1975.3.886]

Reed pen, ink and w/c. $8\frac{7}{8} \times 4\frac{9}{16}$ (226 × 116).
PROV. T. Girtin; bt by him, 1927. Tom Girtin.
COMMENT. Compare same girl from slightly different angle in Witt Collection 544 (Plate 33).

566 *c.*1821
Interior of a Room [B.1975.4.584]

w/c. $2\frac{7}{16} \times 3\frac{1}{2}$ (61 × 82).
PROV. Gilbert Davis.
COMMENT. The mouldings are similar to those in The Dining Room at Cassiobury Park, dated 1821 in the Fry Collection (375, Plate 22).

567 *c.*1825
Two Peasant Girls Carrying Baskets
[69.4.16.8.PM.8146]

w/c. 12 × 9 (306 × 228).

568 *c.*1830
Sophy: Study of a Young Girl Reading
[B.1975.4.827]

Inscribed in a later hand: 'Sophy Steadman [sic] (related to Hunt) from a family album'.
Pencil. Size: paper $7\frac{7}{8} \times 4\frac{3}{4}$ (198 × 120), subject $4\frac{1}{2} \times 4\frac{1}{4}$ (114 × 108). Signed.
Bt 1972.
COMMENT. Sophia (Sophy) was the daughter of Hunt's sister Mrs Sophia Steedman, and received a legacy under Hunt's will of £50.

569 *c.*1830
Portrait of a Lady [B.1977.14.5062]

Pencil and w/c. $4\frac{1}{2} \times 3\frac{1}{2}$ (114 × 89). Signed.
PROV. L. G. Duke.

570 *c.*1830
Girl in a Long Dress with a Red Belt
[B.1977.14.5060]

Pencil and w/c. $3\frac{1}{2} \times 2\frac{3}{4}$ (90 × 70). Signed.
PROV. L. G. Duke.

571 (Plate 71) *c.*1830
Girl with a Black Dress [B.1977.14.5059]

w/c. $7\frac{11}{16} \times 3\frac{7}{8}$ (195 × 98).
PROV. L. G. Duke.

572 *c.*1830
Boy Writing a Letter [B.1977.14.5061]

Pencil and w/c. 3 × 3 (75 × 75). Signed.
PROV. L. G. Duke.

573 Dated 1834
The Gamekeeper

w/c. $15 \times 9\frac{1}{2}$ (382 × 242). Signed and dated 1834.
Bt 1963.
PROV. Mr Paul Mellon.
EXH. British Watercolour Drawings in the Collection of Mr and Mrs Paul Mellon, The Art Gallery of Greater Victoria, 1971, No. 22.
COMMENT. Compare: (1) The Gamekeeper, Exh. 1824 or 1825, Fry Collection (377); (2) A Gamekeeper from Nature, dated 1828, Mr and Mrs D. J. Methven Collection (444); (3) The Gamekeeper standing in a Wood, illustrated Quilter, *Preferences*, 1892.

574 *c.*1835
Negro Boy [B.1975.4.583]

Pencil and w/c heightened with white. $6\frac{5}{16} \times 4\frac{1}{4}$ (160 × 108).
Bt 1970.
PROV. Barnet Lewis. J. Haydock.
BIB. Repr. Pl. XV, F. G. Stephens, 1865.
COMMENT. Compare A Brown Study, Victoria and Albert Museum (533).

575 Dated 1836

Interior of a Barn with Bench, Vice and Tools [70.5.27.10.PM.8145]

w/c heightened with white. $13\frac{5}{8} \times 9\frac{5}{8}$ (346 × 245).
Signed and dated 1836.
Bt 1970.

576 *c*.1845

A Lady Reading Sitting on a Sofa [B.1975.3.862]

Mrs Hunt aged about 33.
w/c heightened with white. $11\frac{5}{16} \times 7\frac{11}{16}$ (287 × 195).
PROV. T. Girtin. Tom Girtin.
BIB. Repr. Pl. XIII, F. G. Stephens, 1865.

577 *c*.1845

Two Peasants by a Window [B.1975.4.581]

Inscribed on old backing board: 'Wm. Hunt 1845', and 'from Admiral Popham'.
Black chalk and w/c. $7\frac{15}{16} \times 4\frac{13}{16}$ (202 × 121).
Bt 1964.

3
Still Life
including live animals and birds

ABERDEEN, Art Gallery and Museums

578 *c.*1825
A Dead Dove

w/c. 12 × 9 (305 × 228).
Gift. Trustees of Sir Thomas Jaffrey, 1956.
EXH. (perhaps) Ruskin Hunt Exhibition 1879–80, No. 141 as A Pigeon, lent by Ruskin. Ruskin's note on No. 141, where he refers to it as Dead Dove, describes it as 'a pure water-colour drawing before his style was perfectly formed. Full of interest but too conventional and slight in background.' Two other pigeons (also referred to in the note as Dead Doves), Nos 139 and 145, were included in the Exh., No. 139 as 'finished work of central time' and No. 145 as 'replica of No. 139 with completer background'. The present whereabouts of Nos 139 and 145 are unknown.
COMMENT. Similar in style to Woodcock in Oxford, Ashmolean Museum, which is dated 1825 (686, Plate 53).

579 *c.*1860
A Peach and Grapes

w/c on prepared ground. 6 × $7\frac{3}{4}$ (152 × 196) oval. Signed.
Bequest. Alexander Webster, 1921; bt by him, 1871.

ACCRINGTON, Haworth Art Gallery

580 1840–50
Chaffinch Nest with Briar Rose [16]

w/c. 11 × 7 (280 × 178). Signed.

ANDERSON, Dr Roger, Minneapolis, Minnesota

581 *c.*1845
Bird's Nest and Lilac Branch

w/c heightened with white. $9\frac{3}{4}$ × $13\frac{1}{2}$ (248 × 342). Signed.

BAKER, Richard, London

582 *c.*1845
Plums and Redcurrants on a Mossy Bank

w/c on prepared ground. $7\frac{1}{4}$ × $8\frac{7}{8}$ (184 × 225). Signed.

BATH, Victoria Art Gallery

583 *c.*1840
Camellia in a Vase with Melon and Peach [P.1917.19]

w/c. $13\frac{1}{2}$ × $9\frac{1}{2}$ (343 × 242). Signed.
Bequest. Hon. Caroline Jervis, 1917.
COMMENT. Compare Fruit (Melon and Other Fruit) in Cambridge, Fitzwilliam Museum (615, Colour Plate 23) and Basket with Melon and Other Fruit, Witt Collection (765).

BIRKENHEAD, Williamson Art Gallery and Museum

584 *c.*1840
Fruit – Sloes and Plums [BIKGM.2087]

w/c on prepared ground. 12 × 17 (306 × 433). Signed.
Bt 1933.

BIRMINGHAM, City Museum and Art Gallery

585 *c.*1827
Lobster, Crab and Cucumber [32/91]

w/c heightened with white. $5\frac{3}{4} \times 10\frac{1}{2}$ (147 × 266). Signed.
EXH. (1) Arts Council Touring Exhibition of British Watercolours 1760–1930, from the Birmingham Museums and Art Gallery, 1980, No. 59, repr. p. 17. (2) Hunt Exhibition 1981.
COMMENT. Strong resemblance stylistically to A Rabbit and Lobster (mistitled A Dead Hare and a Cooked Lobster), Yale Center (774, Plate 55), exh. OWCS, 1827, No. 216. The work is therefore dateable *c.*1827.

586 (Plate 85) 1835–40
Black Grapes and Pear [2408]

w/c on prepared ground. $7\frac{3}{4} \times 11$ (197 × 280). Signed.
Bequest. H. C. Brunning, 1908.

587 1845–50
Bird's Nest, Apple Blossom and Primroses [166/05]

w/c. $8\frac{3}{4} \times 11\frac{3}{4}$ (197 × 298). Signed.
Bt 1905.
EXH. (1) British Royal Family Exhibition, Tokyo, 1967, No. 123. (2) Hunt Exhibition 1981.

BLACKBURN, Museum and Art Gallery

588 1825–30
Foxgloves [779]

w/c. $5\frac{1}{4} \times 3$ (133 × 76). Signed.
Bequest. Miss S. J. Duckworth, 1969.

589 Dated 1837
Flower Study [451]

w/c. $6\frac{1}{4} \times 11\frac{1}{2}$ (160 × 290). Signed and dated 1837.
Bequest. Mrs E. A. Yerburgh, 1948.

590 *c.*1840
Still Life, Grapes [379]

w/c on prepared ground. $7\frac{7}{8} \times 11$ (200 × 280). Signed.
Bequest. E. Hamer, 1940.

591 *c.*1850
Fruit Study [452]

Pear and two peaches.
w/c on prepared ground. $4\frac{1}{2} \times 6\frac{1}{2}$ (114 × 165). Signed.
Bequest. Mrs E. A. Yerburgh, 1948.

592 *c.*1860
Flowers and Holly [450]

w/c. $4\frac{3}{4} \times 8$ (120 × 205). Signed.
Bequest. Mrs E. A. Yerburgh, 1948.

BOLTON, Museum and Art Gallery

593 (Plate 81) *c.*1835
Still Life of Slaughtered Goose and Basket [P.35.1973]

w/c heightened with white. $10\frac{1}{4} \times 10\frac{1}{4}$ (261 × 261). Signed.

594 *c.*1845
May Blossom and Hedge-Sparrow's Nest [P.45.1963]

w/c heightened with white. $7\frac{3}{4} \times 11\frac{1}{4}$ (192 × 286). Signed.
Bt 1955.
PROV. G. W. Isherwood.

BOURNEMOUTH, Russell-Cotes Art Gallery and Museum and The Rothesay Museum

595 1830–35
Bird's Nest [224]

w/c. $7\frac{1}{2} \times 5\frac{1}{2}$ (190 × 140).
Gift. Sir Merton Russell-Cotes, 1922.

596 1840–45
Flowers in a China Mug, sometimes called The Overflowing Mug [304]

w/c heightened with white. $10\frac{1}{2} \times 7$ (267 × 178). Signed.

BRADFORD, Art Galleries and Museums

597 *c*.1840
Rose and Bird's Nest [14–32]

w/c. $12\frac{7}{8} \times 10$ (327 × 254). Signed.
Gift. Francis V. Gill, 1932.
PROV. Dr Joseph Needham.

BRANDT, Estate of the late Walter, London

598 1845–50
Still Life, Peaches, Black Grapes and Strawberries

w/c on prepared ground. $6 \times 8\frac{1}{4}$ (152 × 210). Signed.

THE BRANTWOOD TRUST, Brantwood, Coniston, Cumbria

599 (Plate 104) Exh.1858
Peach and Grapes [735]

w/c on prepared ground. $8 \times 10\frac{3}{4}$ (203 × 273) oval.
Bt from Sharp Estate, 1960.
PROV. John James Ruskin (John Ruskin's father), from his accounts: 'March 1858, Hunt Dg Grapes £40'. John Ruskin. Arthur Severn Family. F. J. Sharp.
EXH. (1) OWCS, 1858, No. 314 as Fruit. (2) Ruskin Hunt Exhibition 1879–80, No. 134.
COMMENT. During most of the time that Ruskin lived at Brantwood (1871–1900) this drawing hung over his bedroom fireplace, surrounded by some of his Turners. Ruskin describes the drawing in these terms: 'Here you see the most beautiful painting of fruit that Hunt ever did, and it hangs among the Turners like a brooch'. Ruskin, *Works*, Vol. XXXIV, p. 670.

BRIGHTON, The Royal Pavilion, Art Gallery and Museums

600 *c*.1855
Grapes and Strawberries [100717]

w/c on prepared ground heightened with white. $5\frac{1}{4} \times 7\frac{1}{4}$ (133 × 183). Signed.
Bequest. A. G. E. Godden, 1933.

BRITISH MUSEUM, London

601 *c*.1827
Cauliflower, Potatoes and Brown Jug [1944.10.14.109]

w/c heightened with white. $6\frac{3}{8} \times 9\frac{1}{8}$ (162 × 232). Signed.
Gift. Miss M. H. Turner, 1944.
EXH. (1) (probably) OWCS, 1827, No. 55 as Cauliflower etc. (2) Hunt Exhibition 1981.

602 1830–35
Dead Velvert Duck [1944.10.14.107]

With red legs lying on rocks with sea and boats in the distance.
w/c heightened with white on wings and head. $5\frac{7}{8} \times 10\frac{7}{8}$ (149 × 277). Signed.
Gift. Miss M. H. Turner, 1944.

603 1930–40
Bird's Nest [1944.10.14.108]

Hedge sparrow's and chaffinch's eggs making a necklace, and brown jug.
w/c heightened with white. $6\frac{1}{4} \times 6$ (159 × 152). Signed.
Gift. Miss M. H. Turner, 1944.
EXH. Hunt Exhibition 1981.

604 *c*.1840
Hollyhocks in a Vase with Apple [1889.7.24.365 (LB5)]

Pencil and w/c heightened with white. $4\frac{3}{8} \times 3$ (110 × 75). Signed.
COMMENT. Compare earlier study of a Hollyhock, Fry Collection (628).

605 *c*.1841
The Wonderful Cat, Juvenile Night Pantomime [1934.9.22 No. 82]

In an illustrated letter postmarked 13 January 1841, Hastings, written by Hunt to George Peckitt Esq., 16 White Conduit Grove, Islington, London.
Pen and sepia ink. $11 \times 7\frac{1}{4}$ (280 × 185).
EXH. Hunt Exhibition 1981.
COMMENT. The letter refers to 'Christmas without having the misfortune to tumble out of his chair as you and myself recclect [sic] him to have done once upon a time'. Separately mounted from Album A.7. See under 607.

606 (Colour Plate 25) *c*.1845
Long-Tailed Tit's Nest [1915.3.13.36]

With holly leaves and berries.
w/c heightened with white. 13 × 9 (330 × 228). Signed.
Bequest. Rev. C. J. Sale, 1915.
PROV. Joseph Gillot; his sale, Christie's, 4 May 1872, Lot 469. Bt Rev. C. J. Sale.

606(a) *c*.1850
Peach with Black and White Grapes [1915.3.13.35]

w/c on prepared ground heightened with white. 6 × 7 (152 × 179). Signed.
Bequest. Rev. C. J. Sale, 1915.

607
Album A.7 [1934.9.22]

Consists of 'Drawings by William Henry Hunt and others from a scrap book once in the possession of Mrs Baxter of Compton Terrace, Highbury, a great niece of the artist'. Hunt drawings numbered 1–124 inclusive with a number of gaps. They comprise mainly portrait and figure drawings, a number of members of his family; e.g. Nos 2–7 inclusive, of his sister-in-law Maria Hunt; Nos 9–14 inclusive, of his nephew Charles Steedman (born 1826) as a baby (No. 9) and at varying ages up to 18 (No. 14); his niece Sophia Steedman (born 1830) as a baby (No. 18); and other members of the Steedman family. Nos 60 and 61 are of chess players. The album also includes (91–120 inclusive) shore scenes around Hastings and a few landscapes mainly in pencil and small in size. No. 93 is of shipping and is more elaborate than the usual landscape/seascape – $6\frac{5}{8} \times 8\frac{5}{8}$ (167 × 218) – and inscribed on verso: 'W. Hunt, 6 Marchmont Street.' As Hunt lived at that address from 1825 to 1842, No. 93 is dateable between those years. No. 121 is of Caroline Place, Hastings, in pen and sepia ink and inscribed in Hunt's handwriting: 'this our prospect one way, with the sea to our right'. Also inscribed verso: '1 Caroline House, Caroline Place, Hastings'. The album also includes the following small pencil drawings of animals: Nos 83 and 84, Cats; 85 and 86, Pug Dog Asleep; 87, two Pigs.
Bt 2 September 1934 from Mr A. Brandon through the Florence Fund.

BURNLEY, Towneley Hall Art Gallery and Museums

608 *c*.1845
Grapes and a Pineapple [WA/CO.27]

w/c on prepared ground. $12\frac{1}{4} \times 9$ (312 × 228). Signed.
Bt 1923.

609 *c*.1845
Grapes, a Pear and Nuts [WA/CO.107]

w/c on prepared ground. $8\frac{1}{2} \times 12$ (216 × 305). Signed.
Bequest. Amos Preston, 1943.

BURY, Art Gallery

610 *c*.1840
Plums [76]

Spray of blackberries in foreground.
w/c. $8\frac{3}{4} \times 13\frac{1}{2}$ (223 × 342). Signed.
Gift. Wrigley Family, 1901.
PROV. Thomas Wrigley (a local paper manufacturer) who died 1880.

611 *c*.1845
Hedgesparrow's Nest [74]

w/c heightened with white. $8\frac{3}{4} \times 11\frac{1}{2}$ (223 × 292). Signed.
Gift. Wrigley Family, 1901.
PROV. Thomas Wrigley (a local paper manufacturer) who died 1880.

612 1850–60
Fruit Piece [77]

Peaches and hazel nut.
w/c on prepared ground. $5\frac{1}{2} \times 9\frac{1}{2}$ (140 × 242). Signed.
Gift. Wrigley Family, 1901.
PROV. Thomas Wrigley (a local paper manufacturer) who died 1880.

BYAM SHAW, James, London

613 1820–30
Cat

w/c. $2\frac{1}{2} \times 2\frac{1}{2}$ (64 × 64).
PROV. Gift from Gilbert Davis.

CAMBRIDGE, Fitzwilliam Museum

614 (Plate 84) Dated 1835
Study of a Rose [3338]

w/c heightened with white. $5\frac{3}{8} \times 9\frac{1}{4}$ (138 × 235). Signed and dated 1835.
Bequest. Marlay, 1912.

615 (Colour Plate 23) *c.*1840
Fruit (Melon, Black Grapes, Plums and Red Currants) [1795]

w/c on prepared ground. $10\frac{1}{8} \times 14\frac{1}{4}$ (257 × 362). Signed.
Bequest. Arthur W. Young of Trinity College, Cambridge, 1936.
COMMENT. Compare melon in Bath, Victoria Art Gallery (583) and Basket with Melon in Witt Collection (765).

616 (Plate 100) 1840–50
Study of Fruit [741]

Black grapes, figs and plum.
w/c on prepared ground. $8 \times 11\frac{1}{2}$ (203 × 292). Signed.
Gift. C. Fairfax Murray, 1912.

617 *c.*1850
Study of Flowers [740]

Roses and various flowers in jug on table with bird's nest and basket.
w/c heightened with white. $19\frac{7}{8} \times 15\frac{1}{4}$ (505 × 387). Signed.
Gift. C. Fairfax Murray, 1912.

CAMBRIDGE, Massachusetts, Fogg Art Museum, Harvard University

618 1840–50
Hawthorn and Bird's Nest [1898.1]

Chaffinch nest with five eggs.
w/c heightened with white. $6\frac{9}{16} \times 10\frac{3}{8}$ (167 × 258). Signed.
Bt 1898.

619 *c.*1855
Still Life with Fruit [1943.475]

Quince, black grapes and rose hips.
w/c on prepared ground heightened with white. $5\frac{3}{4} \times 8\frac{7}{8}$ (147 × 225). Signed.
Bequest. Grenville L. Winthrop, 1943.

620 (Plate 113) Exh. 1859
Shells [1943.1336]

Mussel shells and limpet.
w/c heightened with white. $4\frac{1}{2} \times 6\frac{1}{2}$ (114 × 165). Signed.
Bequest. Grenville L. Winthrop, 1943.
EXH. (1) OWCS, 1859, No. 225 as 'Sea Shells. Painted for J. Ruskin, Esq.' (2) Ruskin Hunt Exhibition 1879–80, No. 180 as Shells, then lent by Mr Barnes. Mr Barnes also lent No. 182, A Bit of Mont Blanc, which was exhibited at the OWCS, 1856, No. 253 also as: 'Painted for J. Ruskin, Esq.' Mr Barnes must therefore have acquired both these works from Ruskin, for whom they had been painted.

COURTAULD Institute of Art, University of London

621 *c.*1828
Two Ducks Hanging from a Shelf [2196]

w/c slightly heightened with white. $10\frac{1}{8} \times 7\frac{1}{2}$ (257 × 190).
Bequest. Sir Robert Witt, 1952.
COMMENT. Similar version, signed and dated 1828, $10\frac{1}{2} \times 7\frac{1}{2}$ (267 × 190), formerly with Fine Art Society, London, but present ownership unknown.

DANIELS, David, New York City

622 1840–50
Hedge-sparrow's Nest with Primroses and Violets

w/c. $7\frac{1}{2} \times 9\frac{5}{8}$ (190 × 245).

DERBY, Museum and Art Gallery

623 *c.*1850
Apple Blossom and Hedge Sparrow's Nest

w/c heightened with white. 8 × 11 (203 × 280).
Bequest. Col. Richard Sale, 1904. Col. Sale, of the Royal Bengal Engineers, was a member of an old Derby family, and died in 1903.

DEVONSHIRE Collection Chatsworth, Derbyshire

624 *c.*1827
Dog in a Bed

Greyhound or whippet.
Black and red chalk. $7\frac{1}{4} \times 9\frac{5}{8}$ (183 × 244). Signed.

625 *c.*1827
Spaniel on a Chair

w/c heightened with white. $10\frac{1}{4} \times 6\frac{5}{8}$ (260 × 168).

DUDLEY Museum and Art Gallery, West Midlands

626 (Plate 99) *c.*1850
Fruit

Grapes, plums and peach.
w/c on prepared ground. $9\frac{1}{2} \times 13$ (242 × 330).
Signed.
Bt 1904.
COMMENT. This unfinished work is of particular interest as showing Hunt's special method of using Chinese white mixed with gum to make a prepared ground on which he would subsequently paint in pure watercolour.

EXETER, Royal Albert Memorial Museum

627 *c.*1845
Primroses and Bird's Nest

w/c slightly heightened with white. $14\frac{1}{8} \times 12\frac{1}{4}$ (358 × 310) oval.
Bequest. Sir Harry Veitch, 1924.

FRY, Mr and Mrs Cyril, London

628 1820–25
Study of a Hollyhock

Pencil and w/c. $3\frac{3}{4} \times 2\frac{1}{2}$ (93 × 62).
EXH. Hunt Exhibition Fry Collection 1967.
BIB. Fry Cat., 1967, No. 35(a).
COMMENT. Compare later Hollyhocks in a Vase, British Museum (604).

629 *c.*1841

A series of 12 letters, each decorated at the top with a small watercolour drawing, including a peacock, flowers in a vase, a spray of lilac, a hyacinth, fruit, a bird's nest and 2 landscapes. The letters are addressed to a Miss Moore, who was evidently a pupil living in Cheyne Walk. Hunt writes from three different addresses in Hastings and from one address in London. Some of the letters are dated with the day of the month, but none with the year. Apart from references to Miss Moore's health, Hunt's drawings, and Miss Moore's copies of them, the letters contain requests for orders from Mr Moore for theatre seats, and this may have been the form of Hunt's remuneration for helping Miss Moore with her studies.
w/c.
Gift. From L. G. Duke.
COMMENT. Note by L. G. Duke: 'The letters may all be dated c.1841 as "London Assurance" referred to in one of them was a comedy by Dion Boucicault, which was produced at Covent Garden in that year'. Hunt's great fondness for the theatre is referred to in Roget, Vol. II, p. 197.

630 (Plate 112) *c.*1850
Study of Two Onions

Inscribed verso: 'purchased by W. Hunt's niece'.
w/c. $5\frac{1}{2} \times 8\frac{1}{4}$ (145 × 220).
EXH. Hunt Exhibition Fry Collection 1967.
BIB. Fry Cat., 1967, No. 53.

631 *c.*1850
Strawberries on a Mossy Bank

w/c. $3\frac{3}{4} \times 5\frac{1}{2}$ (92 × 137).
EXH. Hunt Exhibition Fry Collection 1967.
BIB. Fry Cat., 1967, No. 55(b).

632 *c.*1850
Bird's Nest with Briar Rose

w/c heightened with white. $7\frac{3}{8} \times 8\frac{1}{8}$ (190 × 214).
Signed.
EXH. Hunt Exhibition Fry Collection 1967.
BIB. Fry Cat., 1967, No. 61. Repr. Maas, *Victorian Painters*, 1969, p. 208.

633 (Plate 97) *c.*1850
Flowers in a Pewter Mug

Lily, tulip and pansies.
w/c heightened with white. $10\frac{5}{8} \times 6\frac{7}{8}$ (270 × 175).
Signed.
EXH. Hunt Exhibition Fry Collection 1967.
BIB. Fry Cat., 1967, No. 54.

634 (Colour Plate 27) Exh. 1859
An Oyster Shell and an Onion

w/c heightened with white. $4\frac{3}{4} \times 6\frac{1}{2}$ (123 × 165).
Signed.
PROV. John Ruskin. James Orrock. Sir William Lever who presented it to a Red Cross Sale, Christie's, 16 April 1915, Lot 615. A. Passingham. Miss N. Armitage: Christie's, 14 October 1969, Lot 101.
EXH. (1) OWCS, 1859, No. 226 as 'Painted for J. Ruskin, Esq.' (2) Hunt Exhibition 1981.

BIB. Roget, Vol. II, p. 196 records of this work that 'the old man used to pause in his work which he was trying his very best to accomplish and cry out "How difficult it is to paint this oyster-shell!"'

GATELEY, Alan B., West Midlands

635 Exh. 1840
Dead Kingfisher and Fishing Tackle

w/c. 8 × 12 (203 × 305). Signed.
EXH. OWCS, 1840, No. 280 as 'Kingfisher, etc.'
BIB. Probably the drawing of a kingfisher referred to by William Collingwood, p. 505 (this passage is quoted in Part I, Chapter 4).

636 *c.*1850
Plums and Snail Shell

w/c. 8 × 11 (203 × 280). Signed.

GATESHEAD, Shipley Art Gallery

637 (Plate 103) 1845–50
Fruit Piece [C.11745]

Blackberries and hazel nuts.
w/c heightened with white. $8\frac{1}{4} \times 15\frac{1}{2}$ (209 × 395). Signed.
Gift. H. C. Richardson, 1947.

SMITH, Hammond, Leicester

638 1845–50
Chaffinch Nest and Primroses

w/c heightened with white. 11 × 9 (280 × 228). Signed.

HASTINGS, Museum and Art Gallery

639 *c.*1838
Basket and Fruit [911.36.2]

Large wicker basket on its side with apple, plums and black currants.
w/c. $7\frac{3}{4} \times 19\frac{3}{4}$ (200 × 500). Signed.
Gift. Miss Clara Allen, 1911.
EXH. Hunt Exhibition 1981.
COMMENT. Notes, verso, state: 'Mr Hunt begs Miss Isabella Prout will do him the favour to accept the enclosed trifle for her scrap book. . . . This drawing by Mr Hunt belongs to Isabella Anne Prout – given to her by him for singing "Wapping Old Stairs" at Mr John Maw's West Hill House, Hastings 1838 or 1840. The said I. A. Prout bequeaths it at her death to her brother – eventually to the Hastings Museum.'

640 *c.*1840
Three Apples [925.32]

w/c. $6\frac{5}{8} \times 8\frac{5}{8}$ (170 × 220). Signed.
Bt 1925.

HENRY E. HUNTINGTON Library and Art Gallery, San Marino, California

641 *c.*1820
Begging Dog [59.55.739]

w/c. $6\frac{1}{8} \times 3\frac{3}{8}$ (156 × 86). Signed.
PROV. Gilbert Davis; bt by him, 1950.
BIB. Repr. OWCS, 28th Annual Volume 1950, Plate XV.

642 (Plate 49) *c.*1820
Dog Studies [59.55.740]

Pencil and brown wash. $10\frac{3}{4} \times 7\frac{1}{4}$ (274 × 184). Signed.
PROV. Gilbert Davis; bt by him, 1948.

643 *c.*1826
Dead Duck – A Mallard [59.55.742]

w/c. $4\frac{1}{2} \times 6\frac{1}{2}$ (115 × 162). Signed.
PROV. Gilbert Davis; bt by him, 1949.
COMMENT. Compare mallards in Dead Game in Witt Collection (758) which was perhaps exhibited OWCS, 1826, Nos 6 or 250, or 1828, No. 243.

644 Dated 1838
Grapes [59.55.748]

w/c slightly heightened with white on prepared ground. $7\frac{1}{4} \times 11$ (184 × 280). Signed and dated 1838.
PROV. Gilbert Davis; bt by him, 1949.
COMMENT. Compare Black Grapes and Basket (764).

645 1840–50
Peach and Grapes [59.55.759]

w/c on prepared ground. $8 \times 11\frac{1}{2}$ (203 × 292) oval.
PROV. Gilbert Davis; bt by him, 1947.

646 *c.*1860
Wild Roses and Shell [59.55.762]

w/c heightened with white. $4\frac{1}{4} \times 5\frac{1}{4}$ (107 × 133). Signed.
PROV. Gilbert Davis; bt by him, 1947.

KENDAL, Town Hall (in Mayor's Parlour)

647 *c.*1840
Primroses [112]

With chaffinch's nest.
w/c slightly heightened with white. $8\frac{7}{8} \times 13$ (227×330).
Bequest. Mrs W. H. Heelis (Beatrix Potter), 1946.

LEAMINGTON SPA, Art Gallery, Warwickshire

648 1835–40
Apples and Nuts [311/48]

w/c. $9\frac{1}{4} \times 13\frac{1}{2}$ (235×343).
Bequest. G. H. Smythe, 1948.

649 *c.*1845
Grapes and Pomegranate [310/48]

w/c. $8\frac{1}{2} \times 11$ (216×280).
Bequest. G. H. Smythe, 1948.

LEICESTER, Museums and Art Galleries

650 *c.*1845
Birds' Nests [2A.1895]

Two chaffinch nests.
w/c slightly heightened with white. $7\frac{1}{2} \times 11\frac{1}{8}$ (190×283). Signed.
Bt 1895.

LIVERPOOL, Walker Art Gallery

651 1840–45
Primroses, Apple Blossom and Bird's Nest [92]

w/c heightened with white. $9 \times 11\frac{7}{8}$ (227×302). Signed.
Gift. Henry S. Young, 1932.

652 Exh. 1846
Plum, Peach and Grapes [894]

w/c on prepared ground. $8\frac{3}{4} \times 11\frac{5}{8}$ (208×296) oval. Signed.
Gift. Moss Family, 1922.
PROV. G. W. Moss.
EXH. (1) OWCS, 1846, No. 233 as Peaches, Grapes etc. (2) Leeds National Exhibition of Works of Art, 1868, No. 2121. (3) Walker Art Gallery, Liverpool, Grand Loan Exhibition of Pictures, 1886, No. 1043. (4) Manchester, Royal Jubilee Exhibition, 1887, No. 1756.

653 (Plate 111) Exh. 1861
John Ruskin's Dead Chick [895]

w/c heightened with white. $4\frac{1}{4} \times 6\frac{1}{8}$ (108×154). Signed.
Gift. Henry S. Young, 1932.
PROV. John Ruskin. Walter F. Morrice; sold Christie's, 12 May 1922, Lot 22. Harold E. Young.
EXH. (1) OWCS, 1861, No. 258 as 'A Chick. One of a series painted for J. Ruskin, Esq., to be presented to Schools of Art'. (2) Ruskin Hunt Exhibition 1879–80, No. 146 as Dead Chicken. (3) Hunt Exhibition 1981.
BIB. Ruskin, *Works*, Vol. XIV, p. 441; notes on 146, Dead Chicken: 'Done by the old man, in all kindness and care, at my own request, for me to give as types of work to country schools of art. Yet no kindness or care could altogether enable him to work rightly under the direction of another mind; and the project was ultimately given up by me, the chicken, finished as it is, having been one of my chief disappointments.'

MACDONALD-BUCHANAN, Major J., London

654 Dated 1827
Black Grapes in a Basket

w/c. 8×10 (203×254). Signed and dated 1827.
PROV. John Varley.
EXH. (perhaps) OWCS, 1827, No. 234 as Grapes.
COMMENT. Compare White Grapes in a Basket, also signed and dated 1827, in Witt Collection (759, Plate 54).

McLAREN, Mr and Mrs A., London

655 *c.*1850
Pineapple, Grapes, Peaches, Tomato and Basket

w/c on prepared ground heightened with white. $9\frac{3}{4} \times 15$ (250×380). Signed.

MANCHESTER, City Art Gallery

656 *c.*1840
Pot of Asters [1917.17]

w/c heightened with white. $16\frac{1}{2} \times 11\frac{1}{4}$ (418×286). Signed.
Bequest. James Blair, 1917.

657 (Colour Plate 26) 1845–50
Roses [1917.13]

w/c heightened with white. $11\frac{1}{2} \times 8\frac{1}{2}$ (292 × 217). Signed.
Bequest. James Blair, 1917.

658 (Plate 108) *c.*1850
Spring Flowers and Birds' Nests [1917.14]

Chaffinch and hedge sparrow nests and primroses.
w/c. $8\frac{1}{2} \times 13\frac{1}{2}$ (216 × 343). Signed.
Bequest. James Blair, 1917.
PROV. R. Wade; sold Christie's, 9 March 1872. George Gurney; sold Christie's, 17 July 1903, Lot 17.
EXH. (1) Ruskin Hunt Exhibition 1879–80, No. 154, as lent by George Gurney. (2) Hunt Exhibition 1981.

659 (Plate 110) *c.*1850
Bird's Nest and Blossom [1933.31]

Chaffinch nest and blackthorn.
w/c heightened with white. $11\frac{1}{2} \times 13$ (293 × 330) oval. Signed.
Gift. Mrs W. Heelis (Beatrix Potter), 1933.

660 1850–60
Plums [1920.586]

w/c on prepared ground. $6\frac{1}{2} \times 7\frac{1}{2}$ (166 × 191). Signed.
Bequest. Dr Lloyd Roberts, 1920.

661 1850–60
Grapes, Peach and Strawberry [1920.593]

w/c on prepared ground. $5\frac{1}{2} \times 8\frac{1}{4}$ (140 × 210). Signed.
Bequest. Dr Lloyd Roberts, 1920.

662 1850–60
Peach and Purple Grapes [1890.49]

w/c on prepared ground. $4\frac{7}{8} \times 6$ (125 × 152). Signed.
Gift. Roger R. Ross, 1890.

663 *c.*1860
Wild Roses [1920.604]

w/c on prepared ground heightened with white. $6 \times 3\frac{3}{4}$ (153 × 96). Signed.
Bequest. Dr Lloyd Roberts, 1920.
PROV. M. Birket Foster. Dr Lloyd Roberts; bt by him, 1898.
COMMENT. Compare Manchester, City Art Gallery (664), same size, prov. and bequest, and dated 1860.

664 Dated 1860
May Blossom [1920.607]

w/c on prepared ground heightened with white. $6 \times 3\frac{3}{4}$ (153 × 96). Signed and dated '60.
Bequest. Dr Lloyd Roberts, 1920.
PROV. M. Birket Foster. Dr Lloyd Roberts; bt by him, 1898.
COMMENT. Compare Manchester, City Art Gallery (663), same size, prov. and bequest.

MANCHESTER, Whitworth Art Gallery, University of Manchester

665 (Plate 56) *c.*1827
Still Life: Turtle, Crab and Fish [D/19/1900]

Reed pen, brown ink and w/c. $7 \times 13\frac{3}{4}$ (177 × 348). Signed.
Gift. G. W. Agnew, 1900.
COMMENT. Strong resemblance stylistically to A Rabbit and a Lobster (mistitled A Dead Hare and a Cooked Lobster on a Bench), Yale Center (774, Plate 55), which was exh. OWCS, 1827, No. 216. It is therefore dateable *c.*1827. Compare almost identical Turtle as a single work, Witt Collection (760).

666 *c.*1840
Vase of Roses [D.35.1887]

With straw basket behind and strawberries on ground.
w/c heightened with white. $11\frac{1}{4} \times 7\frac{3}{4}$ (287 × 197). Signed.
Bt 1891 for £270 with funds given by the Guarantors of the Royal Jubilee Exhibition, Manchester, 1887.

667 *c.*1850
White Hawthorn and Bird's Nest [D/34/1887]

Chaffinch nest with five eggs.
w/c heightened with white. $9 \times 10\frac{7}{8}$ (229 × 277). Signed.
Gift. Guarantors of the Royal Jubilee Exhibition, Manchester, 1887.

668 (Plate 101) Exh. 1851
Fruit and Tankard [D/24/1887]

Elaborate silver-gilt and carved ivory tankard with wine glass, black grapes and peaches on green tablecloth.
w/c on prepared ground. $14\frac{3}{8} \times 12$ (366 × 306). Signed.
Gift. Guarantors of the Royal Jubilee Exhibition, Manchester, 1887.
EXH. (1) OWCS, 1851, No. 312, as Ivory Cup etc. (2) Hunt Exhibition 1981.

669 1850–60
Bird's Nest and Apple Blossom [D/1/1902]

Chaffinch nest with three eggs.
w/c heightened with white. $8\frac{7}{8} \times 11\frac{3}{4}$ (226 × 298) oval. Signed.
Gift. Sir William Agnew Bart, 1902.

670 1850–60
Bird's Nest and Hawthorn [D/3/1902]

Chaffinch nest with white feather.
w/c heightened with white. $8\frac{1}{8} \times 11\frac{1}{8}$ (210 × 286) oval. Signed.
Gift. Sir William Agnew Bart, 1902.
EXH. Hunt Exhibition 1981.
BIB. John Nicoll, *The Pre-Raphaelites*, 1970, pp. 16 and 122.

MATHER, Mr and Mrs Charles, Philadelphia, Pennsylvania

671 c.1845
Flowers in a Jug

w/c heightened with white. $10\frac{1}{2} \times 7\frac{1}{2}$ (267 × 191). Signed.

671(a) c.1827
Dead Game Hanging, with Lobster and Cabbage on a Barrel

w/c heightened with white. $10\frac{1}{2} \times 7\frac{1}{2}$ (267 × 191). Signed.
COMMENT. Compare A Dead Hare and a Cooked Lobster on a Bench, Yale Center (774, Plate 55) which was exh. OWCS, 1827, No. 216, as Rabbit and Lobster.

NATIONAL MUSEUM OF WALES, Cardiff

672 c.1850
Flowers in a Vase [98.157]

w/c heightened with white. $10\frac{1}{4} \times 7\frac{1}{8}$ (260 × 184). Signed.
Gift. Pyke Thompson Family, 1898.
PROV. James Pyke Thompson; bt by him, 1895.

673 (Plate 106) c.1855
Fruit Piece [21]

Apple, black and white grapes and strawberry.
w/c on prepared ground. $5\frac{1}{4} \times 7\frac{3}{4}$ (133 × 197). Signed.
Gift. Pyke Thompson Family and Turner House Collection, 1921.
PROV. James Pyke Thompson; bt by him, 1895.

NEWCASTLE-UPON-TYNE, Laing Art Gallery

674 c.1820
Study of a Dog's Head [27/192W/C]

Pencil and w/c. $3\frac{3}{4} \times 4\frac{1}{2}$ (95 × 114). Signed.
Bequest. J. R. Holliday, 1927.
COMMENT. Compare Studies of a Dog, Mrs G. M. Tuft Collection (736, Plate 50).

675 (Plate 83) Dated 1831
Bird's Nest with Blossom [37/132W/C]

Chaffinch nest with three eggs.
w/c heightened with white. $7\frac{1}{2} \times 12$ (191 × 305). Signed and dated 1831.
Bequest. G. E. Henderson, 1937.

676 (Plate 109) c.1850
Bird's Nest [40.86]

w/c heightened with white. $6 \times 8\frac{3}{4}$ (152 × 223). Signed.
Gift. Samuel Smith, 1940.

NEWPORT, Museum and Art Gallery, Gwent

677 1840–50
Moss Roses [45–19]

w/c heightened with white. $9\frac{1}{2} \times 14$ (242 × 355). Signed.
Bt 1945.
EXH. Empire Art Loan Exhibitions Society, 1947–48, Australia, New Zealand, London.

678 1840–50
Grapes and Medlars [45–18]

w/c. $6\frac{1}{4} \times 8$ (159 × 203). Signed.
Bt 1945.

NORWICH, Castle Museum

679 *c.*1860
Still Life of Fruit – Three Grapes and an Apple [12.132.198]

w/c on prepared ground. $4\frac{5}{8} \times 6\frac{1}{8}$ (116 × 156). Signed.
Gift. R. W. G. Allars, 1938.
COMMENT. Stylistically similar to May Blossom, Manchester, City Art Gallery, dated 1860 (664).

NOTTINGHAM, Castle Museum

680 *c.*1850
Hedge-Sparrow's Nest and Primroses [20.28]

w/c heightened with white. Diameter $11\frac{3}{4}$ (298) circular. Signed.
Bt 1920.

681 *c.*1850
Plums [20.29]

w/c on prepared ground. Diameter $12\frac{1}{4}$ (312) circular. Signed.
Bt 1920.

OPPÉ, D. L. T., London

682
Sketch of a Dog [1180]

Pencil. $3\frac{1}{2} \times 2\frac{1}{2}$ (89 × 63).
PROV. A. Paul Oppé; bt by him, 1921.
COMMENT. From Hunt Box (120) containing 30 drawings, all in pencil, consisting of 18 landscapes, 11 figures and 1 sketch of a dog.

OWEN, Mrs Felicity, Devonshire

683 1840–50
Onions, Pomegranates and Cobnuts

w/c. $5\frac{7}{8} \times 8\frac{7}{8}$ (149 × 226).

OXFORD, Ashmolean Museum

(None of the following works has an accession number.)

All the following six works formed part of the Ruskin Art Collection, which now belongs to the Ashmolean Museum.
The Ruskin Art Collection was formed by Ruskin in 1872 when he was Slade Professor at Oxford. It was divided into two series, each of three hundred examples, for the purpose of giving practical instruction in drawing. The first series was for members of the University, and the examples referred to as the Educational Series (contracted Edu.). The second series was for general students, defined by Ruskin as 'well-educated young people of from twelve to fifteen, entering first on the study of drawing'. This series was referred to as Rudimentary (contracted R), though in Ruskin's words 'it contains some examples of the highest art'.

684 (Colour Plate 21) *c.*1825
Still Life with Earthenware Pitcher, Coffee Pot and Basket

Pencil and w/c slightly heightened with white. $6\frac{3}{4} \times 9\frac{7}{8}$ (170 × 250). Signed.
PROV. The Ruskin Art Collection (R 59).
EXH. Hunt Exhibition 1981.
BIB. Ruskin's Cat. of the Rudimentary Series. Ruskin, *Works*, Vol. XXI, p. 182, includes the following entry for this work: 'R 59. Study of Earthenware Pitcher . . . W. Hunt. Put beside the Leonardo [Study of Drapery by Leonardo was R 58] partly to exhibit the completion of the older work by contrast with the imperfection of the modern, which in this case has probably been hurried either as a lesson or for sale, – but principally because the painting of the coffee-pot and brown jug is as good as such objects deserve, and insuperably good in the intelligent variety of local and reflected colour. All students are to copy the coffee-pot as soon as they are able. The form of the brown jug is also a useful example of the kind of curves and proportions which are essentially vulgar as compared with outlines like those of the Greek vases in No. 51.'
COMMENT. Compare Still Life: Copper Jug, Blue Vase etc., Yale Center (773, Plate 51) and Still Life with Copper Jug etc., Witt Collection (757).

685 (Plate 52) Dated 1825
Study of Copper Pot and Horn Mug

w/c heightened with white. $4\frac{1}{2} \times 5\frac{1}{4}$ (116 × 133). Signed and dated 1825.
PROV. The Ruskin Art Collection (R 60).
BIB. Ruskin's Cat. of the Rudimentary Series. Ruskin, *Works*, Vol. XXI, p. 183, includes the

following entry: 'R 60. Study of Copper Pot and Horn Mug . . . W. Hunt. Standard example of colour-execution on objects more or less rustic and picturesque yet having great subtlety in some parts, as, for instance, here the edge of the horn mug. There is scarcely any difference between this and the finest Venetian execution, except that the Venetian, being almost invariably of beautiful things, is itself always graceful and beautiful to the utmost degree. For instance, had the rim of the mug been of silver instead of pewter, Hunt's execution would have become a little more delicate, but as in England our powers of enjoyment are more rustic than refined – so that we may any day produce a Bewick, a Gainsborough, or a William Hunt, but have little chance of producing a Filippo Lippi – the manner of execution in this drawing is that for the most part best adapted to the national temper which, if compelled to be refined, nearly always becomes mechanical.'

686 (Plate 53) Dated 1825
Study of a Woodcock

w/c, brown and yellow, slightly heightened with white. $5\frac{1}{8} \times 8\frac{5}{8}$ (129 × 220). Signed and dated 1825.
PROV. The Ruskin Art Collection (R 179).
EXH. OWCS, 1825, No. 333.
BIB. See under 687.

687 *c.*1825
Study of Two Woodcock, in fully developed manner

w/c, brown and yellow, slightly heightened with white. $6 \times 9\frac{1}{8}$ (153 × 231). Signed.
PROV. The Ruskin Art Collection (R 180).
BIB. Ruskin's Cat. of the Rudimentary Series. Ruskin, *Works*, Vol. XXI, p. 254 includes the following entry: 'Now, as soon as you have succeeded in drawing that Egyptian bird rightly, and in putting the blue smoothly on its plumes, within the red lines, you will find yourself able to draw the wing of the real Tringa Candida, R 177, this being represented somewhat meagrely and flatly, therefore conveniently, for you by the Dutch ornithologist. And from the Tringa Candida there will be scarcely any difficulty in passing on to the painting of any patterned bird in flat colours, if you are only patient and accurate enough. And, once able to draw patterns and lay plumes truly, the step to the kind of brush-work used in painting my partridge, R 178, is a very short one indeed.

But to reach near Hunt's birds, R 180, will be a much longer business, and needs a new piece of study to be gone through, namely, of light and shade.'
COMMENT. The dating of this work presents particular difficulty. The term in the title 'in fully developed manner' is not explained in Ruskin's Cat. Stylistically R 180, though similar to R 179, looks freer. The backward sloping signature also differs from the signature of R 179, though this is no real criterion as Hunt often used different forms of signature at about the same period. On balance it seems best to date the work at about the same date as R 179 – namely *c.*1825.

688 *c.*1850
Grapes and a Yellow Snail Shell

w/c on prepared ground slightly heightened with white. $5\frac{3}{8} \times 3\frac{1}{2}$ (137 × 92).
PROV. The Ruskin Art Collection (Edu. 192).
COMMENT. This is only part of the drawing. According to the Ruskin Drawing School Cat. in the Ashmolean, Ruskin cut the drawing in two, placing the other half, of Apples and Grapes, with another series called the Working Series in Cabinet I No. 40. This latter half has now been lost.

689 (Colour Plate 22) *c.*1850
Grapes and a Peach

w/c on prepared ground slightly heightened with white. $4\frac{1}{2} \times 6\frac{1}{2}$ (114 × 165). Signed.
PROV. The Ruskin Art Collection (Edu. 213).

PORT SUNLIGHT, The Lady Lever Art Gallery, Cheshire

690 *c.*1850
Bird's Nest with Basket of Primroses
[WHL 212]

w/c. $12\frac{1}{4} \times 16\frac{1}{2}$ (312 × 520). Signed.
PROV. James Orrock; from whom bt, 1907.

691 *c.*1850
Peaches, Purple Grapes and Filberts
[WHL 292]

w/c on prepared ground. $7\frac{3}{4} \times 11$ (197 × 280). Signed.
PROV. James Orrock; from whom bt, 1905.

692 *c*.1850
Greenfinch's Nest and Primroses [WHL 299]

w/c heightened with white. $7\frac{3}{4} \times 10\frac{3}{4}$ (197 × 274). Signed.
PROV. James Orrock; from whom bt, 1905.

693 *c*.1850
Chaffinch's Nest and Primroses [WHL 338]

w/c heightened with white. $9 \times 11\frac{3}{4}$ (228 × 298). Signed.

PRESTON, Harris Museum and Art Gallery

694 *c*.1840
Pink and White Roses in White China Jug [325]

w/c heightened with white. $11\frac{1}{4} \times 7\frac{1}{2}$ (286 × 190). Signed.
Bequest. Richard Newsham, 1883.

695 1840–50
Flowers in a Glass Vase [1301]

w/c heightened with white. $14 \times 9\frac{3}{4}$ (356 × 247). Signed.
Bequest. Rev. J. P. Haslam, 1924, subject to his wife's life interest; received 1949.

696 1840–50
Group of Mixed Flowers in Brown and Fawn Jug [327]

w/c heightened with white. $12 \times 8\frac{1}{2}$ (305 × 216). Signed.
Bequest. Richard Newsham, 1883.

697 *c*.1850
The Contrast – Red and Green Apples [319]

w/c on prepared ground. $5\frac{1}{2} \times 8$ (140 × 203). Signed.
Bequest. Richard Newsham, 1883.
EXH. Hunt Exhibition 1981.

698 *c*.1850
Black Grapes, Peaches, Apricot and Raspberries [320]

w/c on prepared ground. $7\frac{1}{2} \times 11$ (191 × 280). Signed.
Bequest. Richard Newsham, 1883.
EXH. Hunt Exhibition 1981.

699 *c*.1850
Golden Drop Plums and Black Grapes [326]

w/c on prepared ground. $7 \times 9\frac{3}{4}$ (178 × 247). Signed.
Bequest. Richard Newsham, 1883.
EXH. Hunt Exhibition 1981.

700 *c*.1850
Winter Flowers [328]

w/c heightened with white. $8 \times 9\frac{1}{4}$ (203 × 235). Signed.
Bequest. Richard Newsham, 1883.

701 1850–60
Apples and White Grapes [321]

w/c on prepared ground. $6 \times 9\frac{1}{4}$ (152 × 235). Signed.
Bequest. Richard Newsham, 1883.

702 1850–60
Branch of Apple Blossom and Bird's Nest [323]

w/c heightened with white. $8\frac{1}{2} \times 11\frac{1}{2}$ (216 × 293). Signed.
Bequest. Richard Newsham, 1883.

703 1850–60
Bank of Primroses and Bird's Nest with Three Blue Eggs [329]

w/c. $10\frac{1}{2} \times 8\frac{1}{2}$ (267 × 216). Signed.
Bequest. Richard Newsham, 1883.

704 1850–60
Purple Plums, Apricots and Woodnuts [330]

w/c on prepared ground. $7\frac{1}{4} \times 10\frac{1}{2}$ (184 × 267) oval. Signed.
Bequest. Richard Newsham, 1883.
EXH. Hunt Exhibition 1981.

705 1850–60
Bank of Primroses and Blackthorn [331]

w/c heightened with white. $11 \times 8\frac{1}{4}$ (280 × 210). Signed.
Bequest. Richard Newsham, 1883.

706 1850–60
Bird's Nest with Eggs and Apple Blossom [1299]

w/c heightened with white. $7\frac{1}{2} \times 11$ (190 × 280).

Signed.
Bequest. Rev. J. P. Haslam, 1924, subject to his wife's life interest; received 1949.

707 1850–60
Bird's Nest with Three Blue Eggs and Primroses [1300]

w/c. $7\frac{1}{2} \times 10\frac{3}{4}$ (190 × 273). Signed.
Bequest. Rev. J. P. Haslam, 1924, subject to his wife's life interest; received 1949.

708 *c.*1855
China Jug with Heaths and Small Flowers [318]

w/c heightened with white. $11 \times 7\frac{3}{4}$ (280 × 197). Signed.
Bequest. Richard Newsham, 1883.

709 *c.*1855
Ripe and Unripe Plums [322]

w/c on prepared ground. $5\frac{1}{2} \times 9$ (140 × 228). Signed.
Bequest. Richard Newsham, 1883.

710 *c.*1860
Two Apples and Shell [316]

w/c. $5\frac{1}{4} \times 7\frac{1}{2}$ (134 × 190). Signed.
Bequest. Richard Newsham, 1883.
EXH. Hunt Exhibition 1981.

711 Dated 1861
Black Grapes, Quince and Newtown Pippin [324]

w/c on prepared ground. $6\frac{1}{2} \times 8\frac{3}{4}$ (165 × 222). Signed and dated '61.
Bequest. Richard Newsham, 1883.
EXH. Hunt Exhibition 1981.

PRYOR, J. M., Hertfordshire

712 Dated 1833
Dead Pheasants

w/c heightened with white. $15\frac{3}{4} \times 8$ (390 × 203). Signed and dated 1833.

ROCHDALE, Art Gallery

713 *c.*1840
Pineapple, Melon and Plums [ROCDG.485]

w/c on prepared ground. $10\frac{1}{4} \times 14\frac{1}{2}$ (260 × 369). Signed.
Bt 1921.

ROSSETTI, Mr and Mrs Harold, Suffolk

714 *c.*1850
Grapes, Pear and Cherries

w/c on prepared ground. $5\frac{1}{4} \times 6\frac{3}{4}$ (134 × 173). Signed.

715 *c.*1850
Grapes, Peach, Apple and Fig

w/c on prepared ground. $7\frac{1}{4} \times 10\frac{1}{2}$ (184 × 267). Signed.

716 *c.*1850
Hedge Sparrow's Nest and May Blossom

w/c heightened with white. $11\frac{1}{2} \times 16\frac{3}{8}$ (293 × 417). Signed.

717 *c.*1860
Grapes and Two Peaches

w/c on prepared ground. $8 \times 11\frac{1}{8}$ (203 × 282). Signed.

ROYAL ACADEMY OF ARTS, London

718
Jupp Catalogue [JU.9.5]

This consisted of 16 volumes compiled by E. J. Jupp (1812–77) and presented by him to the Royal Academy. Vol. IX comprised 12 drawings by Hunt all in pencil, and with one exception, Boat and Wagon – $6\frac{1}{8} \times 8\frac{5}{8}$ (155 × 220), all small as follows: Beach and Rocks; Storm; Dark Trees in a Landscape; three of Babies; three of Dogs; two of Cats.
COMMENT. The volume contains a letter by Hunt dated 21 July 1847 from 62 Stanhope Street, Hampstead Road, to a Mr Mackinley: 'The frame is after my own fancy – hope that it would harmonise with the furniture in your drawing room. I trust you will accept of the same with best respects to Mrs Mackinley and my young moth'.

ROYAL SOCIETY OF PAINTERS IN WATER-COLOURS, London

719 *c.*1845
Jug with Rose and Other Flowers and Chaffinch Nest [RWS.PB.34]

w/c heightened with white. $9\frac{1}{8} \times 11\frac{3}{8}$ (232 × 289).
Bequest. R. W. S. Parsons, 1979.

RUSKIN GALLERIES, Bembridge School, Isle of Wight

720 *c.*1860
Cob Nuts [246]

w/c heightened with white. $4 \times 4\frac{3}{4}$ (102 × 122).
Bt 1946.

RUST, David E., Washington DC

721
Black Grapes and Wicker Basket

w/c on prepared ground. $7\frac{1}{4} \times 8\frac{1}{4}$ (184 × 210).
Signed.

SANTA BARBARA, Museum of Art, California

722 *c.*1850
Autumn Still Life

Pineapple, grapes and fig.
w/c on prepared ground heightened with white.
$8\frac{3}{4} \times 12\frac{1}{4}$ (222 × 311). Signed.
Gift. Esther Robles, 1959.
COMMENT. Compare Pineapple and Other Fruit, Victoria and Albert Museum (744).

SHEEPSHANKS, Captain R., Suffolk

723 Dated 1835
Melon, Black and White Grapes in Basket

w/c on prepared ground. $11 \times 18\frac{3}{4}$ (280 × 477).
Signed and dated 1835.
PROV. John Sheepshanks; by descent through members of the Sheepshanks family to present owner.

724 *c.*1845
Tulips in a Glass

w/c heightened with white. $10\frac{1}{2} \times 7\frac{1}{2}$ (266 × 190).
Signed.
PROV. John Sheepshanks; by descent through members of the Sheepshanks family to present owner.

SHEFFIELD, Graves Art Gallery

725 1850–60
Peaches and Grapes [1873]

w/c on prepared ground. $9\frac{1}{8} \times 11\frac{1}{2}$ (233 × 293).
Signed.
Gift. E. Robinson, 1949.

726 (Plate 102) 1850–60
Still Life: Grapes and Pineapple [835]

w/c on prepared ground heightened with white.
$8\frac{1}{8} \times 11$ (205 × 280).
Gift. J. J. Graves, 1946.

727 *c.*1860
Still Life: Plums and Peach [832]

w/c on prepared ground. $8\frac{3}{8} \times 10\frac{5}{8}$ (214 × 270).
Signed.
Gift. J. J. Graves, 1946.

728 (Plate 98) Dated 1860
Blossom [944]

Apple blossom.
w/c heightened with white. $7\frac{3}{4} \times 5\frac{1}{2}$ (197 × 140).
Signed and dated '60'.
Gift. J. J. Graves, 1946.
EXH. Victorian Paintings, Matlock, and Nottingham University, 1967.

SMITH, Hammond. *See* **638**

SOUTHPORT, Atkinson Art Gallery

729 *c.*1860
Fruit [475]

Grapes and one apple.
w/c on prepared ground. $7\frac{1}{4} \times 8$ (184 × 203). False signature.
Bequest. J. H. Bell, 1929.

730 *c.*1860
Fruit [492]

Grapes and apples.
w/c on prepared ground. $9\frac{1}{4} \times 13\frac{1}{2}$ (235 × 343).
False signature.
Bequest. J. H. Bell, 1929.

STOKE-ON-TRENT, City Museum and Art Gallery

731 *c*.1850
Apple Blossom [106/58]

w/c heightened with white. 12 × $8\frac{1}{2}$ (305 × 216).
Signed.
Gift. Miss E. H. H. Morley, 1958.

TATE GALLERY, London

732 1840–50
Primroses and Bird's Nest [3564]

w/c heightened with white. $7\frac{1}{2}$ × 11 (191 × 280).
Signed.
Bequest. Miss Moss, 1920.

733 *c*.1850
Apples [1974]

Two Cox's apples and white snail shell on mossy bank.
w/c heightened with white. $5\frac{1}{4}$ × $7\frac{1}{2}$ (134 × 191).
Signed.
Bequest. C. Fraser, 1905.

734 *c*.1855
Fruit [1972]

Peach, apricots, plums, black and white grapes and red currants.
w/c heightened with white. $8\frac{1}{2}$ × $10\frac{3}{4}$ (216 × 274).
Signed.
Bequest. C. Fraser, 1905.

TORBOCK, H. C., Cumbria

735 1830–35
A Frisian Cow in a Stall

Inscribed verso: 'At Mr Bernal's Sale April, 1853.'
Pencil and w/c. 7 × $12\frac{1}{2}$ (178 × 318).
PROV. R. Bernal.

TUFF, Mrs G. M., London

736 (Plate 50) *c*.1820
Studies of a Dog

Pencil and w/c. $5\frac{7}{8}$ × $8\frac{1}{4}$ (148 × 210). Signed.
COMMENT. Compare Study of a Dog's Head, Newcastle, Laing Art Gallery (674).

737 *c*.1831
Chaffinch Nest, Leaves and Beetle

w/c heightened with white. $6\frac{1}{2}$ × 10 (161 × 254).
COMMENT. Compare Bird's Nest with Blossom, dated 1831. Newcastle, Laing Art Gallery (675, Plate 83).

VICTORIA AND ALBERT MUSEUM, London

738 *c*.1835
Glass Vase and Flowers [1759.1900]

Red and purple anemones and tulip.
w/c heightened with white. $10\frac{3}{8}$ × 7 (263 × 185).
Signed.
Bequest. H. S. Ashbee, 1900.

739 1840–45
Grapes, a Melon and Plums [1032.1873]

w/c on prepared ground heightened with white.
$8\frac{3}{8}$ × $12\frac{3}{8}$ (213 × 314).
Gift. Mrs R. Ellison, 1860.

740 *c*.1845
Hawthorn Blossoms and Bird's Nest [1470.1869]

w/c heightened with white. $6\frac{7}{8}$ × 13 (175 × 330).
Bequest. Rev. C. H. Townshend, 1869.

741 *c*.1845
Wild Roses and Bird's Nest [1502.1869]

w/c. $7\frac{3}{8}$ × $10\frac{7}{8}$ (188 × 276). Signed.
Bequest. Rev. C. H. Townshend, 1869.

742 *c*.1850
Grapes and Peaches [1486.1869]

w/c on prepared ground. $7\frac{1}{4}$ × $10\frac{3}{4}$ (184 × 273).
Signed.
Bequest. Rev. C. H. Townshend, 1869.

743 *c*.1850
Primroses and Birds' Nests [1525.1869]

Hedge-sparrow and chaffinch nests.
w/c. $13\frac{1}{2}$ × $13\frac{7}{8}$ (343 × 353). Signed.
Bequest. Rev. C. H. Townshend, 1869.
EXH. Hunt Exhibition 1981.
BIB. Repr. Pl. 14, Neville Lytton, *Water Colour*, 1911.

744 *c.*1850
Pineapple and Other Fruit [1752.1900]

Black grapes and pear.
w/c on prepared ground heightened with white.
$9\frac{1}{2} \times 12\frac{3}{4}$ (242 × 342). Signed.
Bequest. H. S. Ashbee, 1900.
COMMENT. Compare Autumn Still Life, Santa Barbara Museum of Art (722).

745 *c.*1850
Plums [1922.1900]

w/c on prepared ground. 12 × 15 (305 × 381) oval. Signed.
Bequest. H. S. Ashbee, 1900.

746 1855–60
Plums [FA.525]

In wicker basket.
w/c on prepared ground. $8\frac{1}{4} \times 11\frac{3}{4}$ (210 × 298). Signed.
Gift. Mrs R. Ellison, 1860.
EXH. Hunt Exhibition 1981.
BIB. Repr. in colour facing p. 92, H. M. Cundall, *History of Water Colour Painting*, 1908.

747 1855–60
Jug with Plums [1926.1900]

w/c on prepared ground. $15\frac{5}{8} \times 11\frac{1}{8}$ (391 × 283). Signed.
Bequest. H. S. Ashbee, 1900.
EXH. Hunt Exhibition 1981.

WITT, C. W., Bucks.

748 (Plate 48) *c.*1820
Cock and Hens in a Barn [95]

w/c heightened with white. $12\frac{1}{8} \times 16$ (307 × 408).
COMMENT. Distant view of (probably) Bushey Church from barn door opening.

749 *c.*1831
Hedge-Sparrow Nest, Apple Blossom and Tortoiseshell Butterfly [130]

w/c heightened with white. $7\frac{3}{4} \times 13$ (197 × 330). Signed.
COMMENT. Compare with Bird's Nest with Blossom, dated 1831, Newcastle, Laing Art Gallery (675, Plate 83).

750 *c.*1850
Plums [101]

With gooseberry and cherries.
w/c on prepared ground heightened with white.
$10\frac{7}{8} \times 15$ (276 × 382).

WITT, Mrs E. M., Bucks.

751 *c.*1825
White Daisies and Ears of Wheat [100]

w/c heightened with white. $4\frac{7}{8} \times 8\frac{1}{2}$ (125 × 216).

WITT, Miss Frances, London

752 *c.*1850
May Blossom

w/c heightened with white. $5\frac{3}{4} \times 6\frac{1}{8}$ (147 × 153). Signed.

WITT, Sir John and Lady, London

753 *c.*1825
Two Hedge Sparrow Nests with Eggs [141]

Inscribed: 'From W. Hunt to J. C. Hall and by him to Frederick Hall'.
w/c. $4 \times 5\frac{1}{2}$ (101 × 140). Signed.
Bt 1927.

754 *c.*1825
Hare [1084]

w/c. $9\frac{1}{4} \times 7\frac{1}{2}$ (235 × 190).
Bt 1964.
PROV. Hesketh Hibberd.
EXH. (perhaps) OWCS, 1825, No. 335, A Hare.

755 *c.*1825
Dead Pheasant [1241]

Inscribed (in Hunt's handwriting): 'with W. Hunt's compliments to Mrs. Beckford'.
w/c. $5\frac{3}{4} \times 7\frac{3}{4}$ (146 × 197). Signed.
Bt 1965.

756 *c.*1825
Spray of Hazel Nuts [1438]

w/c. $9 \times 13\frac{5}{8}$ (228 × 347).
Bt 1967.

757 *c.*1825
Still Life with Copper Jug, Blue Vase, Glass Bottle and Wooden Barrel [2111]

w/c slightly heightened with white. $7\frac{1}{8} \times 10\frac{1}{2}$ (182 × 267).
Bt 1980.
COMMENT. Compare same copper jug and blue vase in Yale Center (773, Plate 51) and Still Life with Earthenware Pitcher, Coffee Pot and Basket, Oxford, Ashmolean Museum (684, Colour Plate 21; see entry).

758 *c.*1826
Dead Game: Mallards and Various Birds [2112]

w/c. $5\frac{1}{2} \times 8\frac{5}{8}$ (140 × 218). Signed.
Bt 1980.
EXH. (perhaps) OWCS, 1826, Nos 6 or 250, or 1828, No. 243 (all as Dead Game).
COMMENT. Compare Huntington Library (643).

759 (Plate 54) Dated 1827
White Grapes in a Basket [1943]

w/c heightened with white. $7\frac{7}{8} \times 11\frac{1}{4}$ (198 × 287). Signed and dated 1827.
Bt 1974.
EXH. (perhaps) OWCS, 1828, No. 284, Grapes from Nature, the second Grapes which Hunt exhibited.
COMMENT. Compare Black Grapes in a Basket, also signed and dated 1827, in Collection of Major J. Macdonald-Buchanan (654).

760 *c.*1827
Turtle [381]

Reed pen, brown ink and w/c. $6\frac{1}{2} \times 10\frac{3}{4}$ (166 × 274). Signed.
Bt 1936.
PROV. F. A. White. His catalogue entry stated: 'Bought by my father either at the Old Water-Colour Society or at the artist's sale, I am not sure which'. A Turtle was Lot 297 at the artist's sale, Christie's, 17 May 1864, and fetched 3 guineas.
COMMENT. Compare almost identical turtle in Still Life: Turtle, Crab and Fish, Manchester, Whitworth Art Gallery (665, Plate 56). Both works bear a strong resemblance stylistically to A Rabbit and a Lobster (mistitled A Dead Hare and a Cooked Lobster on a Bench), Yale Center (774, Plate 55), exh. OWCS, 1827, No. 216. They are therefore dateable *c.*1827.

761 *c.*1830
King Charles Spaniel [2123]

Pencil and w/c heightened with white. $5\frac{3}{4} \times 4$ (145 × 100).

762 Dated 1832
Still Life with Gooseberries, Cherries and Other Fruit [1986]

w/c slightly heightened with white. $8\frac{5}{8} \times 12\frac{1}{4}$ (218 × 312). Signed and dated 1832.
Bt 1976.
EXH. (1) OWCS, 1833, No. 302 Fruit. (2) Hunt Exhibition 1981.

763 (Plate 82) *c.*1835
Carrots, Celery, Mushrooms, Cheese and a Jug [2006]

w/c slightly heightened with white. $6\frac{3}{4} \times 12\frac{1}{2}$ (173 × 318). Signed.
Bt 1977.
EXH. Hunt Exhibition 1981.

764 *c.*1838
Black Grapes and Basket [1437]

w/c on prepared ground slightly heightened with white. $7\frac{1}{2} \times 11\frac{1}{4}$ (192 × 282).
Bt 1967.
COMMENT. Compare Grapes, dated 1838, Huntington Library (644).

765 *c.*1840
Basket with Melon, Peaches, Grapes and Plums [1987]

w/c on prepared ground. $9\frac{1}{2} \times 13$ (242 × 330). Signed.
Bt 1976.
COMMENT. Compare Bath, Victoria Art Gallery (583) and Cambridge, Fitzwilliam Museum (615, Colour Plate 23).

766 *c.*1845
Chaffinch Nest and May Blossom [1236]

w/c heightened with white. $9\frac{1}{2} \times 14\frac{3}{4}$ (242 × 374). Signed.
Bt 1965.

767
Four Stags [140(f)]

Pencil. $2 \times 3\frac{1}{8}$ (51 × 80).
Bt 1927.

768
Album [2106]

Containing 22 pen and 27 pencil studies of single figures and groups of figures, 11 pencil studies of cats and dogs, 1 study of a goat (in coloured chalks) and 1 pencil study of a fountain – all small. Bt 1980.

WOLVERHAMPTON, Art Gallery and Museums

769 *c.*1860
Apples and Holly Berries [W.130]

w/c on prepared ground. $6 \times 7\frac{1}{2}$ (152×191). Bequest. Cartwright, 1887.
EXH. Hunt Exhibition 1981.

770 *c.*1860
Still Life [W.110]

Grapes and apple.
w/c on prepared ground. $6\frac{3}{4} \times 9\frac{3}{4}$ (172×248). Bequest. Cartwright, 1887.
EXH. Hunt Exhibition 1981.

WORTHING, Museum and Art Gallery, Sussex

771 *c.*1850
Roses and Bird's Nest [1954/536]

Red and white roses in a jug, and hedge sparrow's nest.
w/c heightened with white. $10\frac{3}{4} \times 15$ (273×380). Signed.
Bt 1954.

YALE CENTER FOR BRITISH ART (Paul Mellon Collection), New Haven, Connecticut

772 *c.*1825
A Terrier Sitting

Looking up to right.
w/c. $4\frac{1}{2} \times 4\frac{13}{16}$ (115×122). Signed.
Bt 1966.
PROV. Sir Bruce Ingram. Mr Paul Mellon.

773 (Plate 51) *c.*1825
Still Life: Copper Jug, Blue Vase, Blue and White Ginger Jar, Pepper Pot and Basket [B.1975.3.1038]

Pencil and w/c. $7\frac{1}{2} \times 10$ (190×255). Signed.
PROV. W. Ward. T. Girtin; bt by him, 1912. Tom Girtin.
EXH. Royal Academy, London, Girtin Collection, 1962, No. 52.
COMMENT. Compare same copper jug and blue vase in Witt Collection (757) and in Still Life with Earthenware Pitcher, Coffee Pot and Basket, Oxford, Ashmolean (684, Colour Plate 21; see entry).

774 (Plate 55) Exh. 1827
A Dead Hare and a Cooked Lobster on a Bench [B.1975.3.867]

Pencil, reed pen, brown ink and w/c. $4\frac{1}{4} \times 8\frac{15}{16}$ (108×227). Signed with brush in red.
PROV. T. Girtin; bt by him, 1919, in New York. Tom Girtin.
EXH. OWCS, 1827, No. 216 as Rabbit & Lobster.
COMMENT. Compare Whitworth Art Gallery, Manchester (665, Plate 56; see entry).

775 (Colour Plate 24) 1845–50
Bird's Nest with Sprays of Apple Blossom [B.1975.3.965]

w/c heightened with white. $10 \times 12\frac{1}{8}$ (255×307).
PROV. T. Girtin; bt by him, 1947. Tom Girtin.

776 *c.*1850
Plums and Mulberries [B.1977.14.5923]

w/c on prepared ground. $7\frac{7}{8} \times 9\frac{9}{16}$ (200×243) oval. Signed.
PROV. Martin Hardie; bt by him, 1961.
COMMENT. Note by Martin Hardie on the mount: 'Banal, debased Victorian-realistic, representational, it may be, but a brilliant piece of virtuosity. One can not only see the bloom on the plum, but see where it has been removed by human touch'.

777 *c.*1850
Apple, Black Grapes and Cobnut [B.1975.3.863]

w/c on prepared ground. $5\frac{1}{16} \times 7\frac{3}{8}$ (129×188).
PROV. T. Girtin; bt by him, 1946. Tom Girtin.
EXH. (1) Sheffield, Graves Art Gallery, Early Watercolours from the Collection of Thomas Girtin, 1953, No. 72. (2) Royal Academy, London, The Girtin Collection, 1962, No. 48.

ZIFF, Professor Jerrold, Champaign, Ill.

778 *c.*1850
Two Birds' Nests

w/c heightened with white. $8\frac{3}{4} \times 11\frac{1}{2}$ (223×292) oval. Signed.

Subject Index to the Catalogue

Numbers are those of the Catalogue. Some works are included under more than one heading

PART III

Works Exhibited during Hunt's Lifetime

1

Works Exhibited at the Society of Painters in Water-Colours, 1814-1864*

1814

41 View of Windsor Castle.
94 View of the Bell Tower Windsor.

1815

25 The Seat of John Barren, Esq., Westerham, Kent.
33 Portrait of a Young Lady.
39 Portrait of a Young Gentleman.
210 A View at Hastings.
229 A View at Hastings.
336 A View from Richmond Hill.

1819

32 A Sketch from the East Cliff, Hastings.

1824

62 Gamekeeper.
286 The Miller.

1825

6 Snipes.
133 Gamekeeper.
139 A Poacher.
194 The Gardener.
276 Rabbit.
309 Pheasant.
333 Woodcock.
335 A Hare.
340 A Sketch from Nature.
341 Gamekeeper.
343 Sketch from Nature.
344 A Sketch from Nature in Cassiobury Park.

1826

6 Dead Game.
69 A Gamekeeper in the service of Charles Dixon, Esq.
108 Tame Rabbit.
161 The Can and Horn.
181 A Brother of the Angle.
250 Dead Game.
255 Young Pigeon.
256 Hen Pheasant.

1827

55 Cauliflower etc.
165 Paper Lanthorn.
216 Rabbit and Lobster.
223 Flowers.
224 Rabbit.
227 Flower Girl.
234 Grapes.
238 Sea Gull.
248 A Sportsman.
267 Brace of Partridges.
268 Lettuce.
276 Study from Nature.
290 Interior of a Cow-House.
304 Widgeon.
331 Teal.
344 Game.

1828

18 Westminster Scholar.
27 Sketch from Nature.
40 Sketch from Nature.
82 Study from Nature.

*As listed by F. G. Stephens, 'William Henry Hunt', *Fraser's Magazine*, November 1865.

94 A Study from Nature, of an Old Man who sailed with Captain Cook on his first voyage.
98 A Sketch from Nature.
142 Sketch from Nature.
190 An Interior.
195 Fruit from Nature.
206 Study from Nature.
243 Dead Game.
284 Grapes from Nature.
307 A Study from Nature.
312 A Butcher's Boy.
326 Fishermen's Children looking out for their Father's Boat.
329 A Paper Lanthorn.
330 Mary, Queen of Scots' Room, Hardwick.
337 Study from Nature.
346 Library of His Grace the Duke of Devonshire at Hardwick.
353 Sketch from Nature
359 A Gamekeeper from Nature.
365 The Gallery at Hardwick.

1829

7 Saturday Evening.
8 A Peasant Boy.
13 A Lady reading by Lamp-light.
18 Cow Boy.
30 The Boudoir.
37 The Sempstress.
45 A Recess in the Drawing Room of John Shorter, Esq., at Hastings, Sussex.
52 An Interior of a Mill, Cashiobury, Herts.
59 A Blacksmith's Shop at Strathfieldsay, Hampshire.
67 A Cow Shed.
74 Fruit.
91 A Young Lady Sleeping.
109 The Romp.
139 Meditation.
145 A Water Carrier.
149 The Weary Traveller.
189 A Cottage at Strathfieldsay.
194 Reading by Lamplight.
214 A Lady Reading by Lamplight.
227 A Study from Nature.
232 An Interior of a Cow-house.
242 A Cottage at Bushy [*sic*], Herts.
261 A young Lady, Reading.
271 Children at a Cottage Door.
275 A Blacksmith's Shop at Strathfieldsay.
280 A Radish Stall.
293 A Water Carrier.
350 Going to School.
351 Fruit.
360 An Interior.
366 A Study.
377 A Fisherman.
378 A Paper Lanthorn.
394 A Fisherman Mending Nets.

1830

25 Scenery in Cassiobury Park.
40 An Interior.
49 Lower Decks of the Ship Enchantress, in His Majesty's Preventive Service, Rye Harbour.
70 Anticipation.
79 Young Fishermen.
112 A Gardener's Store Room.
130 A Sketch.
177 Fishing Boys.
196 Bird's Nest and Lilac.
207 Cottages at Oxford.
215 A Sea Gull.
222 A Clay Pit.
231 A Brick Kiln.
240 A Sketch.
246 Fruit.
259 A Gypsey Boy.
268 Interior of a Potter's Shed.
273 A Fishing Boy.
283 Sea Gull and Teale.
302 A Fishing Boy.
314 Fruit and Bird's Nest.
325 A Brick Kiln.
332 Fruit etc.
339 Grapes and Currants.
343 A Study.
362 A Girl Reading to her Grandfather.
366 A Paper Lanthorn.

1831

48 A Fishing Boy.
68 A Child with Pitcher.

86 Prayer.
'Prayer is the Soul's sincere desire
Unutter'd or express'd
The motion of a hidden fire
That trembles in the breast.'
Montgomery

130 An Old Mariner.
133 A Peasant Boy.
134 An Old Smuggler.
141 Pug, a Sketch.
165 A Smuggler of Hastings.
166 Little Red Riding Hood.
178 A Peasant Girl.
189 The Mendicant.
204 A Peasant Girl.
213 The Idle Boy.
239 Taking Luncheon.
242 A Boy with Prandle Net.
252 Still Life.
253 Study of an Old Man.
260 A Fisherman.
262 Still Life.
322 Grapes etc.
331 Melon and Grapes.
333 Peasant Girls.
351 Pine Apple etc.
366 Candle-light Effect.
376 A Gipsey Girl.
378 Grapes etc.
388 Grapes.
400 A Cottage Girl.
402 Study of an Old Man.
403 Hydrangea.
425 A Fishing Boy.
426 Bird's Nest.

1832

9 Study of a Head.
18 Head of a Smuggler – A Study.
28 An Old Man's Head – A Study.
34 The Gleaner.
41 A Smuggler.
66 The Lesson.
93 Interior of a Fisherman's Cottage.
128 An Interior.
132 A Boy – a Study from Nature.
156 The Lump of Pudding.
165 A Fisherman.
167 An Old Fisherman.
170 Hot Bread and Milk.
219 Hyacinth.
226 Interior of a Barn.
227 Peasant Girl.
237 Pink and White Thorn.
242 Reading.
263 An Interior of a Kitchen.
282 Blackberries.
287 A Bittern.
291 Japanese Roses.
305 Poppies.
314 Interior, with Girl Sleeping.
319 Sundries.
334 Grapes.
339 Bird's Nest.
341 The Page.
355 An Old Man Reading.
360 The Seamstress.
371 A Nap.
376 Blowing Bubbles.
382 An Old Man's Head – a Study.
412 Plums etc.

1833

23 Still Life.
42 A Gypsey Girl.
44 A Study.
93 A Group of Models.
130 Interior of a Barn.
131 An Amateur Musician.
226 Juvenile Students.
236 An Interior.
237 A Sempstress.
287 Ishmael.
290 A Peasant Girl.
295 Candle-light Effect.
297 A Flower Girl.
302 Fruit.
309 Picking a Fowl.
313 Grapes.
326 A Lady in Swiss Costume.
340 The Loiterers.
345 Sweet Peas, etc.
349 A Young Negro.
352 A Mendicant.
354 Lanthorn Light.
363 A Sketch.
364 A French Peasant.
374 Study of a Head.
383 Study of a Head.
386 Boy with a Sea Gull.
388 Study of a Head.

392 Devotion.
398 A Study.

1834

13 Flowers.
20 The Maid and the Magpie.
72 An Interior.
79 A Sketch.
147 An Interior.
160 A Sketch.
253 Winter.
291 A Fisher Boy.
293 A Sketch.
301 Candlelight Effect.
307 A Negro Boy.
313 Peasant Girls.
323 Boy with Pitcher.
341 Fruit.
350 Fruit.
367 The Conclusion.
373 The Father's Boots.
380 A Peasant Girl.
382 The Commencement.

1835

11 A Sailor Boy.
18 A Woodcutter.
62 Wild Rabbit and Pheasant.
70 A Specimen of the Circular, Angular, and Lineal Principles of Composition.
86 Arithmetical Calculation.
102 A Candlelight Effect.
112 Candlelight.
173 Kitchen in the Rye House, North Hodderdon.
182 An Interior at Strathfieldsay.
189 A Boy with a Shrimp Net.
192 A Lady Reading.
200 A Lady Sewing.
207 A Rustic Scene at Strathfieldsay.
234 Birds.
261 Fruit.
307 Apple Blossoms etc.
311 Return from the Masquerade.
315 Peasant Girls.
321 Grapes.
323 A Monk.

1836

12 Interior of an Old Priory.
58 Free and Easy.
60 Boy with Ducks.
88 Scared.
95 Contentment.
98 Massa Sambo.
99 A Sleeping Boy.
132 Girl with a Basket.
154 Devotion.
163 Fruit.
168 The Idle Boy.
192 Boy with a Goat.
203 A Peasant Girl.
210 An Old Pilot.
222 A Farmer's Boy.
229 A Paper Lantern.
236 Flowers.
245 Flowers.
265 Flowers.
268 Flowers and Bird's Nest.
277 Candlelight.
313 A Study of a Head.
322 Boy with Shrimp Basket.
331 Interior of a Fisherman's Cottage.
338 The Cricketer.

1837

1 An Oak Tree near Guildford.
4 A Cow House.
6 Interior of a Kitchen.
9 Girl in a Wood-house.
14 Interior of St Mary's Guilford [*sic*].
62 Jim Crow.
69 A Puffer.
84 Trees near Guilford [*sic*].
90 The Toilet.
105 Piety.
109 The Day of Rest.
126 Interior of a Wood House.
169 Grapes.
180 Tired.
184 Fetching a Light.
187 Begging.
195 Winter.
213 Morning.
221 Pied Pheasants.
237 A Fly Catcher.
251 The Barber.
255 Admiration.
277 A Study.
285 Going to Bed.

347 Mischief.
356 Doing Penance.
364 Hide and Seek.

1838

32 Flowers.
41 Luncheon.
49 A Marine Effect.
74 A Peasant Girl.
82 An Interior.
106 The Young Mother.
108 Dead Wood-Pigeon.
122 A Student.
137 An Incipient Smuggler.
156 A Sleeping Match Girl.
182 Cymon and Iphigenia.
192 The Forlorn Sailor Boy.
200 A German Stove.
218 Flowers.
262 Interior of a Wood House.
268 Plums.
273 A Laughing Boy.
278 A Genius.
280 The Village Chimes.
282 Sleeping Girl.
290 Bubbles.
295 Milk Porridge.
301 A Turnip Bogle.
318 Spelling Book.
327 Boy Reading.
343 Fortune Teller.

1839

6 Bird's Nest, etc.
23 Sailor Boy.
51 A Rustic.
67 Juvenile Palmistry.
84 The Rustic Toilet.
92 Interior of a Stable.
98 Candlelight Effect.
127 All Fours.
129 Fruit.
134 Plums.
141 A Hermit.
178 Miss Jem-ima Crow.
212 Girl Sleeping.
270 A Cricketer.
271 Interior at Guildford.
275 Flowers.
276 A Shrub.
278 The Lesson.
292 Panic-struck.
308 A Sketch.
325 The Narcotic.
332 Grapes.
338 A Kitchen.
342 Gooseberries.

1840

7 A Pozer.
16 A Cottage.
22 A Popular Omen.
24 Peasant Girl.
40 Girl Sleeping.
45 Fruit and Flowers.
48 A Brother of the Angle.
58 Camellia Japonica, etc.
68 Iris, etc.
100 Grandmother's Spectacles.
107 Astonishment.
116 A Brown Study.
124 Mulatto Girl.
133 Lady and Mandolin.
165 A Hard Word.
170 Grapes, etc.
173 A Sand Boy.
177 Master Izaac Walton.
208 Hollyhock, etc.
217 Peasant Boy.
236 A Young Cricketer.
245 A Young Archer.
259 Pitcher of Flowers.
265 Ploughboy.
276 Fruit.
280 Kingfisher, etc.
287 Interior – Girl Sleeping.
298 A Long Song.
299 Melon, etc.
305 Boy Sleeping.
308 Preserved Ginger.
313 Miriam.
316 Bottle of Minnows.
321 An Interior.

1841

4 Remnants of the Tournament.
13 A Cottage Door.
23 Threading Birds' Eggs.
60 The Good Shepherd Boy.
69 A Young Fisherman.

84 Bullace.
88 A Winter Effect.
99 Asking a Blessing.
105 Giving himself (H)Airs.
126 An Irish Pilgrim Boy.
148 Fruit.
153 Boy with Ballads.
162 A Self-taught Genius.
166 A Laboratory.
168 Whittington.
178 A Masquerader.
189 Birds' Nests, etc.
193 A Cockscomb.
198 Fruit and Flowers.
203 Bullfinch, etc.
249 A Mulatto Girl.
267 Models.
273 Flowers.
281 Damascenes, etc.
284 Devotion.

1842

20 A Sleeping Trooper.
38 A Rollicking Trooper.
55 An Unwelcome Visitor.
85 A Peasant Boy.
107 Apples and Plums.
108 A Trooper.
121 Fruit.
127 A Monk.
140 '2nd Carrier. Lend me thy lanthorn, quotha? Marry I'll see thee hanged first.' Shakespeare.
146 Flowers.
151 A Farmer's Boy.
159 A Sleeping Boy.
167 Saying grace.
218 Study of a Boy.
229 An Interior.
252 Making the Pot Boil.
258 Morning Prayers.
265 A Sleeping Infant.
289 Devotion.
296 Grapes and Melon.
299 Interior of West Hill House, the residence of J. H. Mawe, Esq.
304 Fruit.

1843

10 Still Life.
53 An Interior.
59 A Cottage Interior.
70 Grapes etc.
72 Grapes and Melon.
80 Bird's Nest, etc.
82 Sloes, etc.
105 A Poet.
128 A Study of a Head.
185 Apples, etc.
190 An Interior.
200 An Interior in Devonshire-place.
216 Roses.
251 Bird's Nest.
268 Lilac, etc.
273 Damsons, etc.
280 The Shadow on the Wall.
288 Waking up.
297 Fruit.
298 Tulips, etc.
306 A Pet.
307 Apples, Plums, etc.
315 Plums, etc.
331 Flowers.
338 Bird's Nest and Flowers.
346 Peonies.
348 A Beggar Boy.
356 A Flower Girl.
360 A Peasant Girl.
362 Melons, Plums, etc.

1844

26 A Flower Girl.
35 The Gardener's Daughter.
52 An Interior.
61 A Study of Heads.
67 Fruit.
84 A Yew Tree.
92 The Toilet.
96 A Peasant Boy.
97 Apricots and other Fruit.
106 Nutting.
131 Tulips.
140 Rose, Lily, etc.
162 An Old Pollard.
186 A Rose, etc.
190 A Bird's Nest.
192 Lilac, etc.
205 A Jug of Flowers.
210 A Cottage.
220 The Forsaken.

227 Dahlia, etc.
237 An Aspirant and Done up [Boy with a Cigar].
249 A Rose and Fruit.
258 Birds' Nests.
267 Grapes, etc.
272 Roses, Grapes, etc.
281 Fruit, Flowers, etc.
289 A Group of Flowers.
293 Flowers.
297 Study of a Head.
312 A Penitent.
318 Pineapple and other Fruit.

1845

10 Romish Devotion.
38 Interior of part of a Church.
42 Pigeons.
44 A Sea View.
68 Interior, with Still Life.
211 A Stable Boy.
218 A Stable.
226 A Mishap.
234 Writing.
244 Pineapple and Grapes.
246 An Interior, in the Elizabethan Style.
251 Pineapple Grapes Melon, etc.
256 Bird's Nests.
258 A Quince, etc.
266 A Paper Lantern.
270 A Rabbit, etc.
279 Drawing by Candlelight.
301 Hollyhocks, etc.
310 Flowers.
312 Candlelight Studies – a Sketch.
319 Candlelight.

1846

14 Plucking a Fowl.
123 Saturday.
131 Anticipation.
211 Melons Grapes, etc.
227 Sunday.
233 Peaches, Grapes, etc.
239 Yellow Corridor, – T. Mackinlay's, Esq.
244 A Primrose Girl.
252 Going to the Fair.
255 Boy Sleeping.
258 Still Life.
260 Veneration.
262 Pineapple etc.
276 Roses.
287 Drawing.
297 A Peasant Girl.
308 Grapes, Pomegranates, etc.
309 Prayer.
316 An Interior, J. Maw's, Esq., Hastings.

1847

69 A Hermit.
160 A Tramper.
188 A Page.
211 Birds' Nests.
212 Devotional offerings.
232 Christmas Pie.
233 Lamplight.
245 Black and Green Grapes.
267 Drawing by Two Lights.
276 Trampers at Home.
285 Hedge Sparrow's and Robin's Nests.
290 Plums.
298 A Monk.
314 Grapes.
315 Butcher's Boy.

1848

39 Flowers.
69 Interior, at the Residence of T. McKinlay, Esq., Soho Square.
104 Fast Asleep.
112 The Orphan.
137 Flowers – The Crown Imperial, etc.
225 A Branch of May.
242 Cabbage Roses.
245 Candlelight Effect.
246 Grapes and Bird's Nest.
252 Grapes and Peaches.
268 Geranium, etc.
276 An Interior, at the Residence of John Curteis, Esq., Devonshire Place.
278 Roses.
285 May Blossom.
286 Roses.
289 A Soap and Water Bubble.
293 The Sister's Pet.
295 Apples and Plums.
296 The Expectant.
299 An Interior.
305 Wild Roses.
310 Rehearsing the Lesson.

312 Primroses etc.
313 Roses and Bird's Nest.
316 Bird's Nest and Primroses.
327 Boy with Paper Lantern.
337 What shall I play?
340 Hot Bread and Milk.
345 Pineapples, Peaches etc.

1849

78 Wild Flowers.
227 An Old Pollard.
234 A Basket of Plums.
237 Reading.
248 A Pigeon.
259 Plums and Grapes.
265 Primroses etc.
266 Candlelight Effect.
284 Pineapple, etc.
289 Roses.
296 May Blossoms.
306 Lilac.
312 Apricots etc.
315 Grapes and Peaches.
319 Sunday School Girl.
329 Apple Blossom.
333 Group of Flowers etc.
339 Plums.
344 Mary.
347 A Farm House Pantry.
354 Bullace.
355 A Lane Scene.
357 A Basket of Primroses.

1850

165 Hare, Wood-pigeon, etc.
240 A Jug of Roses.
241 The Oratory.
249 A Masquerader.
262 A Female Head.
275 Primroses.
280 Prayer.
281 Grapes, Figs, etc.
284 Bird's Nest, etc.
288 Apple Blossom.
300 Roses.
306 Reading.
319 Blackberries.
321 A Broom Dasher.
333 Grapes Apricots and Plums.
336 Pineapples, Grapes, etc.
343 Plums.
345 Wild Roses.
351 Devotion.
374 The Emigrant's Daughter.
378 Dead Birds.

1851

249 Plums, etc.
259 May.
264 Winter.
283 Pineapple, Grapes, and Quinces.
284 Spring.
398 Primroses and Bird's Nest.
304 Apple Blossom.
308 Jug of Flowers.
312 Ivory Cup, etc.
322 Grapes and Plums.
326 Primroses.

1852

223 Remnants of Garlands.
231 Wood Pigeon, etc.
234 Grapes and Quince.
243 The Village Pet.
248 Snow Drops.
261 Plums.
267 Primroses.
282 Apple Blossoms, etc.
292 Crocuses.

1853

209 A young Rustic.
220 A Masquerader.
250 A Wood Pigeon.
254 Devotion.
259 [No title].
280 Apple Blossom.
283 A Study.

1854

232 Fruit.
233 May Blossom.
263 Primroses.
273 Fruit.
296 [No title].
298 Diffidence.

1855

155 A Usurper.
229 Le Malade Imaginaire.

247 A Mendicant.
256 Fruit.
262 Primroses and Pear Blossom.
270 Confidence.
271 A Group of Fruit.
285 From Nature.

1856

212 Fruit.
219 Fruit.
253 A Bit of Mont Blanc. (Painted for J. Ruskin, Esq.)
256 An Itinerant.
271 Devotion.
274 Fruit.
278 Fruit.
285 Fruit.
292 Fruit.

1857

228 A Poacher.
261 Primroses, etc.
286 Quinces, etc.
294 Apple Blossom, etc.
311 Roses, etc.

1858

232 Fruit.
244 Fungi.
298 Wild Flowers.
306 The Thames, from Richmond Hill.
314 Fruit.
327 A Branch of May.

1859

203 Bird's Nest and Primroses.
225 Sea Shells. Painted for J. Ruskin, Esq.
226 An Oyster Shell and Onion. Painted for J. Ruskin, Esq.
261 A Pineapple and Grapes.
267 Fruit.
271 A Quince and Grapes.

1860

216 Pilchards – Study of Gold. One of a series painted for J. Ruskin, Esq., to be presented to Schools of Art.
220 Devotion.
221 Apple and Grapes.
229 Mushrooms. – Study of Rose Grey. One of a series painted for J. Ruskin, Esq., to be presented to Schools of Art.
237 Grapes, Peach and Plum.
238 A Branch of Apples.
240 A Study of Heads.
241 Grapes, Apricot, and Plum.
242 Old Hughs.
259 Apples, Holly, and Shell.
261 Apples, Grapes, etc.

1861

238 Pine-Apple.
255 Grapes, etc.
258 A Chick. One of a series painted for J. Ruskin, Esq., to be presented to Schools of Art.
259 Study of a Head.

1862

250 An Apple, Pear, and Grapes.
255 A Wood Pigeon.
258 Apples and Grapes.
262 A Branch of May and Bird's Nest.
297 Grapes and Peach.
305 Grapes and Plums.

Winter 1862

8 The Cricketer.
51 Blowing Bubbles.
65 Old London Bridge.
86 The Gipsy's Tent.
115 Rocks at Hastings.
154 Tramps.
212 The Fly-Fisher.
248 The Old Stile.
249 St Martin's Church.
340 Pamber Church, and Fishermen.
396 The Itinerant Show Girl.
404 Devotion.
423 Bedtime.
428 Rose Cottage.
433 An Eel-Trap.
435 Miscellaneous.
443 Miscellaneous.
445 The Old Chair.

1863

225 Apples and Grapes.
231 Grapes and Strawberries.

237 Apples and Grapes.
242 A Study by Lamp-Light.
248 A Wild Convolvolus.
249 Grapes and Apple. One of a series of drawings presented to Edwin W. Field, Esq., by the Members of the Society of Painters in Water Colours.
253 A Sketch.
266 Primroses and Bird's Nest.
271 Roses, etc.
277 A Bird's Nest.
279 Grapes Apples, etc., etc.
288 Quinces, Plums, etc.
296 Grapes and Holly.

Winter 1863

26 Four Landscapes.
95 A Frame containing ten subjects.
105 A Frame containing nine subjects.
177 A Frame containing nine subjects, including the Sketches of Topsey and the Pet of the Village.
197 Six Sketches at Hastings.
203 1. Sketch of a Turtle. 2. Ditto of a Fawn.
290 1. A Study of a Peacock. 2. Mary Queen of Scots' Room, at Hardwicke Hall.
312 A Frame containing six subjects.
333 A Frame containing nine Sketches in colour.
341 A Frame containing five Sketches of Boats.
352 Two Landscapes.
359 1. A View at Hastings. 2. A Landscape.
364 A Frame containing four studies of Clouds and one Landscape.

1864

272 Peaches Grapes, and Strawberries.
275 Flower Girl (painted 1863).
278 Roses, etc.
280 Bird's Nest, Wild Rose, etc.
285 Plums.
298 Grapes, Apples, etc.
311 Peaches and Grapes.
316 1. Branch of May Blossom. 2. Primroses. 3. Wild Rose.
371 Apples Grapes and Strawberries.
332 Apple, Grapes, etc. (The last finished work by the Artist.)
340 Apples, Grapes, etc.

Winter 1864

127 Sketches at Bramley, Hants.
375 Study of a Head. Lent by Carl Haag, Esq.
383 Study from Nature.
395 An Inn Yard, Hemel Hempstead.
397 Dead Bird (Lent by W. Collingwood Smith, Esq.).
399 Sketches in Pencil.
412 Rocks, Hastings.

2

Works Exhibited at the Royal Academy, 1807-25

1807	51	Scene near Hounslow	in oil
	15 Broad Street, Golden Square		in oil
1807	78	View near Reading, Berkshire	in oil
1807	190	Scene near Leatherhead	in oil
1808	525	Selling Fish	in oil
1809	25	A Sketch	in oil
1809	193	A Sketch	in oil
1811	182	A Landscape	in oil
	8 Old Belton Street, Long Acre		in oil

1822	569	Sketch from Nature	
	36 Brownlow Street, Drury Lane		
1822	884	Sketch of the porch of St Martin's Church	in water-colour
1822	918	Sketch of the Winter Dining Room at Cassiobury, the Seat of the Earl of Essex	in water-colour
1823	502	Sketch from Nature	
1823	629	Sketch from Nature	
1824	744	A Study from Nature	
1825	450	Sketch from Nature in Cassiobury Park	
	6 Marchmont Street, Brunswick Square		

3

Coloured Lithographs entitled 'Hunt's Comic Sketches, drawn on stone by Thomas Fairland from original drawings exhibited at the Water-Colour Society', published by Henry Graves, 1844

Published titles	*Present writer's descriptions*
Frontispiece	
Adam's Pale Ale	Boy drinking from jug
The Boy and the Wasp	Boy ducking away from a wasp
Astonishment	Boy spilling a bowl of milk
A Poser	Boy holding a slate
How are you?	Boy holding jug
The Fly Catcher	Boy sitting with fly on open book
An Apple Dumpling	Boy eating dumpling with dog
Too Hot	Boy blowing on spoonful of gruel with bowl on his knees
The Gleaner	Girl with sheaf of corn
The Bubble	Boy blowing coloured bubble from pipe
The First Cigar – The Aspirant	Boy smoking
The First Cigar – Used Up	Boy feeling sick after smoking
Adam's Pale Ale – A Junior Member of the Temperance Society	Coloured version of Frontispiece
The Pet	Boy holding pig
Done Up	Boy in nightshirt with candle – yawning
The Long Sermon	Boy yawning wearing top hat
A Young Shaver, Giving Himself H(Airs)	Boy with shaving brush and lather in bowl
All Fours	Two boys playing cards

Domestic Felicity	Boy seated on barrel talking to a ginger cat
The Attack	Boy eating pie } from the original drawings in the collection of John Sheepshanks Esq.
The Defeat	Boy after eating pie } from the original drawings in the collection of John Sheepshanks Esq.
The Shrimper	Boy with shrimping net
Master James Crow	Coloured boy warming his hands at the stove
Miss Jim-Ima Crow	Coloured girl with coffee pot, bellows and open fire
The Pet Lamb	Boy cuddling lamb
The Corn Question or The Puzzled Politician	Boy reading newspaper
Master Izaak Wâlton, Eyeing a Bite	Boy on bank fishing
The Child's Prayer	Young girl praying at side of bed with patchwork quilt
Saturday	Girl leaning on dressing table
Sunday	Girl in a mauve dress
A Sleeping Nymph	Girl asleep in barn
The Rival Artists – The Mechanical Genius	Boy on barrel with slate and abstract figure
The Rival Artists – The Natural Genius	Same boy with slate and naturalistic figure
Margate	Mother and seasick-looking son on boat

4

Works Exhibited at the Exposition Universelle, Paris Salon, 1855

Palais des Beaux-Arts, 1 May 1855

AQUARELLE SECTION

p. 115 *Hunt (W) 62 Stanhope Street, Hampstead Road*

1031	Une jeune fille avec une corbeille de fleurs	Apartient à W. [John] Sheepshanks
1032	L'Attaque du pâté	– do. –
1033	Le pendant de l'attaque	– do. –
1034	Raisins et prunes	S. Maw
1035	Primevères et nid d'oiseau	– do. –
1036	Roses	– do. –
1037	Lièvre et ramiers	– do. –
1038	Timidité	– do. –
1039	Le chanteur de ballade	L. Pocock
1040	Le joueur de cricket	C. Birch
1041	Une froide matinée	– do. –

Hunt awarded 3rd Class.

G. Cattermole awarded 1st Class with eleven works; L. Haghe 2nd Class with two works. W. Callow, W. Dyce, Copley Fielding, J. F. Lewis and S. Palmer (one work) also exhibited.

In the Oil Painting Section, C. R. Leslie (1st Class), E. Landseer, J. Linnell, J. Holland and W. Holman Hunt also exhibited.

5

Works Exhibited at the Exhibition of Art Treasures of the United Kingdom, Manchester, 1857

Drawings in watercolours		1–965
William Hunt		518–547
		Owner
518	Fruit	S. Ashton
519	Mulatto Girl	Wm. Leaf
520	Interior at Hastings	– do. –
521	Preparing for the Soirée	Albert Hall
522	The Ballad Singer	James Fallows
523	Consulting the League	– do. –
524	The Orphans	John Hick
525	The Laboratory	Jacob Bell
526	The Attack	G. W. Moss
527	The Defeat	– do. –
528	Fruit, Grapes, Apricots, etc.	– do. –
529	Too Hot	C. Langton
530	Girl with Pitcher	– do. –
531	Devotion	J. J. Jenkins
532	Apple Blossom, Cowslips and Bird's Nest	James Platt
533	Grapes, Peaches, etc.	B. Freeland
534	Lady in a Corridor	Thos. Birchell
535	Girl at work in a Chamber	B. Freeland
536	Too Much Play	Hon. Edmund Phipps
537	Too Much Work	Hon. Edmund Phipps
538	Devotion	J. Dillon
539	Boy with a Dog	– do. –
540	A Girl's Head	F. D. P. Astley
541	Grandfather's Boots	Thomas Griffith
542	Plums	Thos. Wrigley
543	Fruit	Thos. Robinson
544	Stable Boy	Charles Oddie
545	An Itinerant	F. W. Topham
546	Poppy etc.	H. A. J. Munro
547	The Artist	William Hunt

Other artists then living	*Numbers exhibited*
G. Cattermole	445–474
D. Cox	480–496
D. Roberts	734–770
C. Stanfield	834–850

Artists dead	*Numbers exhibited*
Turner	296–380
De Wint	261–275
J. Varley	202–212
Girtin	66–82

Appendixes

CATALOGUE

OF

THE WHOLE OF

THE REMAINING WORKS

Of that highly-talented Artist,

WILLIAM HUNT,

DECEASED:

Comprising a large number of SKETCHES in Pencil and Water-Colours; highly interesting finished STUDIES and DRAWINGS;

ALSO,

A FEW PICTURES AND WATER-COLOUR DRAWINGS

BY OTHER ARTISTS;

ENGRAVINGS AND ARTISTIC ACCESSORIES,

Frames, Painting Materials, &c.:

WHICH

Will be Sold by Auction, by

MESSRS. CHRISTIE, MANSON & WOODS,

AT THEIR GREAT ROOMS,

8, KING STREET, ST. JAMES'S SQUARE,

On MONDAY, MAY 16, 1864,

And following Day,

AT ONE O'CLOCK PRECISELY.

---o---

May be viewed Friday and Saturday preceding, and Catalogues had, at Messrs. CHRISTIE, MANSON and WOODS' Offices, 8, *King Street, St. James's Square, S.W.*

APPENDIX I

Christie's Catalogue of Sale of Hunt's works, 16/17 May 1864

First Day's Sale

On Monday, May 16, 1864,

AT ONE O'CLOCK PRECISELY

		[*Number in lot*]
1	Twenty-five slight studies of figures, shipping, &c.	
2	Twenty-five ditto	
3	Twenty-five ditto	
4	Twenty-five ditto	
5	Twenty-five ditto	
6	Twenty-five ditto	
7	Twenty-five ditto	
8	Twenty-five ditto	
9	Twenty-five ditto	
10	Twenty-five ditto	
11	Twenty-five ditto	
12	Twenty-five ditto	
13	Twenty-five ditto	
14	Twenty-five ditto	
15	Twenty-five ditto	
16	Twenty-five ditto	
17	Twenty-five ditto	
18	Twenty-five ditto	
19	Twenty-five ditto	
20	Twenty-five ditto	
21	Twenty-five ditto	
22	Twenty-five ditto	
23	Twenty-five ditto	
24	Twenty-five ditto	
25	Twenty-five ditto	
26	Twenty-six ditto	
27	A girl at Malines; and two other figures	3
28	Sketch for 'Very Hot'; and two others	3
29	A turnip and leaves; and one other	2
30	A lady and child in conversation	
31	A girl sleeping on a sofa	
32	A cottage; and four others	5
33	St Mark's Place, after Guardi	2
34	A church – *in pencil, &c.*	7
35	Sketches of figures	7
36	Cottages, &c. – *in colours – unfinished*	5
37	A farmyard, &c. – *in colours*	4
38	Unfinished sketches	16
39	Foliage, &c.	6
40	An interior, &c. – *Indian ink*	10
41	A lady at an easel, &c. – *in colours*	3
42	Figures – *in colours – unfinished*	8
43	Various – *pen and pencil*	35
44	The grandfather, &c. – *Indian ink*	5
45	Figures – *pen and pencil*	43
46	Ditto	42

		[*Number in lot*]
47	Ditto	29
48	Ditto	22
49	Various	47
50	Hastings Beach, &c. *Signed, York*	30
51	A park scene, &c. *Signed*	17
52	Windsor Castle, &c. *Signed*	20
53	Various	40
54	Figures, &c.	40
55	Ditto	40

SKETCHES IN CHALK

56	The beach at Hastings	
57	A girl's head; and a man's head	2
58	Two studies of heads	
59	Two female heads	
60	Two girls' heads	
61	Two girls' heads	
62	Two ditto	
63	Heads of a boy and girl	
64	A girl in a hat; and a boy's head	
65	Male and female heads	2
66	Male and female heads	2
67	Shipping and buildings – *pencil*	
68	Coal brig, Hastings Beach – *ditto*	
69	A boy and pony	
70	A donkey, in a stable	
71	A view of Hastings	
72	Cottages under the cliffs, Hastings	
73	Broom girls	
74	A female nude figure; and a male figure	

WATER-COLOURS

		[*Number in lot*]
75	Thames barge – a sketch	
76	Cave at Hastings	
77	Hemel Hempstead – *unfinished*	
78	At Hastings, view from the heights	
79	Cottage and barn at Bramley, Hants	2
80	Sketches at Hastings; and figure of a boy	6
81	A tank at Hastings	
82	Study of a pollard	
83	'Going to market,' a girl in a landscape, with a basket of poultry	
84	Dead calm off Hastings	
85	Landscape, with water and a group of trees – two in one frame	
86	An elderberry tree in blossom	
87	A lake scene, with a castle	
88	Park scenes	2
89	A group of trees, near a building	
90	A man reading, after Etty	
91	Two studies of buildings, after Bridges	
92	Electioneering at Hastings	
93	A landscape and figures, after Molyn	
94	Head of a Turk, in a red cap	
95	A boat, and a horse and cart	2
96	A landscape, with figures, after S. Rosa	
97	Two landscapes	
98	Two studies of skies; and two others – in two frames	
99	Boats at Hastings	2
100	A lady at a window; and one other – sketch	
101	Two, after Van Dyck and Maes	
102	Boats at Hastings	
103	Buildings and figures, after Prout	
104	Study of a dog; and a winter scene	
105	Two small landscapes	
106	A pump	
107	Two sketches of fruit	
108	Three sketches at Hastings	
109	Three men's heads	
110	A cottage and elderberry tree	
111	A Scotchman; and one other head	
112	Beach at Hastings	2
113	A cow at a stall	
114	A dead bird; and two other sketches	
115	A landscape – evening; and one other	
116	A group of trees; and study of a sky	
117	A dead bird	
118	A man's portrait	
119	A brewhouse, Bramley [Hants] – candlelight; and a coast scene – moonlight	
120	Pork jars	

[*Number in lot*]

121 Three landscapes; and a study of a sky – in two frames
122 A fisherman, with a basket
123 Two sketches at Hastings; and two landscapes
124 A boy's head; and a girl's head
125 A Scotchman smoking a pipe
126 A landscape, with a figure, after Mulready
127 A barn at Bramley; and three studies of skies – in two frames
128 A landscape; a sky; and two sketches at Hastings – in two frames
129 On the Thames; and at Hastings 2
130 A church porch
131 Four sketches at Hastings – in two frames
132 A larder
133 A pig; and two other studies
134 Figures of a man and a boy
135 A fisherman; and one other figure
136 Three sketches of figures
137 Houses at Hastings; and one other
138 A boy asleep
139 Study of a terrier
140 Carting hay – morning and evening
141 Hastings Beach 2
142 Rocks at Hastings; and boats – winter scene 2
143 Two sketches at Hastings; and two landscapes – in two frames
144 The school-ship off Greenwich
145 A peasant leaning on a grindstone
146 A study of a bank
147 The beach at Hastings
148 A stone-wall at Oxford
149 Haystack and cart-hovel 2
150 Hastings Castle
151 A fishing-boat, Hastings
152 Stone-wharf opposite Somerset House
153 The fish-market, Hastings
154 Boats and figures, Hastings
155 Open sea, Hastings
156 'An Interesting Youth'
157 Hearing School Lesson

[*Number in lot*]

158 Fishing-Boats, Hastings
159 Portico of St Martin's-in-the-Fields, with Figures
160 Butler's Cave, Hastings
161 Hastings, looking seaward over Houses and Beach
162 Bushy [*sic*] Churchyard, Herts, with the Tombs of Hearne, Edridge, and Alexander Munro [*sic*]
163 A Bricklayer's Labourer with his Hod
164 View of a Mansion, with a Lake and Trees
165 Interior of a Scullery
166 A Gentleman in a Court Dress
167 A Star-fish and Fungi 2
168 A Girl Reading near a Window
169 A Boy and Girl with a Dog
170 A Girl's Head
171 A Man Reading
172 A Boy Fishing
173 A Back-yard, Belton Street
174 A Gateway and House at Chiswick
175 A Figure of a Monk
176 Aldenham Churchyard, with Figures
177 Cottages and Boats at Oxford
178 The Kitchen at Cashiobury
179 Old Houses at Hemel Hempstead
180 Cottage in Cashiobury Park
181 Fishermen Mending Nets
182 An Inn Yard, Hemel Hempstead
183 Buildings, Hemel Hempstead
184 A View in the Isle of Wight, after Linnell
185 A Male Academy Figure
186 'THE MISHAP.' *Very fine*
187 THE DWARF AT HASTINGS
188 'THE CONNOISSEUR'
189 BLACK AND WHITE GRAPES AND A BASKET
190 A GIRL IN FANCY COSTUME SLEEPING – lamplight
191 THE BEDROOM AT HARDWICK, WITH A FEMALE

192 THE MUSIC LESSON – candlelight
193 IN THE GARDEN AT CHISWICK
194 THE DINING-ROOM AT CASHIOBURY
195 THE ANTEROOM, CASHIOBURY
196 THE HOUSEKEEPER'S ROOM, CASHIOBURY
197 A GIRL SEATED READING A LETTER
198 A GIRL AT HER DEVOTIONS
199 A COTTAGE AT CASHIOBURY

End of First Day's Sale.

Second Day's Sale

On Tuesday, May 17, 1864,

AT ONE O'CLOCK PRECISELY

200 Twenty-five slight studies of figures, shipping, &c.
201 Twenty-five ditto
202 Twenty-five ditto
203 Twenty-five ditto
204 Twenty-five ditto
205 Twenty-five ditto
206 Twenty-five ditto
207 Twenty-five ditto
208 Twenty-five ditto
209 Twenty-five ditto
210 Twenty-five ditto
211 Twenty-five ditto
212 Twenty-five ditto
213 Twenty-five ditto
214 Twenty-five ditto
215 Twenty-five ditto
216 Twenty-five ditto
217 Twenty-five ditto
218 Twenty-five ditto
219 Twenty-five ditto
220 Twenty-five ditto
221 Twenty-five ditto
222 Twenty-five ditto
223 Twenty-five ditto
224 Twenty slight sketches – *in water-colours, &c.*
225 Twenty ditto
226 Twenty ditto
227 Seventeen ditto
228 Six slight sketches – unframed
229 Five portraits of members of the Old Society of Water-Colours: Mr Fielding, Mr Nash, Mr Scott, and two others
230 Rocks at Hastings
231 The cofferdam, New London Bridge; and a sketch at Hastings
232 The ruined castle, Hastings; and one other sketch
233 The Look-out, Hastings
234 A river scene, with figures fishing, after Callcott
235 The eel-pot
236 A cottage
237 Three views at Hastings; and one at Richmond
238 Cottage on the cliffs, Hastings
239 Farm-buildings at Aldenham
240 On the White Rocks, Hastings

[*Number in lot*]

241 A fishing-boat, Hastings
242 The Old King's Mews, Trafalgar Square – *a copy*
243 Rocks at Hastings – moonlight
244 Cliffs at Hastings – winter
245 Two sketches at Hastings; and two others
246 A bank at Hastings
247 Rocks at Hastings
248 Buildings and boats
249 Interior of a barber's shop
250 Hay-barge on the Thames; and a study of cliffs
251 An ivory tankard
252 Cliffs at Hastings – upright; and two others in two frames
253 An arm-chair; and one other study
254 The Lady Chapel, at Basingstoke
255 A dog asleep; and a study
256 A sketch of fir-trees – upright
257 An elderberry-tree and ladder
258 A gamekeeper on horseback
259 Sketches of trees at Bramley 2
260 Study of a buoy at Hastings
261 A child's head – oval; and a charity boy 2
262 The shepherd, after Cristall
263 A landscape and three studies of sky, in two frames
264 The Look-out at Hastings
265 A bank and gate
266 A lady at her toilette – *unfinished*
267 Boats and figures on Hastings Beach
268 Study of sea and sky at Hastings
269 The gamekeeper
270 A barge on the Thames – *water colours*; Blowing bubbles; and one other – *in chalks*
271 THE COVER-SIDE
272 A MAN AND DONKEY
273 BUILDING OF NEW LONDON BRIDGE
274 THE SWISS COTTAGE, CASHIOBURY
275 MOUNTEBANKS IN ST MARK'S PLACE. *A capital copy after Canaletti*
276 'VERY HOT'
277 CHICKSANDS PRIORY
278 HEAD OF A GIRL IN A HAT AND FEATHERS
279 A DEAD FAWN
280 THE MAGDALENE, AFTER ETTY
281 A COTTAGE, CASHIOBURY PARK
282 A BARN AT BUSHEY
283 AT HASTINGS
284 LAMBETH PALACE
285 THE BELFRY, MAPLEDURHAM CHURCH
286 FISHING-BOAT WITH SAIL, HASTINGS
287 ROCKS AT HASTINGS
288 A COTTAGE AT BRAMLEY
289 PLUMS AND GRAPES – landscape background
290 A NEGRO'S HEAD – *oval*
291 THE ISLE OF WIGHT, AFTER J. LINNELL
292 A COTTAGE IN CASHIOBURY PARK
293 A GAMEKEEPER
294 CASHIOBURY
295 A STUDY OF PARK PALINGS
296 A COTTAGE AT BRAMLEY
297 A TURTLE
298 HASTINGS BEACH, WITH FIGURES
299 BUILDINGS AND FIGURES AT VENICE. *A capital copy from Canaletti*
300 A COAL BRIG, HASTINGS BEACH
301 EEL FISHERS
302 PAMBER CHURCH
303 AN OLD FONT
304 THE MILLER AT CASHIOBURY
305 OLD LONDON BRIDGE – BOATS, &C., IN THE FOREGROUND
306 A COLONNADE IN VENICE. *Copy of a picture by Guardi*
307 'A VALIANT KNIGHT:' a boy standing near a group of armour
308 A STUDY OF A POLLARD, near a pond
309 THE JUVENILE ARTIST
310 OLD LONDON BRIDGE, boats and a sailing barge in the foreground
311 FARMYARD, WITH FIGURES, BRAMLEY, HANTS
312 SOUTHWARK AND BLACKFRIARS BRIDGES, FROM THE THAMES

DRAWINGS IN WATER-COLOURS

			[*Number in lot*]
313	J. Man	A coast scene, &c.	6
314	Rowlandson	The extravagant wife, &c.	13
315	Turner, R.A.	A lake scene, &c.	2
316	Wilkie	Sketches – *in pen*	3
317	Academy figures – *in oils*		3
318	Sketches by Stothard, Wheatley, &c.		5
319	Stothard	An illustration to a novel	
320	C. Bega	Two female figures – *in red chalk*	
321	G. Chambers	A canal scene, Amsterdam	
322	G. Chambers	Gravesend	
323	De Wint	A lake scene	
324	J. Varley	Hampstead Heath, with cattle	
325	G. Chambers	Dutch boats in a stiff breeze	
326	De Wint	A landscape, with a church and pond	
327	Langendyck	Scene in the French revolution, 1794	
328	Wright	Two illustrations to Shakespeare	
329	Schweikardt	Two studies of cattle – *in chalks and Indian ink*	
330	Bega	A woman sleeping; and three others	
331	Canaletti	A view in Venice, with figures – *in Indian ink*	
332	Prout	A snow-scene, &c.	5
333	C. Stanfield, R.A.	Figures on a road under a rocky height	
334	Vickers	London from the Thames – *pencil*	
335	Martin	A woody landscape – *Indian ink*	
336	Unknown	A man with a beard – *on ivory, in gilt frame*	
337	R. P. Burcham	Two studies of fungi	
338	Unknown	A group of fruit	
339	Unknown	A landscape, with figures and sheep – *unfinished*	
340	J. Varley	Two small landscapes	
341	Unknown	View of Greenwich; and a river scene, with boats	
342	Unknown	A sprig of holly and a shell	2
343	Unknown	A beach scene, &c.	2
344	Unknown	A woody river scene	
345	J. Varley	Two landscapes; and a river scene – *in two frames*	
346	Edwards	Cashiobury House – *in pencil*	
347	J. Varley	Windsor Castle	
348	G. White, 1732	Portrait of a lady – *in crayons*	

PICTURES

349	W. Davis, Worcester	A girl's head
350	Brauer	A man's head; and one other
351	Chavet	The toilette
352	T. Stothard, R.A.	A combat

ARTISTIC ACCESSORIES, &c.

353 A HANDSOME IVORY TANKARD, carved with Bacchanalian figures in high relief; lined and mounted with silver gilt, foot, cover and handle, chased with a female Caryatid

354 A large tortoiseshell comb
355 A grès-de-Flandres jug, with chequers and initials, G. R.
356 Another, with flowers and G. R.
357 Another, with larger ornaments and G. R.
358 A smaller ditto, with masks in relief
359 Another, with spots; and one with rings
360 Another, with tulip ornaments and metal lid
361 A pair of smaller ditto, with masks
362 A two-handled jar, with initials W. H.
363 Four brown jugs
364 A brown ginger-jar; two metal pots; and a mill
365 A quantity of mounts and drawing-boards
366 A tin box, with glass; two plaster-casts; and two easels
367 Eight gilt frames
368 Eight ditto
369 Eight ditto
370 Eight ditto
371 Twenty ditto
372 Twenty ditto
373 Thirty sketch-books, with a few sketches and memoranda
374 A camera-lucida; a box of instruments; and three boxes, with beads, &c.
375 Four mahogany boxes, with paints; a pallet; a box of brushes; a box with various paints; and one with bottles
376 A tin colour-box; a ditto pallet; and a box with three pallets; a grinder and mullet; and various paints and brushes
377 A deal box; and various costumes
378 Ten frames, with lithographs, &c.
379 Twenty-nine lithographs
380 One hundred ditto – various
381 Eight etchings

ENGRAVINGS, &c.

		[*Number in lot*]
382	Portrait of David Cox, by Bellin, &c.	11
383	Etchings, after Ostade, Suyderhoef, &c.	23
384	The Castle of Indolence, after Rimer, &c.	
385	After Watteau, &c.	6
386	After old masters	18
387	After Hunt, by Turner and Ryall – *India proofs, &c.*	12
388	Lithographs, after Hunt	31
389	Girtin's Views in Paris, &c.	64
390	Grapes, after Hunt – chromolithograph	
391	The Approving Critic, &c., ditto	4
392	Landscapes, &c. – chromolithographs	
393	Portrait of Mr Hunt, and other Photographs, after his works	31
394	Photographs – various	71
395	Fenton's Photographs of the Crimea	21

APPENDIX II

Ruskin's Notes on Hunt for his Exhibition of Prout and Hunt at the Fine Art Society, 1879-80, with a List of Hunt's Works Exhibited*

Preface

1. It has been only in compliance with the often and earnestly-urged request of my friend Mr Marcus Huish, that I have thrown the following notes together, on the works of two artists belonging to a time with which nearly all associations are now ended in the mind of general society; and of which my own memories, it seemed to me, could give little pleasure (even if I succeeded in rendering them intelligible) to a public indulged with far more curious arts, and eager for otherwise poignant interests, than those which seemed admirable, though not pretending to greatness, and were felt to be delightful, though not provoking enthusiasm, in the quiet and little diverted lives of the English middle classes 'sixty years since'.

2. It is especially to be remembered that drawings of this simple character were made for these same middle classes, exclusively; and even for the second order of the middle classes, more accurately expressed by the term *bourgeoisie*. The great people always bought Canaletto, not Prout, and Van Huysum, not Hunt. There was indeed no quality in the bright little water-colours which could look other than pert in ghostly corridors, and petty in halls of state; but they gave an unquestionable tone of liberal-mindedness to a suburban villa, and were the cheerfullest possible decorations for a moderate-sized breakfast-parlour opening on a nicely-mown lawn. Their liveliness even rose, on occasion, to the charity of beautifying the narrow chambers of those whom business or fixed habit still retained in the obscurity of London itself; and I remember with peculiar respect the pride of a benevolent physician,[1] who never would exchange his neighbourhood to the poor of St Giles's for the lucrative lustre of a West End square, in wreathing his tiny little front drawing-room with Hunt's loveliest apple-blossom, and taking the patients for whom he had prescribed fresh air the next instant on a little visit to the country.

3. Nor was this adaptation to the tastes and circumstances of the London citizen a constrained or obsequious compliance on the part of the kindly artists. They were themselves, in mind, as in habits of life, completely a part of the characteristic metropolitan population whom an occasional visit to the Continent always thrilled with surprise on finding themselves again among persons who familiarly spoke French; and whose summer holidays, though more customary, amused them nevertheless with the adventure, and beguiled them with the pastoral charm, of an uninterrupted picnic. Mr Prout lived at

*Ruskin, *Works*, Vol. XIV, pp. 373–84 and 440–54.

Brixton, just at the rural extremity of Cold Harbour Lane, where the spire of Brixton Church, the principal architectural ornament of the neighbourhood, could not but greatly exalt, by comparison, the impressions received from that of Strasburg Cathedral, or the Hôtel de Ville of Bruxelles; and Mr Hunt, though often in the spring and summer luxuriating in country lodgings, was only properly at home in the Hampstead Road, and never painted a cluster of nuts without some expression, visible enough by the manner of their presentation, of the pleasure it was to him to see them in the shell, instead of in a bag at the greengrocer's.

4. The lightly rippled level of this civic life lay, as will be easily imagined, far beneath the distractions, while it maintained itself meekly, yet severely, independent of the advantages, held out by the social system of what is most reverently called 'Town.' Neither the disposition, the health, nor the means of either artist admitted of their spending their evenings, in general, elsewhere than by their own firesides; nor could a spring levée of English peeresses and foreign ambassadors be invited by the modest painter whose only studio was his little back-parlour, commanding a partial view of the scullery steps and the water-butt. The fluctuations of moral and aesthetic sentiment in the public mind were of small moment to the humble colourist, who depended only on the consistency of its views on the subject of early strawberries; and the thrilling subjects presented by the events or politics of the day were equally indifferent to the designer who invited interest to nothing later than the architecture of the fifteenth century. Even the treasures of scientific instruction, and marvels of physical discovery, were without material influence on the tranquillity of the two native painters' uneducated skill. Prout drew every lovely street in Europe, without troubling himself to learn a single rule of perspective; while Hunt painted mossy banks for five-and-twenty years, without ever caring to know a sphagnum from a polypody, and embossed or embowered his birds' eggs to a perfection, which Greek connoisseurs would have assured us the mother had unsuspectingly sat on, without enlarging his range of ornithological experience beyond the rarities of tomtit and hedge-sparrow.

5. This uncomplaining resignation of patronage, and unblushing blindness to instruction, were allied, in both painters, with a steady consistency in technical practice, which, from the first, and to the last, precluded both from all hope of promotion to the honours, as it withheld them from the peril of entanglement in the rivalries, connected with the system of exhibition in the Royal Academy. Mr Prout's method of work was entirely founded on the quite elementary qualities of white paper and black Cumberland lead; and expressly terminated within the narrow range of prismatic effects producible by a brown or blue outline, with a wash of ochre or cobalt. Mr Hunt's early drawings depended for their peculiar charm on the most open and simple management of transparent colour; and his later ones, for their highest attainments, on the flexibility of a pigment which yielded to the slightest touch and softest motion of a hand always more sensitive than firm. The skill which unceasing practice, within limits thus modestly unrelaxed, and with facilities of instrument thus openly confessed, enabled each draughtsman in his special path to attain, was exerted with a vividness of instinct somewhat resembling that of animals, only in the slightest degree conscious of praiseworthiness, but animated by a healthy complacency, as little anxious for external sympathy as the self-content of a bee in the translucent symmetry of its cell, or of a chaffinch in the silver tracery of her nest – and uniting, through the course of their uneventful and active lives, the frankness of the bird with the industry of the insect.

6. In all these points of view, the drawings to which I venture, not without hesitation, to call the passing attention of the public, can claim regard only as examples of genius both narrowed and depressed; yet healthy enough to become more elastic under depression, and scintillant enough to be made more vivid by contraction. But there are other respects in which these seemingly unimportant works challenge graver study; and illustrate phases of our own national mind – I might perhaps say, even of national civilization – which coincide with many curious changes in social feelings, and may lead to results not easily calculable in social happiness.

7. If the reader has any familiarity with the galleries of painting in the great cities of Europe, he cannot but retain a clear, though somewhat monotonously calm, impression of the character of those polished flower pieces, or still-life pieces, which occupy subordinate corners in their smaller rooms; and invite to moments of repose, or frivolity, the attention and imagination which have been wearied in admiring the attitudes of heroism, and sympathizing with the sentiments of piety. Recalling to his memory the brightest examples of these which his experience can supply, he will find that all the older ones agree – if flower pieces – in a certain courtliness and formality of arrangement, implying that the highest honours which flowers can attain are in being wreathed into grace of garlands, or assembled in variegation of bouquets, for the decoration of beauty or flattery of noblesse. If fruit or still-life pieces, they agree no less distinctly in directness of reference to the supreme hour when the destiny of dignified fruit is to be accomplished in a royal dessert; and the furred and feathered life of hill and forest may bear witness to the Wisdom of Providence by its extinction for the kitchen dresser.

8. Irrespectively of these ornamental virtues, and culinary utilities, the painter never seems to perceive any conditions of beauty in the things themselves, which would make them worth regard for their own sake; nor, even in these appointed functions, are they ever supposed to be worth painting, unless the pleasures they procure be distinguished as those of the most exalted society. No artists of the old school would ever think of constructing a subject out of the herbs of a cottage garden, or viands of a rural feast. Whatever interest was then taken in the life of the lower orders involved always some reference to their rudenesses or vices; and rarely exhibits itself in any other expression than that of contempt for their employments, and reproach to their recreation.

9. In all such particulars the feelings shown in the works of Hunt, and of the school with which he was associated, directly reverse those of the preceding age. So far from being garlanded into any polite symmetry, his primroses fresh from the bank, and hawthorns white from the hedge, confess at once their artless origin in the village lane – have evidently been gathered only at the choice, and thrown down at the caprice, of the farmer's children; and cheerfully disclaim all hope of ever contributing to the splendours or felicities of the great. The bloom with which he bedews the grape, the frosted gold with which he frets the pine, are spent chiefly to show what a visible grace there is in the fruits of the earth, which we may sometimes feel that it is rude to touch and swinish to taste; and the tendernesses of hand and thought that soothe the rose-grey breast of the fallen dove, and weave the couch of moss for its quiet wings, propose no congratulation to the spectator on the future flavour of the bird in a pie.

10. It is a matter of extreme difficulty, but of no less interest, to distinguish, in this order of painting, what part of it has its origin in a plebeian – not to say vulgar – simplicity, which education would have invested with a severer charm; and what part is grounded on a real

sense of natural beauty, more pure and tender than could be discerned amid the luxury of courts, or stooped to by the pride of nobles.

11. For an especial instance, the drawing of the interior, No 174, may be taken as a final example of the confidence which the painter felt in his power of giving some kind of interest to the most homely objects, and rendering the transitions of ordinary light and shade impressive, though he had nothing more sacred to illuminate than a lettuce, and nothing more terrible to hide than a reaping-hook. The dim light from the flint-glass window, and the general disposition and scale of the objects it falls on, remind me sometimes, however unreasonably, of the little oratory into which the deeply-worn steps ascend from the Beauchamp Chapel at Warwick. But I know perfectly well, and partly acknowledge the rightness of his judgment, though I cannot analyze it, that Hunt would no more have painted that knightly interior instead of this, with helmets lying about instead of saucepans, and glowing heraldries staying the light instead of that sea-green lattice, than he would have gone for a walk round his farm in a court dress.

12. 'Plebeian – not to say vulgar' – choice; but I fear that even 'vulgar', with full emphasis, must be said sometimes in the end. Not that a pipkin of cream in Devonshire is to be thought of less reverently than a vase of oil or canister of bread in Attica; but that the English dairymaid in her way can hold her own with the Attic canephora, and the peasant children of all countries where leaves are green and waters clear, possess a grace of their own no less divine than that of branch and wave. And it is to be sorrowfully confessed that the good old peach and apple painter was curiously insensible to this brighter human beauty; and though he could scarcely pass a cottage door around his Berkshire [Hampshire] home without seeing groups of which Correggio would have made Cupids, and Luini cherubs, turned away from them all, to watch the rough ploughboy at his dinner, or enliven a study of his parlour-maid at her glass (158) with the elegance of a red and green pincushion.

13. And yet, for all this, the subtle sense of beauty above referred to was always in his mind, and may be proved and partly illustrated, by notice of two very minute, but very constant, differences between his groups of still life and those of the Dutch painters. In every flower piece of pretension, by the masters of that old school, two accessory points of decoration are never absent. The first of these is the dew-drop, or rain-drop – it may be two or three drops, of either size, on one of the smoothest petals of the central flower. This is always, and quite openly, done to show how well the painter can do it – not in the least with any enjoyment of wetness in the flower. The Dutchman never got a wet flower to paint from. He had his exquisite and exemplary poppy or tulip brought in from the market as he had occasion, and put on its dew-drops for it as a lady's dressing-maid puts on her diamonds, merely for state. But Hunt saw the flowers in his little garden really bright in the baptismal dawn, or drenched with the rain of noontide, and knew that no mortal could paint any real likeness of that heaven-shed light; – and never once attempted it: you will find nothing in any of his pictures merely put on that you may try to wipe it off.

14. But there was a further *tour de force* demanded of the Dutch workman, without which all his happiest preceding achievements would have been unacknowledged. Not only a dew-drop, but, in some depth of bell, or cranny of leaf, a bee, or a fly, was needful for the complete satisfaction of the connoisseur. In the articulation of the fly's legs, or the neurography of the bee's wings, the Genius of painting was supposed to signify her accepted disciples; and their work went forth to the European world, thenceforward, without question, as worthy of its age and country. But, without recognizing in myself, or desiring

to encourage in my scholars, any unreasonable dislike or dread of the lower orders of living creatures, I trust that the reader will feel with me that none of Mr Hunt's peaches or plums would be made daintier by the detection on them of even the most cunningly latent wasp, or cautiously rampant caterpillar; and will accept, without so much opposition as it met with forty years ago, my then first promulgated, but steadily since repeated assertion, that the 'modern painter' had in these matters less vanity than the ancient one, and better taste.

15. Another interesting evidence of Hunt's feeling for beauty is to be found in the unequal distribution of his pains to different parts of his subject. This is, indeed, one of the peculiar characteristics of our modern manner, and in the abstract not a laudable one. All the old masters, without exception, complete their pictures from corner to corner with a strictly driven level of deliberation; and whether it be a fold of drapery, a blade of grass, or a wreath of cloud, on which they are subordinately occupied, the pencil moves at the same tranquil pace, and the qualities of the object are rendered with the same fixed attention. In this habitual virtue, the dull and the brilliant, the weak and the mighty, concur without exception; holding it for their first point of honour to be thorough craftsmen, and to carry on the solicitude of their skill throughout the piece, as an armourer would hammer a corslet, or a housewife knit a stocking, leaving no edge untempered, and no thread unfastened. Modern petulance and incompetence lead, on the contrary, to the flaunting of dexterity in one place, and the pretence of ease in another – complete some portions of the subject with hypocritical affection, and abandon others in ostentatious contempt. In some few cases, the manner arises from a true eagerness of imagination, or kindly and natural desire for sympathy in particular likings; but in the plurality of instances, the habit allies itself with mistaken principles of art, and protects impatience and want of skill under the shield of philosophy.

16. Few modern pieces of oil-painting are more accomplished or deliberate than those of Meissonier; and in the example placed on the table in the centre of the room,[2] his subject was one which he certainly would not have treated, consciously, with prosaic indignity of manner, or injurious economy of toil. Yet the inequality of workmanship has depressed what might have been a most sublime picture almost to the level of a scenic effect. The dress of the Emperor and housings of his steed are wrought with the master's utmost care; but the landscape is nearly unintelligible, and the ground a mere conventional diaper of feeble green and grey. It is difficult to describe the height to which the picture would have risen above its present power, if a ruined French village had been represented with Flemish precision amidst the autumnal twilight of the woods; and the ground over which the wearied horse bears his dreaming rider, made lovely with its native wild-flowers.

17. In all such instances, the hold which a true sense of beauty has over the painter's mind may be at once ascertained by observing the nature of the objects to which his pains have been devoted. No master with a fine instinct for colour would spend his time with deliberate preference on the straps and buckles of modern horse furniture, rather than on the surrounding landscape or foreground flowers, though in a subject like this he would have felt it right to finish both, to the spectator's content, if not to his amazement. And among the numerous rustic scenes by Hunt which adorn these walls, though all are painted with force and spirit, none are recommended to our curiosity by an elaborate finish given to ungraceful objects. His final powers are only employed on motives like the dead doves in Nos 139 and 145, accompanied by incidents more or less beautiful and seemly.

18. I must even further guard my last sentence, by the admission that the means by which his utmost intentions of finish are accomplished, can never, in the most accurate sense, be

termed 'elaborate.' When the thing to be represented is minute, the touches which express it are necessarily minute also – they cannot be bold on the edge of a nutshell, nor free within the sphere of a bird's nest – but they are always frank and clear, to a degree which may seem not only imperfect, but even harsh or offensive, to eyes trained in more tender or more formal schools. This broken execution by detached and sharply-defined touches became indeed, in process of years, a manner in which the painter somewhat too visibly indulged, or prided himself; but it had its origin and authority in the care with which he followed the varieties of colour in the shadow, no less than in the lights, of even the smallest objects. It is easy to obtain smoothness and unity of gradation when working with a single tint; but if all accidents of local colour, and all differences of hue between direct and reflected light, are to be rendered with absolute purity, some breaking of the texture becomes inevitable. In many cases, also, of the most desirable colours, no pigments mixed on the palette, but only interlaced touches of pure tints on the paper, will attain the required effect. The indefinable primrose colour, for instance, of the glazed porringer in the foreground of No 174 could not possibly have been given with a mixed tint. The breaking of grey through gold by which it has been reached is one of the prettiest pieces of work to be seen in these rooms; it exhibits the utmost skill of the artist, and is an adequate justification of his usual manner.

19. Among the earliest statements of principles of art made in the *Stones of Venice*,[3] one of those chiefly fortunate in obtaining credit with my readers was the course of argument urging frankness in the confession of the special means by which any artistic result has been obtained, and of the limitations which these appointed instruments, and the laws proper to the use of them, set to its scope. Thus the threads in tapestry, the tesseræ in mosaic, the joints of the stones in masonry, and the movements of the pencil in painting, are shown without hesitation by the greatest masters in those arts, and often enforced and accented by the most ingenious; while endeavours to conceal them – as to make needlework look like pencilling, or efface, in painting, the rugged freedom or joyful lightness of its handiwork into the deceptive image of a natural surface – are, without any exception, signs of declining intelligence, and benumbed or misguided feelings.

20. I therefore esteem Hunt's work all the more exemplary in acknowledging without disguise the restrictions imposed on the use of water-colour as a medium for vigorously realistic effects; and I have placed pieces of it in my Oxford school as standards of imitative (as distinguished from decorative) colour, in the rightness and usefulness of which I have every day more confirmed trust. I am aware of no other pieces of art, in modern days, at once so sincere and so accomplished: only let it be noted that I use the term 'sincere' in this case, not as imputing culpable fallacy to pictures of more imaginative power, but only as implying the unbiassed directness of aim at the realization of very simple facts, which is often impossible to the passions, or inconsistent with the plans, of greater designers.

Notes

142. THE BUTTERFLY

Before saying anything more of the Hunt series, I want my readers once more clearly to understand what I have brought it here for – namely, to show them what real painting is, as such, wholly without inquiry concerning its sentiment or story. The Prouts are here for an exactly opposite reason – not at all to show you what mere pencilling is, as such, but what it can pencil for us of European scenery and history. Whereas this butterfly is here, not at all to teach you anything you didn't know about butterflies; nor the peach and grapes to teach you anything you didn't know about those familiar fruits; nor even that boy in his father's boots to teach you anything you didn't know before about boys and boots.[4] They are here merely to show you what is meant by painting, as distinguished from daubing, from plastering, from rough casting, from chromo-tinting, from tray-varnishing, from paper-staining, and in general from the sort of things that people in general do when you put a brush into their hands and a pot within reach of them..

Now that little brown-red butterfly (which Mr Gurney is so fortunate in possessing) is a piece of real painting; and it is as good as Titian or anybody else ever did. And if you can enjoy it, you can enjoy Titian and all other good painters; and if you can't see anything in *it*, you can't see anything in *them*, and it is all affectation and pretence to say that you care about them.

And with this butterfly in the drawing I put first, please look at the mug and loaf in the one I have put last, of the Hunt series, No 171. The whole art of painting is in that mug – as the fisherman's genius was in the bottle. If you can feel how beautiful it is, how ethereal, how heathery and heavenly, as well as to the uttermost muggy, you have an eye for colour, and can enjoy heather, heaven, and everything else below and above. If not, you must enjoy what you can, contentedly, but it won't be painting; and in mugs, it will be more the beer than the crockery – and on the moors, rather grouse than heather.

Going back to No 142, you will perhaps ask me why the poppy is so poor and the butterfly so rich? Mainly because the poppy withered, and the butterfly was pinned and permanent. But there are other reasons, of which more presently.

144. HERRING AND PILCHARD[5]

Supreme painting again, and done with his best pains; for these two subjects, and

146. DEAD CHICKEN[6]

were done by the old man, in all kindness and care, at my own request, for me to give as types of work to country schools of art. Yet no kindness or care could altogether enable him to work rightly under the direction of another mind; and the project was ultimately given up by me, the chicken, finished as it is, having been one of my chief disappointments. And here anent, let me enter into some general account of the tenor of his drawings. They may be broadly divided into the following classes, into one or other of which every work of importance from his hand will distinctly fall.

CLASS 1

Drawings illustrative of rural life in its vivacity and purity, without the slightest endeavour at idealisation, and still less with any wish either to caricature or deplore its imperfections. All the drawings belonging to this class are virtually faultless, and most of them very beautiful. It is, I am glad to say, thoroughly represented in this room, which contains several examples of the highest quality – namely, 121, 168, 171, 172, 173, 175; besides two pieces of still life (169, and the interior, No 174), properly belonging to the group.

CLASS 2

Country life, with endeavour to add interest to it by passing sentiment. The drawings belonging to this class are almost always over-finished, and liable to many faults. There are three in this collection – 120, 165, 166.

CLASS 3

Country life, with some expression of its degradation, either by gluttony, cowardice, or rudeness. The drawings of this class are usually very clever, and apt to be very popular; but they are, on the whole, dishonourable to the artist. There are five examples here – namely, 157, 158, 161, 163, 164.

CLASS 4

Flower pieces. Fruit is often included in these; but they form a quite separate class, being necessarily less finished drawings – the flowers sooner changing their form. Including the fungi among these, there are eight fine ones in the room – 148, 150, 149, 152, 147, 151, 154, 156.

CLASS 5

Fruit pieces, on which a great part of the artist's reputation very securely rests. Five first-rate ones are here, and several of interesting, though inferior, quality.

CLASS 6

Dead animals. Alas! if he could but have painted living ones, instead of those perpetual bunches of grapes. But it could not be. To a weakly, sensitive, nervous temperament, the perpetual changes of position, and perpetual suggestion of new beauty in an animal, are entirely ruinous: in ten minutes they put one in a fever. Only the very greatest portrait-painters – Sir Joshua and Velasquez – can draw animals rightly.

I begin with this last class, and reascend to the highest.

138. DEAD HARE AND GAME

A most notable drawing of early practice, quite wonderful in textures of fur and in work of shadows, but tentative, and in many points failing.

141. DEAD DOVE (A)

A pure water-colour drawing, before his style was perfectly formed. Full of interest, but too conventional and slight in background.

139. DEAD DOVE (B)

Finished work of central time.

145. DEAD DOVE (C)

Replica, I suppose, of B, with completer background, and of highest quality. I must be pardoned for saying so of my own drawing; but of course, after long and affectionate relations with the painter, it would be strange if I had not some of his best works.[7]

143. PINE MELON, AND GRAPES

We were obliged to put this drawing low down, for, in spite of its dark background, it killed everything we put near it. To my mind it is the most majestic piece of work in the room. The grapes are the vintage of Rubens, and the shadows are the darkness of Tintoret. It is wholly free from any pettiness of manner, and in force, spring, and succulence of foliage it is as if the strength of nature were in it, rather than of human hand. I never saw it until now, and have learned from it more than, after my fifty years of labour, I thought anything but a Venetian picture could have taught me.

132. 'LOVE WHAT YOU STUDY, STUDY WHAT YOU LOVE'

All *Modern Painters* in a nutshell of a sentence, and the painted nutshell perfect.

130. GRAPES

Consummate. Can't be better anywhere.

131. MR SIBETH'S QUINCES

All that's best in this kind.

125. BULLACES

Very fine, but conventional in background.

129. GRAPES

Perfect work, but wasted. Why he did so many grapes, and scarcely ever sloes, or finely russet apples, or *growing* strawberries, always mystified me.

126. PLUMS

Finest work, but a little dull. My own favourites of his plums were such variegated ones as 133 and 135; but I somehow never got any. This drawing, however, was the one of which Hunt said to me innocently – seeing it again after some ten years – 'It's very nice, isn't it?'

128. PLUMS

The bit of oak-leaf here is very wonderful and interesting as an example, and what Hunt meant by saying to me once, 'I like to see things "fudged" out.' It is to be remembered, however, that this was his own special liking; and it must not be followed by the general student. The finest forms of anything cannot be 'fudged' out, but must be drawn, if possible, with the first line, at least with the last one, for ever.

149. DR DRAGE'S FUNGI

A perfect gem; 'Venetian red' in its best earthly splendour: it could only be more bright in clouds.

147. MR FRY'S HAWTHORN

A little overworked, but very glorious. Soft and scented, I think, if you only wait a little, and make-believe very much.

155. (MINE.) HAWTHORN AND BIRDS' NESTS

The hawthorn this time a little *under*worked, but very good; and nests as good as can be.

148. LILAC. (MR SIBETH'S)

Fine, but curiously redundant. The upper branch by itself, or the lower with only the laburnum, or both together without the third, would have been beautiful; but two's company, and three's none.

150. VASE WITH ROSE AND BASKET WITH FRUIT
151. FLOWERS AND FRUIT

Two resplendent ones; everything that he could do best in this kind – absolutely right in colour, absolutely in light and shade, and without any rivalship in past or present art.

162. THE GAMEKEEPER[8]

Early study. Please observe that Hunt learned his business, not in spots but in lines. Compare the entirely magnificent sketch of the riverside, No 124, which is as powerful in lines as Rembrandt, and the St Martin's Church, No 123, which is like a bit of Hogarth.

157. THE INVALID

Full of humour; but there is no place for humour in true painting. See also No 164, 'The Young Artist,' and 'The Wasp,' No 163. If I could have the currant-pie without the boy, I should be content.

161. GIPSIES

Very powerful; historic in its kind.[9]

166. PRAYING BOY.[10] (MR QUILTER'S)

Over-finished, as its companion, No 165, an endeavour at doing what he did not understand. So also the large study of himself, No 176, with the 'Mulatto,' No 122, and 'Wanderer,' No 120. His mode of work was entirely unfitted for full life-size.

121. MR QUILTER'S STABLE-BOY[11]

172. MR ORROCK'S SHY SITTER,[12] AND THE BLESSING (171)

On the contrary, he is here again in his utmost strength – and in qualities of essential painting – unconquerable. In the pure faculty of the painter's art – in what Correggio, and Tintoret, and Velasquez, and Rubens, and Rembrandt, meant by *painting* – that single bunch of old horse-collars is worth all Meissonier's horse-bridles, boots, breeches, epaulettes and stars, together.

The other drawings of the highest class need no commentary. There is not much in the two little candle-lights, Nos 168, 175, but all that is, of the finest; and the three drawings with which I close our series, 'The Shy Sitter,' No 172, 'The Fisherman's Boy,' No 173, and 'The Blessing,' No 171, things that the old painter was himself unspeakably blessed in having power to do. The strength of all lovely human life is in them; and England herself lives only, at this hour, in so much as, from all that is sunk in the luxury, sick in the penury, and polluted in the sin of her great cities, Heaven has yet hidden for her old men and children such as these, by their fifties, in her fields and on her shores, and fed them with Bread and Water.

NOTES

1. Probably Mr R. Wade, who resided in Dean Street, Soho, and formed a collection of Hunt's works; dispersed in 1872.

2. 'Napoleon in 1814'.

3. The reference seems rather to be to the *Seven Lamps of Architecture*, Chapter 2, 'The Lamp of Truth'.

4. No 173, 'My Father's Boots.'

5. Listed by Ruskin in the exhibition catalogue as 'Herrings and Red Mullet'. – J.W.

6. Six of the drawings thus done for Ruskin were exhibited in the gallery of the Old Water-Colour Society between the years 1856 and 1881. 'Some of these – in particular, one of "Mushrooms: Study of Rose-Grey" (1860) – were exquisite. But the generous donor ultimately gave up the project. The old man used to pause in the task, which he was trying his very best to accomplish, and cry out, "How difficult it is to paint this oyster-shell!" After painting some "Pilchards: Study of Gold" in 1860, one of the most striking of the series, he wrote, however, "If you want studies of colour, fish is the sort of thing to look at"' (Roget's *History of the Old Water-Colour Society*, ii, 196).

7. Bought by Ruskin's father. 'I got a piece of advice from Hunt,' he wrote to his son in 1852, 'never to commission a picture. He could not have done my pigeon so well had he felt he was doing it for anybody' (Collingwood's *Life of Ruskin*, p 137). Ruskin, on hearing of the purchase, wrote from Venice:- '10*th Jan.* [1852]. – I forgot – my head being full of Turner and Tintoret yesterday – to thank you for your kindness both to Hunt and me in buying the ringdove – no subject could possibly be better fitted to show his powers. I would – if I had given him a commission, which he says I ought not – have commissioned him just for that. You must come some day to visit Mr Fawkes with me, and see Turner's ringdove – a rainbow made of down: but I doubt not Hunt's will be *very nearly* equal to it.'

8. Reproduced at p 180 of Mr Harry Quilter's *Preferences in Art*.

9. Reproduced at p 184 of Mr Harry Quilter's *Preferences in Art*.

10. Otherwise called 'Devotion.'

11. Generally known as 'The Eavesdropper.' Reproduced at p 177 of Mr Harry Quilter's *Preferences in Art*. Mr Quilter says: 'I remember Sir Frederick Burton saying many years ago to my father – perhaps in a fit of generous enthusiasm – that this is the finest water-colour in the world' (p 182).

12. No 172 is reproduced as frontispiece in the illustrated (1880) edition of the *Notes*.

Hunt's Works Exhibited★

		Contributed by
120	The Wanderer	Mr Jas. Orrock
121	The Eavesdropper	Mr W. Quilter
122	Head of a Mulatto Girl	Mr F. Wigan
123	St. Martin's Church	Mr Ellis [256]
124	Somerset House	Mr J. C. Robinson [239, Plate 8]
125	Bullaces	Mr W. Quilter
126	Plums	Mr Ruskin
127	Black Grapes and Strawberries	Mr Edmund Sibeth
128	Magnum Bonum Plums	,,
129	Black and White Grapes	,,
130	Grapes	Mr W. J. Galloway
131	Quinces	Mr Edmund Sibeth
132	'Love what you study, study what you love'	Mr George Gurney
133	Plums and Blackberry	Mr Jas. Orrock
134	Black Grapes and Peach	Mr Ruskin [599, Plate 104]
135	Fruit	Mr Alfred Harris
136	Black and White Grapes	Mr Jas. Orrock
137	Grapes, Casket, and Peaches	Mr A. W. Lyon
138	Hare (dead)	,,
139	A Pigeon	Mr W. Quilter
140	Acorn	Mr J. W. Knight
141	A Pigeon	Mr Ruskin [perhaps 578]
142	Flowers and Fruit with Butterfly	Mr George Gurney
143	Pine, Melon, and Grapes	The Fine Art Society†
144	Herrings and Red Mullet	Mr George Gurney
145	A Pigeon	Mr Ruskin
146	Dead Chicken	,, [653, Plate 111]
147	A Bird's Nest, with May Blossom	Mr Fry
148	Lilac and Bird's Nest	Mr Edmund Sibeth
149	Fungi	Dr Drage
150	Vase with Rose, and Basket with Fruit	Mr Edmund Sibeth
151	Flowers and Fruit	Mr Jas. Orrock
152	Apple Blossom	Mr George Gurney
153	Dog-roses and Bird's Nest	Mr R. D. Farnworth
154	Primrose and Bird's Nest	Mr George Gurney
155	Birds' Nests and May Blossom	Mr Ruskin
156	Primroses	Mr Jas. Orrock

★Where present owners have been identified, reference numbers of this writer's Catalogue are added within square brackets. Nos 121, 161, 162 and 166 in Ruskin's list, whose present ownership is not known to the present writer, are illustrated in Harry Quilter's *Preferences in Art, Life and Literature*. Nos 126 and 155 are illustrated in Ruskin's *Works*, Vol. XIV, opposite pp. 445 and 446 respectively.

†'Now Mr A. T. Hollingsworth's' – *Ill. Ed.*

157	The Invalid	Mr S. J. Thacker
158	Sunday Morning	Mr J. J. Wigzell [407, Plate 74]
158*a*	'Study of a Head'	Mr G. Peck
159	The Pitcher Girl	Mr Jas Orrock
159*a*	Sketch for the drawing of the Flycatcher	Mr H. G. Hine
160	Sketch for the drawing of the Cricketer	Mr Carl Haag
161	The Gipsies	Mr W. Quilter
162	The Gamekeeper	,,
163	Boy startled by a Wasp	Mr John Rhodes
164	A Young Artist	Mr George Gurney [278]
165	Prayer	Mr Prescott Hewett
166	Devotion	Mr W. Quilter
167	Girl's Head	Mr W. J. Galloway
168	Boy with a lighted Candle	Mr W. Beacall
169	The Blacksmith's Shop	Mr W. H. Urwick
170	By the Wayside	Mr S. J. Thacker
171	The Blessing	Mr Jas. Orrock
172	The Shy Sitter	,,
173	My Father's Boots	Mr John Rhodes
174	An Interior	Mr Ruskin [286]
175	Boy with Lantern	Mr J. J. Elliott
176	Portrait of Hunt (painted by himself)	Mr Sutton Palmer [451, Plate 80]
176	[sic] Grapes – Muscatel, Peach, and Spray of Raspberries	Mr George Gurney
177	Portrait of Saml. Prout, by Wm. Hunt [reproduced in the illustrated edition of the *Notes by Mr Ruskin on Samuel Prout and William Hunt*]	Mr Haydon [319]
178	Portrait of Wm. Hunt, by himself	Mr Osler
179	A Green Melon, Grapes, and Plums	Sir John Swinburne, Bart.
180	Shells	Mr Barnes [620, Plate 113]
181	Dead Pigeons	,,
182	A Bit of Mont Blanc	,,
183	Bird's Nest and Apple Blossom	Mr W. Barfoot
184	The Art Critic	,, [259]

APPENDIX III

List of the Chief Past Collectors of Hunt's Works, with Dates of Sale and Number of Works Sold

*Part I**

	Date of Sale	*Number of Works*
Dr T. Monro	26 June 1833	168
Ralph Bernal	21/22/23 April 1853	44
James Anderson Rose	1 March 1861	7
Lewis B. Mozeley	17/18 April 1863	12
	27 May 1865	14
Dr R. Wade (Executors)	9 March 1872	18
Joseph Gillot	4 May 1872	26
William Quilter	9 April 1875	39
	18 May 1889	6
George Gurney	17 March 1883	7
	11 July 1903	2
W. E. Sibeth	29 March 1884	6
George Schlotel	25 April 1884	7
Edwin H. Lawrence	6 May 1892	5
M. Birket Foster	28 April 1894	2
Charles Frederick Huth	6 July 1895	5
John Morley	16 May 1896	6
Henry Jenkins	27 March 1897	2
J. Grant Morris	23 April 1898	5
Gilbert Winter Moss	28 April 1900	5
James Orrock	4 June 1904	14
Lord Northwick	7 July 1921	11

* At Christie's, with the exception of Lord Northwick's collection, sold at Sotheby's.

Part II

J. P. Heseltine	Eight works repr. Pl. 11 to 18 inclusive in J. P. Heseltine, *John Varley and his Pupils, W. Mulready, J. Linnell and W. Hunt – Original Drawings in the Collection of J.P.H.*
A Paul Oppé	Collection of English drawings (including 59 works by Hunt) bequeathed in 1957 to his son D. L. T. Oppé
L. G. Duke	Collection (including five works by Hunt) sold 1965 to the Yale Center for British Art, Paul Mellon Collection, New Haven, Connecticut
Gilbert Davis	Collection (including thirty-nine works by Hunt) sold 1959 to Huntington Library and Art Gallery, San Marino, California
Thomas Girtin	Collection (including twenty-five works by Hunt) sold by his son Thomas Girtin 1970 to the Yale Center for British Art, Paul Mellon Collection, New Haven, Connecticut

Indexes

Index of Owners*

Numbers are those of the Catalogue

**For arrangement of entries, see Basis of Catalogue and Abbreviations used, item 2, page 141.*

Index of Hunt's Catalogued Works

referred to in text of Part I: *Life and Work* and Appendix II

Numbers in brackets are those of the catalogue

General Index